Facts & Folklore

An Historical Guide to

Southern Gulf Islands

Landmarks, Events, Activities, Parks, Beaches, Shops & Services

Vicky Lindholm

Hidden Lighthouse Publishers

Hidden Lighthouse Publishers
A division of Diskover Office Software Ltd.
Email: info@hiddenlighthouse.com
www.hiddenlighthouse.com

A great deal of care has been taken to ensure that all information presented in this book is accurate and up-to-date. However, neither the author nor the publisher can be held responsible for any errors.

Cover design, page design and composition by Vicky Lindholm
All photos by Vicky Lindholm,
with the exception of those listed under Credits.

Front cover photo:
Sunset waters © Marek Roszkowicz,
Agency: Dreamstime.com

Back cover photo:
Aerial photo of the southern Gulf Islands

ISBN 978-0-9783367-4-5

Corporate orders:
Granville Island Publishing
www.granvilleislandpublishing.com
604-688-0320
1-877-688-0320

Dedication

To my best friend
who went where no billygoat has
gone before

Contents

Maps:

Bad Waters

Before the British arrived, First Nations people lived in the southern Gulf Islands. They were known as the *Coast Salish* and were members of the *Nanaimo*, *Chemainus*, *Cowichan*, *Saanich* and *Songhees* tribes.

By the 1850's, the British had started negotiating with First Nations for the right to occupy their land. However, when some of the Indians in the Gulf Islands would migrate during the summer, the British would simply take their land.

In the early 1860's, a settler from Washington State decided to join a Mayne Islander in working his newly acquired land. On an Easter weekend, he set out to move his family to Mayne in two boats.

When they encountered a storm, the settler and one of his daughters took shelter on Saturna Island. As they sat by their campfire, the settler was shot in the back. His daughter ran, but was caught and killed.

Shortly thereafter, two other settlers were shot, on Pender Island. One of the settlers died of his wounds, but the other lived to describe his attackers as Indian.

When the British learned of the attacks, they sailed a gunboat, called the HMG *Forward*, to Mayne Island. They took a half-breed Indian aboard to act as their interpreter. He guided them to where they could investigate the sites of the attacks.

The result of their investigation prompted them to sail just north of Salt Spring Island, to where a Coast Salish group of Indians lived on a neighboring island. There, they anchored their gunboat in the bay in front of the Indian village.

Unknown to the British, Indian warriors were hiding on the bay when they arrived. When the British fired, the warriors returned their fire and a 16-year-old sailor was killed. He was the first and last British serviceman killed in action in British Columbia.

After several hours, the British attack proved futile. Defeated, they pulled their boat out of the bay. It was the only tactical defeat ever inflicted by a tribal group over the British Royal Navy.

It is estimated that the Indians numbered just over 100 people, most of which were children. In spite of this, it took two additional expeditions by the British, with three ships and 500 men, to overtake them.

The Indian village was then burned and later confiscated. Seven natives were captured on Galiano Island. They were then tried and executed for the murders on Saturna and Pender Islands. The Indian war chief was never captured.

This battle was one of the largest military operations in the entire history of British Columbia. Unfortunately, it is not mentioned in most recorded histories.

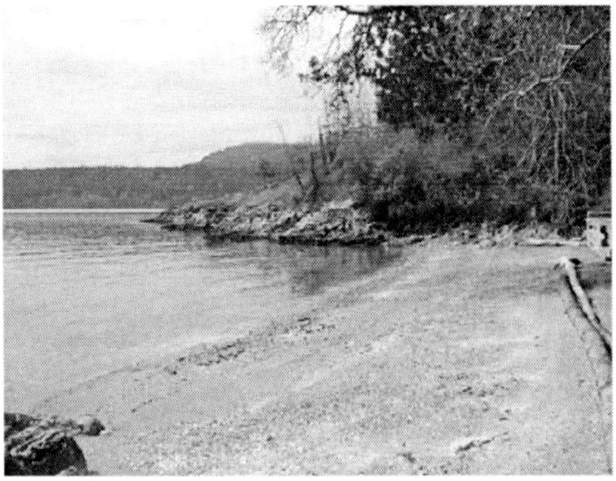

By the late 1860's, the British had given up negotiating with the Indians. Instead, they implemented a system of creating Indian reserves within the boundaries of lands claimed by white settlers.

A point on Saturna was named because of the killings that had occurred there. Now a part of the Gulf Islands National Park Reserve, it is called *Murder Point*. Today, there are First Nations reserves on each of the southern Gulf Islands.

SOUTHERN GULF ISLANDS

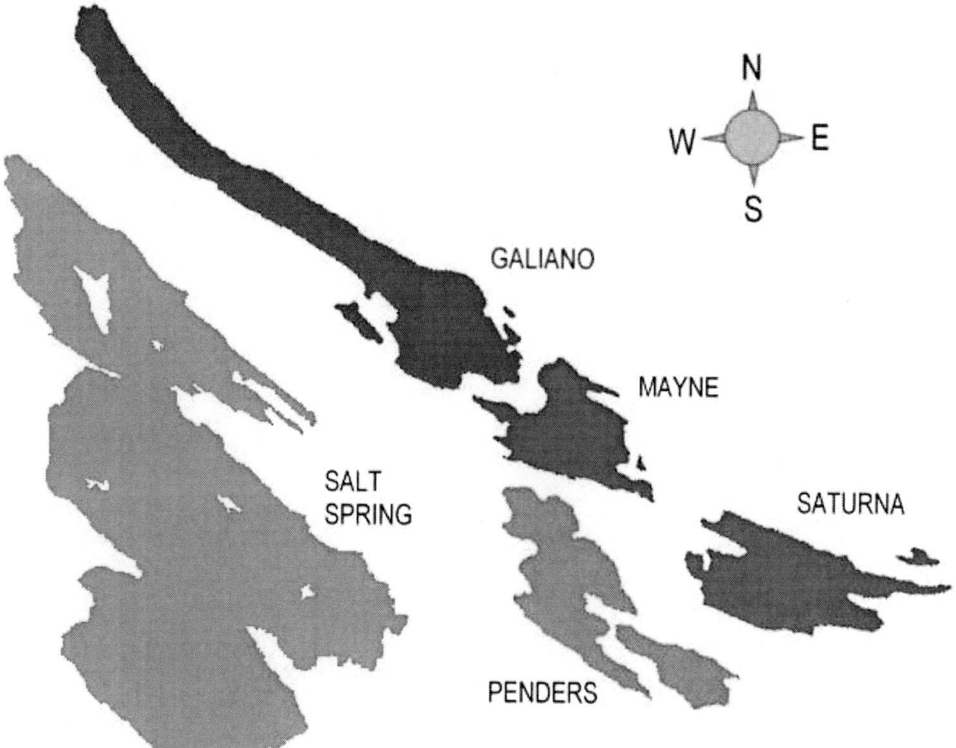

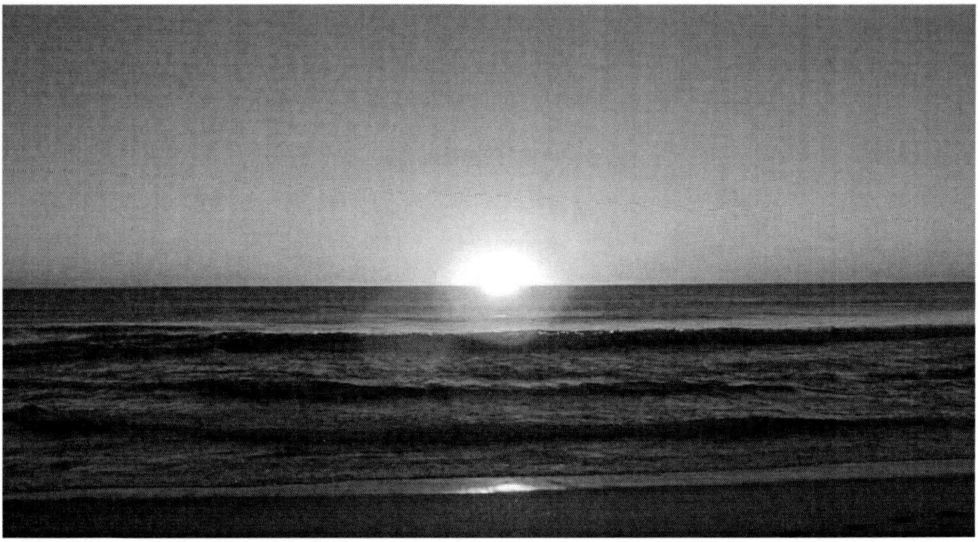

Sunset in the Islands

Just sit right back and you'll hear a tale...

The southern Gulf Islands are centrally located between Vancouver Island and the mainland. They include *Salt Spring, Mayne*, *Pender*, *Galiano* and *Saturna*. Of these Islands, Mayne, Pender, Galiano and Saturna make up what is known as the outer Gulf Islands.

The Islands lie in the rain shadow of the Vancouver Island Mountains, which protects them from storms that blow in from the Pacific Ocean. Often referred to as the *Banana Belt of Canada*, they have Canada's only Mediterranean-type climate.

Although most of the Gulf Islands are uninhabited, the Islands have a combined population of over 14,000 permanent residents.

The rolling hills and roads on the Islands are reminiscent of an English *Illahee* (countryside). There are few streetlights, curbs or sidewalks, making them quite a quaint attraction.

The Islands enjoy an average of 2,000 hours of sunshine, annually. With the longest frost-free season in Canada, spring begins as early as February.

Because it rarely snows, a winter weekend can be quite cozy with some logs on a *paia* (fire). So much so that an early settler said this about them:

"We didn't notice until we left the Gulf Islands just how quiet it had been… But we loved it… When I think back on it, it was a really nice life."

Mrs. Peter Georgeson

Mayne Island

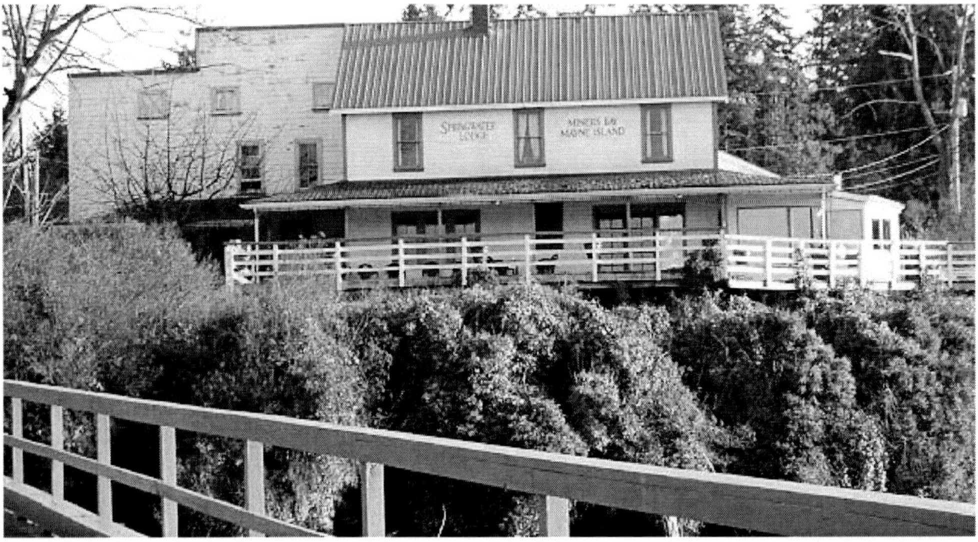

Miners Bay Wharf

It was in the summer of 1862 that the notorious killer, Boone Helm, stopped an Englishman, named Tom Collinson, on a trail during the gold rush...

Helm aimed a shotgun at Tom's head, while his partner took Tom's six-shooter and his pack. Then, they chased him down the trail at gunpoint, claiming his cash for their own, but missing a large amount of gold dust in his shirt pocket.

William Tompkins Collinson was born in the 1830's and emigrated with his family from England to Canada. In the 1870's, he moved to Mayne Island with his Indian wife, where he earned the nickname 'Baron Munchausen of Mayne'.

The story-telling Tom Collinson was an avid carpenter, having built several buildings on a bay on Mayne, including the very first store.

In 1880, Tom became **the Postman** for Mayne, operating the first post office from the home he had built there. He was later made Justice of the Peace, around the time this was said about him:

"Tall, lean Mr. Collinson was the postmaster, and held the record for having the largest feet, and being the island's champion liar - or shall we say, Romantic. No matter what the topic of conversation, he could lie... about his experiences and utterly impossible exploits... with a perfectly straight face, and then tell the same episode next time, with varying circumstances. It was a real gift!"

Winifred Grey

Things to Know

Mayne is a relaxed island. At only 23 sq km, it is the smallest of the southern Gulf Islands. While idyllic meadows and wildflowers are its most distinguishing characteristics, the history behind the landmarks gives Mayne Island its unique charm.

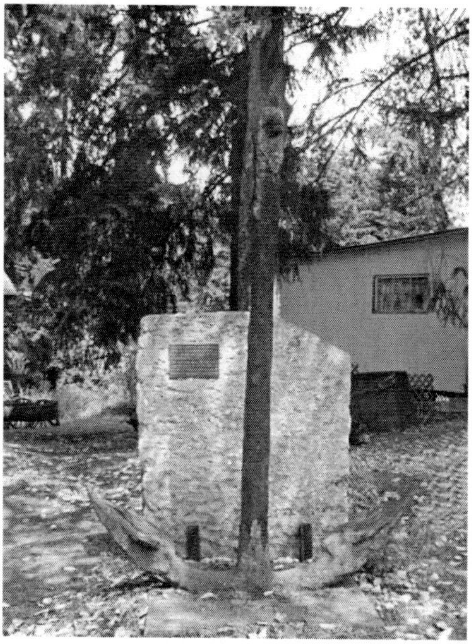

Mayne has a population of about 900 permanent residents, a large percentage of which are over 55 years of age and retired. During the tourist season, the population swells to around 3,000.

Miners Bay

Before the 1850's, less than 500 settlers lived at the south end of Vancouver Island, and the only white people travelling between Vancouver Island and the mainland were employees of the Hudson's Bay Company.

When gold was discovered on the Fraser River, tens of thousands of *fifty-eighters* (miners living in the year 1858) came to British Columbia to seek their *tolla* (fortune) in the gold mines.

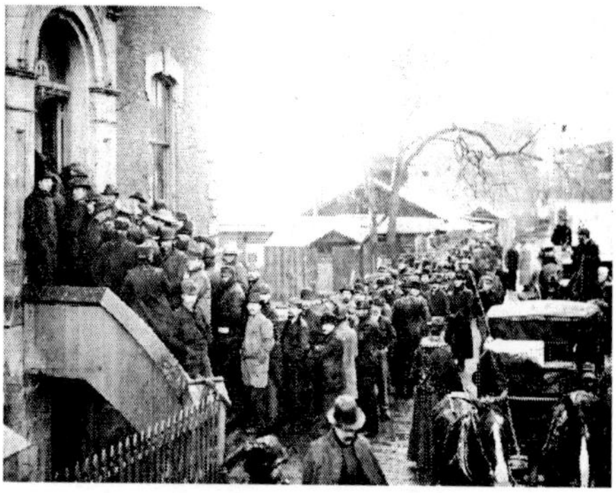

Miners in Victoria in the mid-1800's
BC Archives A-04498

Many came from the United States, by way of a steamer ship that docked at Vancouver Island. Some gold miners continued the perilous journey to the mainland in a canoe or rowboat.

Since Mayne Island is located midway between Vancouver Island and the Fraser River, many of these miners began stopping overnight at the bay on its west side. The bay and its surrounding areas soon became known as *Miners Bay*.

Over time, Mayne Island became one of the earliest summer resorts to ever exist on the West Coast of Canada. A surprising number of accommodations date back to the turn of the century when it developed into an important Pacific Northwest resort island.

At that time, only approximately 100 residents lived on the Island. Nevertheless, they rapidly began to establish tourist facilities to capitalize on its growing popularity.

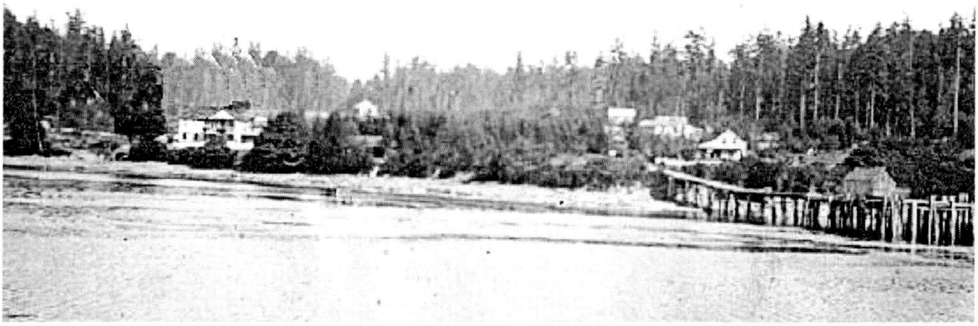

Miners Bay in the early 1900's, seen from the water, BC Archives A-09773

Today, Miners Bay is 'downtown' to Mayne Islanders. It is a seaside village where businesses and residents co-exist.

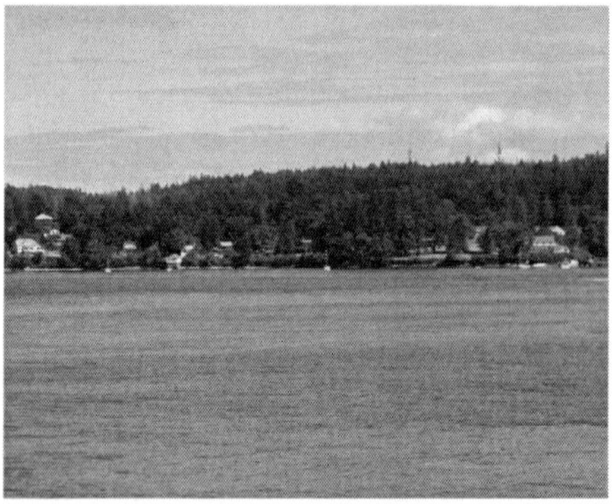

Miners Bay as it appears today

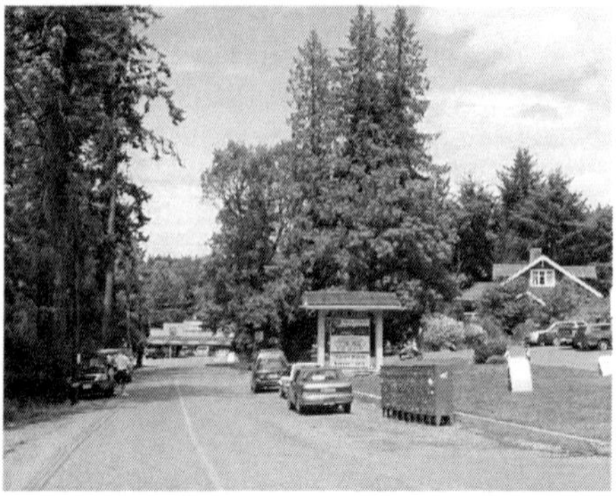

Miners Bay Wharf

The first wharf to ever exist in the outer Gulf Islands was built in Miners Bay in the 1870's. The wharf accommodated ships coming through the waterway that is officially called *Active Passage*, but was then known locally as *Plumper Pass*.

In the 1880's, the first wharf was replaced with a larger wharf that was twice as wide and extended an additional 15 m into the Pass. When the first steamer arrived at the new wharf, the settlers saluted it by firing their rifles.

Much later, in the 1930's, a bench was built at the foot of the wharf. For several decades, Mayne Islanders gathered to socialize around the bench on *boat days* (when boats would dock at the wharf).

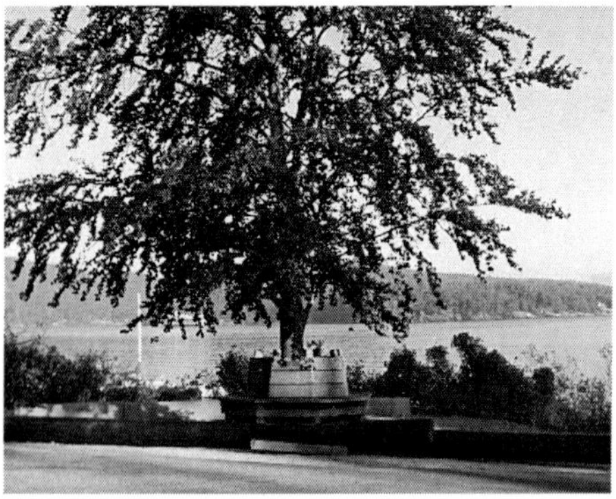

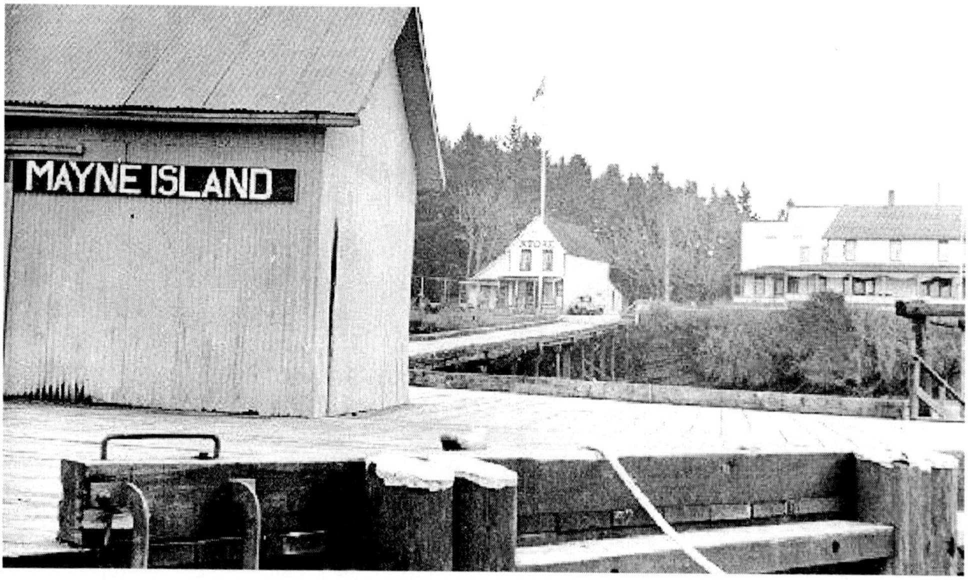

Miners Bay wharf in the 1930's, the post office shown in the background, BC Archives D-07435

In the 1950's, the Miners Bay wharf was upgraded to accommodate the ship named *Princess Elaine*. Much later, in the 1990's, it was destroyed by fire and a new wharf was built to replace it.

Today, it is used by sea planes and to transport schoolchildren to neighboring schools. The bench still sits there, although the little tree that was planted in the center is just a bit larger now.

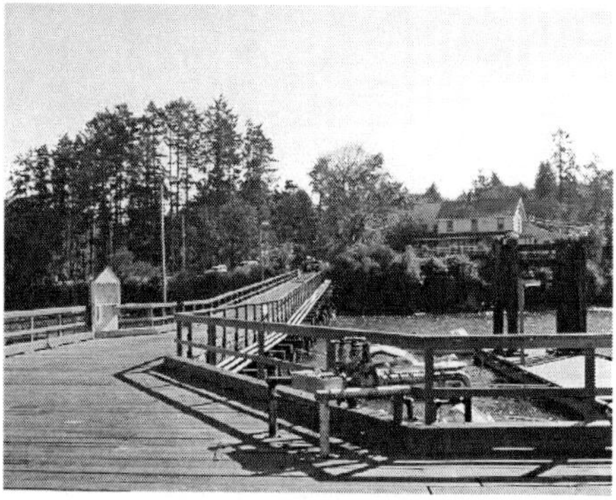

Miners Bay wharf as it appears today

Mayne Island Post Office

In the 1880's, a request for a post office on Mayne was approved by the Postmaster General.

When a letter slot was cut into the side of his house, postal service began from **the Postman's** home. His 1879 tax records indicate that the total tax paid for the property on which the post office sat was 75 cents.

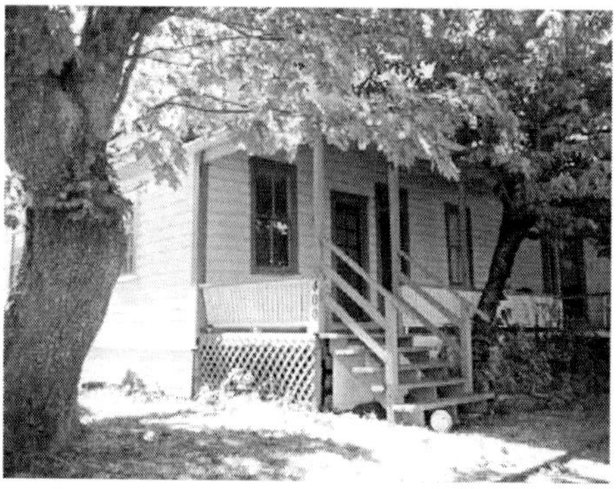

In the 1890's, **the Postman** built a new home and store at the head of the new wharf, moving the post office to its second location. At that time, the address of the post office was simply 'Plumper Pass'. It was later renamed the *Mayne Island Post Office*.

The Mayne Island Post Office was the first to serve the outer Gulf Islands. Steamer ships would first deliver the mail to Salt Spring Island, and then it would be delivered in a mailbag to Mayne. The mailbag would be taken down to the boat on a wheelbarrow.

The first building to serve as the post office was torn down in the 1970's. The second building still sits in front of the wharf on the bay. It operates as the *Springwater Lodge*.

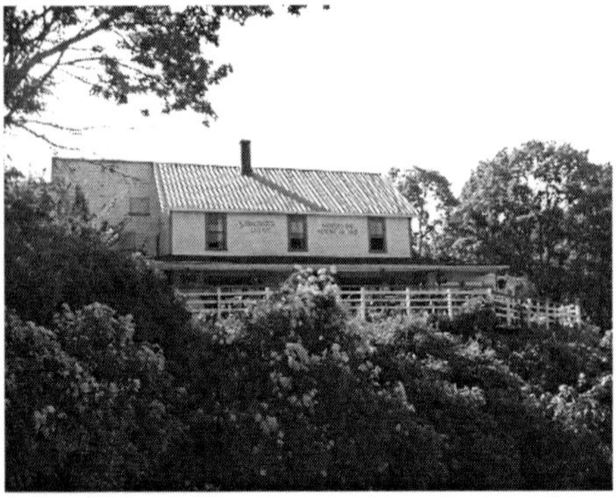

At the turn of the century, **the Postman** built a third building, on the north side of the wharf. Then, he moved his store and post office there.

He retained ownership of the building, but later sold his retail business to another settler who operated it as *Deacon's Store*.

Soon, the hands of **the Postman** set to work on yet another building, for a retired Commander of the British Royal Navy. Located just up the street, it was operated as the *Mayne Store*.

For decades, the post office operated from various stores at Miners Bay, including the Mayne Store and what would eventually become the *Miners Bay Trading Post*.

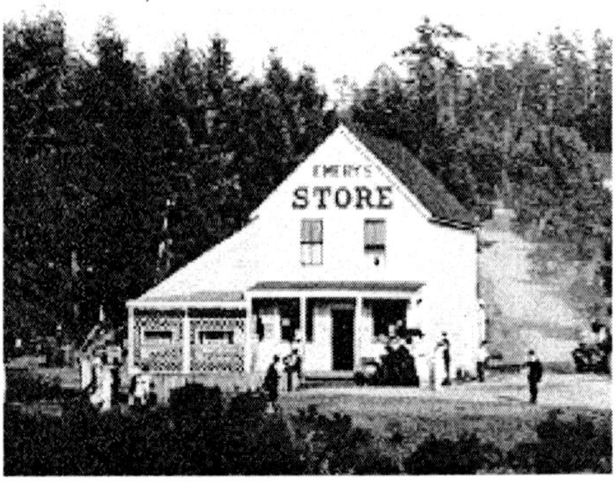

The third post office, in the 1920's
BC Archives B-03269

Deacon's Store changed owners many times, becoming *Emery's Store, Bennett's Store* and others. It was torn down in the 1960's.

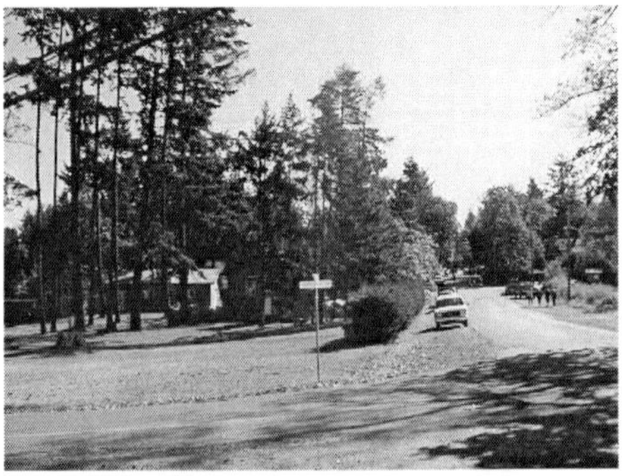

The site of the third post office as it appears today

The Mayne Store, which was built up the street from the first post office, served as the telephone headquarters for the outer Gulf Islands in the 1940's. It now serves as a private residence on Georgina Point Road.

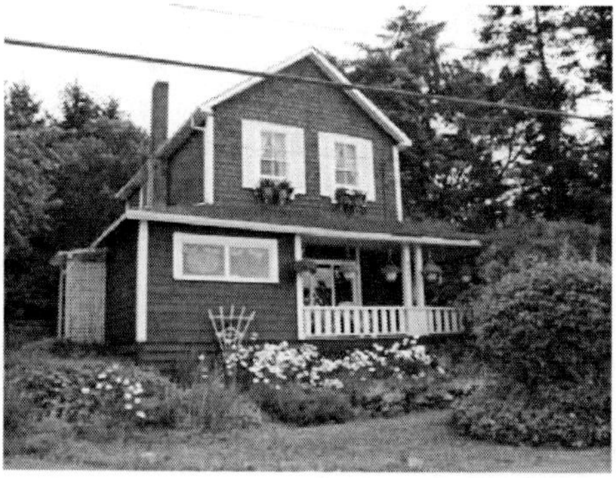

In the 1970's, the post office was moved to another building at Miners Bay. Today, that building operates as a hair salon and the post office sits in a storefront on Fernhill Road. In the year of this writing, the post office was celebrating its 125th Anniversary.

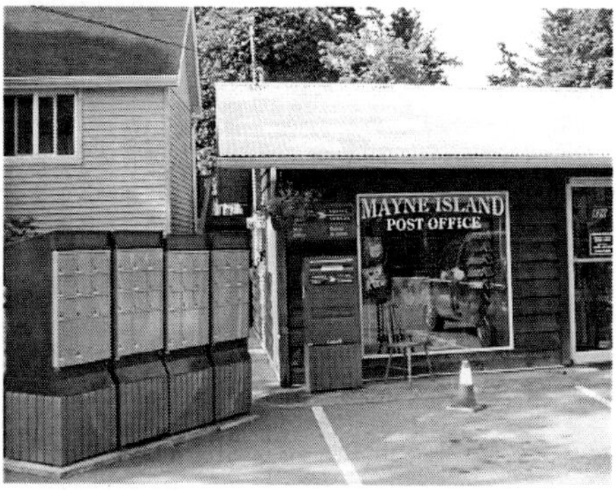

Miners Bay Trading Post

In the 1920's, a general store was built just east of the wharf at Miners Bay. It changed owners several times until the 1950's, when it was run as a franchise called *Bambrick Store Ltd.* Reportedly, it was the only store on Mayne for a while.

Because there was no health centre on the island at the time, three of its rooms were partitioned off to create a clinic for the doctors. This continued for many years.

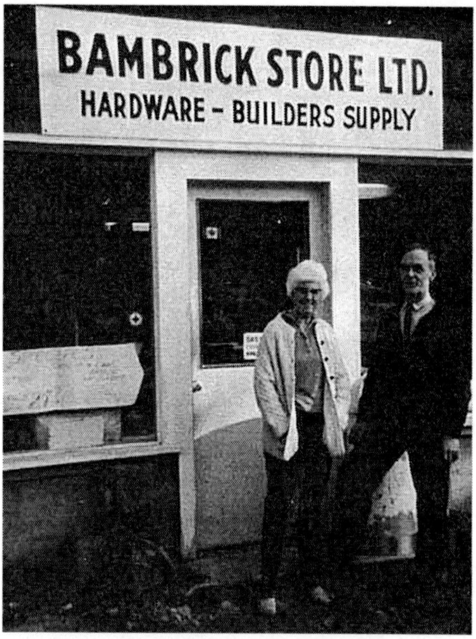

Miners Bay Trading Post in the 1950's
Galiano Archives 2004026691

In the 1960's, new owners changed the name of the store to *Hopkins Trading Post.* During much of the 1950's and 60's, the post office operated from this store. The name was then changed to *Mayne Island Trading Post*, and then to *Miners Bay Trading Post*.

In the 1970's, an apartment that had been built above the Trading Post caught fire. The fire spread to the store beneath it and a new building was constructed to replace it.

The Miners Bay Trading Post was the second business to be issued a liquor license in all of British Columbia. At the time of this writing, it was operating as a grocery and liquor store.

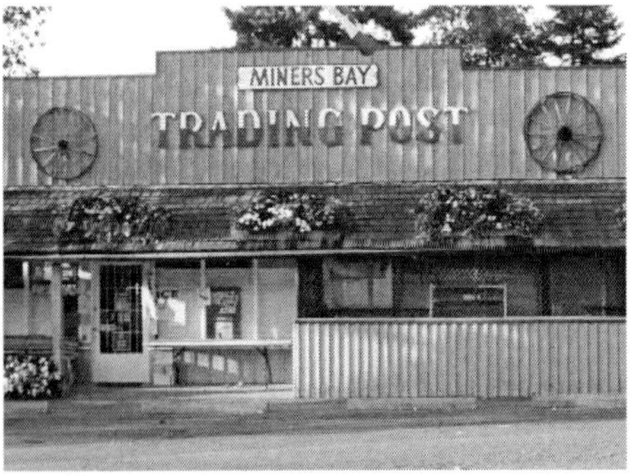

Mayne Island Agriculture Hall

By the 1890's, Mayne had become the social center of the Gulf Islands. Even residents of the larger island of Salt Spring would spend their weekends on Mayne.

Around the turn of the century, a community hall was built at Miners Bay. Because the Maple Leaf Club was formed to care for it, it was originally called the *Maple Leaf Hall*. Later, it was officially renamed the *Mayne Island Agriculture Hall*. Dances held there never ended before dawn because it was considered unsafe to go home until then.

Today, the agriculture hall is known locally as the *Ag Hall*. The site of many community events, dances and markets, the hall and its fair grounds hosted its first fall fair in the 1920's. The *Mayne Island Fall Fair* is the oldest fall fair in the outer Gulf Islands and continues to be a regular event at the fair grounds.

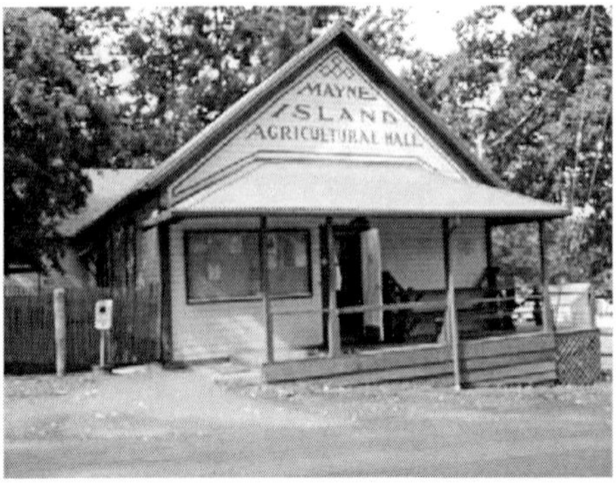

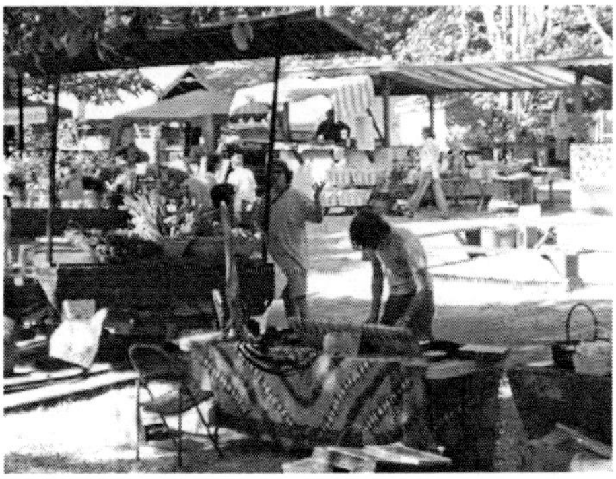

The fair grounds are also the site of the famous *Mayne Island Farmer's Market* and the annual *Christmas Craft Fair*.

The Mayne Island Agriculture Hall, which is located on Fernhill Road, is host to many functions, from musical concerts put on by the Mayne Island Concerts Society to performing arts presentations put on by the Mayne Island Little Theatre.

Active Pass Auto & Marine

Until the introduction of gasoline-powered vehicles, boat was the only means of transportation to and from Mayne. However, in the 1920's, automobiles began to appear, the first of which was a 1914 Model 'T' Ford.

In the 1940's, a roadside gas pump was set up at Miners Bay. The oil and gas drums were transported from the Miners Bay wharf by hand. In the 1960's, a pump was installed with a pipeline that led to modern storage tanks. A few years later, a building was constructed to enclose an automobile repair service.

Today, you can gas up your *chikchik* (wagon) at the *Active Pass Auto and Marine* station, from what is still a single gas pump. The station offers 24 hour towing and a two-bay garage. At the time of this writing, it also provided for movie rentals, fishing licenses, tackle and bait.

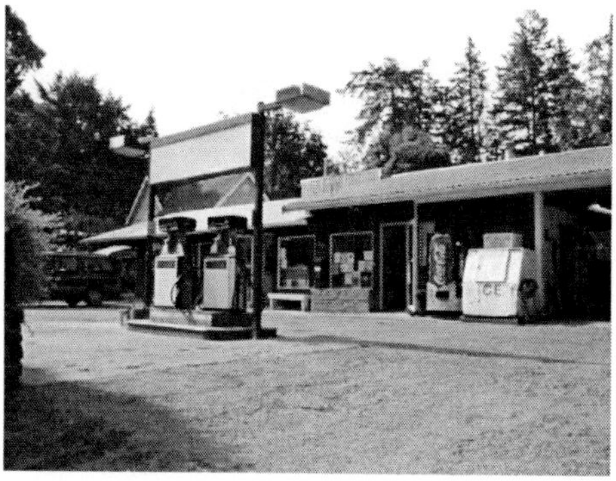

Mayne Street Mall

The *Mayne Street Mall* is a newer building that was built at Miners Bay to house local businesses.

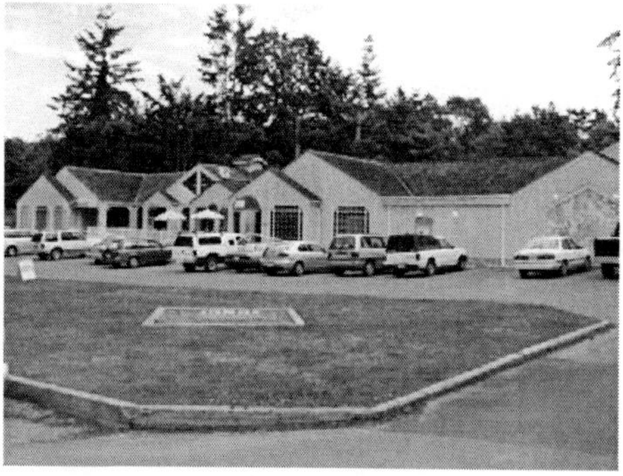

At the time of this writing, the businesses in the Mayne Street Mall included realty and insurance offices, a grocery store and deli, as well as a bakery and café.

Mayne Island Bank

The *Mayne Island Bank* is noticeably absent from the Island. However, at the time of this writing, there was an Automated Teller Machine (ATM) at the Miners Bay Trading Post, as well as at the Mayne Inn on Bennett Bay.

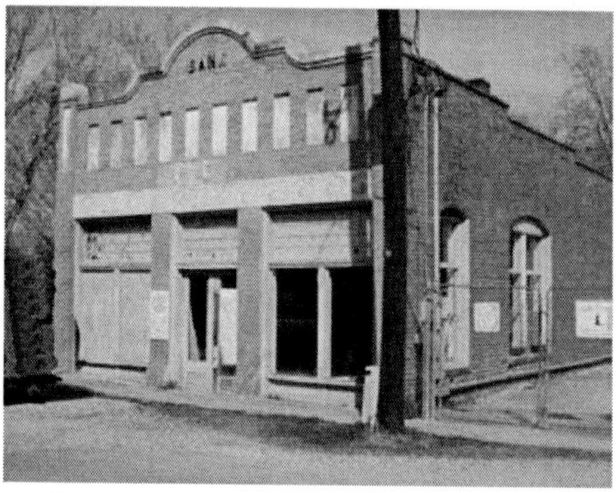

Not the Mayne Island Bank

First Nations Reserve

In the 1870's, First Nations was allotted a reserve on Helen Point, on the west side of Mayne.

A decade earlier, the area had made history when a half-breed Indian was brought aboard a British gunboat, to guide the Royal Navy to where they could investigate the sites of Indian attacks. The Indians had attacked two settlers on Saturna Island, and a settler and his daughter on Pender Island.

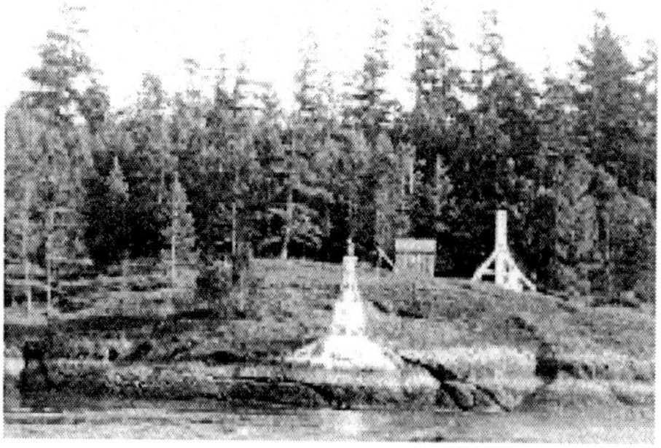

Helen Point in the 1940's BC Archives I-20664

In the 1950's, the Saanich Tribe was divided into five bands. At that time, the *Tsartlip Band* was created.

Recently, the Tsartlip Band began plans to log a portion of Helen Point. When news of the planned logging became general knowledge, opposition arose.

When the logging was complete, the Tsartlip were presented with an award by Tourism Victoria, as a testimonial to the intelligent stewardship they showed during the process.

The reserve on Helen Point is still owned by the Tsartlip Band today, but is occupied by members of the Cowichan Tribe. Helen Point contains the oldest, recorded, human settlement remains in the southern Gulf Islands.

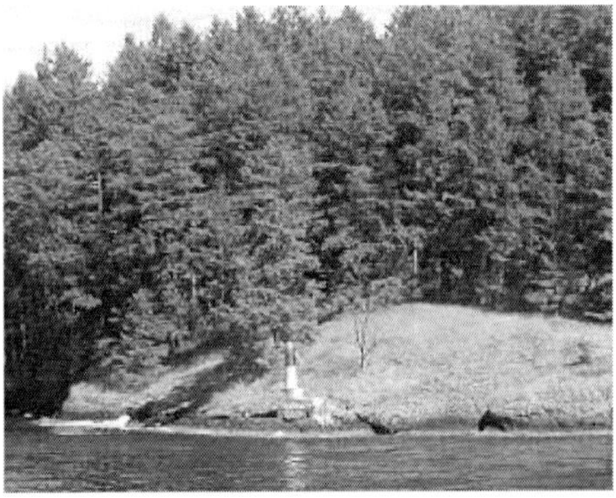

Helen Point as it appears today

Mayne Inn

In the year 1911, a French company began construction of a brick plant on Bennett Bay, on the east side of Mayne. The plant included a large wharf that extended into the bay. A boarding house was also built to accommodate the workers.

At the onset of World War I, the plant was closed, without ever becoming operational.

The Tudor-style boarding house remained empty until the 1940's, when it was converted into a hotel called *Hollandia Hotel*. In the 1950's, the name was changed to *Arbutus Lodge* and then to the *Mayne Inn* in the 1960's.

A decade later, the owners of the Inn attempted to build a large commercial dock beside one of the best swimming beaches on Mayne.

The project was estimated to cost as much as $60,000. However, before they received the necessary re-zoning, they started work on the dock. Later, with half of the project completed, they were ordered to halt the work and begin its demolition.

Today, the Mayne Inn is still operational. In the year prior to this writing, the new owners expanded the Inn by adding more guest suites called *Mayne Island Resort & Beach Homes*. The Inn is located on Arbutus Drive.

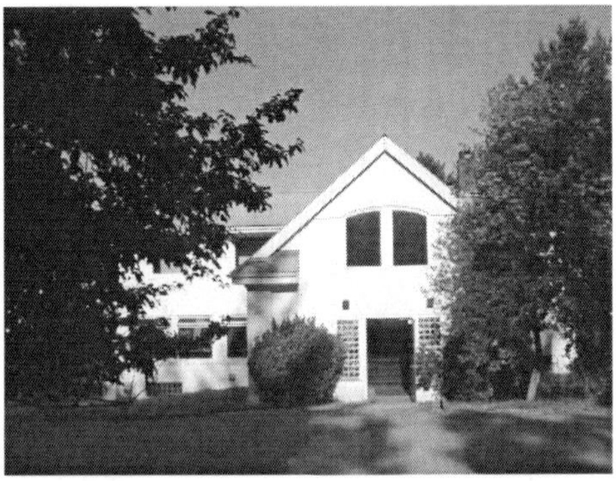

Springwater Lodge

In the 1890's, after his eldest children had left home, **the Postman** turned the two-story home he had built by the wharf into a boarding house. He ran the boarding house for about 15 years, in an effort to supplement his income.

After the turn of the century, **the Postman's** daughter took over the operation of his boarding house, renaming it the *Grandview Lodge*. Soon, it had a false front and a six-bedroom wing off the side.

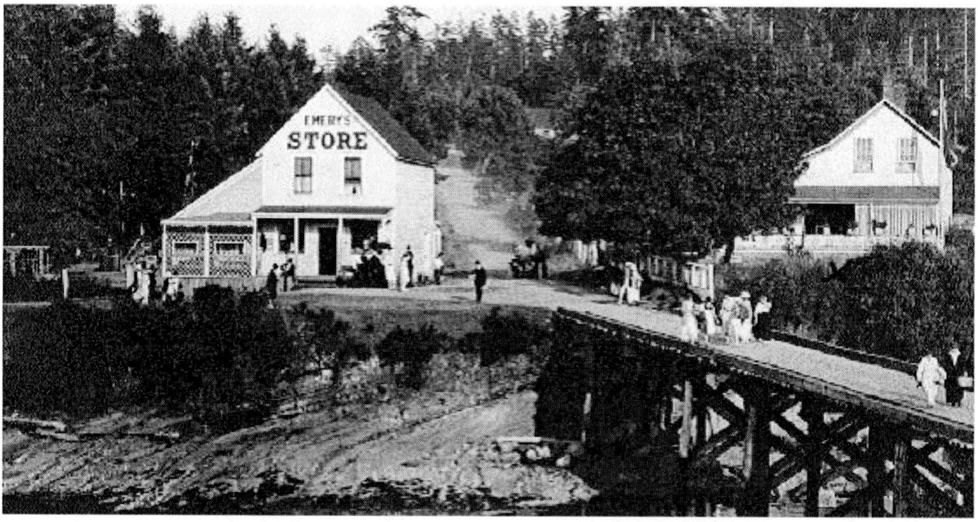

The Springwater Lodge in the early 1920's, BC Archives B-03269

By the 1930's, the lodge had developed such a good reputation that the owners were able to add indoor plumbing, electric lights and a walk-in refrigerator, in spite of the economic depression of that decade. They charged $14 for a single room, meals included.

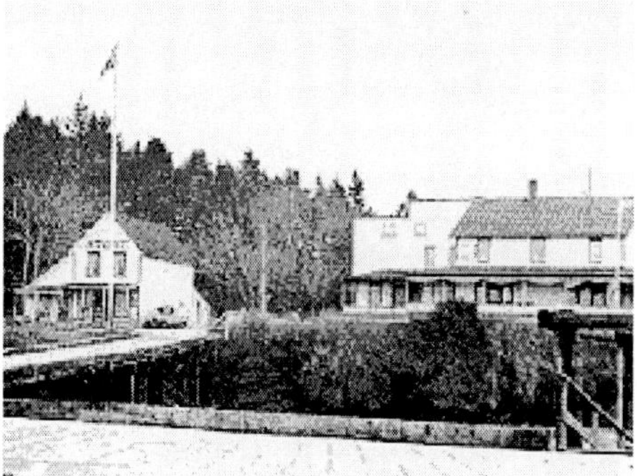

The Springwater Lodge, 1930's
BC Archives D-07435

In the 1960's, new owners changed the name to the *Springwater Lodge*. Reportedly, a '67 Volkswagen van was impounded on Mayne after it crashed into the lodge. The owner who pressed charges was irate and unclothed.

Today, the Springwater Lodge is reputed to be the oldest, continuously operating hotel in all of British Columbia. Parts of **the Postman`s** home still remain.

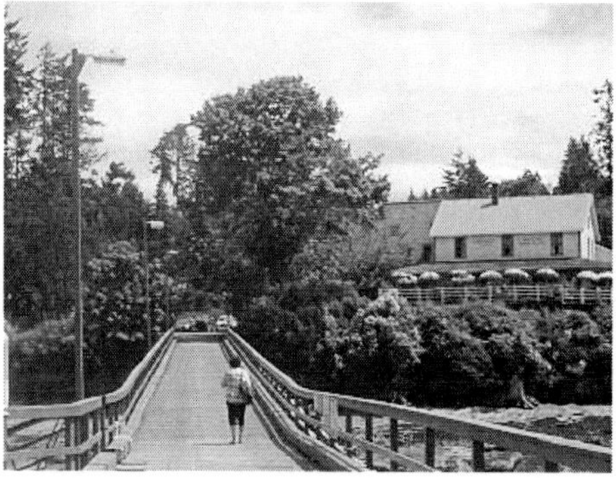

The Springwater Lodge as it appears today

Tinkerer's B&B

In the 1880's, an early settler built a small store and a hotel overlooking Miners Bay. He named the hotel *Mayne Island House*, but it was known locally as *Robson's Hotel*. When it was expanded by new owners, it was renamed the *Mayne Island Hotel*.

Because there were no other saloons in operation in the outer Gulf Islands, Mayne became known as *Little Hell* to the people of the neighboring Islands. This distinction continued until Prohibition.

In the 1920's, the hotel was destroyed by fire and a house was built on the site.

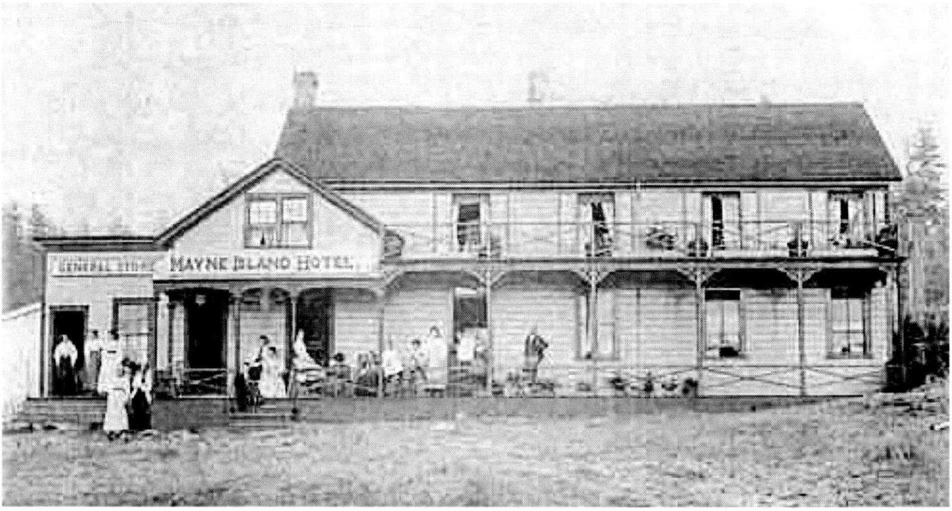

Mayne Island Hotel in the early 1900's – Galiano Archives G57

Much later, in the 1980's, a trained toolmaker and his wife renovated and restored the home that had been built on the site in the 1920's. They called it *Tinkerer's Retreat.* The retreat served them as their summer home.

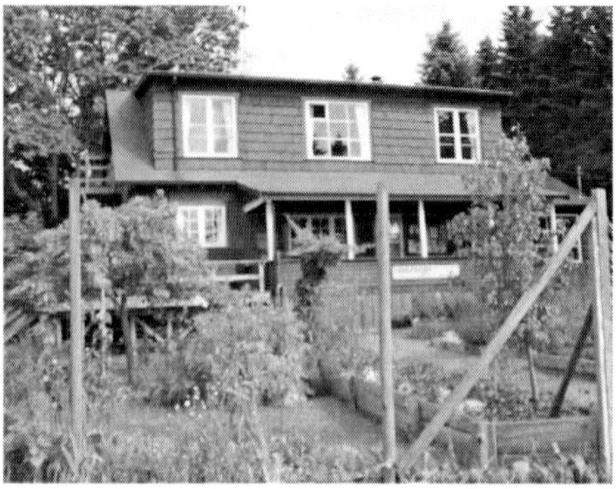

Today, the home operates as the *Tinkerer's Bed and Breakfast.* The building, which is located on Sunset Place, still functions as the couple's summer home. They also use it to run a tool sharpening business, sharpening tools the old-fashioned way.

Mayne Mast Restaurant

In the 1920's, a Japanese fisherman purchased a turn-of-the-century, Victorian style home at Miners Bay. Later, his family purchased a small greenhouse, which they dismantled and moved, piece by piece, to Miners Bay.

After re-assembling the greenhouse alongside his home, the fisherman began to use it to grow hothouse tomatoes. He became successful in this venture and developed a tomato growers cooperative on Mayne.

In the 1930's, the Japanese-Canadian enlarged his home, only to have his family evacuated from it at the start of World War II.

Much later, in the 1970's, the home was converted into a restaurant called the *Five Roosters Restaurant*.

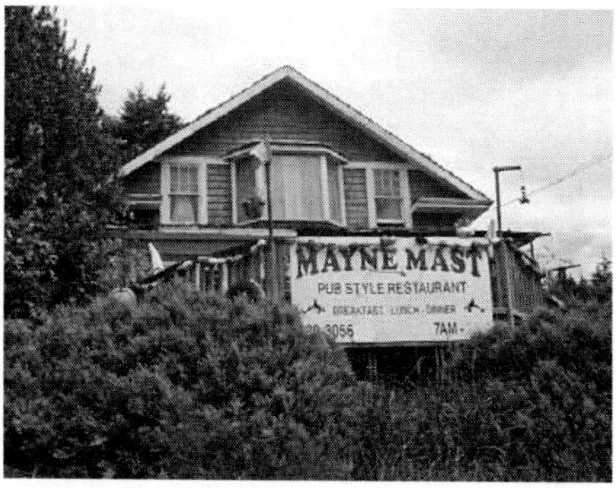

Today, the restaurant, which is located on Village Bay Road, operates as the *Mayne Mast*. As a licensed pub, it offers breakfast, lunch and dinner. At the time of this writing, you could also find a variety of garden gnomes for sale there.

1 Mayne Island Museum
3 St. Mary Magdalene Church
4 The Anchorage
5 Hobbit House
6 Georgina Point Lighthouse
7 Valhalla Gardens
8 Japanese Gardens
9 Meadowmist Farm
10 Glenbrook Farm
11 Fernhill Center Stores
12 Hidden Lighthouse Gifts
13 Island Elements Gifts
14 Glass Blowing Studio
15 Miners Bay Bookstore

Mayne Island Sights & Shops

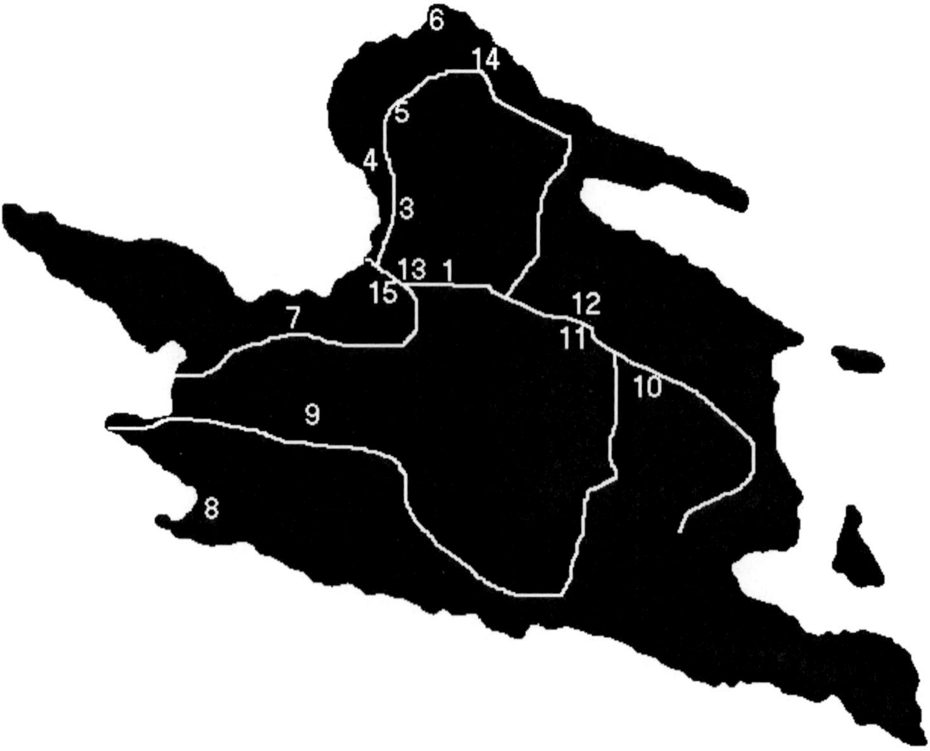

Things to See

Mayne Island is a relaxing getaway with many areas to wander about. Many people come to Mayne simply to stroll out to the lighthouse, gaze at the Victorian architecture, or go for a drive in the country.

There are four major routes on Mayne. Fernhill Road runs east and west, bisecting the Island. Village Bay Road connects Fernhill Road to the ferry terminal and to the south end of the Island.

Horton Bay Road splits off at Gallagher Bay Road, which turns into Mariners Way, connecting several minor roads along the south end of the Island. Georgina Point Road turns into Waugh Road and then into Campbell Bay Road, circumventing the north end of the Island.

Mayne Island Museum

In the 1890's, a famous explorer from Saturna Island donated some land at Miners Bay and the first jail house to exist in the outer Gulf Islands was built there. It was called the *Plumper Pass Lockup*.

The Plumper Pass Lockup became the police headquarters for all the southern Gulf Islands. It measured just 32 sq m, and contained a magistrate's courtroom and two holding cells. The first constable to police the Gulf Islands took residence there.

The reinforced doors of the cells were locked with iron crossbars. The first prisoner to be held in one of the cells was arrested for larceny on Galiano Island. While he was Justice of the Peace, **the Postman** presided over such cases when they were presented in the courtroom.

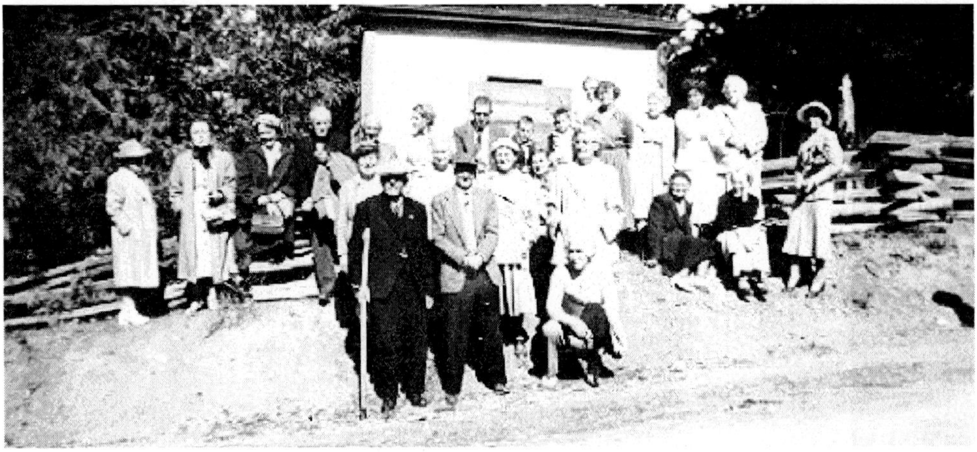

Mayne Island Museum in the 1950's, BC Archives B-07532

Shortly after the turn of the century, ownership of the building that operated as the lockup transferred to a Mayne Island doctor.

Much later, in the 1970's, the lockup was restored by the Mayne Island Agricultural Society, who converted it into the *Mayne Island Museum*.

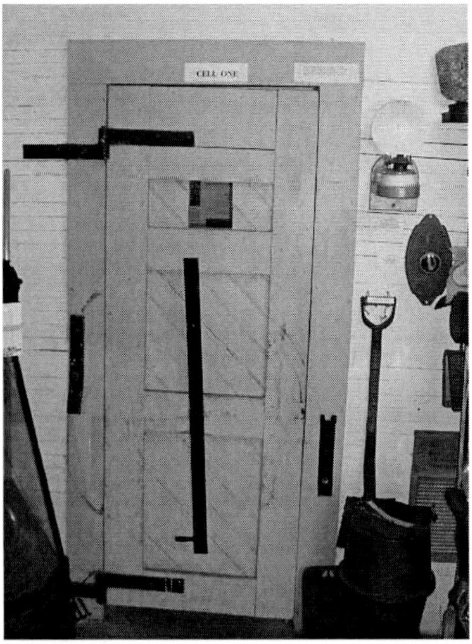

Today, the museum, which is located on Fernhill Road, is home to a variety of artifacts and historical data. (#1 on the map)

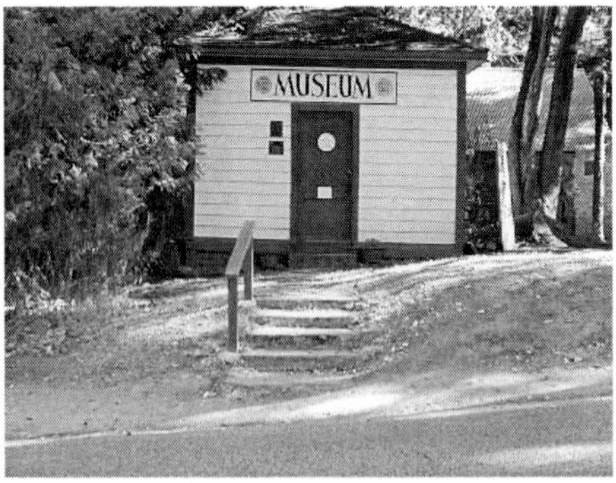

Mayne Island Museum as it appears today

Active Pass Light Station

In the 18th century, the British began surveying the West Coast. During one of their voyages, they landed on a point at the north entrance to the Pass. One hundred years later, in the 1880's, **the Postman** discovered a British one-cent coin that had been lost on that same point. It was dated Seventeen Hundred and Eighty-Four.

Around the time the Postman was examining his newly found coin, construction of a lighthouse began on the point. It was called the *Plumper Pass Lighthouse*.

One of only two major lighthouses constructed before the turn of the century, the Plumper Pass Lighthouse was the most important lighthouse on the entire West Coast of Canada.

The lighthouse was equipped with the first steam-powered foghorn ever used. The light was a coal-oil lamp with wicks and chimneys. It had a revolving, multi-faceted magnifying glass, which was powered by a system of chains and weights and had to be wound up every few hours.

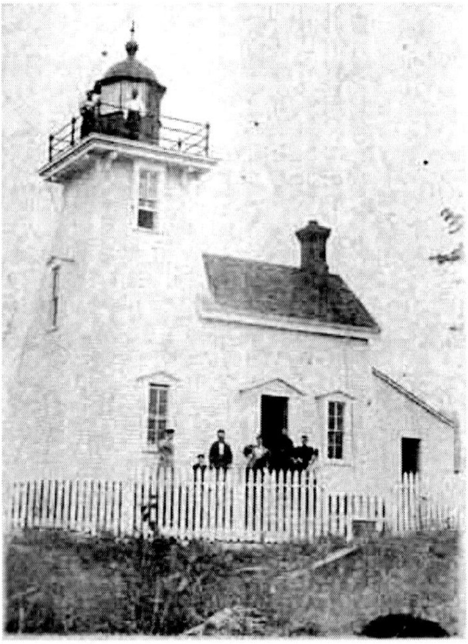

Active Pass Light Station in the late 1800's, Salt Spring Island Archives G39

The resident who took the position as the first lighthouse keeper lived inside the lighthouse with his family. One day, a family friend went around the corner of the lighthouse just as the ship, *Princess Adelaide*, crashed into the rocks in front of him. It had failed to sound its whistle in time.

The lighthouse keeper spent a full day towing passengers to shore in lifeboats. The ship, which had sustained only minor damage, remained on the beach for two more days, before being pulled off by an American tugboat.

In the 1940's, a new light station was built on the point. At that time, one of the original buildings was moved to an organic farm where it is now being used as a house.

The new light station was named the *Active Pass Light Station.* Because the point, itself, had officially been named *Georgina Point*, the lighthouse was renamed the *Georgina Point Lighthouse*.

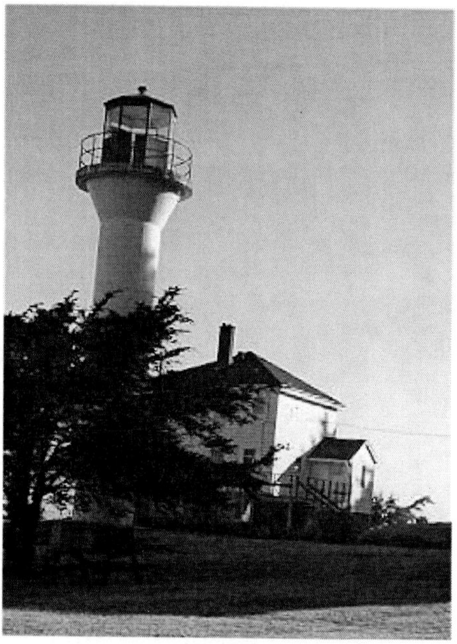

Active Pass Light Station as it appears today

The Active Pass Light Station celebrated its centennial in the 1980's, a distinction held by only a few lighthouses on the entire West Coast.

The tower was recently de-staffed and is now closed. However, the light station, which sits on park grounds, is still open to the public and is accessible from Georgina Point Road. (#6 on the map)

Glenwood Farm

In the 1860's, a prominent settler emigrated from England to Vancouver Island at the age of 14. When he found prospecting for gold too difficult, he set sail for the Gulf Islands and landed in Horton Bay, on Mayne.

As he explored the area on the east side of the Island, he located a valley in which he started growing crops. He called his farm *Glenwood*. It was there that he built his first log home.

A decade later, the young settler formed a partnership with the man who would later become **the Postman**.

Soon, the children attending the Mayne Island School began picnicking at Glenwood Farm, to celebrate the end of each school year. This became a tradition that continued for several years.

Glenwood Farm was eventually developed into a highly successful dairy farm. Around the turn of the century, the settler started supplying cream to the creamery on Salt Spring Island.

During World War I, the farm had become known for its herd of Record of Performance Jerseys, which won prizes at the provincial exhibitions for many years. The settler paid his taxes each year by selling his fattest cow.

Today, Glenwood Farm is the oldest farm on Mayne and is one of the largest of the old homesteads in all the Gulf Islands. Although one of the first houses to be built on the property was destroyed by fire, a descendant who lived in the third house to be built there was still working the farm at the time of this writing.

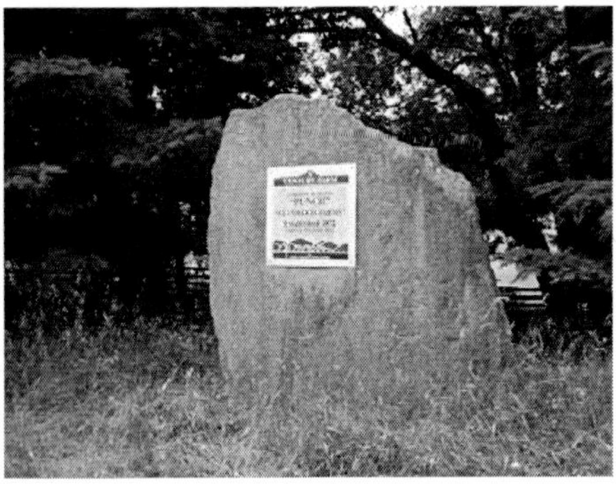

A monument commemorating the farm and the descendant of its first settler exists on Horton Bay Road. (#10 on the map)

Meadowmist Farm

Meadowmist Farm sits in a large valley on the west side of Mayne. In the 1980's, the farm began raising animals to be used for food and other products, such as soap, quilts and clothing.

Today, the farm also raises a novelty bird from Chile, called the *Araucana*. It lays green eggs. Since the farm occasionally raises pigs as well, you might want to purchase some Araucana eggs so you can cook up some 'green eggs and ham'.

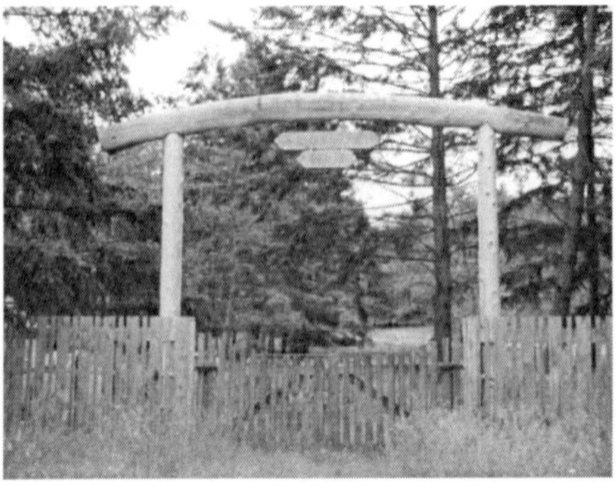

Meadowmist Farm products can be purchased at the farm, as well as in the grocery stores around the Island. The farm is accessible by way of Merryman Drive. (#9 on the map) People are encouraged to visit. The contribution is one *tooney* (two Canadian dollars).

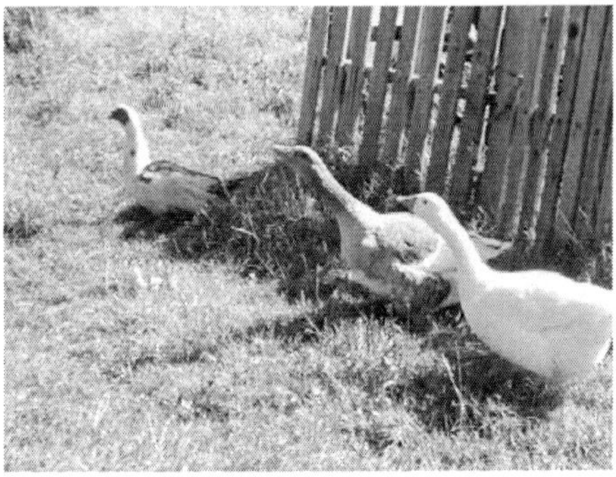

The Anchorage

In the year 1910, a prominent settler purchased some land at the north end of Mayne. There, he established the Island's first hothouse industry and pioneered the use of double-trussed greenhouses.

In his greenhouse operation, he grew some of the first hothouse tomatoes in the province. However, in spite of the fact that he employed Chinese workers for 20 years, he never learned one word of the Chinese language.

In the 1920's, he built a larger operation at Miners Bay, where he specialized in flowers and tomatoes. He called it *Mayne Island Nurseries*. His greenhouse was the largest in all of British Columbia.

Eventually, the settler's hothouse industry became so large that his weekly shipments would often delay the steamer ships at the wharf for hours. As a result, he became well known on the West Coast as 'The Tomato King'.

The successful settler suffered in the stock market crash of the 1920's and, subsequently, he retired in the 1930's.

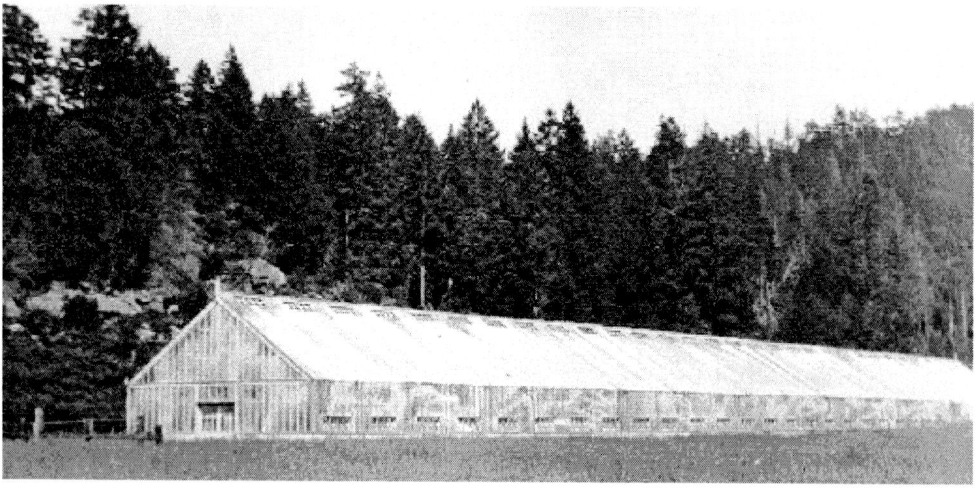

Greenhouses near Miners Bay in the 1940's, BC Archives D-07434

When the Japanese took over his tomato industry, he began catering to guests from his home overlooking the bay. He called his guesthouse *The Anchorage*.

In the 1950's, The Anchorage ceased to operate as a guesthouse. At that time, the hill on which it stood was named after the settler. It is called *Hall Hill*.

Today, the field on Hall Hill is all that remains of Mayne Island Nurseries. However, a descendant of the settler still resides in the home, which is located on Georgina Point Road. (#4 on the map)

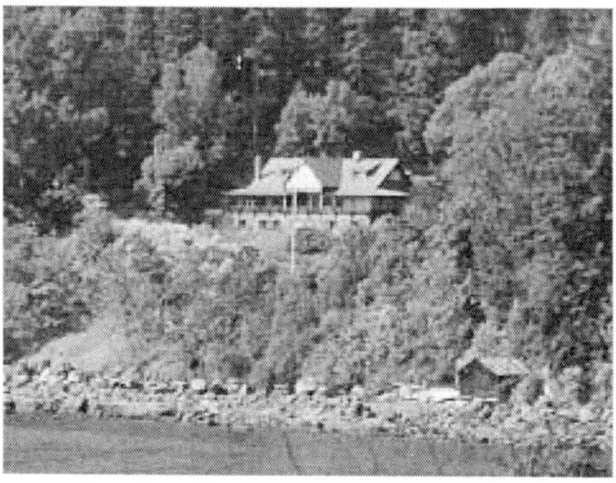

Cob Homes

Cob homes are made from a mixture of sand, clay and straw. The mixture is wet enough to mold, yet dry enough to build up without forms.

There are a few cob homes on Mayne Island. One of the homes is reportedly the first code-approved cob house ever to exist in Canada.

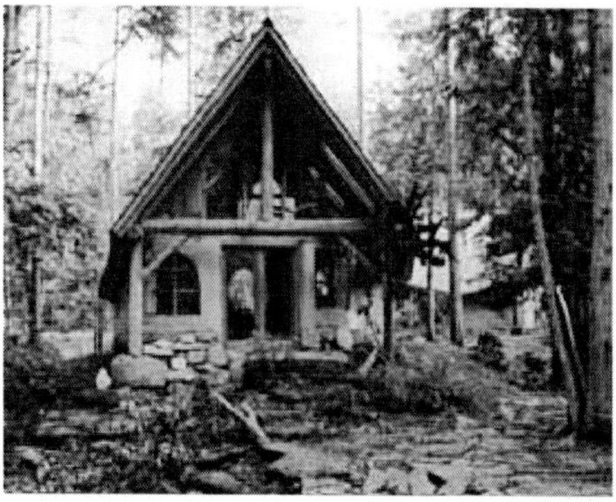

The cob home on Georgina Point Road is run as a cottage rental, called *The Hobbit House*. (#5 on the map) Designed by Charles Andre, it was built using the same method that was used for making cob houses in England and Wales in the 15th and 16th century.

There are also cob homes on Horton Bay Road. Tours of some of the cob homes are available.

St. Mary Magdalene Church

In the 1880's, **the Postman** offered to donate some land for the site of a church, but his offer was not acted upon. Instead, a famous explorer from Saturna Island provided the land. While the church was being constructed, a house that had recently been built on the land was used for services.

In the 1890's, the *St. Mary Magdalene Anglican Church* was built. It was the first church to serve the outer Gulf Islands.

A few years after the church was built, a 180 kg piece of sandstone was discovered on the shore of Saturna. Because a natural basin had been carved into it by the tides, the Vicar, who was the founder of the church, transported it by rowboat so it could be used as the baptismal vessel.

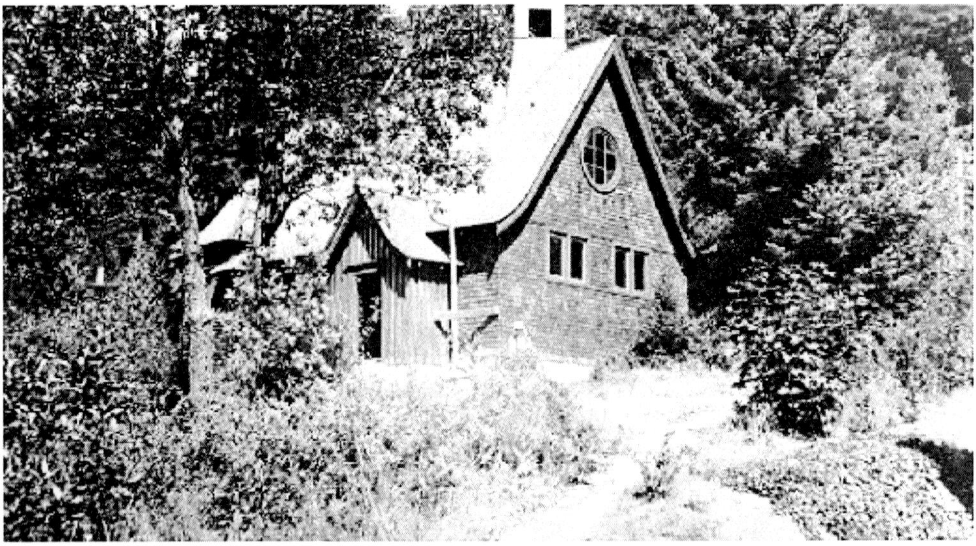

St. Mary Magdalene Anglican Church in the 1890's, BC Archives G-01421

Shortly after the turn of the century, a fire broke out on the church grounds and the house, which had been serving as a residence for the Vicar, was destroyed. Fortunately, the church was saved by its parishioners.

A decade later, the church accommodated an adjoining cemetery. A Cowichan Indian, who lived in a home owned by **the Postman**, held the position as the grave digger.

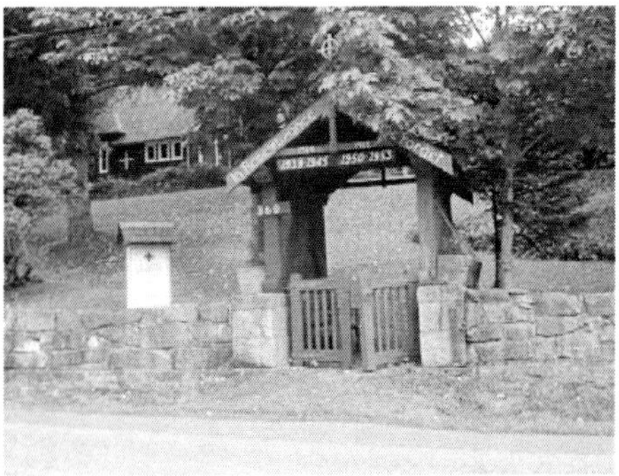

Much later, in the 1950's, the Royal Canadian Legion constructed a *lych* gate in memory of the men who died in the World Wars. It now provides for a traditional, English, church yard entrance where wonderful examples of Arbutus trees grow.

In the 1980's, the church held its first country fair, which continues to be a regular event on the church grounds each summer.

A decade later, another fire ravaged through the forest behind the church. Reportedly, it loosened large boulders and sent them down into the church grounds where they now form part of a Centennial Memorial Garden.

Today, the church, which sits on Georgina Point Road, is still very much the way it was at the turn of the century. The words 'god and ocean' can be read, in Japanese, on the steeple cross. They identify the church and its location in relation to the waters below. (#3 on the map)

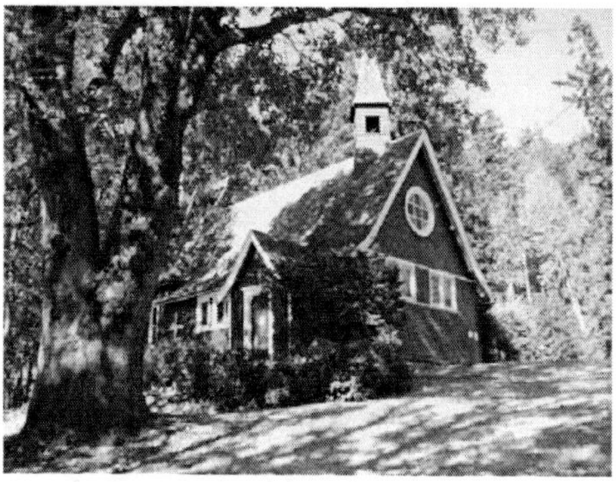

St. Mary Magdalene Anglican Church as it appears today

Valhalla Gardens

Valhalla Gardens is a wonderful flower garden that thrives among a forest of giant Western Red Cedar and Douglas-Fir. Recently, the gardens hosted the first *FestivaLavender* event, which continues to be an annual event. The gardens are located on Village Bay Road. (#7 on the map)

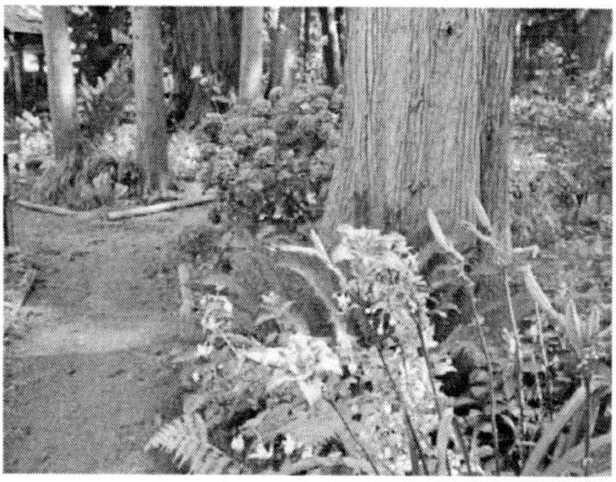

Japanese Memorial Garden

In the 1870's, the first Japanese to come to Canada were known as *Issei*. They settled on Vancouver Island where they encountered racism from the anti-Asian population of British Columbia, as well as from the government.

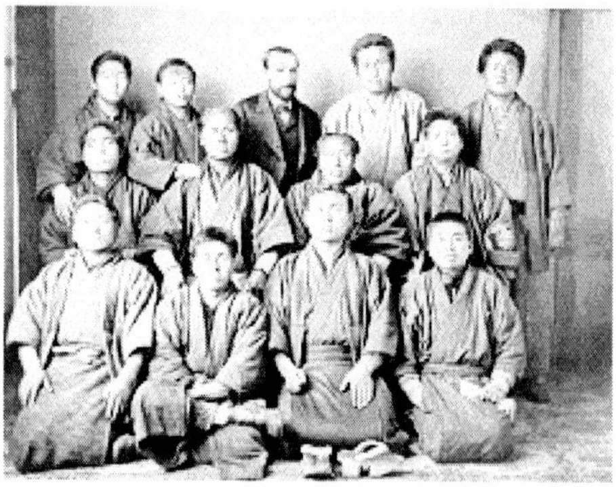

Fishermen in the 1880's, believed to be the first Japanese in Victoria BC Archives B-08405

The government denied the Japanese-Canadians the right to work in a profession, so when they came to Mayne, the first Japanese worked as laborers, cutting wood and making charcoal for the Fraser River canneries.

Soon, Japanese-Canadian fishermen began settling on the southeast side of Mayne, at St. John Point and at what is now Horton Bay. Within their own community they knew

Mayne Island as *Gon Island*, which they named after the first Japanese settler on the Island. Fortunately, they were well received by the Europeans who had already settled on Mayne.

The Japanese-Canadian fishermen soon began concentrating on raising chickens. The families produced market eggs from about 50,000 hens.

When freight increases made poultry farming unprofitable in the 1930's, many began to cultivate hothouse tomatoes and other vegetables, forming a successful marketing cooperative called *Active Pass Growers Association*.

The cooperative boasted almost 35,000 sq m of greenhouses, made from glass imported from Japan.

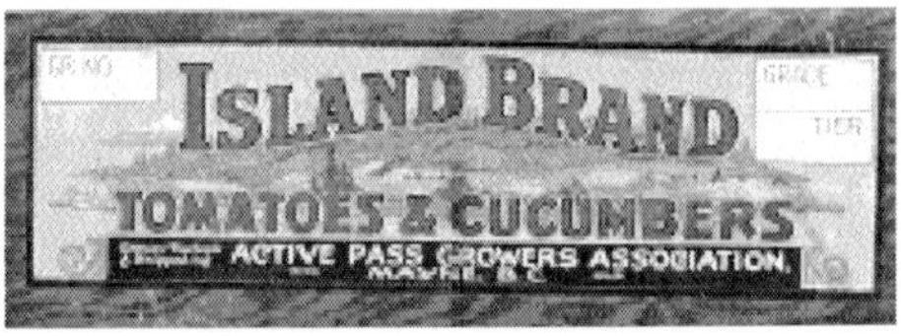

Label used by the Active Pass Growers Association in the 1930's

By the 1940's, the Japanese-Canadian community comprised one-third of Mayne's population. Unfortunately, when the Japanese attacked Pearl Harbor, the Japanese-Canadians were taken from their homes on Mayne and were dispatched to the interior of British Columbia where internment camps had been set up in remote towns.

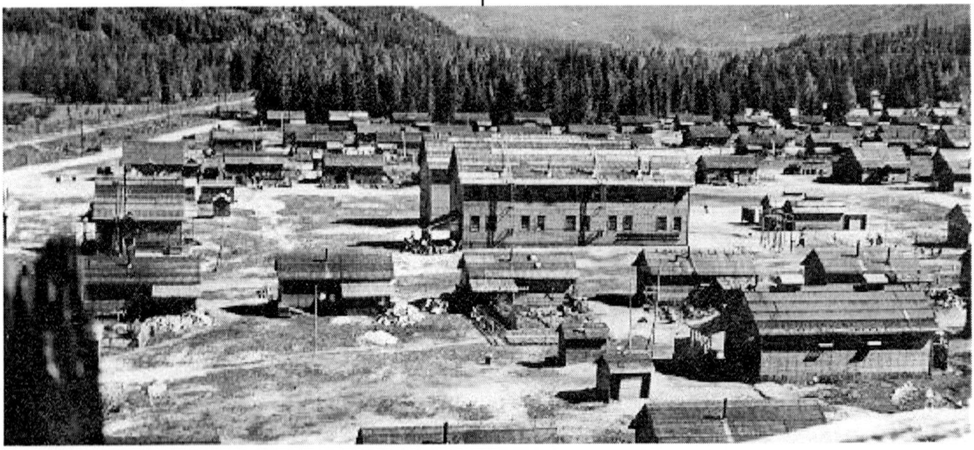

Japanese-Canadian internment camp, south of Slocan City, in the 1940's, BC Archives I-60959

At that time, the Canadian Navy impounded all Japanese fishing boats that existed in British Columbian waters.

Some of the European settlers tried to buy the property that belonged to their Japanese friends, but that soon became a criminal offence.

After World War II, the property of the Japanese-Canadians was sold off by government agents acting on orders made under the provisions of the War Measures Act. The property was often sold to war veterans.

Post-internment, the Japanese-Canadian families were still prohibited from returning to the British Columbian coast. They were only allowed to return to Japan or to travel east of the Rocky Mountains.

Many traveled to the neighboring province of Alberta, to work as laborers on sugar beet farms.

Eventually, the right to vote was returned to the Japanese, who had lost it before the turn of the century. However, very few of them ever returned to Mayne to receive that right.

The *Japanese Memorial Garden* is a development that was completed only recently. Built by residents, on what was once a Japanese-Canadian fruit farm, this heritage park was undertaken to commemorate the Japanese-Canadians who originally settled and worked on Mayne.

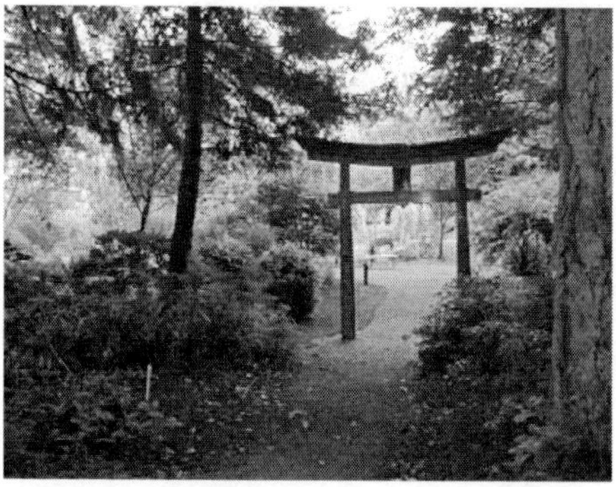

In the garden, Katsura trees, Japanese cherries, flowering plums and rhododendrons surround a large pond.

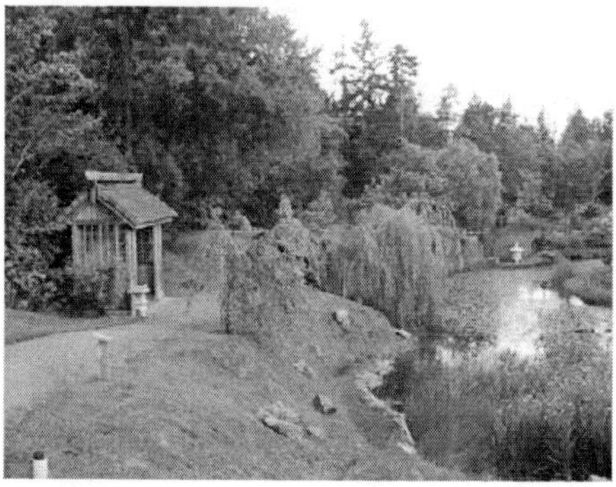

In the year prior to this writing, a small group of individuals who quietly tend to the garden received the Islands Trust Community Stewardship Award for donating their time.

The garden is visited by tourists during the summer and is decorated with an impressive display of festive lights during the Christmas season.

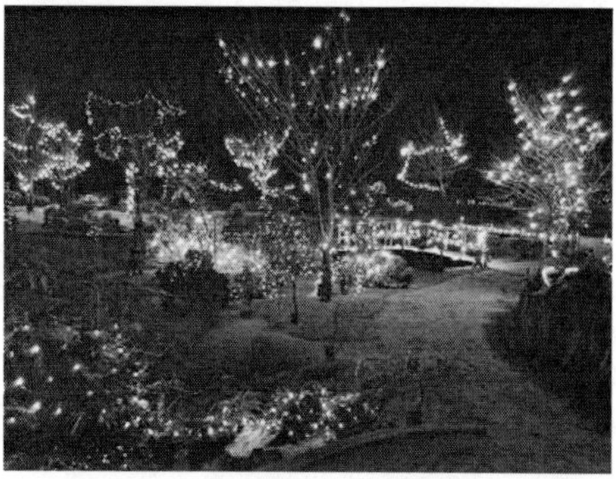

The Japanese Garden is located at Dinner Bay Community Park, which can be accessed by way of Williams Place. (#8 on the map)

Places to Shop

At the turn of the century, **the Postman** would row out to the Hudson's Bay, Spencer's and Woodwards' steamer ships, and then return with parcels in his rowboat.

Today, art galleries, shops and studios provide visitors to Mayne Island the opportunity to pick up a *potlatch* (gift) for someone special. Mayne is home to a variety of fine artists, writers, artisans and filmmakers. Watch for road signs and the chance to meet an artist working in their studio.

En-Vision Gallery

The *En-Vision Gallery* showcases some of British Columbia's leading craftspeople and local talent.

At the time of this writing, the gallery represented the talents of Vitreous Designs, Westcoast Gnomes, as well as of the studio potter, John Charowsky. The gallery can be found at the Fernhill Centre on Fernhill Road. (#11 on the map)

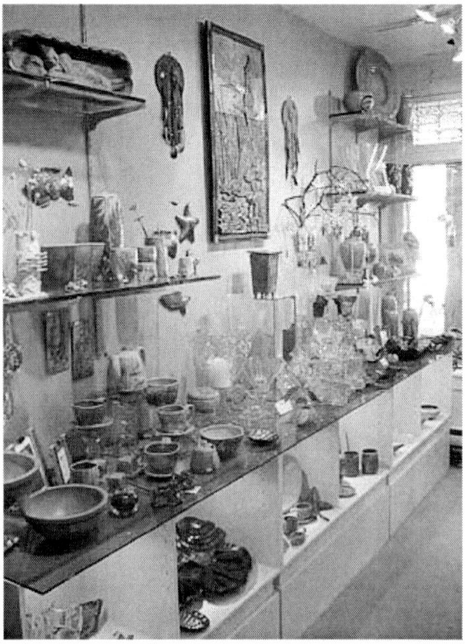

Hidden Lighthouse Gifts

In addition to providing the local Islanders with essentials, *Hidden Lighthouse Gifts and Essentials* has a variety of gifts and collectibles. You will see creations by local artists, unique and unusual gifts, and things of a nautical nature.

The store also sells sporting goods, and hiking and fishing equipment. It can be found across from the Fernhill Centre on Fernhill Road. (#12 on the map)

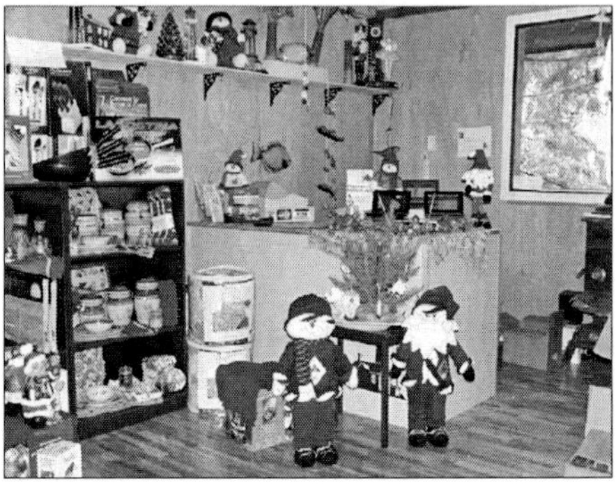

Miners Bay Books

Miners Bay Books can be found at the historic Root Seller Inn at Miners Bay. (#15 on the map) It offers new and used books, gifts, cards, toys and games. The bookstore specializes in West Coast, British Columbian, local author, children's and literary fiction.

Mayne Island Glass Foundry

The *Mayne Island Glass Foundry* is a studio where you can watch glass being blown, cast and pressed into art. It is also a small-scale, glass recycling business.

The studio is dedicated to the process of making environmentally friendly, glass art and to designing super energy-efficient, studio glass equipment. It reports recycling over 29,000 kg of scrap glass since 1996. The studio can be found on Aya Reach Road. (#14 on the map)

Island Elements

At the turn of the century, a Victorian-style home was built at Miners Bay. It was later converted into a gift shop called the *Island Cottage*. At the time of this writing, it was under new management, operating as *Island Elements*. The store is located at Miners Bay, on Fernhill Road. (#13 on the map)

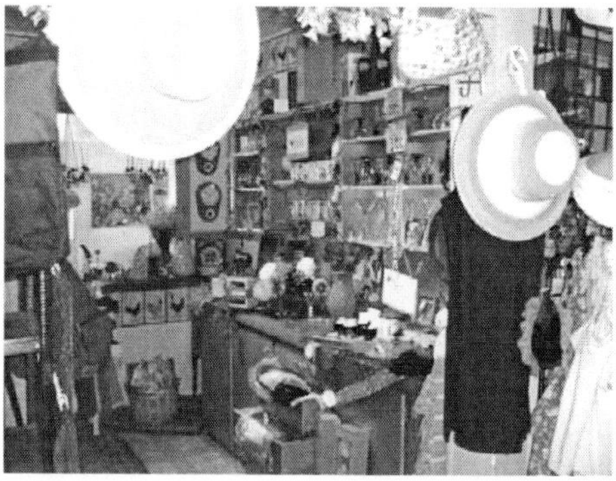

McKenzie Fine Art Gallery

McKenzie Fine Art Gallery features the unique paintings of Jim McKenzie. McKenzie's genre is West Coast realism and his works are available in oil or print. The gallery can be found at the Fernhill Centre on Fernhill Road. (#11 on the map)

Tree Frog Gallery & Natural Clothing

Tree Frog Gallery & Natural Clothing specializes in items produced using organic materials. The gallery can be found at the Fernhill Centre on Fernhill Road. (#11 on the map)

Events to Attend

In the year prior to this writing, a Mayne Islander boarded a ferry to attend a baseball game. Realizing he would be late for the game if he waited for the ferry to dock, he threw himself overboard and started swimming toward Helen Point.

Three ferries launched rescue boats in an effort to come to the man's aid. However, he refused to get into any of the boats and swam all the way to shore. Unfortunately, he never made it to the game because authorities took him to Vancouver Island for a physical examination.

Whether it is an annual event, such as the *LavenderFestival* or the *Country Fair*, or a special event, such as a music festival or play, there is always something to take in on Mayne Island.

The Mayne Island Lions Club has been active for over 30 years. Together, with the Mayne Island Volunteer Firefighter's Association, they host a variety of events throughout the year.

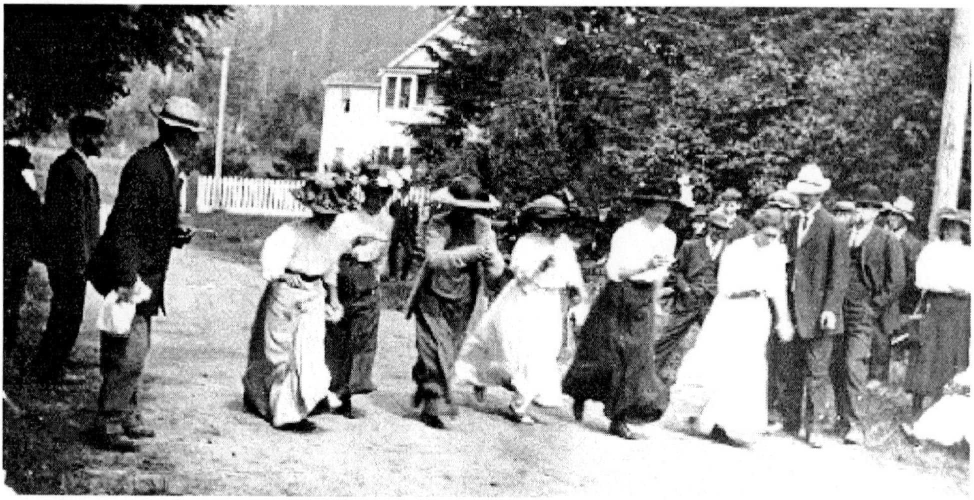

Settlers participating in an 'egg & spoon' race in the early 1900's, BC Archives NA-40411

Folk Night

One day, a young musician from Vancouver, who has recorded an album under a major label, was performing at the Mayne Island Agriculture Hall. During his set break, he was approached by a bearded man who said, "I really like your stuff. I play music too. My name's Raffi".

The Mayne Island Folk Club was formed only recently. The club gets together on *Folk Night*, which is held at the agricultural hall on the first Friday of every month.

The stage is open to all musicians and is then followed by the feature performance of the evening. Musicians and singers like Alison Crowe, Jeremy Fisher, Rick Fines and The Gruff have all performed live at the hall.

Easter Egg Hunt

The annual *Easter Egg Hunt* and parade take place in March at Dinner Bay Community Park. Each year, a Mayne Islander dresses as the Easter Bunny. There is a prize for the best Easter bonnet.

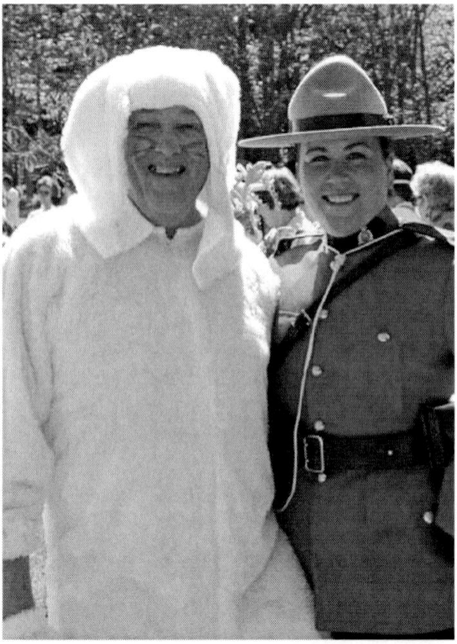

Mother's Day Pancake Breakfast

At the *Mother's Day Pancake Breakfast* you can get some great *deadshot* (flapjacks). The event is held in May at an old schoolhouse on Felix Jack Road.

Canada Day Picnic

The *Canada Day Picnic* is celebrated on July 1 at Dinner Bay Community Park. There is food, games and a variety of festivities.

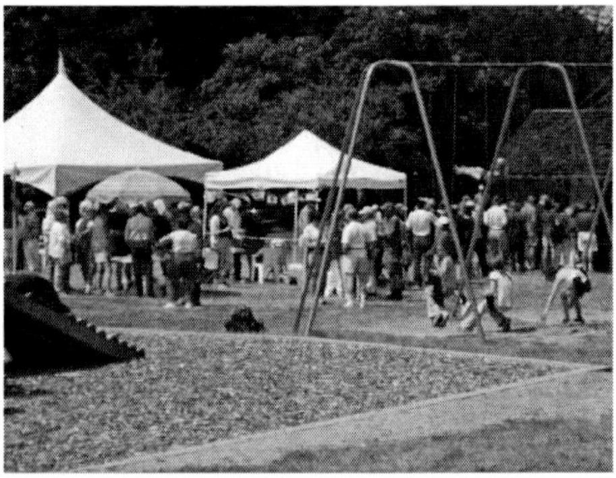

Mayne Island Farmer's Market

The Agriculture Fair Grounds are the site of the famous *Mayne Island Farmer's Market*, which runs every Saturday from July through to October.

The market provides for a cornucopia of fresh produce from local farmers, as well as art from local artists and craftspeople.

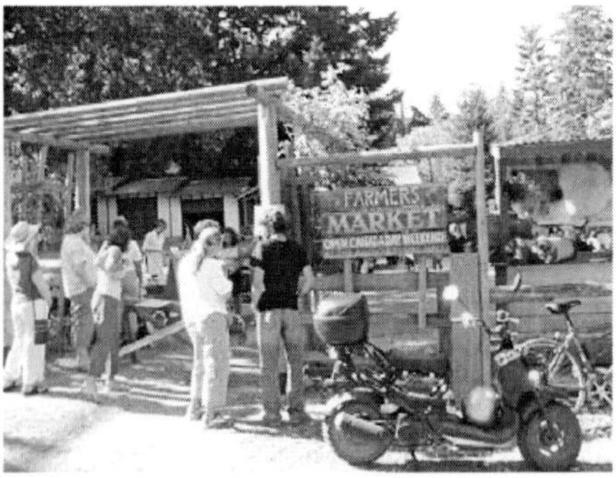

Barn Dance

The first annual *Barn Dance* was held a few years prior to this writing. The event takes place at the Mayne Island School and provides for live music, great food, raffles and a silent auction.

Country Fair

The long-lived *Country Fair* is held early in July at St. Mary Magdalene Church. It is the church's only fundraising event. The fair is complete with games, auctions, baked goods and entertainment.

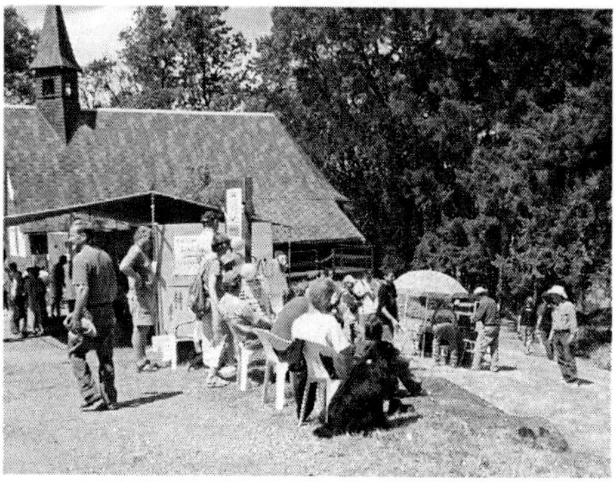

Mayne Island Dog Show

The first annual *Mayne Island Dog Show* took place in the 1990's. The event is held at the end of July in Dinner Bay Community Park. A few years prior to this writing, there were 56 entrants in a variety of categories, from 'Best Jumper' to 'Dog & Owner Look Alike'.

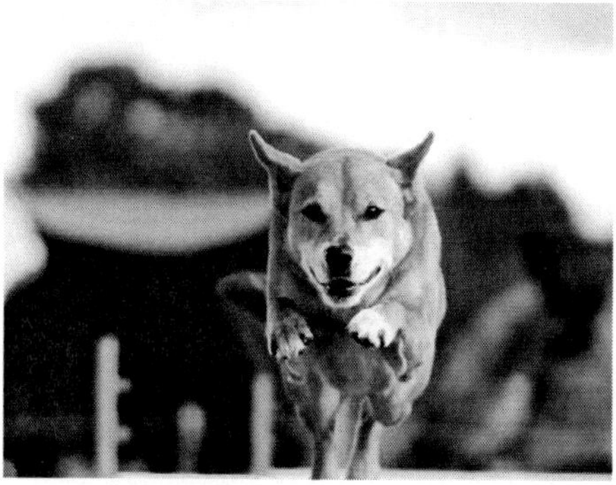

Al'elen Music Festival

Before the turn of the century, the Coast Salish Indians referred to Miners Bay as *Al'elen.* In the year prior to this writing, over 200 people gathered for the first, annual *Al'elen Music Festival*, in Miners Bay Park. The event, which is held at the end of July, provides for music performed at a newly constructed bandstand.

Mayne Island Fall Fair

In the 1920's, an eccentric English woman who was operating a grand hotel started the *Mayne Island Fall Fair.* It grew and expanded until World War II, when it became dormant for seven years.

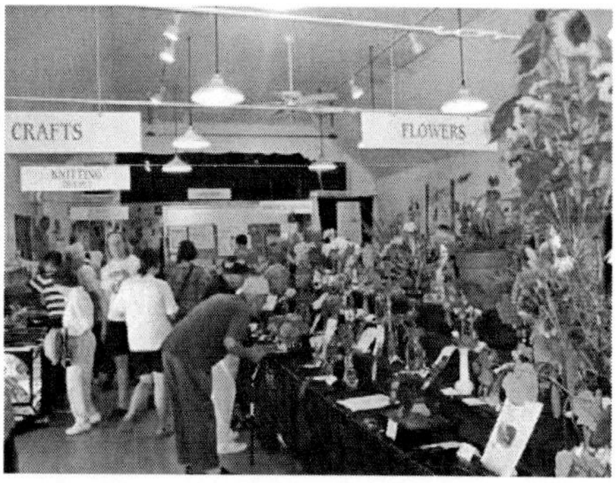

Today, the Mayne Island Fall Fair is the oldest fall fair in the outer Gulf Islands. It takes place in August at the Agriculture Fair Grounds. There is judging in a variety of categories, from produce and baking, to photography and crafts.

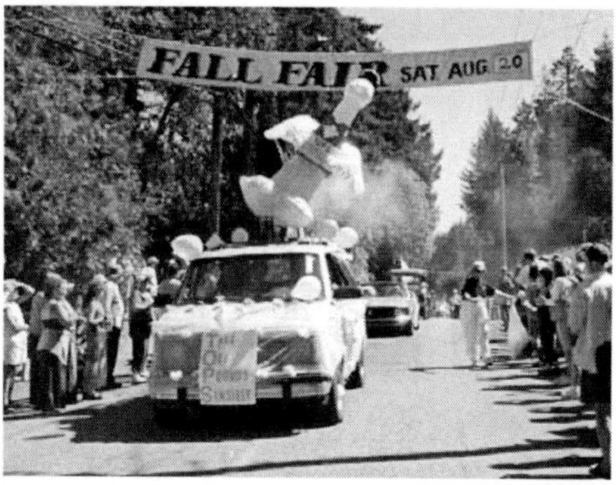

The fair also provides for a colorful parade, great music, games, demonstrations, raffles and other special events.

FestivaLavender

Sequim, Washington is the lavender growing capital of North America, where the largest lavender festival attracts 30,000 visitors each year.

Recently, three women started their own lavender festival on Mayne Island. *FestivaLavender*, which is held at Valhalla Gardens, takes place each year in August. It is much smaller than the Sequim event, but it does have good food, music, contests and lots of lavender exhibits.

FestivaLavender features demonstrations of a variety of products made from the lavender plant, from creams and lotions to baked goods and ice cream. Some Islanders demonstrate uses of lavender that most people will have never seen before.

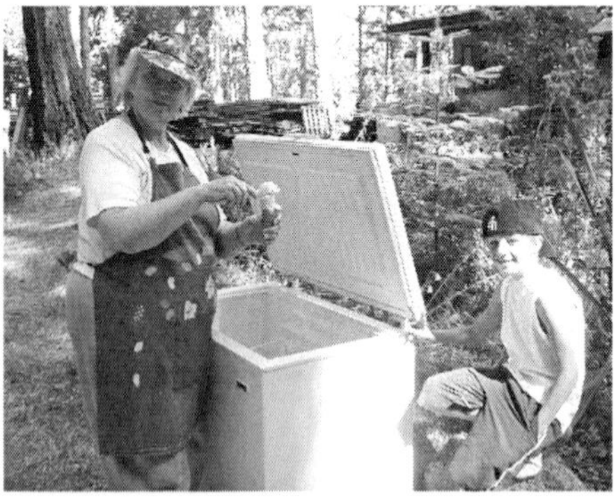

Terry Fox Run

In the 1980's, Terrance Fox, a 20-year-old amputee from British Columbia, inspired all Canadians with his 'Marathon of Hope'. His marathon was a run across the country to raise funds for cancer research.

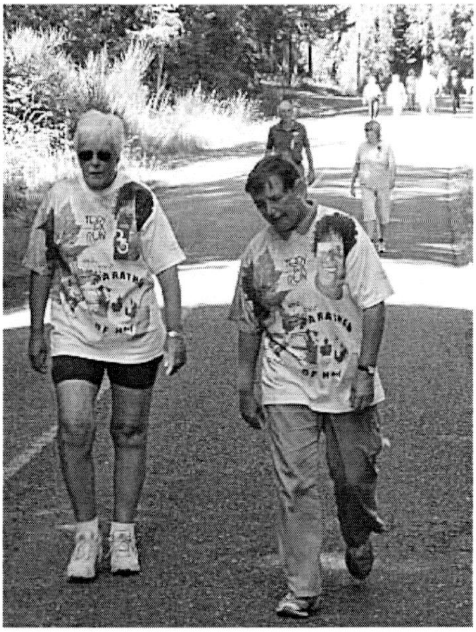

Recently, the Mayne Island Fitness Group organized the Island's first *Terry Fox Run*. The run has since become an annual event and a few years prior to this writing, over 100 people participated in it. Of all the communities participating in British Columbia, Mayne was second in per-capita fundraising.

The one, two, five or ten kilometer run, which takes place on the second Sunday after Labour Day, starts at the Georgina Point Lighthouse.

In the 25th year of the Canada-wide run, the Mayne Island School participated in the first national all-school run.

Mayne Island Cow Pie Run

The *Mayne Island Cow Pie Run* is an annual event that has been taking place in September since the 1990's.

Originally, participants of the run had to avoid cow pies as they ran through cow pastures. However, today, the run takes place entirely on pavement. In the year prior to this writing, the route was 8 km long, and started and ended at Miners Bay.

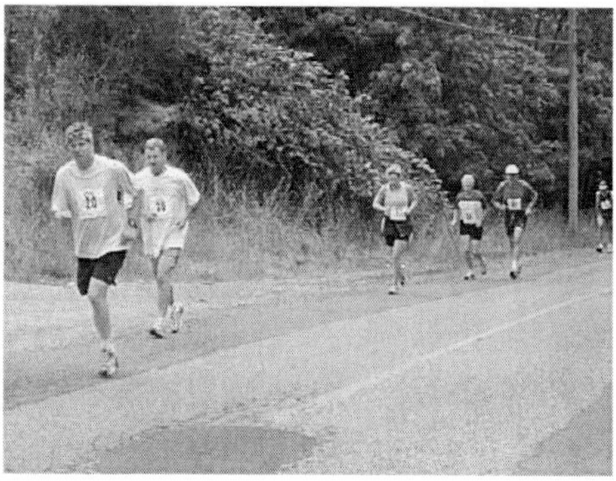

Quilt Show

Recently, 24 Canadian soldiers in Afghanistan were informed that they were going to have to spend Christmas at a remote post. Upon hearing this, the Mayne Island Quilters Guild held a 'Quilt Til You Wilt' day, donating their time and materials to make a quilt for each and every soldier.

Later, all 24 quilts were shipped to where the soldiers were stationed, just in time for Christmas.

Earlier that same year, busloads of quilters from surrounding areas joined the quilter's guild in a quilt exhibition they called 'Blowing In The Wind'.

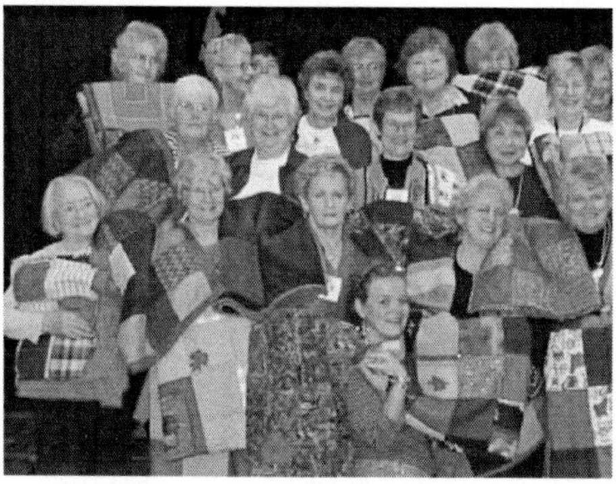

Every four years, the Mayne Island Quilters Guild display their hand-made quilts in a *Quilt Show*. The show attracts quilters from all over the Gulf Islands. At the time of this writing, the guild had 50 members.

Salmon Barbecue

The annual *Salmon Barbecue* occurs in September, on Labour Day Sunday, at Dinner Bay Community Park. The event, which is jokingly referred to as the *Wasp Festival*, provides for barbecued salmon, beer gardens, games and entertainment.

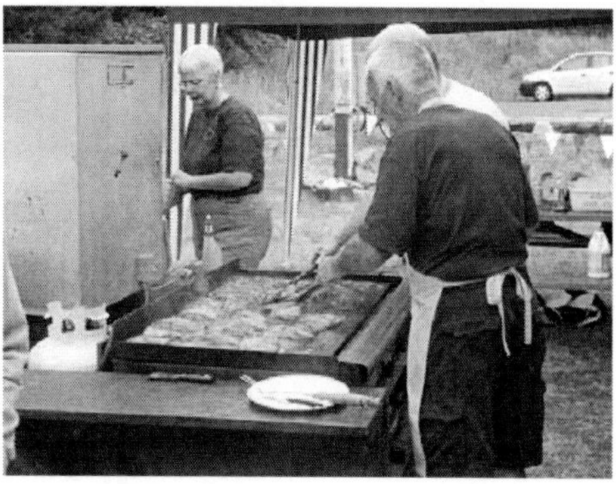

Halloween Howl

The *Halloween Howl* is an annual event held in October at the Mayne Island School grounds. It is hosted by the Mayne Island Volunteer Firefighters Association. There is also a fireworks display.

Christmas Celebrations

For over 40 years, the Bellingham Central Lions Club, in Washington State, has been sending the *Christmas Ship* to the Gulf Islands to bring toys and gifts to the kids.

Known locally as the *Santa Ship*, the Christmas Ship is greeted at the Miners Bay wharf, and then Santa and his 'helpers' distribute gifts to the kids. Additional traditions include a sleigh pulled by fire fighters.

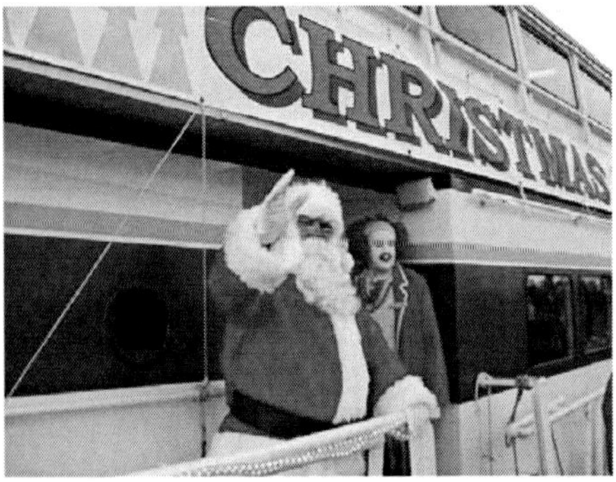

Mayne Islanders continue the Christmas season with two craft fairs. They decorate the tall Douglas-Fir tree in Miners Bay Community Park with lights that can be seen from boats in the Pass. The Japanese Garden, at Dinner Bay Community Park, is also decorated with lights.

The Christmas season is completed with a bonfire at Miners Bay Community Park, where carols are sung around the tree on Christmas Eve.

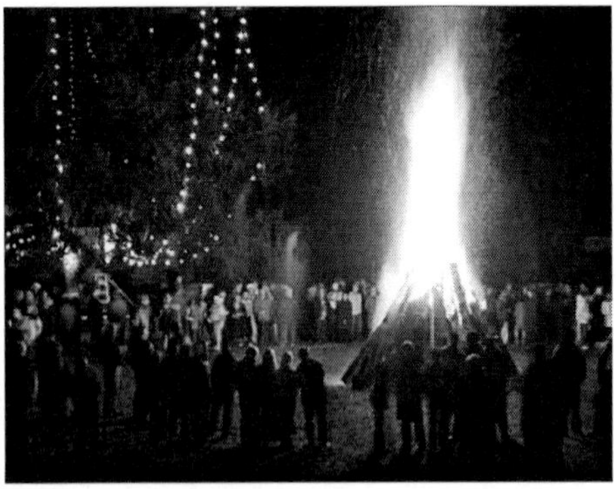

Polar Bear Paddle

The *Polar Bear Paddle* is an annual kayaking event that began just recently. It takes place on New Year's Day in Bennett Bay.

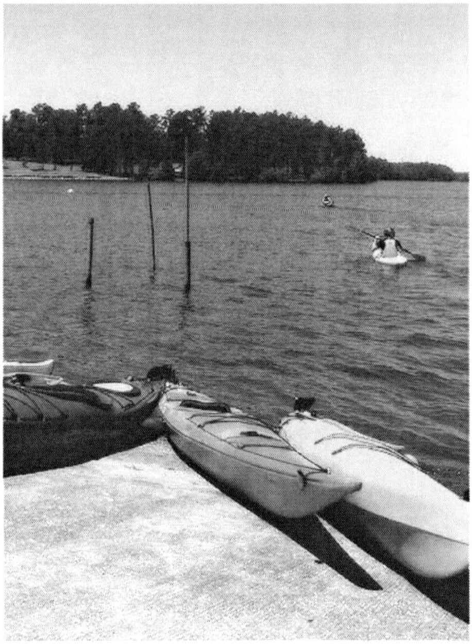

Mayne Island Parks & Beaches

1 Maude Bay
2 Heritage Park
3 Oyster Bay
4 Reef Bay
5 David Cove
6 Campbell Bay
7 Marine Heritage Park
8 Bennett Bay
10 Horton Bay
11 Chu-An Park
12 Arbutus Bay
13 Piggott Bay
14 Conconi Reef Park
15 Gallagher Bay
16 Mount Parke Park
17 Plumper Pass Park
18 Dinner Bay Park
19 Village Bay Park
20 Miners Bay Park
21 Curlew Island

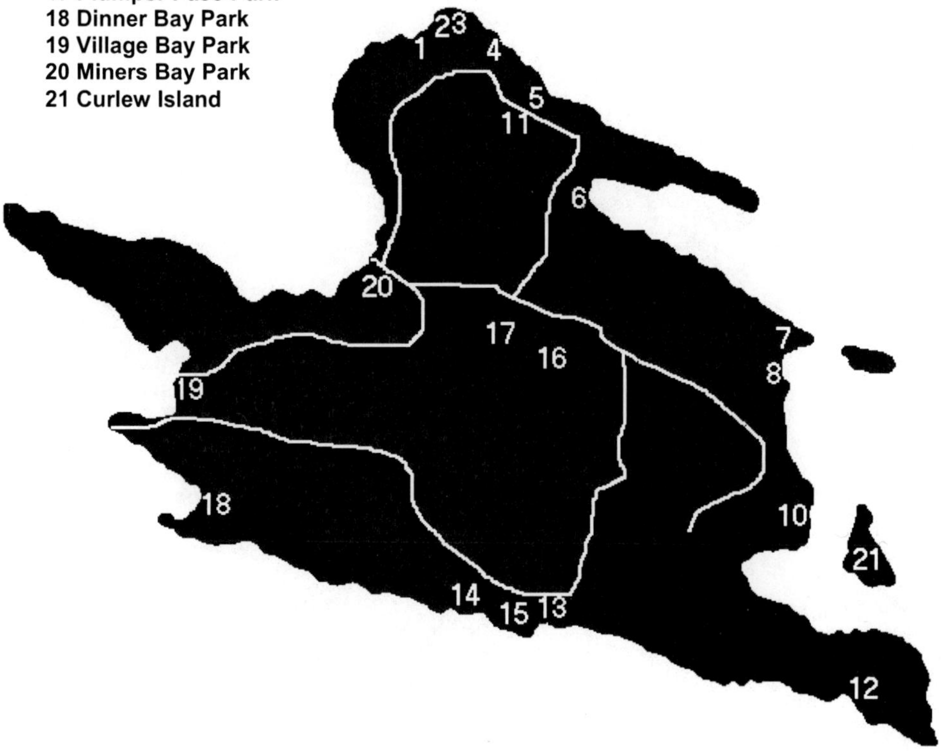

Parks & Beaches to Explore

In the 18th century, Spanish mariners produced the first map to show the outer Gulf Islands. One hundred years later, the English discovered that the map was completely inaccurate. So they commissioned the ship, HMS *Plumper*, to survey the entire coast of British Columbia. The ship's Captain eventually named Mayne Island after his Lieutenant, who spent four years alongside him.

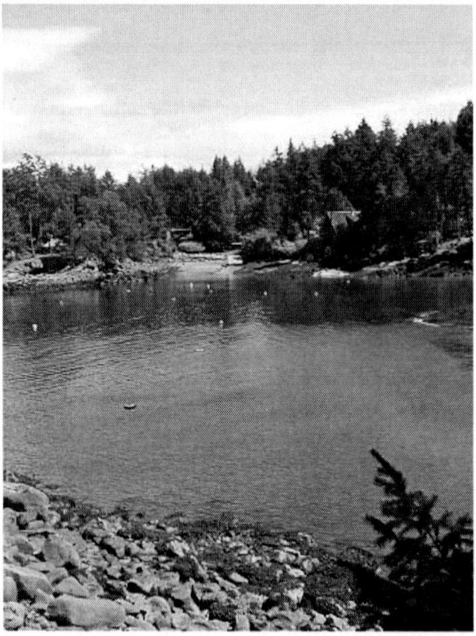

Although there are no rivers or lakes on Mayne today, it has more bays than most of the other Gulf Islands. Many of the bays provide for great *soaking* (swimming). However, there are no provincial parks and no Crown land on the Island. Most of the land is privately owned.

Arbutus Bay

On the southeast side of Mayne, a challenging 300 m trail, off Beachwood Drive, leads to *Arbutus Bay*. (#12 on the map) This pristine, secluded, rocky beach is a perfect spot to watch wildlife.

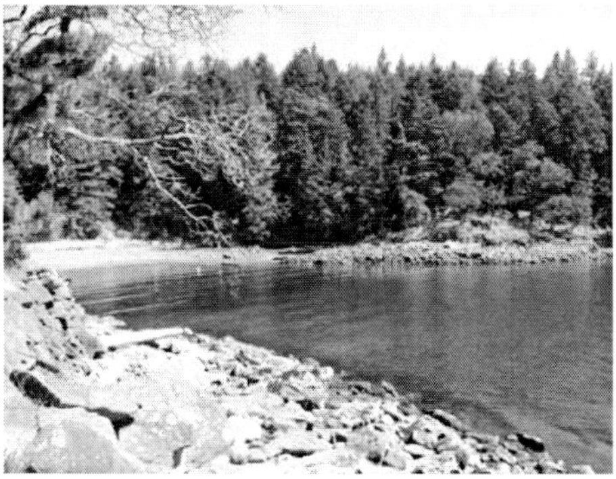

Bennett Bay

In the 1870's, a settler and his family emigrated from Scotland to Mayne. With little or no farming experience, they developed a large, successful farm on a bay on the east side of the Island.

In the 1890's, the settler became the first proprietor of a grand hotel on Georgina Point, where he lived with his family for a while. By then, his wife had become well known as the midwife in the Gulf Islands and one of their own children was the first white man born on Mayne.

When the brick plant was constructed on the bay, the family helped to build the boarding house that was eventually converted into the Mayne Inn.

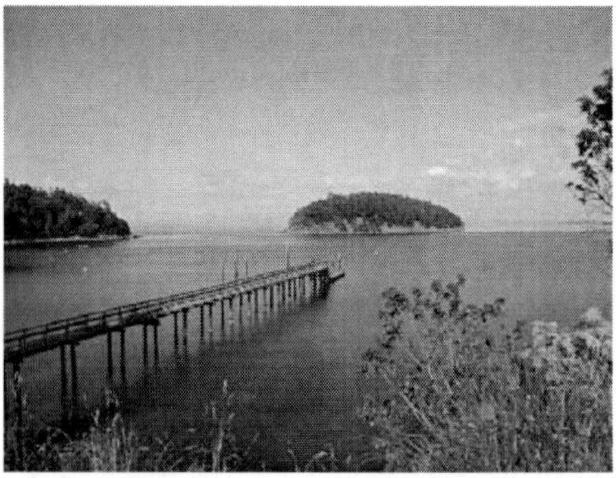

Bennett Bay was named after this family. It provides for glorious views of Georgeson Island. If you launch a boat from the bay, you can sail through Georgeson Passage, toward Campbell Bay, or you can head toward Horton Bay.

A cruise along the shoreline to Saturna Island is also quite intriguing. However, since it is exposed to winds, Bennett Bay offers only temporary boat anchorage.

Bennett Bay also provides for one of the finest sandy beaches in all the Gulf Islands. This great swimming beach can be accessed from Wilkes Road. (#8 on the map)

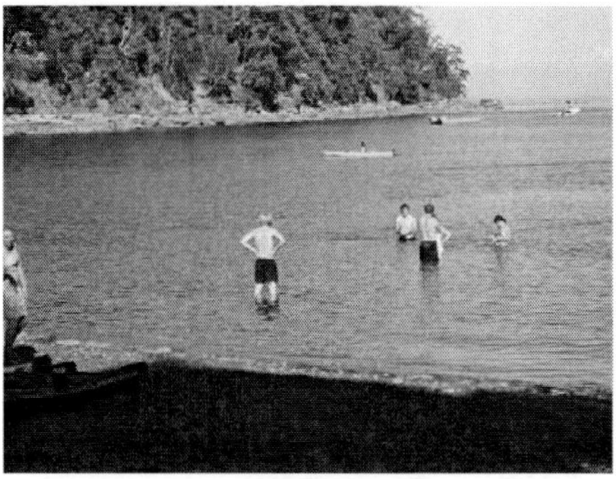

Two smaller, rocky beaches on Bennett Bay are accessible by way of Arbutus Drive. (#9 on the map) Both of these more secluded beaches are best visited at low tide, revealing the tidal pools. They are also good spots for scuba diving at a depth of up to 12 m.

Campbell Bay

Campbell Bay is the deepest bay on Mayne. Located on the northeast side of the Island, it is exposed to winds and offers only temporary boat anchorage. The two small beaches on the bay are accessed by way of unmarked trails on Campbell Bay Road. (#6 on the map)

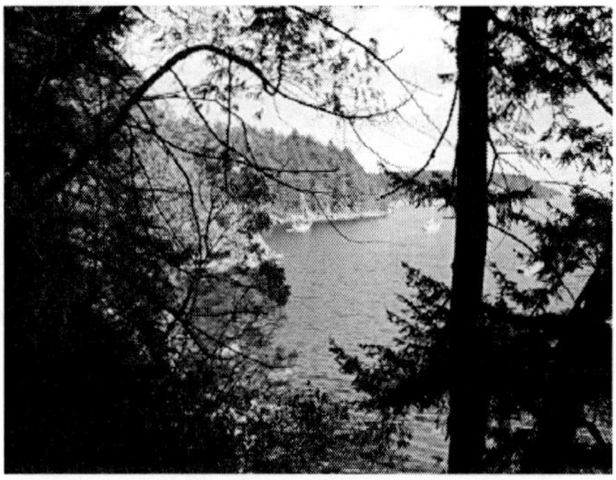

Because rocks that absorb the warmth of the sun surround them, these beaches provide for two of the finest swimming locations in the Gulf Islands. A small sign in the trees identifies Boulder Beach, which is clothing-optional.

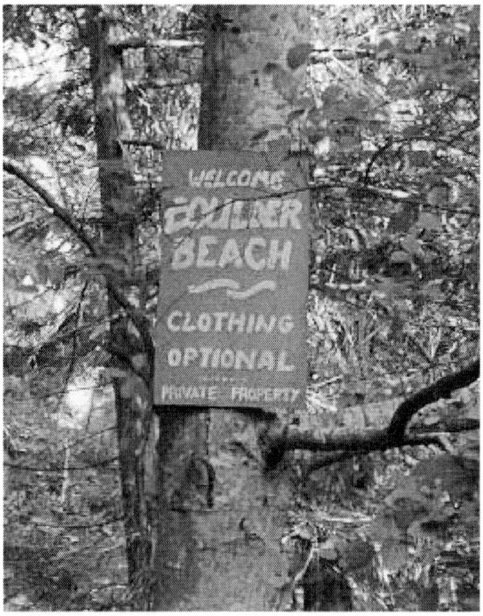

Chu-An Park

Chu-An Park is a linear park on the north side of Mayne. Chu-An, which means *looks out over the sea*, has a viewpoint that does just that.

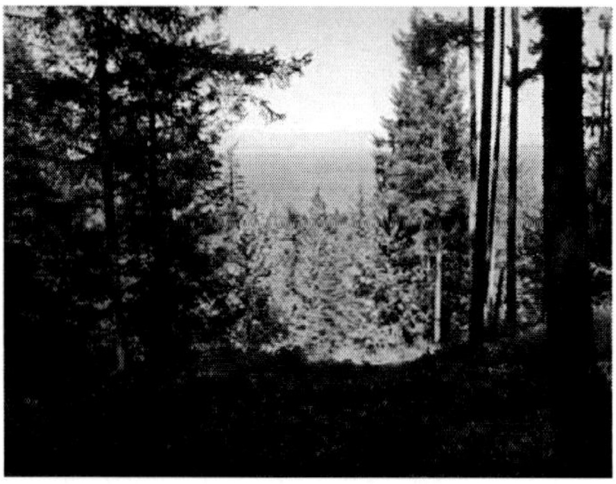

The park is accessible by way of a secret 620 m trail of moderate difficulty, which can be found halfway down the south side of Waugh Road. (#11 on the map)

Conconi Reef Park

Conconi Reef Park is located on the south side of Mayne. A short, but challenging, trail leads through the park. It provides for a spectacular view of the Pender Islands. The trail is accessible by way of a footbridge on the north side of Navy Channel Road.

The pebbled beach in the park is on *Gallagher Bay*. It is accessible via a short, easy trail at the end of the road. (#14 on the map)

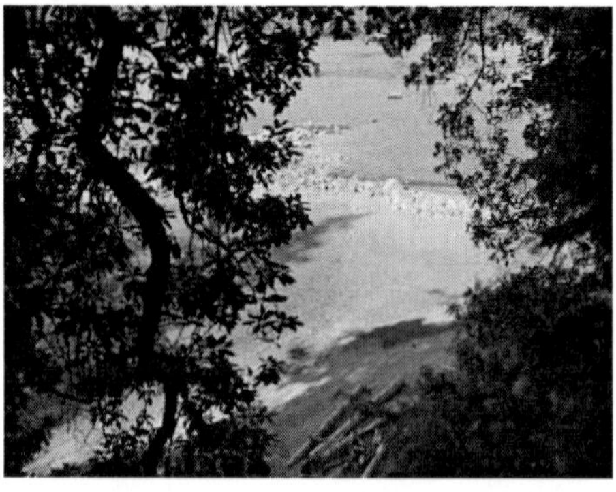

The bay is a good spot to catch cod fish. It is also shallow, with several reefs, which makes it an ideal place to scuba dive at a depth of 12 m. Another access to the beach is located on Piggott Road. (#15 on the map)

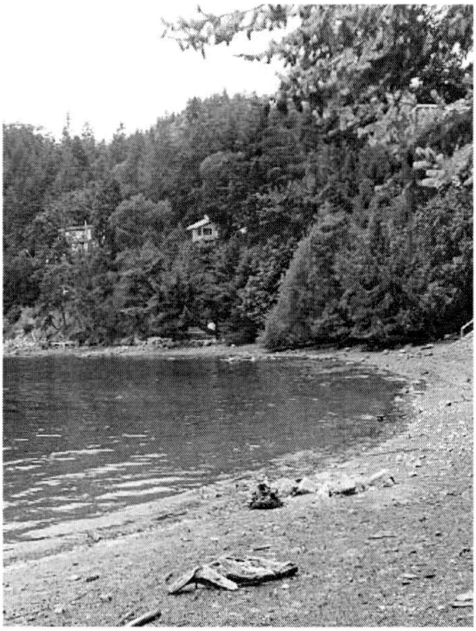

Curlew Island

In the year 1910, a settler emigrated with his family from Norway, and then settled on a small island. He raised goats and grew grapes on his island and would often play his accordion at dances held at the hall on Mayne Island.

After the settler was badly wounded in World War I, he returned to his little island and lived there until his death in the 1930's.

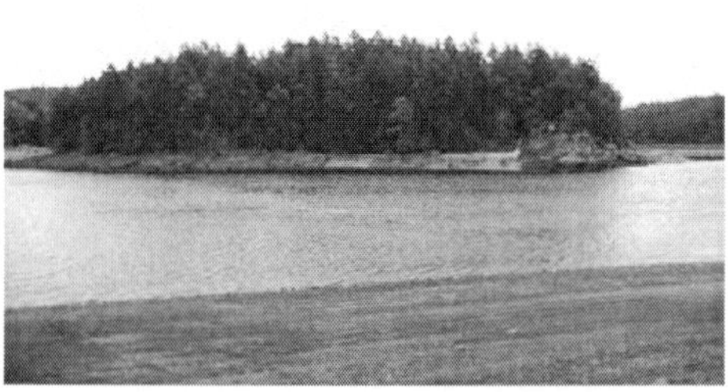

Curlew Island, which sits off the southeast side of Mayne, contains less than .3 sq km of land. It can be explored by way of Horton Bay. (#21 on the map)

The little island is not serviced, except for a group of bighorn mountain sheep. However, it is infested with domesticated peacocks that are living in the wild. If you listen carefully, you can often hear them squeal.

David Cove

In the 1870's, a load of sandstone was bound for San Francisco on a schooner called the *Zephyr.* In a *Squamish wind* (snowstorm) it struck Georgina Shoals on the north side of Mayne, and then sank off a cove. When it sank, it took the Captain and one crewmember with it.

The wreck is reported to be the oldest wreck in all the Gulf Islands and is protected under the Heritage Conservation Act of British Columbia. It was not discovered until the 1970's. A decade later, a large block of sandstone was recovered from the wreck. It can be seen at the Mayne Island Museum.

The cove where the schooner sank was originally named *Hidden Bay*. However, it was later renamed *David Cove*, in honor of an early settler who once lived there. Reportedly, there are two graves beside the cove, where the settler and his daughter rest.

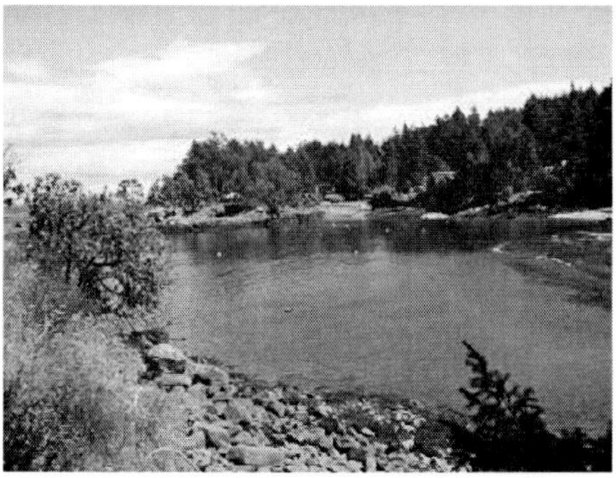

David Cove is a beautiful inlet with a rocky beach that provides for an abundance of clams, mussels, limpets, snails and crabs. It offers some safe boat anchorage.

Further out from David Cove is a favorite spot for scuba diving, where the wreck of the Zephyr exists. The cove can be accessed from the end of Petrus Road. (#5 on the map)

Dinner Bay Community Park

Dinner Bay Community Park was established as a recreational area in the 1980's. It is located on *Dinner Bay*, on the southwest side of Mayne

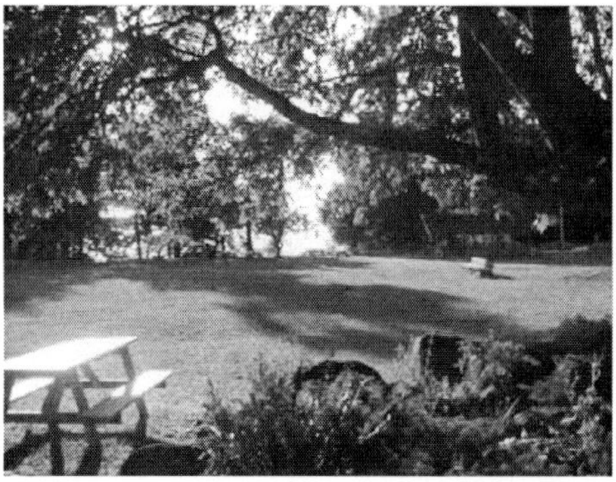

The park has a fenced playground, badminton net, horseshoe pits, baseball diamond, picnic shelters, beachfront swimming area and putting green.

The park is the site of the *Salmon Barbecue* and of the *Canada Day Picnic* celebrations. The park grounds are maintained by the Mayne Island Community and can be rented for events and activities.

The easy, 600 m *Ed Williams Memorial Trail* through the park is accessible by way of Leighton Lane. It winds through woods and along the shore of a pebbled beach. You can access the beach by way of steps at the edge of the park. (#18 on the map)

Because it is exposed to winds and ferry wash, the mooring facilities on Dinner Bay offer only temporary boat anchorage.

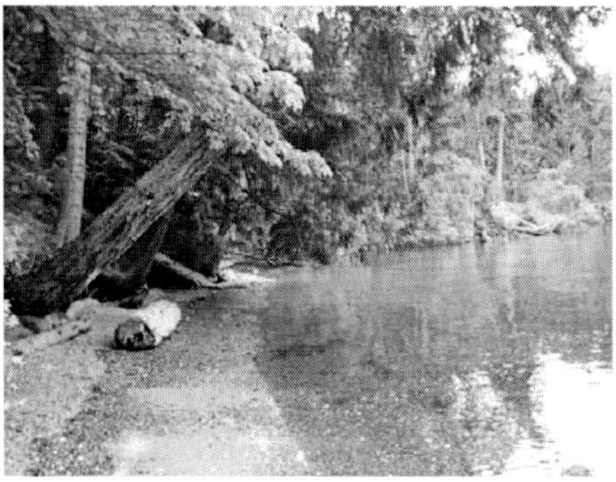

Heritage Park

Recently, a man was swept off his boat called the *Espérance*, while traveling from Vancouver Island to Washington State. He was plunged into the icy waters without a life vest.

Bravely, he heaved his *sakalooks* (pants) over his head to fill the legs with air and used them as a crude life raft. Then, he proceeded to do a slow breaststroke toward a lighthouse in the distance. He swam an exhaustive three hours until he reached the shore of *Heritage Park*.

The site of the Active Pass Light Station, Heritage Park is a federal, shoreline access park that is leased to the Mayne Island Parks and Recreation Commission.

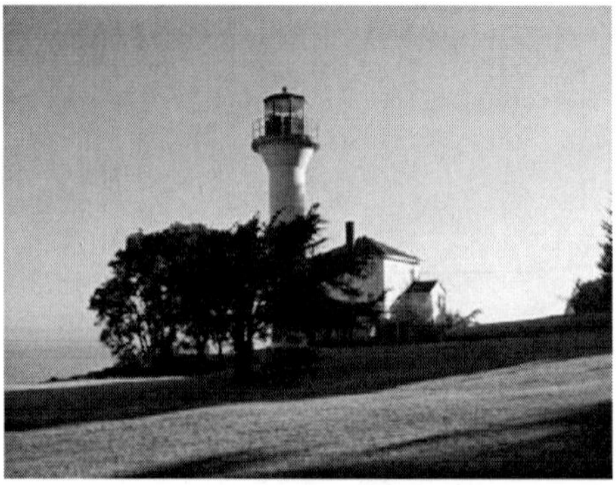

The park grounds are maintained by the Mayne Island Community and can be rented for art shows, book readings, weddings, etc. There are facilities for picnics if you want to stay awhile.

Heritage Park is dancing with Arbutus trees, behind which is a Dahlia Garden. The park provides for breathtaking views of Active Pass and of Galiano Island.

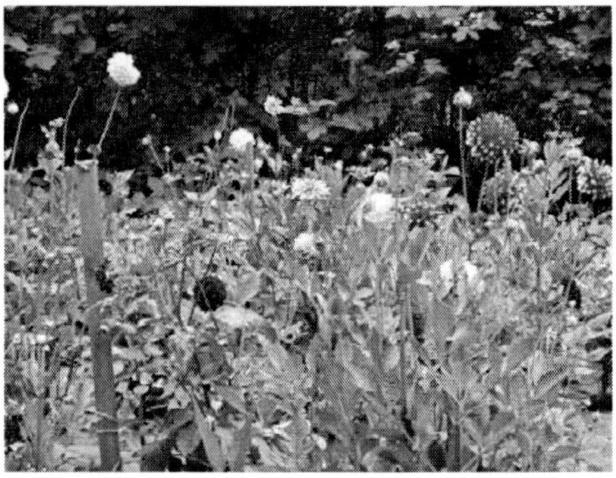

There is a short, easy trail through the park, which leads to a beach. At low tide, you can walk along the beach for *lele* (a long time) looking at the Sea Stars. The park is accessible from Georgina Point Road. (#2 on the map)

Horton Bay

When the first Japanese settled on *Horton Bay*, it was called *Kawashuri Bay*. In the 1930's, when the Japanese formed a marketing cooperative, they built a portable sawmill on that same bay to provide the lumber for the crates used in the shipment of their products.

Today, the home of the first Japanese family to settle on Mayne still sits in a tiny cove in the bay. The family was evacuated from the home at the start of World War II. It was later acquired to serve returning veterans of that same war.

The face of a dock that the family had built up with flat rocks can still be seen at the end of Horton Bay Road, in front of their old boathouse.

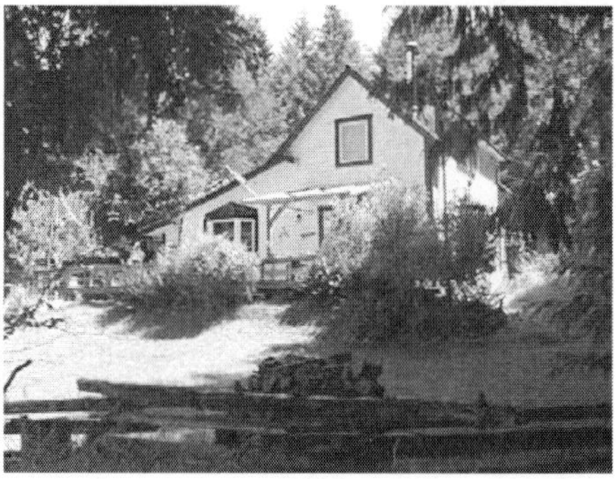

Horton Bay is located on the southeast side of Mayne. It provides for breathtaking views of Curlew Island to the east.

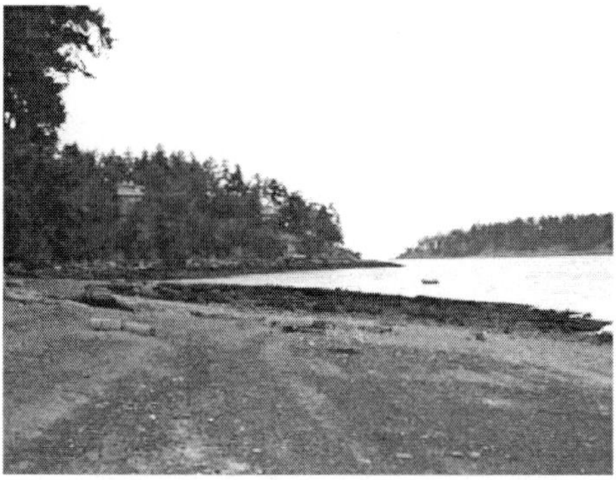

The government wharf at the end of Horton Bay Road makes Horton Bay a great location for boat launching. However, be careful of the *skookumchuck* (strong currents), which are strongest on the east side of Curlew Island.

You can also put a boat in the bay from a pebbled beach that is accessible by way of Steward Road. (#10 on the map) The road leads to a small point, which is known locally as *Spud Point*. Keep in mind that the beach is closed to the harvesting of scallops, mussels, oysters and clams.

Marine Heritage Park

After originally settling on Galiano Island, a prominent settler moved to Mayne in the 1880's and became the first lighthouse keeper at the Active Pass Light Station.

Each night, the stocky lighthouse keeper would light an oil lamp in the tower at sundown and blow it out at sunrise. If the foghorn malfunctioned, he would ring the bell by hand whenever a steamer entered the Pass.

When the lighthouse keeper retired in the 1920's, he received the Imperial Long Service Medal for providing over 35 years of service to the lighthouse. He was succeeded by his son.

Georgeson Island was named after this lighthouse keeper, whose name has become synonymous with the lighthouses in the southern Gulf Islands.

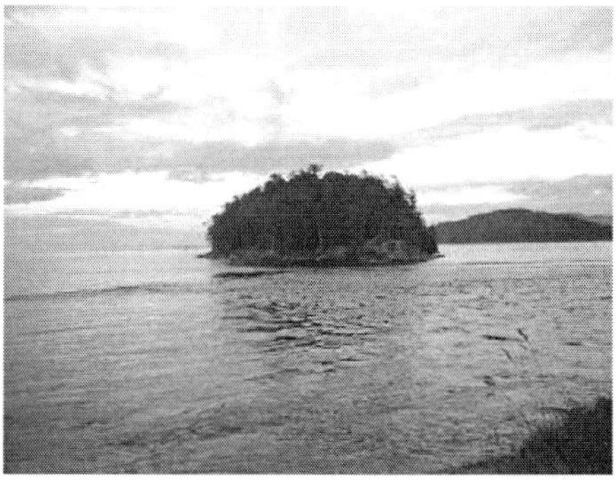

Part of the Gulf Islands National Park Reserve, Georgeson Island is a beautiful ridge on the east side of Mayne. It is highly valued as a seal and sea lion haulout, as well as a nesting site for several species of birds.

The southern shore of the island has great sandstone formations and you can often catch sight of a Bald Eagle flying across Georgeson Passage. However, the island has been designated as a 'no access' area and there is virtually nowhere to land by boat.

The land that was acquired as part of the reserve also includes Bennett Bay and Campbell Point on Mayne Island. The entire area is now protected as *Marine Heritage Park*.

Campbell Point is accessible by way of an easy trail that loops around the point. (#7 on the map) The trail can be accessed from the end of Isabella Lane. There is also a secret access on Wilkes Road.

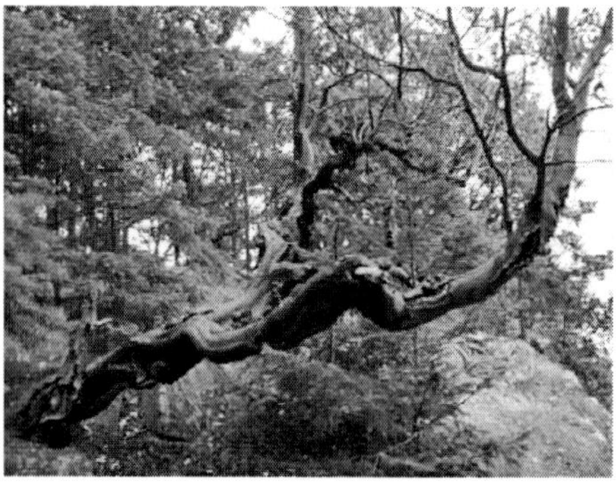

Originally named *Paddon Point*, Campbell Point is highly regarded for its Arbutus trees and is the place to see some of the most incredible examples anywhere on the West Coast.

At the end of Campbell Point, there is a view of Mount Baker, a 3,300 m strato-volcano located in Washington State. It is also a place to see Garry Oak or watch the sea lions while you picnic in the park.

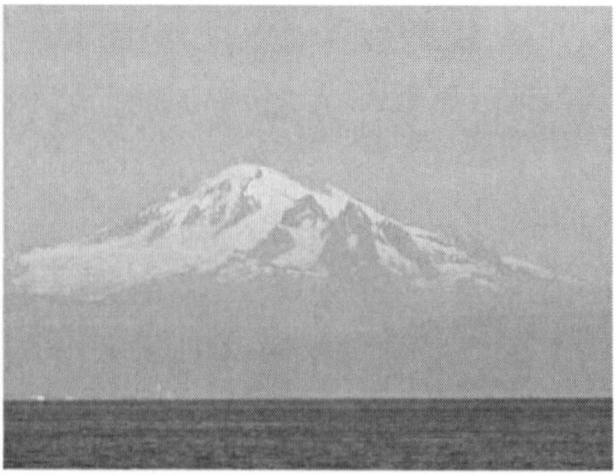

Maude Bay

In the 1920's, the retired Commander who had operated the Mayne Store at Miners Bay attempted to sail his sailboat, the *Half Moon*, from Mayne to England, alone. He was 77 years of age.

The Commander, who had once served on Queen Victoria's own personal yacht, had spent almost 100 days at sea and had traveled over 6,000 km when he was caught in a storm off the coast of California. The storm caused the boom to strike him on the head and left him unconscious.

Although a freighter spotted him, he refused their assistance. Despite having been blinded by the sun, he navigated his boat to Cape Flattery where he was rescued by his son. He returned to his home on Mayne only to succeed in his journey the following year.

Maude Bay was named after this Commander, whose family was the first British middle-class family to settle on Mayne.

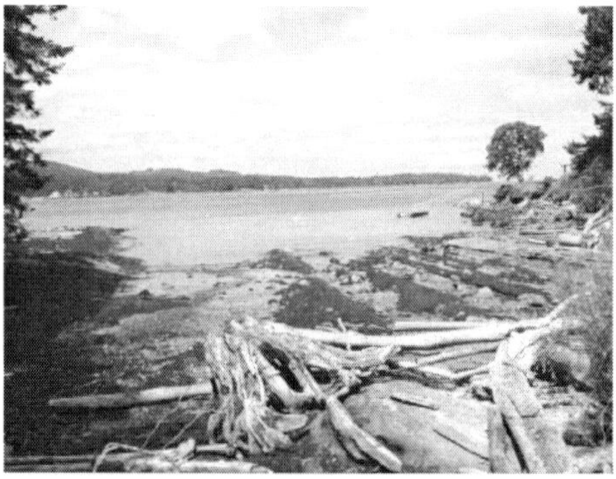

You can see a wide variety of sea life on Maude Bay. Mussels, oysters, limpets and crabs abound. The bay is also known as *Cherry Tree Bay*. From Cherry Tree Bay Road, you can make your way down to the rocky beach using a charming, but broken-down, old dock. (#1 on the map)

Miners Bay Community Park

By the 1890's, **the Postman** had become a member of the Islands Agricultural and Fruit Growers Association. Reportedly, plum, pear and apple orchards could be seen on many of the Island farms at that time, particularly a variety of apples called *King*.

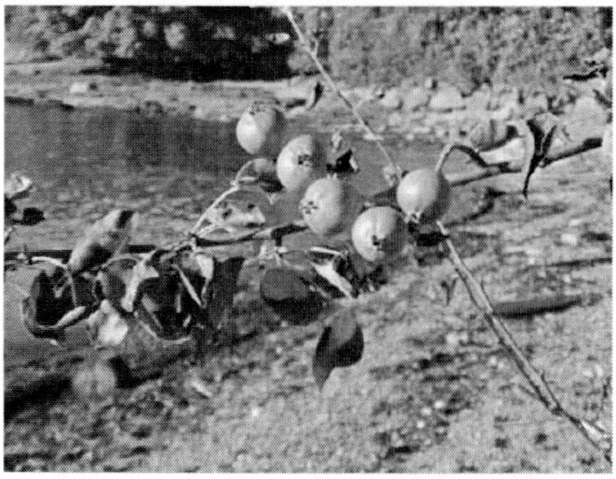

Today, there are still ancient fruit trees growing along the trail that leads to the pebbled beach on *Miners Bay*. The beach is the site of **the Postman's** first home.

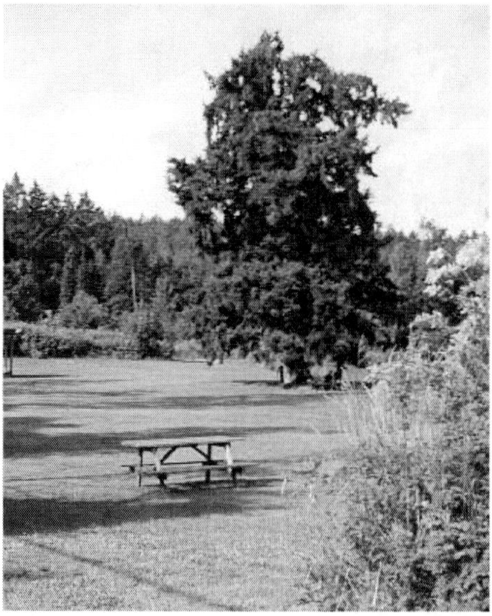

The short trail to the beach passes *Miners Bay Community Park*. It also provides for great berry picking. You can access it from the end of Naylor Road. (#20 on the map)

If you walk beneath the wharf in Miners Bay, you can watch the water as it trickles down the rocks. Although it has limited space and strong tides, you can find docking facilities at the wharf, from which you can walk into the village.

In the summer, the bandstand in the park provides a place for musicians to entertain visitors who come to attend events, such as the *Al'elen Music Festival*. There are also facilities for picnics if you want to stay awhile.

During the Christmas season, the tall Douglas-Fir tree in the park is decorated with a spectacle of lights.

Mount Parke Regional Park

Recently, an aircraft chartered by Purolator Courier was traveling from the mainland to Victoria. As it approached Mayne, it struck some trees on the ridge of a park and sliced through a large number of treetops. Then, it continued over a cliff and crashed into the valley below. Both the pilot and the co-pilot were killed.

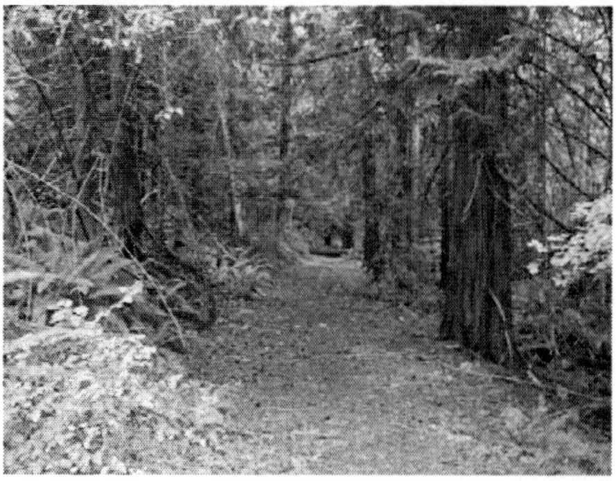

Mount Parke Regional Park is a large parcel of land that was recently bequeathed to Mayne. It is dark with Western Red Cedar, Red Alder, Giant Sword-Fern and Oregon Grape.

Within the park's boundaries sits a 255 m peak that is officially named *Parke Mountain*, but is known locally as *Flag Hill*. The peak is one of the highest points in all the Gulf Islands.

Shortly after its establishment, the threat of large scale, commercial logging of the park caused the Mayne Island Conservancy Society to be formed. The organization ensures that the summit ridge remains part of one intact and contiguous ecosystem.

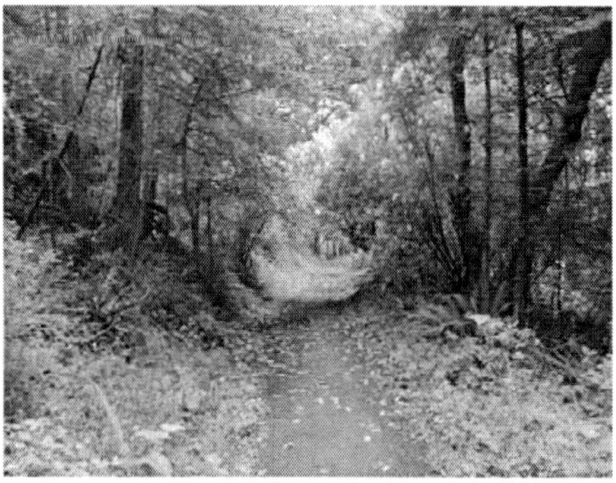

From the park entrance on Montrose Road, an easy, 300 m trail leads to a junction where three other somewhat challenging trails lead into the park. (#16 on the map) All three trails total 5 km.

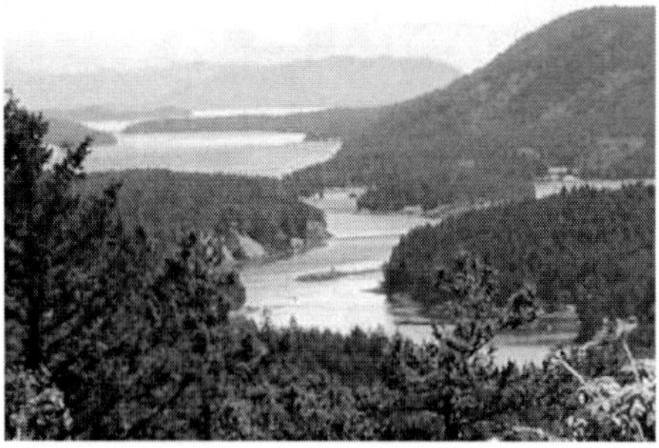

The trail to the left leads to a viewpoint at *Halliday Ridge*, which provides for spectacular, panoramic views of Saturna, Salt Spring and Pender Islands. Beyond the smaller Islands can be seen Vancouver Island, as well as the Olympic Mountains in Washington State.

From Halliday Ridge, the hike continues deeper into the park, to the *Old Gulch Trail*. From there, you can take the *Lowland Nature Trail* straight into a nature appreciation park called *Mary Jeffrey Park*, or you can turn right at the *Arbutus Tree Trail*.

Oyster Bay

On the northern tip of Mayne lies *Oyster Bay*. On its rocky beach are curious driftwood and rock formations. Mussels, limpets, oysters and crabs are plentiful and there is a good supply of snails in the shallow pool.

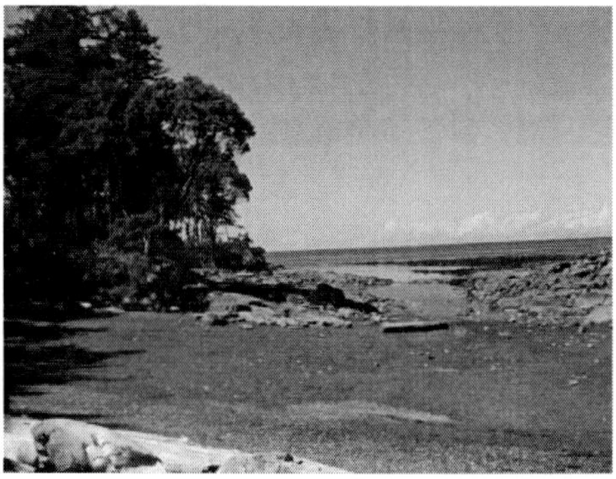

Further out from Oyster Bay, Georgina Shoals is one of the best places in all the Gulf Islands to scuba dive, at a depth of 10 m. You can access Oyster Bay from Bayview Drive. (#3 on the map)

Piggott Bay

In the 1890's, an early settler from the Pender Islands left his brother and moved to Mayne. Whenever he wanted to visit his brother, he would walk to a bay, and then light a fire or blow a horn made out of bull kelp to get his brother's attention. His brother would then row over from North Pender to pick him up at what was then called *Brigg's Landing*.

Other people from the Pender Islands also used the bay as a transfer point when traveling to Mayne, especially when picking up their mail. They would walk to a bay on Pender, and then row across the Channel to Piggott Bay on Mayne.

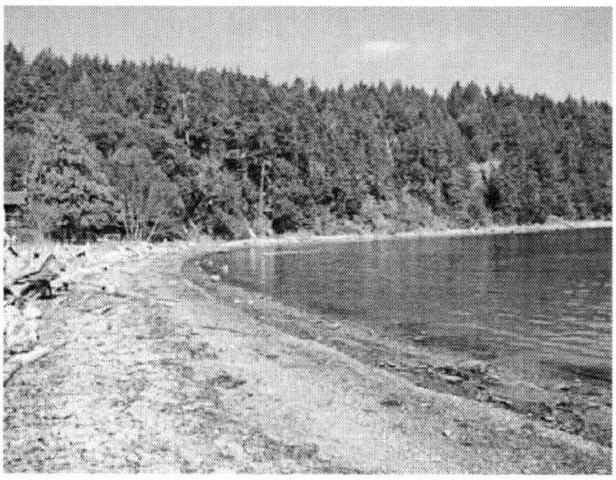

Located on the south side of Mayne, *Piggott Bay* provides for views of Saturna Island. The sandy beach is lined with large pieces of driftwood and clams are plentiful. Because of its warm waters, the bay is a great place for a swim.

You can access the bay from the end of Piggott Road. (#13 on the map) Because it is exposed to the winds, it offers only temporary boat anchorage.

Plumper Pass Park

Plumper Pass Community Park can be accessed by way of a 1.7 km trail that loops around the park. The trail can be accessed from Kim Road and begins in some underbrush that continues to an old road. (#17 on the map)

The park provides for views of the North Shore Mountains and neighboring Bowen Island, as well as some features on the mainland that cannot be seen from other points on Mayne. In the year prior to this writing, a second trail was constructed in the park.

Reef Bay

Reef Bay is located between Oyster Bay and David Cove, on the north side of Mayne. Also known as *Chip Bay*, it is dotted with pieces of driftwood. Mussels, snails, limpets and crabs are plentiful on the rocky beach. The bay can be accessed from Bayview Drive. (#4 on the map)

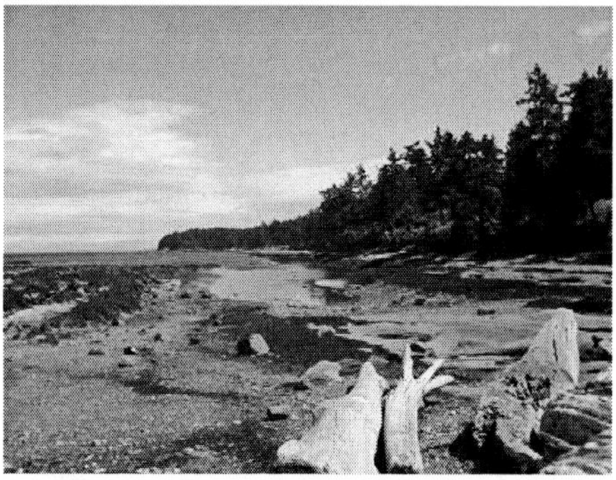

Village Bay

Because the First Nations *rancherie* (village) existed on the southwest side of Mayne in the 1860's, the area eventually became known as *Village Bay*. All of the people who lived there were called *skeh-SUCK* (the Pass) people.

In the 1880's, as Miners Bay was being settled, a prominent settler purchased a large farm sitting in a valley on Village Bay. His family built a barn in the valley and a home at the edge of the farm overlooking the bay.

A decade later, the family converted their home into a very popular resort they called *Kitty's Boarding House*.

When **the Postman** passed away shortly before World War I, the family took over his post office, which was operating from the store beside his home at Miners Bay.

A few years later, the family's boarding house was destroyed by fire. Today, the barn is the only building that remains of their large farm and resort.

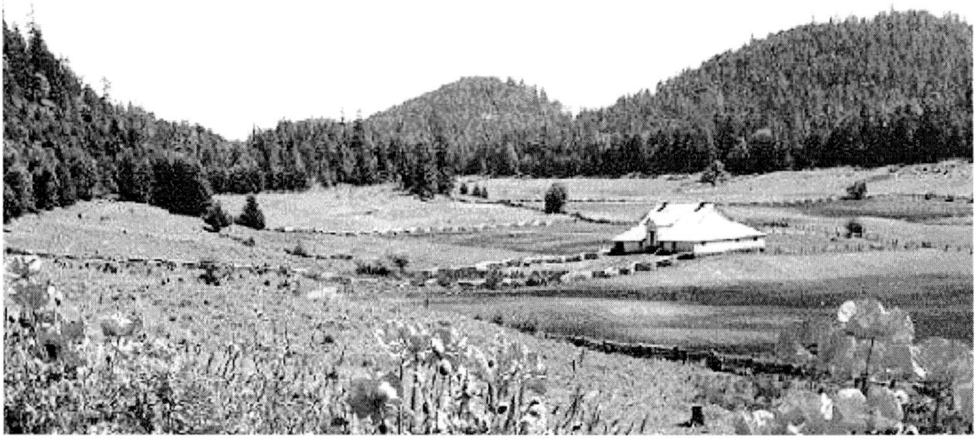

Barn at Village Bay in the 1950's, BC Arcihves NA-40412

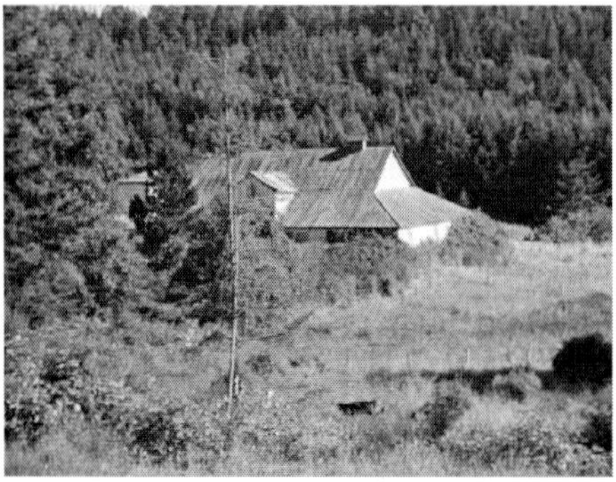

Barn at Village Bay as it appears today

In the 1950's, an end-loading ferry terminal was built on the bay, where Kitty's Boarding House once stood. For the most part, it replaced the wharf at Miners Bay.

A ferry that was later introduced to link the mainland to Salt Spring Island caused the population of Mayne Island to double during the 1970's.

In the 1980's, when a second dock was added to the Village Bay terminal, it became a transfer hub for all the Gulf Islands routes.

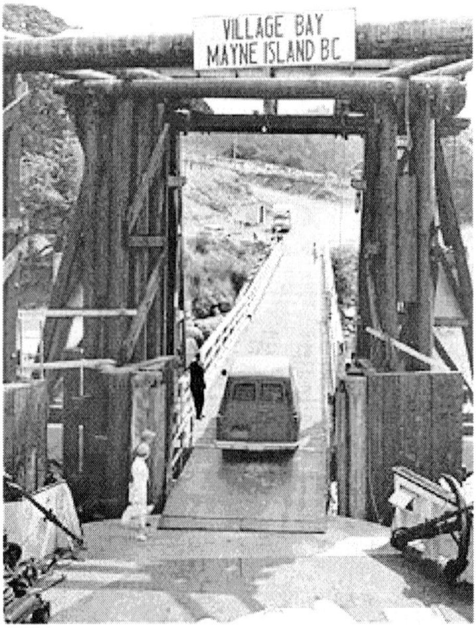

Village Bay ferry terminal, early 1960's
BC Ferries Archives

Today, British Columbia Ferry Services continues to use the land on Village Bay to operate scheduled ferry services from both the mainland and Vancouver Island.

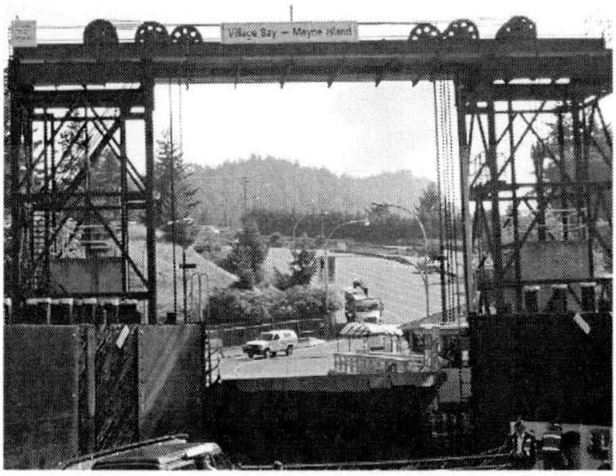

Village Bay ferry terminal as it appears today

The pebbled beach on Village Bay sits in *Village Bay Park*. The park and beach can be accessed from the end of Callaghan Crescent or by way of two, short, easy trails on Dalton Drive and Mariner's Way. (#19 on the map) Keep in mind that the beach is closed to the harvesting of scallops, mussels, oysters and clams.

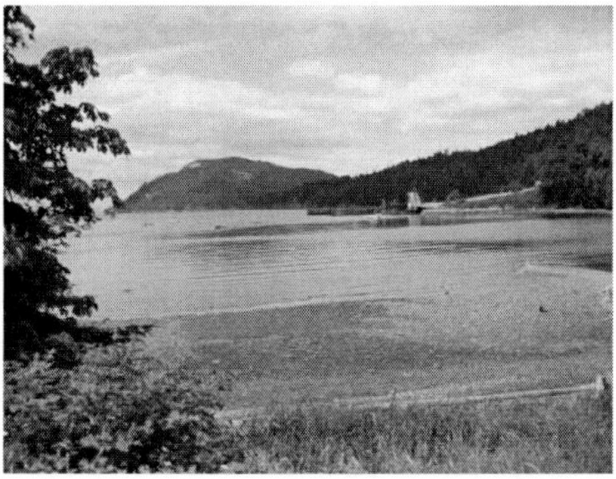

If you launch a boat from Village Bay, a cruise along the shoreline to Dinner Point is quite scenic. However, ferry traffic is heavy in the bay and because it is exposed to winds and ferry wash, the mooring facilities offer only temporary anchorage for small boaters.

Saturna Island

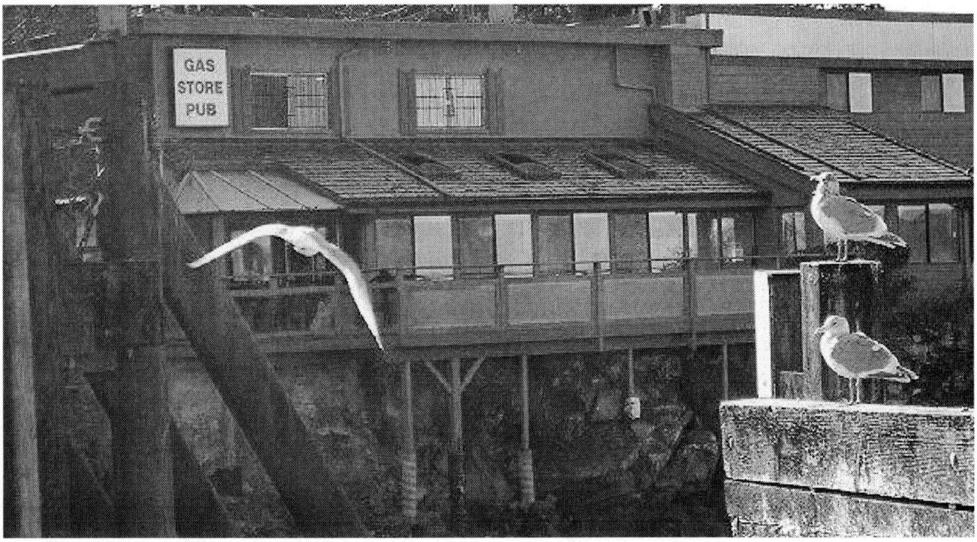

Lyall Harbour Wharf

It was in the spring of 1896 that an Englishman, named Harold Payne, headed for Telegraph Creek to start a trading post in the gold mining fields...

To transport their gear, Harold and two other settlers purchased 150 mules. On the way to the gold fields, they encountered people celebrating Victoria Day. Alarmed, the mules started a stampede that the crowds mistook as part of the celebrations.

Harold Payne was born in the 1870's. In the 1890's, he emigrated from England to Canada and settled on Saturna Island.

The adventurous Harold Payne was a skilled traveler. He had spent 15 years sailing around the world, and had taken many trips to British Columbia and the Arctic. He had dreams of becoming an officer. Unfortunately, they were shattered when he was found to be colorblind.

In the late 1890's, Harold became **the Postman** for Saturna Island, operating a store and post office from buildings he constructed on a bay. Years later, his daughter had this to say about him:

"Of course, Dad would let us. He never told us not to do anything because it was dangerous... Dad used to clear land and put up fences, and go cruising when he felt like it. And in the early days, of course, they always used to go off on these great trips – big game hunting up north with pack horses and guides."

Dora Payne

Things to Know

Saturna is a rugged island. At 31 sq km, it is the second smallest of the southern Gulf Islands. While rocky, sloping terrain and quiet seaside drives are its most distinguishing characteristics, the lack of commercialism gives Saturna Island its unique charm.

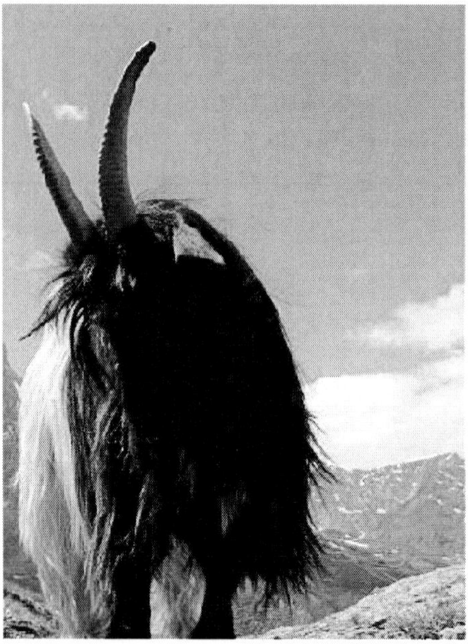

Saturna has more parkland per size and population than any of the other Gulf Islands and five mountains that are taller than 300 m. Its tallest mountain is the second highest peak in the outer Gulf Islands.

Although it is not the smallest of the Gulf Islands, Saturna is the most remote and least inhabited. Because its terrain has made it more difficult to develop than the other Gulf Islands, it has a population of only about 350 permanent residents.

Unlike the other Islands, where families have a continuous history, all of the early settlers have come and gone, leaving a relatively new population.

Most of the permanent residents live near *Lyall Harbour*, where the services and facilities are located. During the tourist season, the population doubles to around 600.

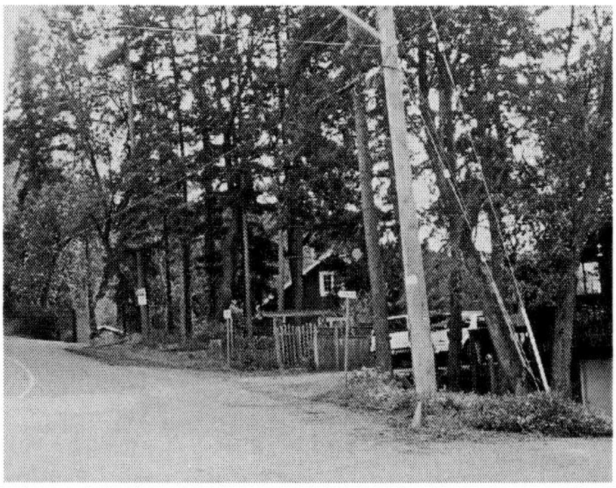

Saturna Beach Wharf

As settlers started to emigrate from England in the late 1860's, residential development of Saturna began on the west side. One of the first land owners to build on the Island purchased property at the harbour.

Other settlements developed in secluded areas that were cut off from the harbour by tall peaks and steep cliffs. Those families who settled there learned to become self-sufficient.

Initially, the settlers would row to Mayne or Pender Island for supplies. They would return by way of a bay.

In the 1890's, a wharf was built in the bay, from a beach called *Pike's Landing*. The wharf accommodated ships coming through the waterway called *Plumper Sound*.

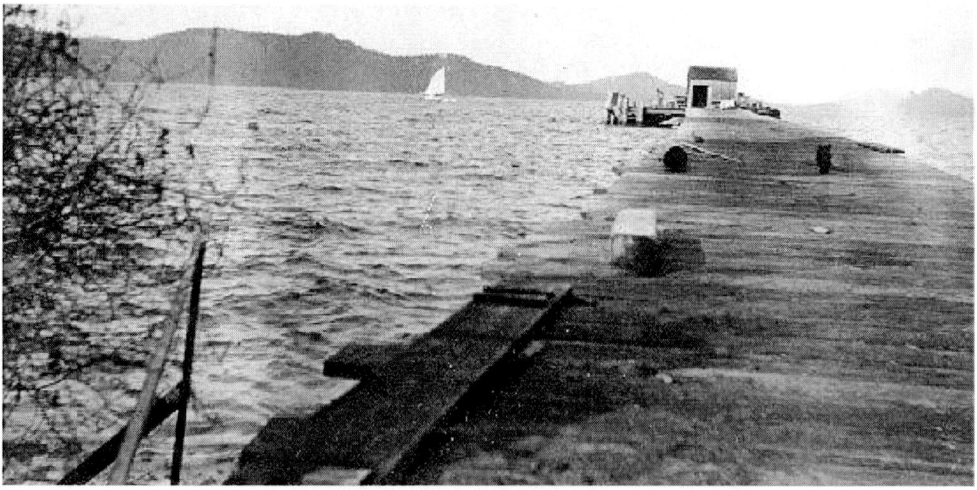

Saturna Beach wharf in the early 1900's BC Archives C-06964

In the 1920's, the wharf was torn down. A decade later, a new wharf was built in the bay and Pike's Landing was renamed *Saturna Beach*.

The Saturna Beach wharf has been moved many times over the years. Today, it can be seen extending into the bay from the same location as the original turn-of-the-century wharf.

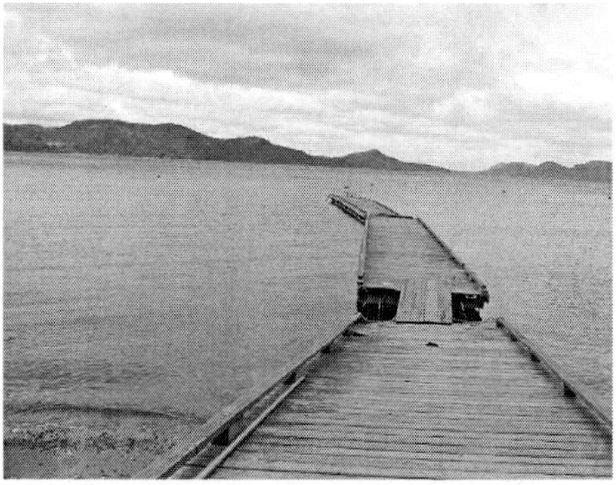

Saturna Beach wharf as it appears today

Saturna Island Post Office

In the 1890's, **the Postman** began operating a post office from a little building he built on Saturna Beach. He would sail a little sailboat to Mayne Island to collect the mail.

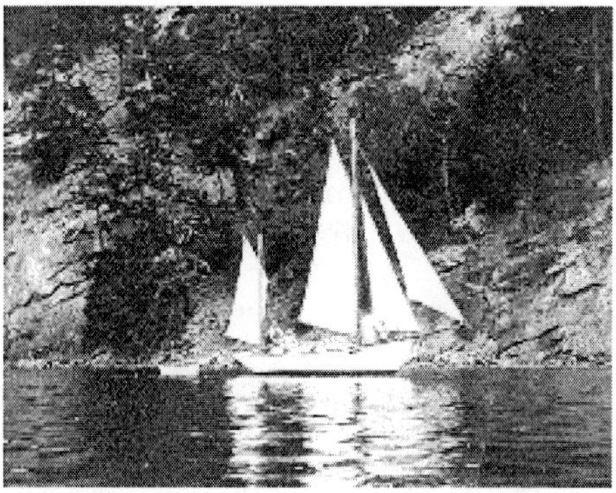

The Postman arriving at Saturna Beach in the 1890's - BC Archives C-07060

When the wharf was built at Saturna Beach, a steamer ship started delivering the mail to the wharf. It soon became the custom to turn the mailbags upside down on the wharf and let the people scramble for their letters.

Postal delivery was the center of Island social life for many years. The settlers would organize games of grass hockey, football or cricket while they waited for the mail. **The Postman** made tea.

Three years later, he transferred the postal service to a police constable.

Soon, the mail was being hand-delivered to the settlers' homes by way of a police boat, called the *Constable*. Those settlers who chose to wait for their mail at the post office would often be served bread and jam, and baked apples.

In the 1930's, the post office was moved to a store at the harbour. Everyone would gather at the community hall to wait for the mail on *boat days* (when boats would dock at the wharf). Two bachelors, who lived between two mountains, would leave a wheelbarrow near the post office, which they would use to transport their mail.

In the 1950's, the store was removed from the harbour. Subsequently, the post office was moved into a building up the road.

Meanwhile, **the Postman`s** little building on Saturna Beach was being used for storage. Unfortunately, it was recently demolished.

Today, the building up the road from the harbour functions as an Internet café and the post office operates from a newer store.

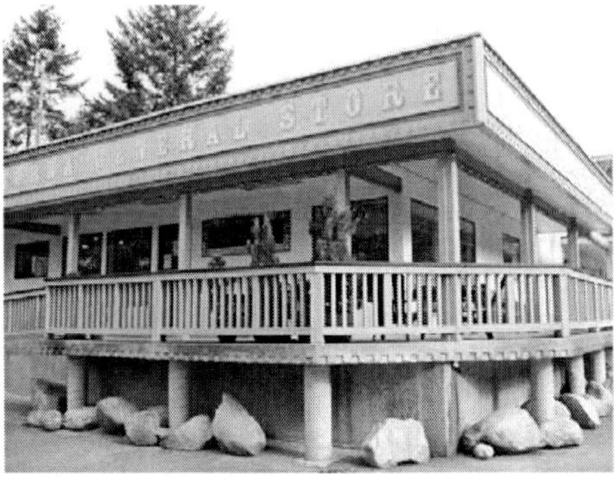

Saturna General Store

In the 1890's, **the Postman** built himself a magnificent white house on Saturna Beach. From his house, he ran the first store ever to exist on Saturna. It was called the *Saturna Island Store*.

When **the Postman** transferred his postal service to the police constable, he also sold him his store on the beach. The constable would deliver orders by boat.

A few years later, **the Postman's** brother-in-law acquired the store. Later, it became the home of the caretaker for a resort. Unfortunately, it burned down in the 1940's.

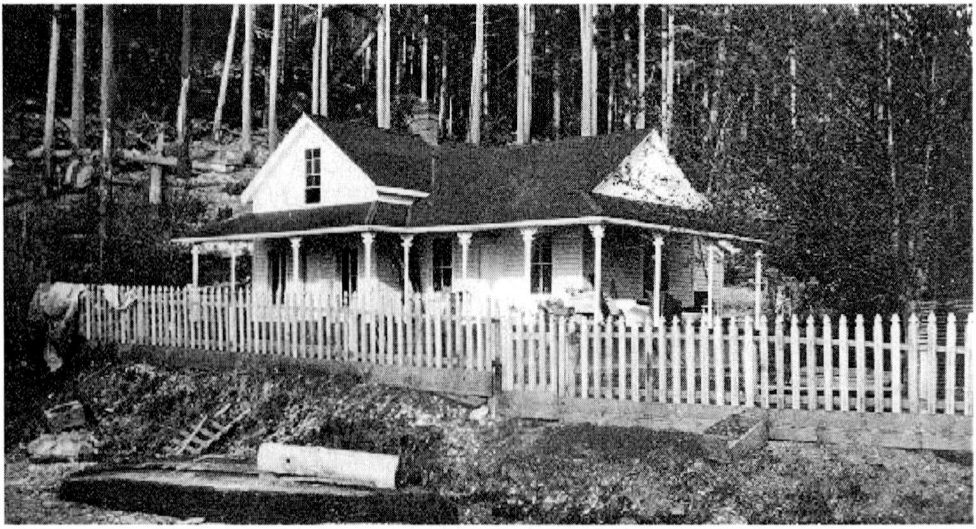

Saturna Island Store, early 1900's - BC Archives C-070007

In the 1950's, a resident built another store, in the center of the Island. Called the *Saturna General Store*, it had apartments on the upper floor. A decade later, the store changed hands and the owners lived in an apartment at the back of the building.

Today, the Saturna General Store functions as a grocery store, liquor store and post office. The new owners also operate an organic bakery that supplies baked goods to the store. The store is located on Narvaez Bay Road.

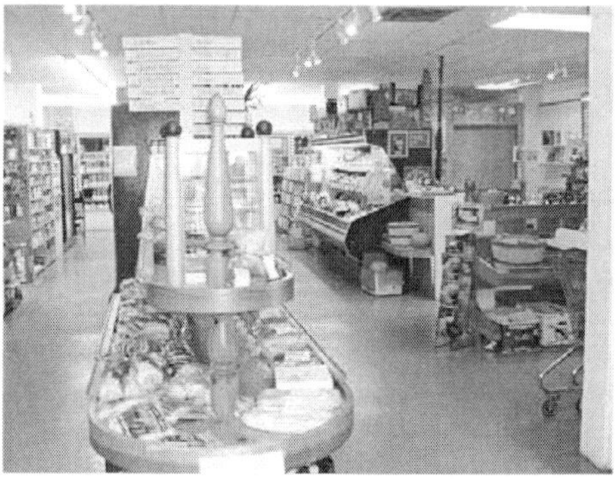

Saturna Point Store

The first store to exist at the harbour was built in the 1920's. Unfortunately, it closed down in the 1950's, when the Saturna General Store opened in the center of the Island.

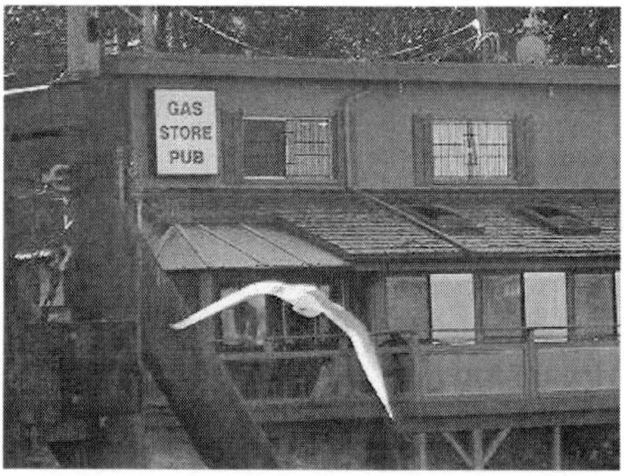

Today, a new store sits at the harbour, across from where the original store was built. Called the *Saturna Point Store*, it provides for gas, groceries and movie rentals. You can also obtain fishing gear and licenses there. The store is located at the end of East Point Road.

Saturna Island Bank

The *Saturna Island Bank* clearly does not exist. However, at the time of this writing, both the Saturna General Store and the Saturna Point Store accepted all forms of electronic payment.

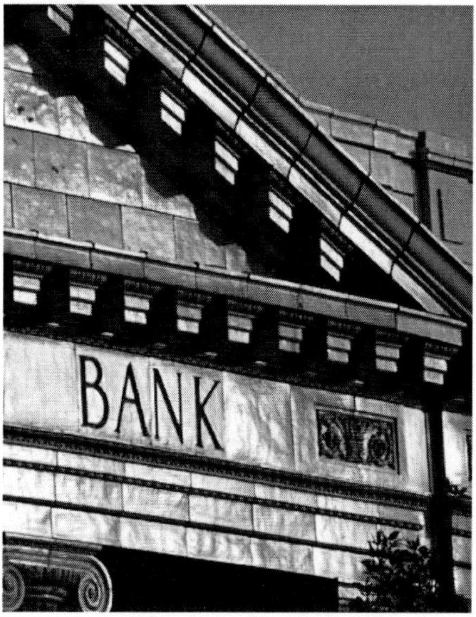

Not the Saturna Island Bank

Saturna Island Community Hall

In the 1930's, a community hall was built near the harbour. It was called the *Saturna Island Community Hall*. For a while, church services were held there. Because there was no electricity, Coleman lamps were hung from a metal rod for light.

The plans for the hall did not include a stage. So it was just large enough to serve as an indoor badminton court. The players had to avoid hitting the badminton birdie into the rod that held the lamps. Over time, a stage was built into the hall.

During the 1950's, whenever there was a dance at the hall, the resident who built the Saturna General Store would pick up some of the other residents in his tractor-trailer and take them to the dance.

Local accordion players provided the dance music and large cedar trays were used to pass coffee around.

Today, the community hall serves as the main venue for indoor events. The rod that once held the Coleman lamps now holds the lights for the stage.

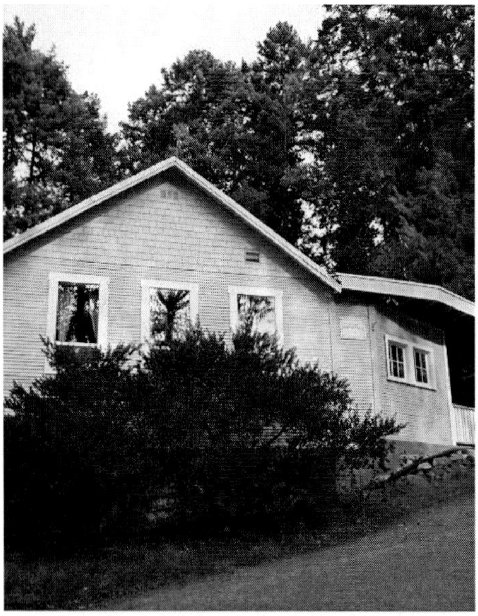

Located on East Point Road, the Saturna Island Community Hall hosts art shows, and theatre and musical performances throughout the year. During the summer, it is host to the annual *Saturna Island Farmer's Market*.

First Nations Reserve

There is a First Nations Indian Reserve on the east side of Saturna. It is located on private land that is jointly owned by the *Tsawout* and *Tseycum* bands.

The reserve is accessible by way of an unmarked trail at the end of Fiddlers Road. The trail leads down to what was once called *Smugglers Cove*, but was later renamed *Fiddlers Cove*. Visitors should obtain permission before hiking it.

Breezy Bay B&B

In the 1880's, a prominent settler brought one of his brothers from England to live with him. The night he arrived on the Island, the Englishman slept rolled up in a coat, on a shelf in a fruit shed.

The brothers came from a wealthy family and received small incomes from England. So, in the 1890's, the Englishman purchased his own property, on a point on the southwest side of Saturna. At that time, the point was called *Old Point*, but was later renamed *Payne Point*.

The Englishman established a farm on the point, where he built a green and white frame house near a bay. Although he was still a bachelor at the time, his home was well kept. The bed was always made and a basin, towels and water jug were always set out.

Six years later, he joined the gold rush, along with his younger brother, **the Postman**.

When he returned to Saturna, the Englishman married and settled in to family life, building a separate schoolhouse on his property for his children's education. In the evening, he would tell them stories at the dining room table.

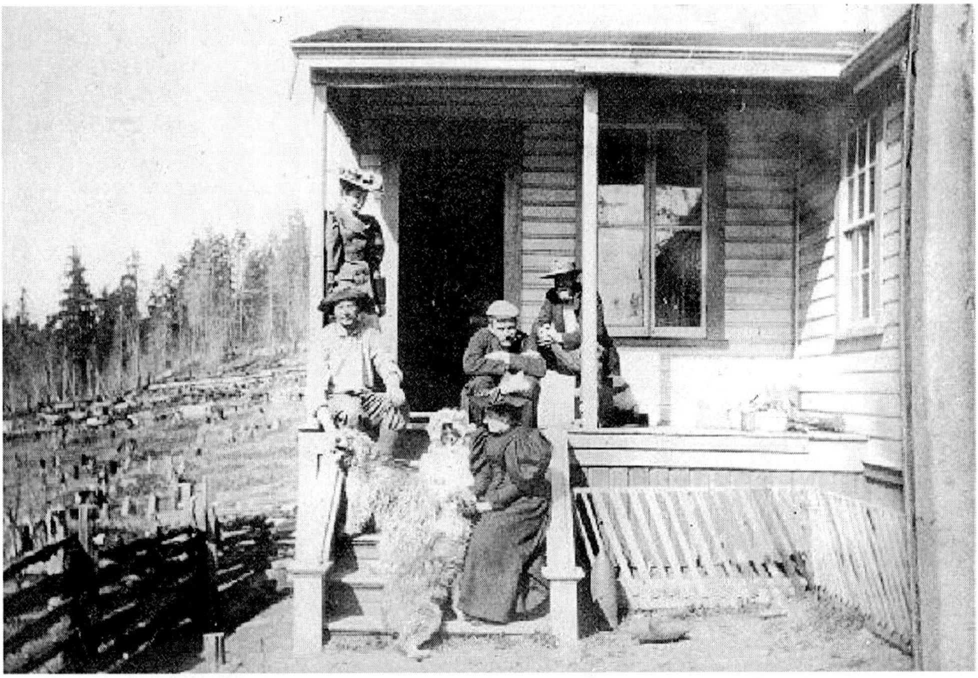

Breezy Bay Bed and Breakfast in 1898, BC Archives C-06980

On either side of Payne Point, the Englishman built docks from which he put his boat in the water. He built a stone dock just north of the Saturna Beach wharf and a wooden dock in a cove on the opposite side of the point.

In the 1930's, the property was sold to the resident who would later build the Saturna General Store. The resident owned a pet goat, which was often seen running along the roof of the house.

Much later, in the 1980's, new owners restored the old house and added a verandah. Today, they run the property as the *Breezy Bay Bed and Breakfast*.

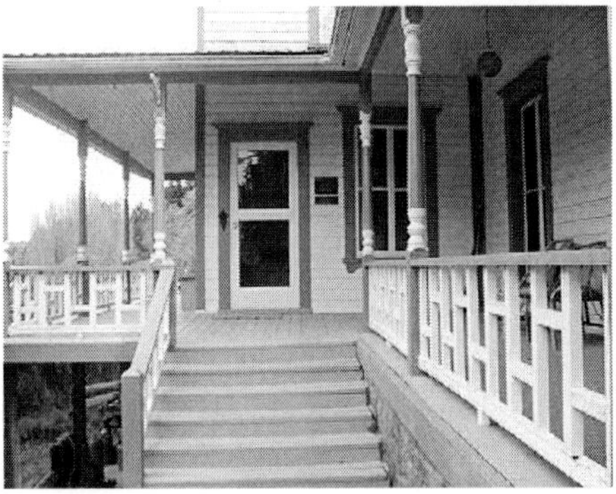

Breezy Bay B&B as it appears today

The B&B is situated on a working organic farm, called *Old Point Farm*. The farm, which is located on Payne Road, is surrounded by orchards. There is a private beach with good kayak access.

Saturna Island Sights & Shops

1 Gallery Rosa
2 Dreamscapes Studio
3 Boot Cove Art Studio
4 Jack Campbell Gallery & Studio
5 Saturna Island Vineyards & Wine Shop
6 Mount Warburton Pike
8 East Point Lighthouse
9 St. Christopher's Church
10 Old St. Christopher's Church
11 Saturna Island Cemetery

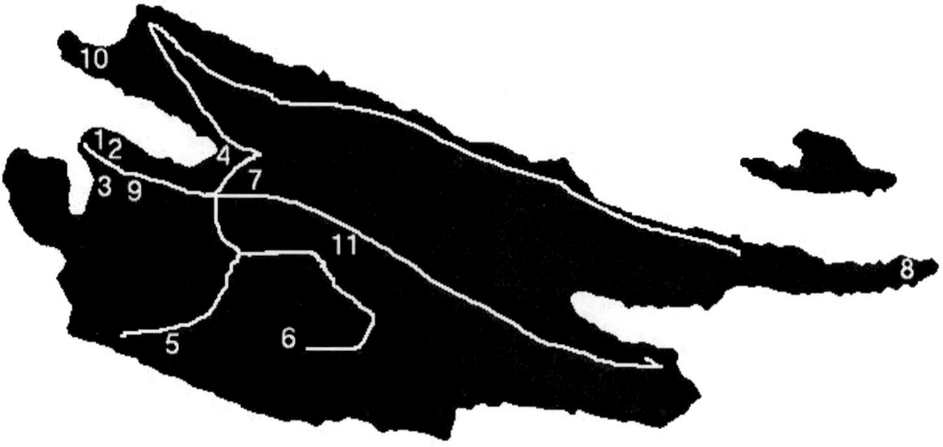

Things to See

Saturna Island is a remote hideaway. Because it is difficult to reach, it is easily the least spoiled of the southern Gulf Islands. Most people come to Saturna to explore its bountiful wildlife and wonder at its natural beauty.

East Point Road, which runs along the entire northern shore of the Island, is the main route on the Island. It turns into Tumbo Channel Road, which turns into Cliffside Road, circumventing the eastern tip of the Island. Narvaez Bay Road runs east and west, bisecting the Island. It connects Narvaez Bay to the ferry terminal.

Old St. Christopher's Church

In the late 1890's, **the Postman** brought his twin brother, who was a Parson, to Saturna. There, the Parson purchased some land on the northwest side of the Island.

On the property sat a Japanese boathouse, which the Parson converted into a small church. His brother-in-law helped him build the church and carved a large wooden cross that was nailed to the front gable.

The church was named *St. Christopher's Anglican Church*. It seated just 20 people and was used for Sunday services.

At that time, there were no roads into the area, so congregations came by boat. The people would attend the church in black lace-up boots and little starched hats and white dresses.

Because the church was never consecrated, it became a private residence when the Parson left.

Unfortunately, a television antenna was soon seen wrapped around the adorable rear gable of the church and a clothesline strung from one of its windows.

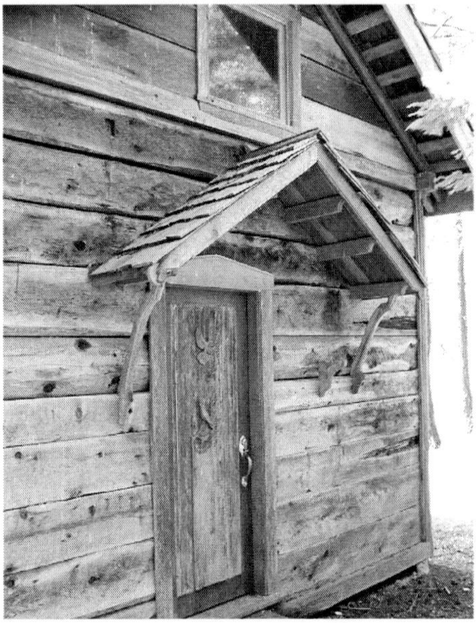

By 1960, a Bishop from Pender Island was ministering to the residents of Saturna and Sunday services were being held in the Saturna Island Community Hall.

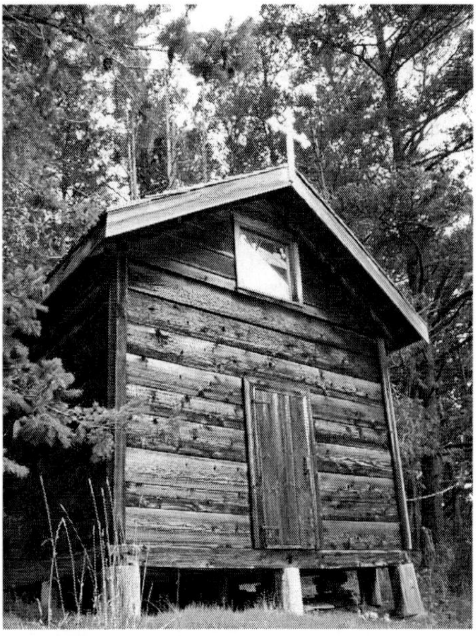

Eventually, St. Christopher's Church was restored. Today, it serves as a private chapel on Church Cove and is accessible from Church Bay Road. (#10 on the map)

New St. Christopher's Church

When some land was purchased for the use of a new church, a Saturna resident proceeded to build a replacement for the old church that sat on Church Cove. Some of the timber for the new church building came from a famous hotel on Mayne Island.

On one side of the new church a wooden cross was encased in a glass wall. On the other side, a glass window was set in a wooden wall.

Steel workers cast the original tower bell. Unfortunately, a visitor pulled the rope, and the bell fell and cracked.

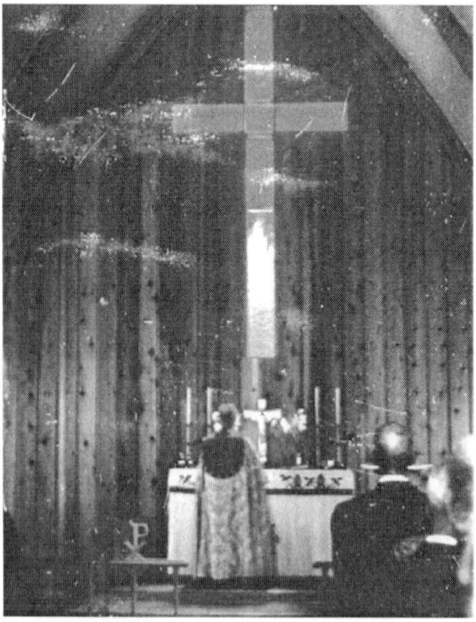

St. Christopher's Church in 1965
Jim & Lorraine Campbell

In the early 1960`s, the new church was dedicated. Later, in the year 1990, a couple donated some books and opened the *Eddie Reid Memorial Library* in the basement of the church.

The new *St. Christopher's Church* is located at the corner of East Point Road and Payne Road, where a baptismal font and shield serve as a memorial to its builder. (#9 on the map)

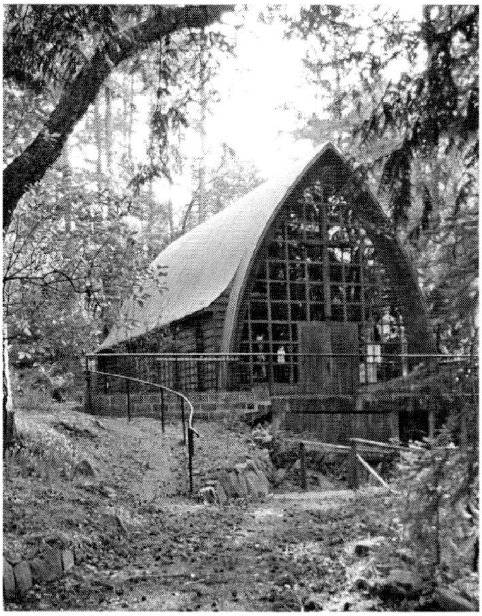

Mount Warburton Pike

In the 1880's, a graduate of Oxford University, in England, immigrated to North America, where he became an explorer. He wore a drooping mustache and often traveled barefoot, hunting for buffalo, wapiti and other big game in the U.S.

Soon, the explorer went into partnership with the oldest brother of the man who would later become **the Postman**. The two settlers purchased a large piece of land at the foot of a tall mountain.

There, on Saturna Beach, the explorer developed a ranch. He built a well-furnished bungalow with a vaulted ceiling and filled it with trophies of the big game he had killed. He also established a stone quarry, on a point at the other end of the property.

The explorer frequently went on sailing trips on his sloop, called the *Fleetwing*. He would leave no word of his whereabouts and sometimes disappeared for months at a time. Whenever he went sailing, he would clean his dirty clothes by fastening them to the end of a long rope and letting them trail in the water.

Referred to as 'Crazy Pike', he was well known for not owning any decent clothes. Once, while on a trip, **the Postman** left his trunk in town to lighten his load. The explorer went into the trunk and borrowed a good suit. It was a strange sight to see him dressed up, with nowhere to go but into the wilderness. He wore the suit until it fell apart.

Eventually, the explorer gained a worldwide reputation as a result of having written two books about his adventures. Unfortunately, during World War I, he ended his life with a penknife, in an English sanitarium.

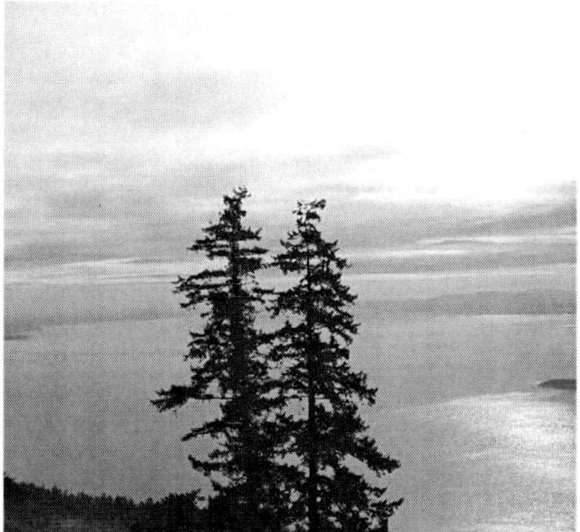

Although the explorer's house burned down in the 1930's, his ranch is still known as the *Old Ranch* and his memory is preserved in *Mount Warburton Pike*.

At 397 m, Mount Warburton Pike is the second highest peak in the outer Gulf Islands and provides for breathtaking panoramic views of the southern Gulf Islands.

The peak is accessible by way of Staples Road and can be reached by car. The road to the top passes the Saturna Island Ecological Reserve, which was set aside to preserve a West Coast Douglas-Fir forest. (#6 on the map)

Saturna Island Cemetery

At the end of World War I, two people starting walking from either end of the Island. Where they met became the site of its first school.

When a new school was built at the harbour in the 1940's, the original school was torn down. At that time, the land became home to the *Saturna Island Cemetery*. The small cemetery is located on Narvaez Bay Road. (#11 on the map)

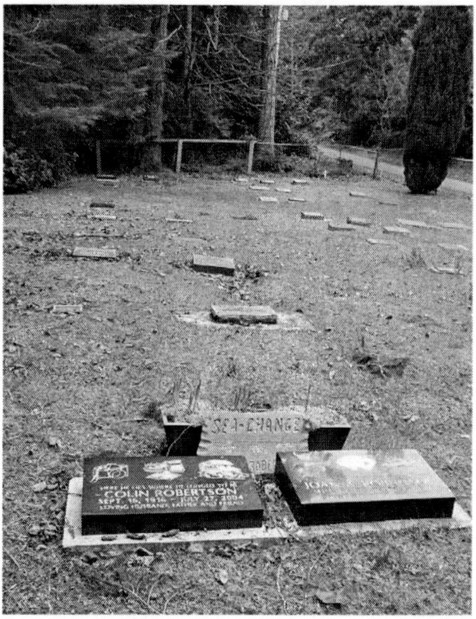

Saturna Island Vineyards

In the 1930's, a Vancouver resident purchased the land that was once owned by the famous explorer. A decade later, his daughter inherited the property, along with her younger brother.

A few years later, she and her brother divided the property between them, and her brother claimed the portion that included Saturna Beach. As a result, she and her husband moved onto a farm further inland.

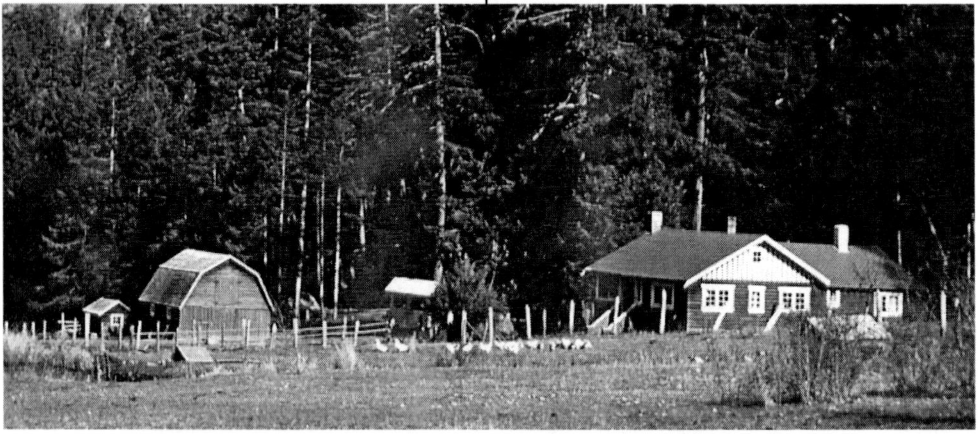

Farm beside Saturna Vineyards in 1956 - Jim & Lorraine Campbell

Separated from their neighbors by a mountain, the woman and her new husband learned to become self-sufficient on their portion of the property.

The couple ploughed up an old pasture and established a potato farm using a potato planter. Unfortunately, the pasture was infested with wireworm, which destroyed their first crop.

Over time, the couple ceased growing potatoes and started raising sheep and cattle. For 50 years, they traveled around the Island by boat because there was no road in to the south end of the Island.

In the 1990`s, the woman's brother sold his portion of the property. When a road was extended into the area, the new owners converted some of his land into a vineyard and began producing award-winning wines.

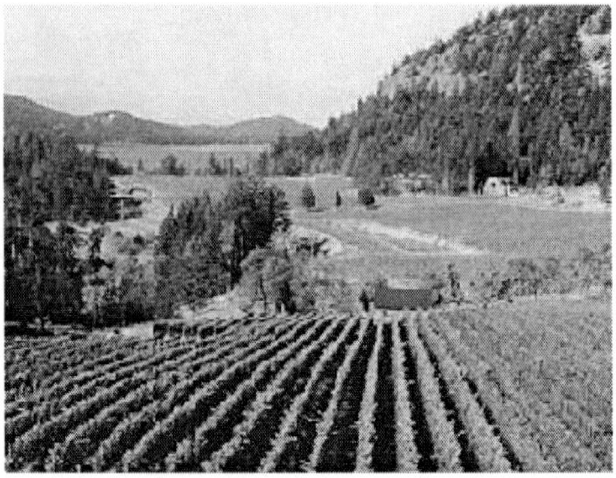

Today, the woman and her family still live on their farm, while her brother's property operates as the *Saturna Island Vineyards*.

The vineyard is one of the largest estate vineyard and winery operations in all of British Columbia. A few years prior to this writing, the winery reported harvesting 25,000 kg of grapes from the vineyard.

Recently, a large building was constructed for the production of the wine. It contains

13 stainless steel fermentation tanks with a state-of-the-art temperature control system and a 4,500 kg grape press.

A mezzanine allows for guided tours throughout the winery. The vineyard and winery, which hosts the *Saturna Island Vineyard Harvest Celebration*, are located on Quarry Road. (#5 on the map).

East Point Lighthouse

In the 1880's, a ship carrying a large supply of coal ran aground on *Boiling Reef.* It was coming through *Boundary Pass* on the east side of Saturna.

The wreckage, which remained on the rocks for a year, prompted the government to purchase some property from the famous explorer so a light station could be built at the Pass.

Two years later, the *East Point Light Station* was built on East Point. It helped to keep the white Empresses and other ships off the reef. One of the first keepers of the lighthouse was the brother of a famous lighthouse keeper on Mayne Island.

The *East Point Lighthouse* at the light station had a circular staircase that led to a wonderful view. The light, which flashed once every 30 seconds, had six wicks and burned coal oil. It operated on a pendulum system and had to be wound up like a grandfather clock, in the morning and at night.

The lighthouse keeper served the light station until the 1920's. He received a Long Service Medal for his service. His sons continued to serve the lighthouse until the year 1940. As a result, the lighthouse was in the family name for over 50 years.

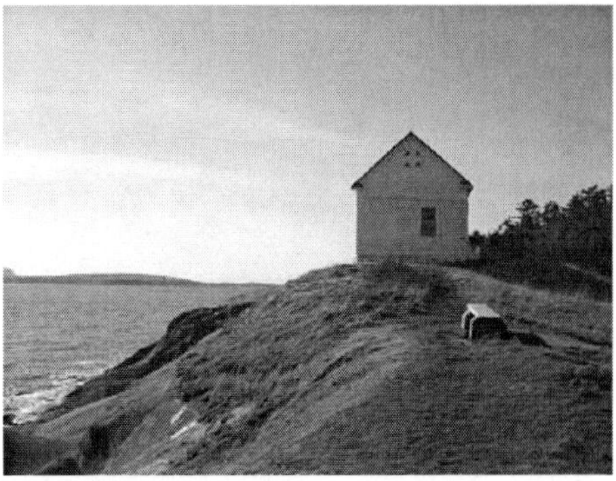

The East Point Lighthouse is located in East Point Park and is accessible from Tumbo Channel Road. (#8 on the map). None of the original buildings remain on the park grounds. The existing lighthouse was built in the 1940's.

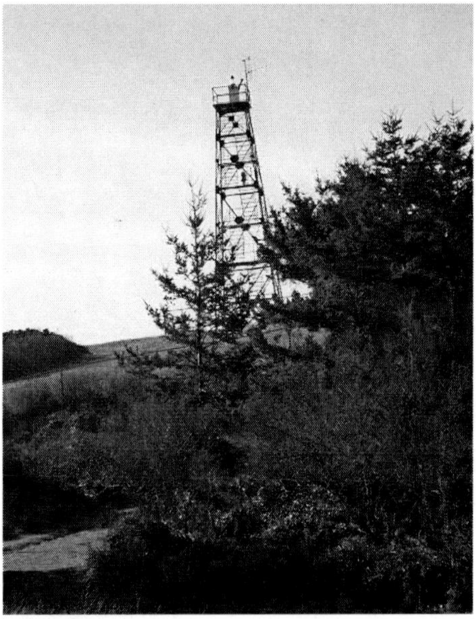

Places to Shop

At the turn of the century, **the Postman's** sister emigrated to Saturna from England and kept house for their brother, the Parson.

The beautiful woman was very artistic and quickly developed a reputation for wandering away to paint. She would often forget about the time and not return home until midnight.

One day, when the woman did not return home, her brothers searched all night, shouting her name out in the dark. In the morning, they found her resting in a shack.

Today, Saturna Island is home to a variety of fine artists and artisans. Art galleries, shops and studios provide visitors to Saturna Island the opportunity to pick up a *potlatch* (gift) for someone special.

Most of the studios are located along East Point Road. Watch for road signs and the chance to meet an artist working in their studio.

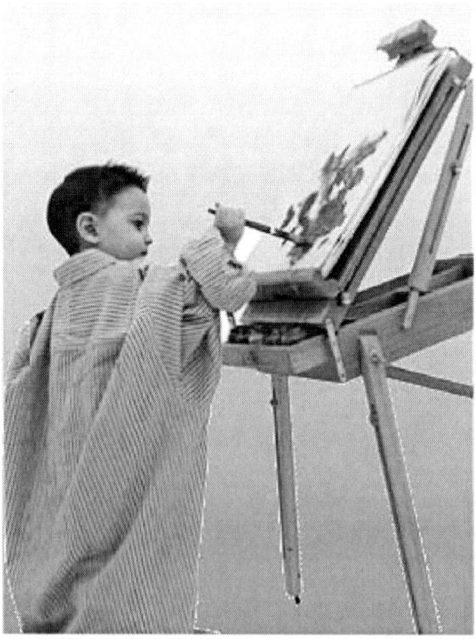

Boot Cove Art Studio

The *Boot Cove Art Studio* offers art in a variety of mediums. The artist uses oil, acrylic, ink, watercolor and other media. Visits can be made by appointment. Phone: (250) 539-3662 (#3 on the map)

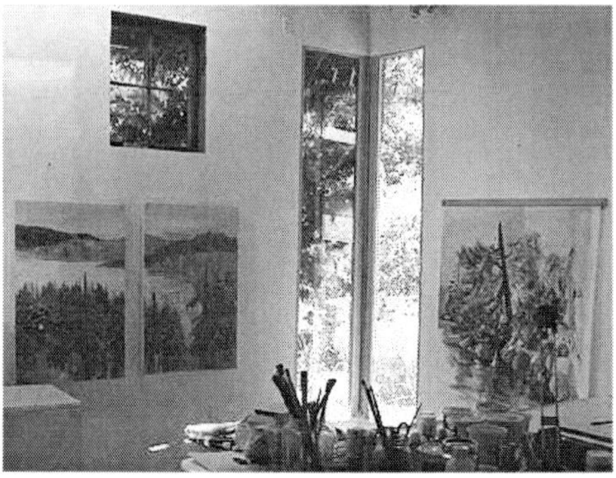

Gallery Rosa

Gallery Rosa sells paintings and prints, local photography, pottery, glass, jewelry, woodturning, wool products and other crafts by local artists. It is located on East Point Road. (#1 on the map)

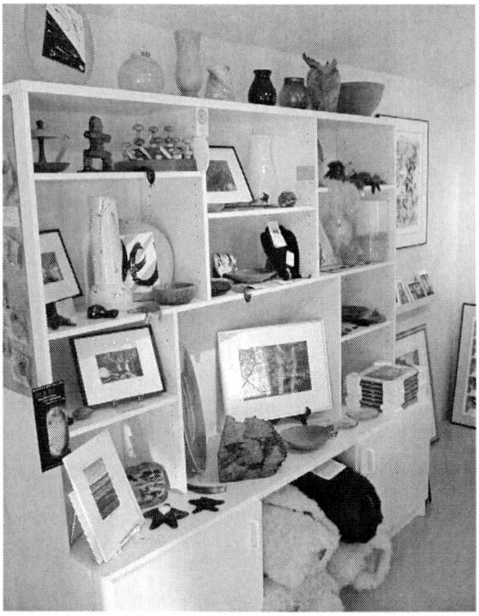

Jack Campbell Gallery & Studio

The *Jack Campbell Gallery and Studio* features Saturna Island and West Coast scenes, as well as figurative compositions.

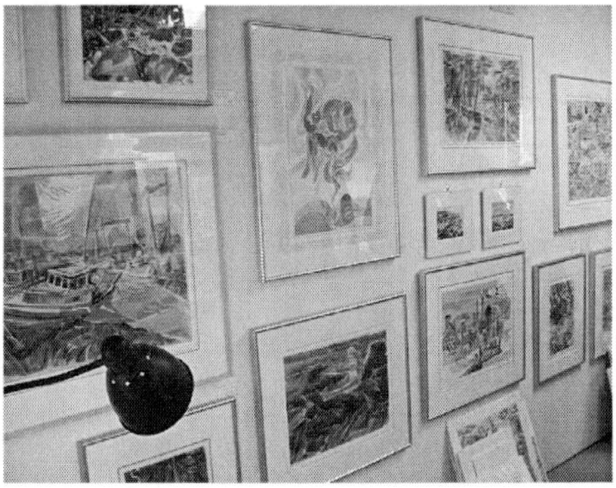

The artist has had over 30 exhibitions in British Columbia. His work is in collections throughout North America and Europe. The studio is located on East Point Road. (#4 on the map)

Dreamscapes Studio

The *Dreamscapes Studio* features creations that make use of a variety of fabrics, in combination with drawing, painting, batik and textile dyeing. The studio offers collages, etchings, scarves and pillows. It is located on East Point Road. (#2 on the map)

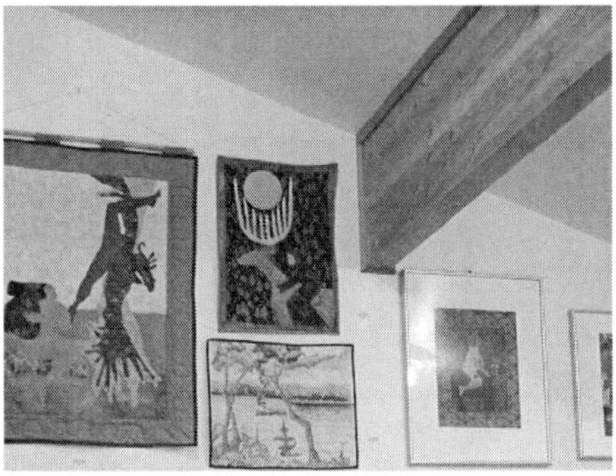

Saturna Vineyards Wine Shop

The *Saturna Vineyards Wine Shop* provides for award-winning wines, as well as local artworks, crafts and gifts. The shop is located at the Saturna Island Vineyards on Quarry Road. (#5 on the map)

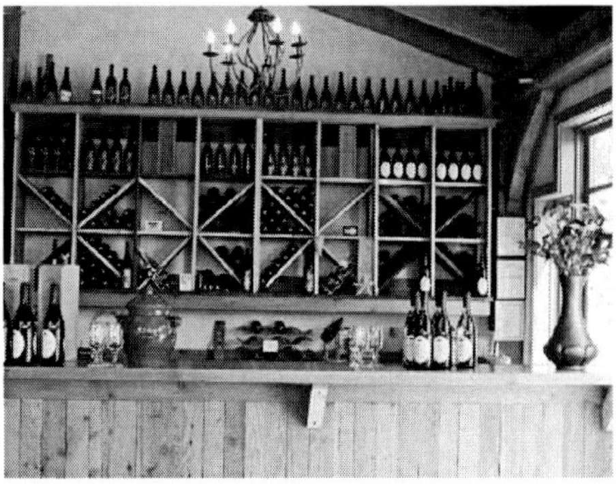

Events to Attend

At the turn of the century, the Englishman who lived on Payne Point decided to teach his daughters to be expert rowers. So he commissioned a boat builder who lived in the lighthouse to build boats for each of them.

The sisters would row `doubles`. The older sister would sit in the bow and if the younger sister did not keep time, she would receive a blow to the back from her sibling.

The Englishman entered his daughters in all the rowing events at the regattas. Because they won all the races, the organizers of the events eventually asked them not to participate.

Whether it is an annual event, such as the *Canada Day Lamb Barbeque* or a *Whole Pig Roast*, or a special event, such as a music festival or play, there is always something to take in on Saturna Island today. The Saturna Island Lions Club hosts a variety of events throughout the year.

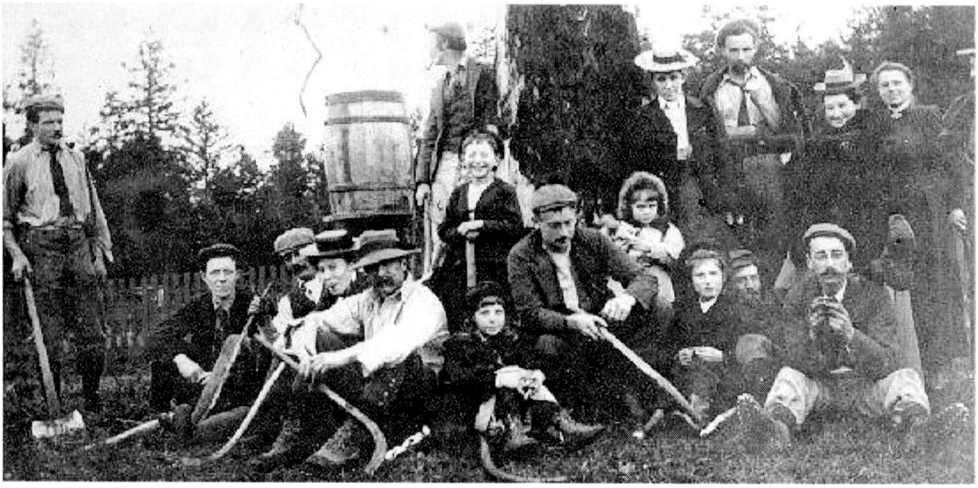

Saturna Island field hockey game in the late 1890's – BC Archives C-06971

Easter Bake Sale

The Easter Bake Sale is an annual event that takes place at Easter at the Saturna Island Community Hall.

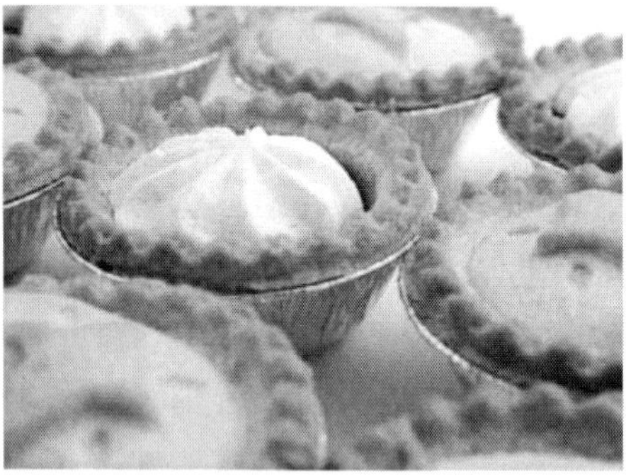

Mother's & Father's Day Brunches

On both Mother's Day and Father's Day, the Saturna Community Hall hosts an annual brunch.

Whole Pig Roasts

On the long weekends in May and November, the Saturna Island Volunteer Fire Department hosts spit-roasted, whole pig dinners at the Saturna Community Hall. The rituals are authentic, with pigs that are placed on a spit and cooked over hot coals. A dance at the hall follows the dinner.

Canada Day Lamb Barbeque

In the late 1940's, well before the vineyards were established on the southwest side of Saturna, the land was leased to an Argentinean sheep farmer.

The Argentinean acquired a small flock of sheep, tending them on the property. Unfortunately, his luck turned bad and the first winter he spent there was very severe.

Ironically, his ram fell down his well the following year. So he decided to sell his flock and move off the Island. He sold all of his sheep, except for two lambs.

The Argentinean had learned how to cook meat in Pratagonia. So he offered to slaughter his two remaining lambs and hold an Argentine-style barbeque for the annual school picnic.

At the picnic, he splayed the lambs out on the iron and roasted them over a fire. The barbeque was so successful that, in 1950, it became an annual event, called the *Canada Day Lamb Barbeque*.

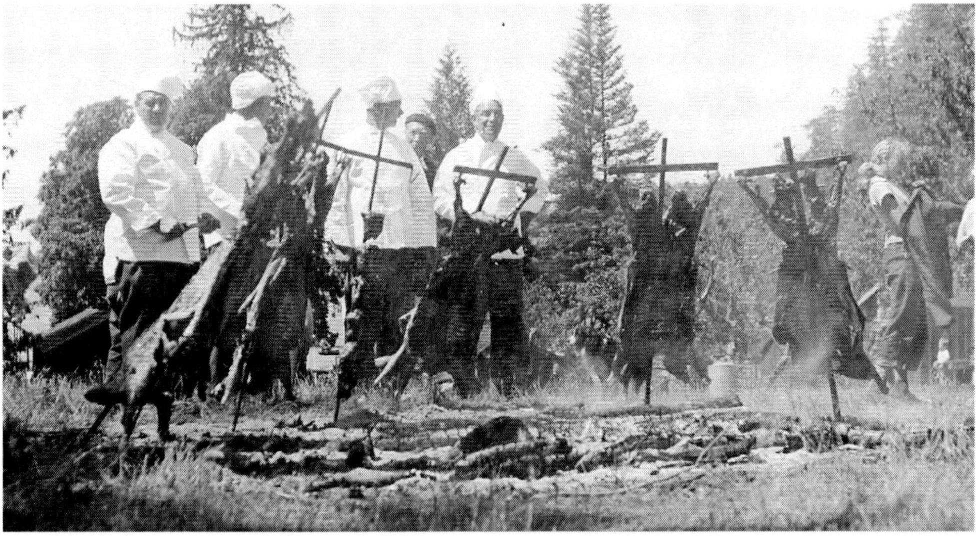

Canada Day Lamb BBQ in 1951 - Jim & Lorraine Campbell

Each year, the Argentinean would set up the lambs on the irons and oversee the barbeque.

Unfortunately, one evening in the 1960's, he died, while preparing the spots for the irons to be set in the ground at the next day's annual barbeque.

The barbeque endured, however, and for 40 years, people traveled to the event by boat because there was no road in to the south end of the Island. In the year 1990, it was moved to a marine park on the northwest side of Saturna.

Today, the Canada Day Lamb Barbeque is one of the largest bashes in all the southern Gulf Islands, drawing hundreds of visitors from all over British Columbia.

Preparations for the barbeque begin long before people arrive. Lit in the early morning, an enormous bonfire is left to burn in a pit until a thick bed of smoldering coals remains.

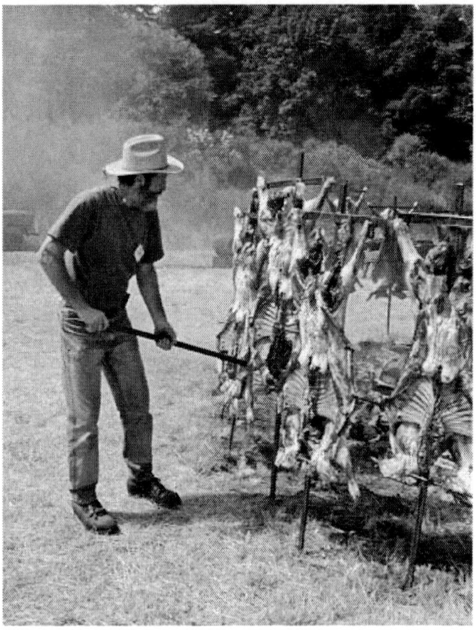

Metal crosses are then staked around the bonfire and whole lambs, which have been split down the middle, are skewered to the crosses to roast.

The event, which is held on July 1, at Winter Cove Park, provides for races, a craft booth, a beer garden, live music and, of course, great food.

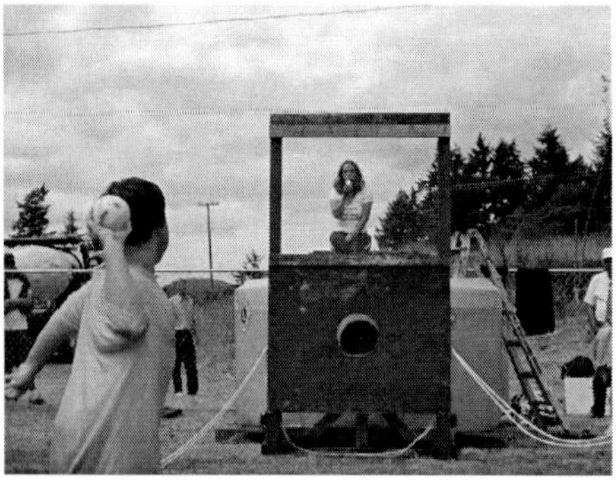

Saturday Market

The *Saturna Island Saturday Market* runs every Saturday from July through to October. The market is held at the Saturna Community Hall and provides for a cornucopia of fresh produce from local farmers, as well as art from local artists and craftspeople.

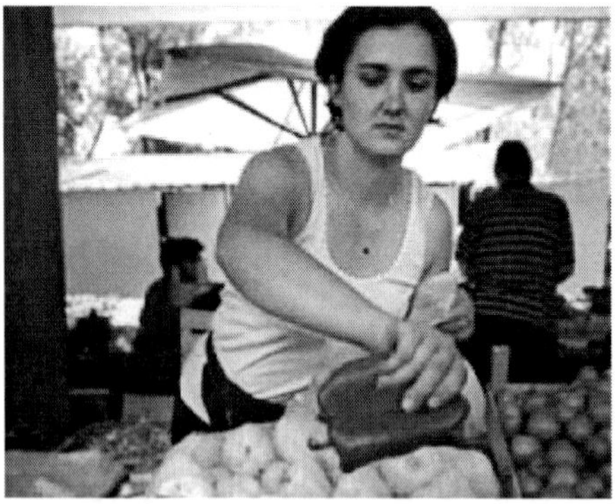

Artists' Studio Tour

The annual *Artist's Studio Tour* takes place each year on the long weekend in August. Look for the blue balloons as guides to the studios on Saturna.

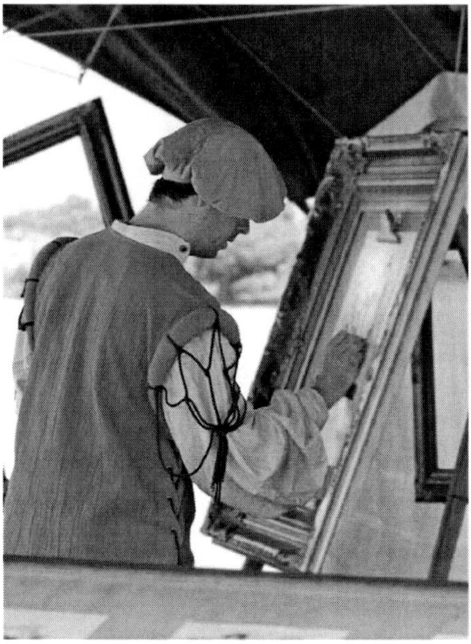

Saturna Island Regatta

The *Saturna Island Regatta* has been taking place every September since the 1990's. During the event, yachtsmen participate in a day of racing. Trophies are awarded, and there are post-race appetizers and cocktails. The race starts and ends at Saturna Beach.

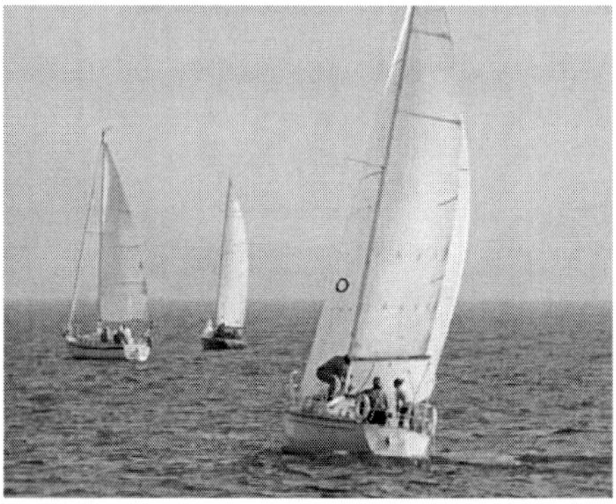

Saturna Vineyards Harvest

The *Saturna Vineyards Harvest Celebration* takes place in September at the Saturna Island Vineyards Bistro on Quarry Road.

The event provides for music, food, wine tasting, grape crushing and other festivities.

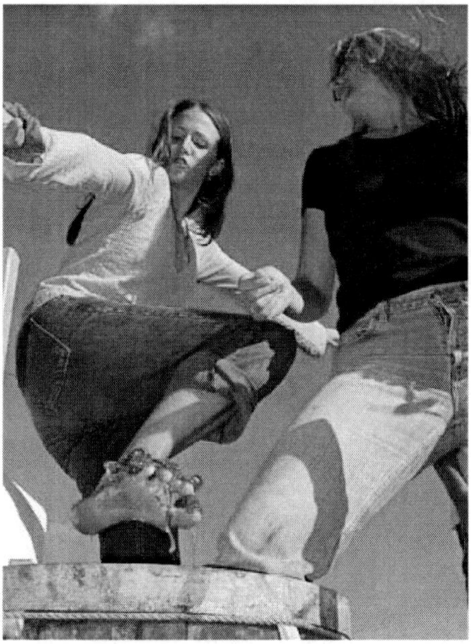

Halloween Howl

The *Halloween Howl* is an annual event held at Halloween at the fire hall on East Point Road.

Hosted by the Saturna Island Fire Department, the event provides for an evening bon-fire, hot dog roast and fireworks display. There is also a contest for the child who can find the largest Maple leaf.

Lyall Creek Salmon BBQ

The *Lyall Creek Salmon Barbeque* takes place in Lyall Creek Park. Hosted by the Lyall Creek Enhancement Society, it celebrates the return of the salmon to the creek.

The event provides for a tour of the estuary, creek bed and dam. The festivities include a bonfire and live music, as well as great food.

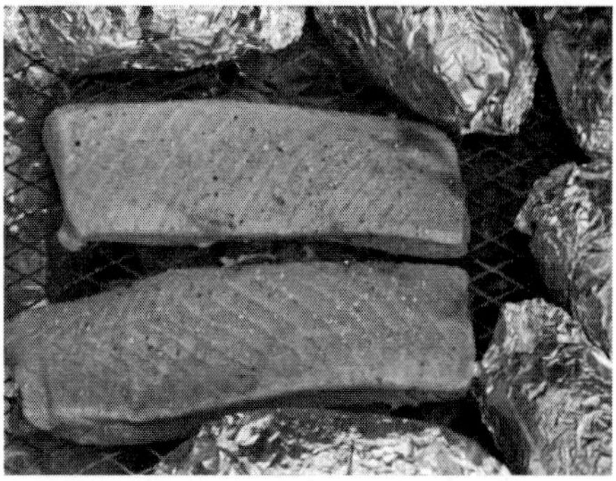

Christmas Celebrations

During the 1950's, the resident who drove people to the dances in his tractor-trailer would also pick them up on Christmas Eve. He would drive them around the Island, while they sang Christmas carols.

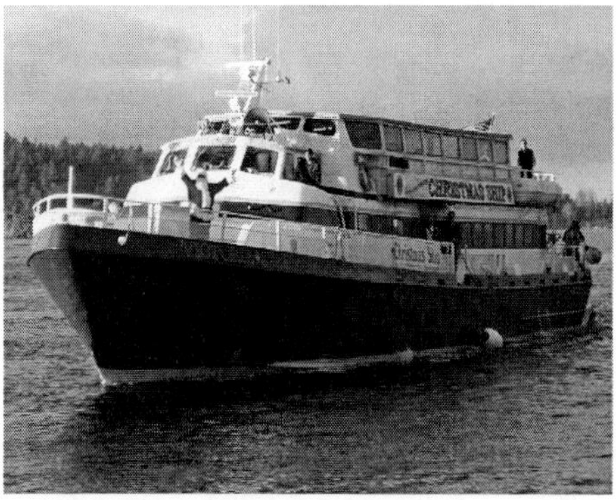

Around that time, the Bellingham Central Lions Club, in Washington State, began sending a ship loaded with toys and gifts to the Gulf Islands. They called it the *Christmas Ship*.

Today, the Christmas Ship is known locally as the *Santa Ship*. Each December, the Santa Ship is greeted at the wharf, and then Santa and his 'helpers' distribute gifts to the kids.

The residents of Saturna continue the Christmas season with a craft fair at the Saturna Community Hall.

Saturna Island Parks & Beaches

1 Winter Cove
3 Russell Reef Provincial Park
4 Lyall Harbour
5 East Point Regional Park
6 Cabbage Island
7 Lyall Creek
8 Narvaez Bay
9 Tumbo Island
10 Taylor Point
11 Thomson Park
12 Boot Cove
13 Veruna Bay

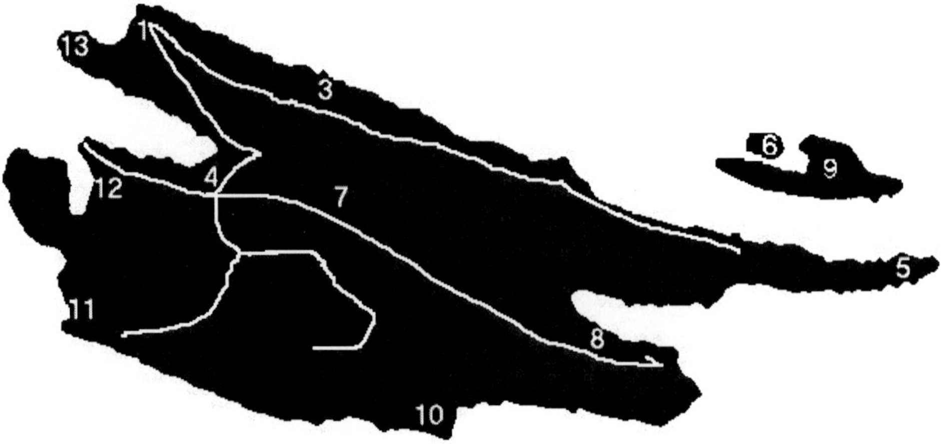

Parks & Beaches to Explore

Before the turn of the century, sheep thrived on the hills of Saturna, roaming wild through the bush. At that time, an Indian sheep farmer lived in a shack on the explorer's ranch. He made a living tending several hundred sheep.

The Indian sheep farmer could run up and down the ridge. At that time, the ridge was called *Prairie Hill*, but was later renamed *Brown Ridge*. Because he could run tirelessly for hours, the other settlers always called on him to help whenever they had to gather their sheep off the mountain.

The Indian ran bent over, as though he was heading into battle with a spear in his hand. He could run as fast as the little dog that helped him.

Sometimes, the other settlers had to round up their sheep for earmarking the lambs. Everyone would yell at the top of their lungs, while the sheep ran ahead. The Indian had a wild, fierce, Indian yell, which he would use whenever the sheep ran in the wrong direction. Dogs would crouch on the ground whenever they heard it.

Eventually, the sheep would be run into a corral where they were shorn and the lambs were taken away.

Today, the hills of Saturna Island provide for some of the best hiking destinations in the Gulf Islands. Almost half of the Island is parkland and is protected within the Gulf Islands National Park Reserve.

The land that was acquired includes Narvaez Bay, the largest acquisition in the Gulf Islands to date. It also includes the Saturna Island Ecological Reserve, Taylor Point, Mount Elford, Mount David, Winter Cove and Brown Ridge.

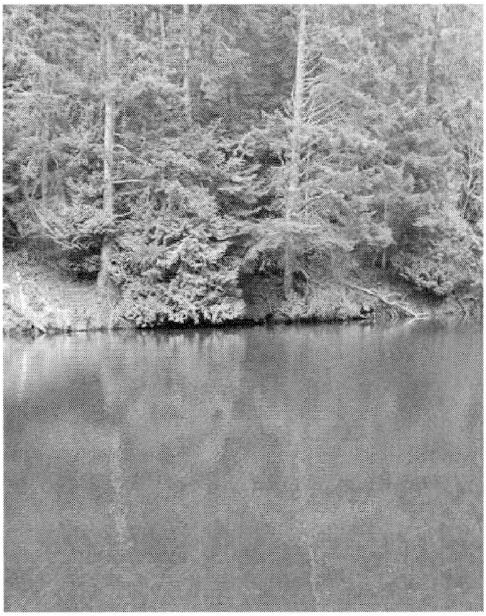

Cabbage Is. Provincial Marine Park

Cabbage Island is located off the northeast side of Saturna Island. The province of British Columbia acquired it in the 1970's. A few years prior to this writing, it was established as a marine park called *Cabbage Island Provincial Marine Park*.

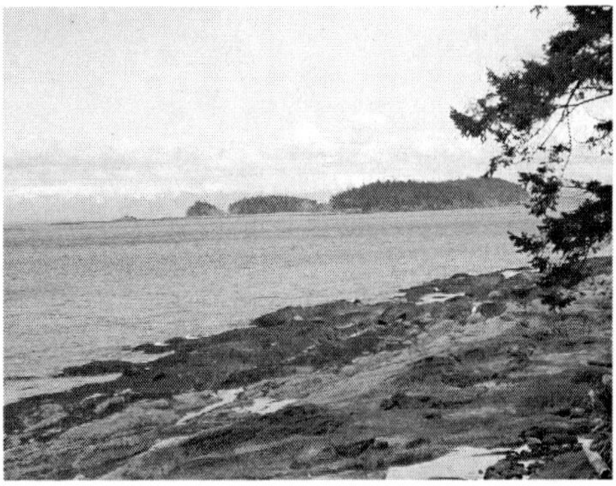

Cabbage Island Park is part of the Gulf Islands National Park Reserve and is an important nesting site for Black Oystercatchers and Bald Eagles.

The sandy beaches in the park provide for good swimming and fishing. Camping is permitted and there are facilities for picnics if you want to stay awhile.

You can boat to Cabbage Island from Russell Reef Park on the north side of Saturna. However, be wary of the tides when crossing Tumbo Channel.

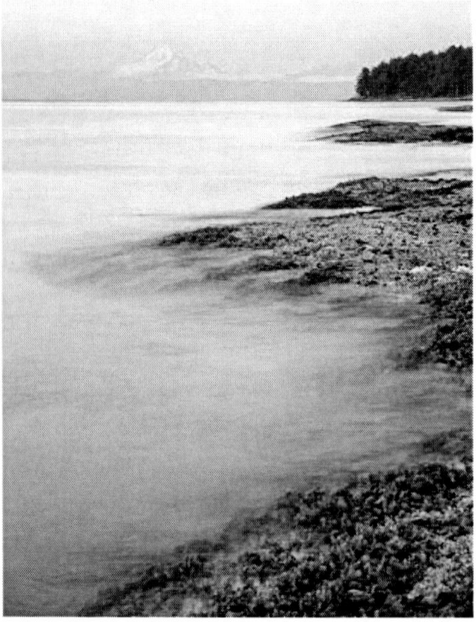

East Point Regional Park

In the 1920's, one of the lighthouse keeper's sons took over the operation of the light station at East Point. He had been the first white child ever to be born on Saturna.

Over time, the son became an expert builder of flat-bottomed skiffs, which he sold to the other residents. They would use the skiffs to get to and from their boats. Some of the skiffs could carry as many as six people.

The boat builder made the skiffs out of clear Cedar, with big, wide planks on the bottom. He also made the oars. He used only an axe to work with the wood.

The boat builder produced a total of 80 boats while he lived at the light station. One of the boats, named *Irene*, was used for over 60 years.

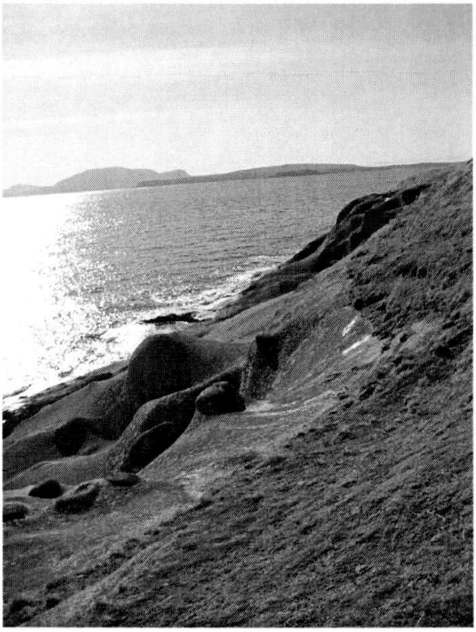

The site of the lighthouse, *East Point Regional Park* provides for spectacular views of Mount Baker in Washington State. Seals and killer whales are frequently spotted in the waters off the point.

The lighthouse was recently de-staffed. However, the park, which is locally referred to as *Lighthouse Park*, is open to the public year-round.

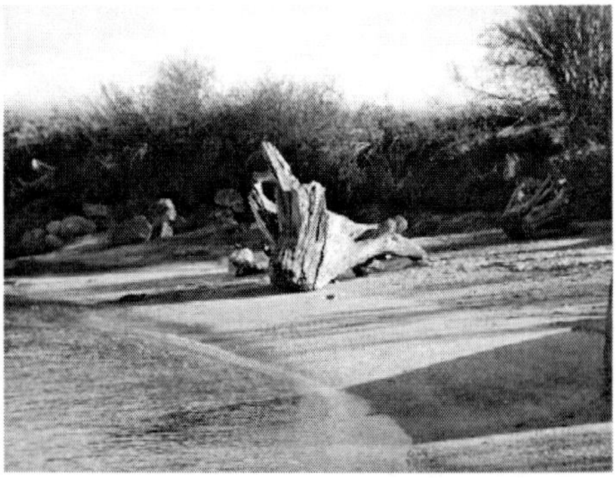

East Point provides for a great *soaking* (swimming) beach called *Shell Beach*. The stunning shoreline is dotted with interesting boulders and intricate sandstone formations.

At low tide, you can walk along the beach, all the way around the point. Along the rocks on the beach are tidal pools, which are home to an abundance of Sea Stars and other sea creatures.

There are two easy trails through the park. The 1.5 km trail to the left is called *Trillium Trail*. It accesses the beach. The trail to the right leads to a rocky ledge above Boiling Reef, where a ship ran aground in the 1880's. Both trails are accessible from the end of Tumbo Channel Road. (#5 on the map)

Lyall Creek Park

Lyall Creek is located in the center of the Island. It includes a 4 km long creek that flows west into Lyall Harbour. The creek is one of the few remaining salmon-bearing streams in the Gulf Islands.

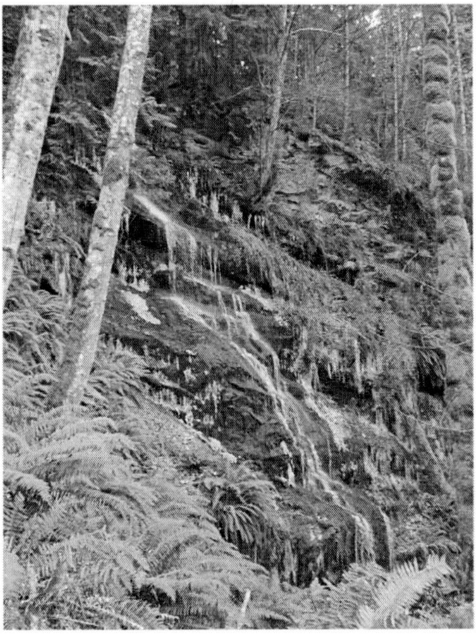

The watershed has seen little human disturbance since the 1970's when it was last logged. Because the area was logged for Douglas-Fir, numerous large Western Red Cedar and Alder trees remain. It is now protected as part of the Gulf Islands National Park Reserve.

Lyall Creek Trail, which descends to the mouth of Lyall Creek, provides for a stunning seasonal waterfall. It joins the two accesses and passes through the trees. The easy 1.5 km trail is accessible via the end of Valley Road. (#7 on the map)

Lyall Harbour

In the 1920's, a wharf was built from Saturna Point into the harbour. For the most part, it replaced the wharf at Saturna Beach. At that time, the road to the harbour was just a narrow, single-lane track.

One day, an old man, who was living in a little shack on the beach nearby, took out an advertisement for a wife. When an interested lady responded to his ad, he sent her a photograph of himself.

Eventually, the lady agreed to move to Saturna to be the man's bride. However, as her ship arrived in the harbour, she saw the old man and realized that the picture he had sent her was 40 years old. As a result, she refused to get off the ship.

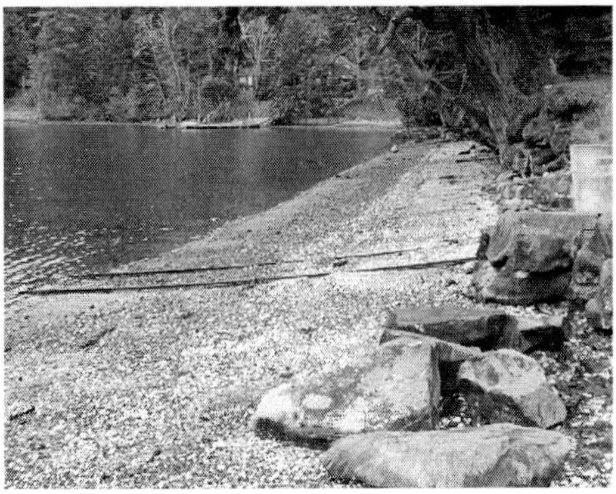

Lyall Harbour fits snuggly between Saturna Point and Winter Point. It provides for a boat launch at one end and a government wharf at the other. The sandy swimming beach at the head of the harbour is accessible by way of Sunset Boulevard. (#14 on the map)

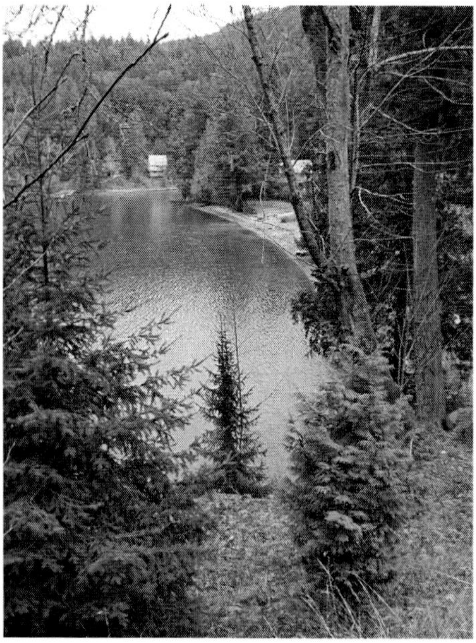

British Columbia Ferry Services uses the land on Saturna Point to operate scheduled ferry services from both the mainland and Vancouver Island.

If you launch a boat from the beach, you can head southwest to *Elliot Bluff*, which is a good scuba diving spot, at a depth of up to 30 m.

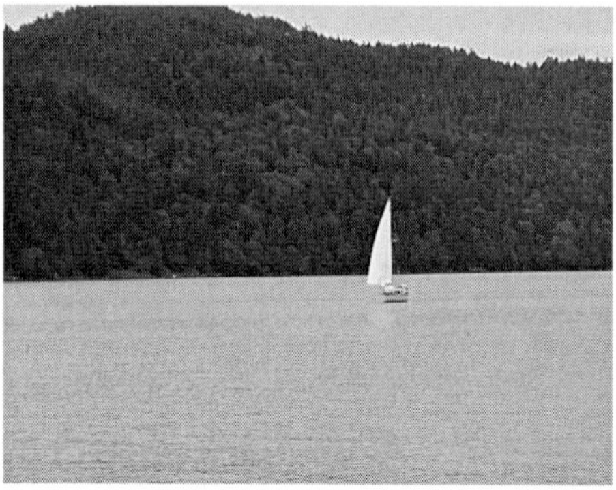

If you head east, *Java Islet* is also a good spot for scuba diving, at a depth of up to 9 m. Once called *Seagull Islet*, Java Islet provides for plenty of kelp beds, abalone and sea urchins.

Narvaez Bay Park

In the early 1890's, a settler with mutton chop whiskers purchased some land on a bay. Having lived several years in the West Indies, he wore a hard, black cummerbund on his head.

The settler's cummerbund was made of tattered pieces of cloth, which included an old school tie, a remnant of silk and some frayed rope. He would often conceal a knife or a gun inside it.

The settler lived on his land only part of the time. The rest of the time, he lived on his leaky boat, named *Edith*.

The top of the boat's cabin was covered with tin and, when it rained, the noise from inside was deafening. Whenever he chopped wood inside the cabin, his axe would hit the canopy, causing the sound to echo around the bay.

The settler was very fond of children. However, he liked to pick them up by the collar or belt, and then dunk them into the bay. Sometimes, he would leave them underwater too long.

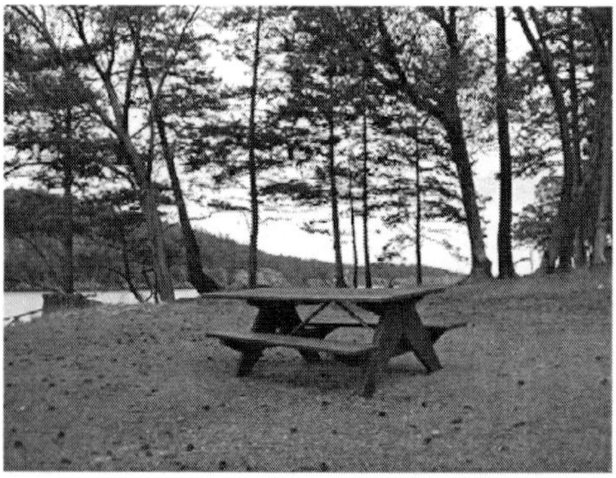

Located on the east side of Saturna, *Narvaez Bay Park* is one of the most diverse ecosystems on the West Coast. A recent addition to the Gulf Islands National Park Reserve, it provides for views of Fiddlers Cove. There are facilities for picnics if you want to stay awhile.

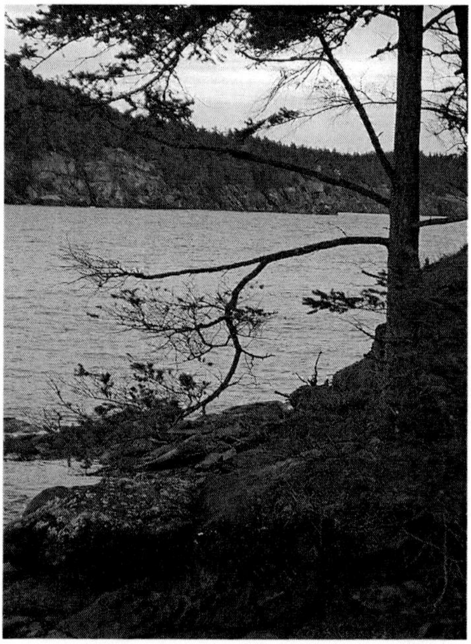

Originally called *Deep Bay*, *Narvaez Bay* is located in the park. Two smaller bays, called *Little Bay* and *Echo Bay*, sit on either side of Narvaez Bay. They provide for great swimming.

The 2 km trail through the park is of moderate difficulty and leads to the bays. It is accessible from the end of Narvaez Bay Road. There are two additional accesses further west. (#8 on the map)

Russell Reef Community Park

Russell Reef Community Park is a small park on the north side of Saturna. It provides for a dense lush forest.

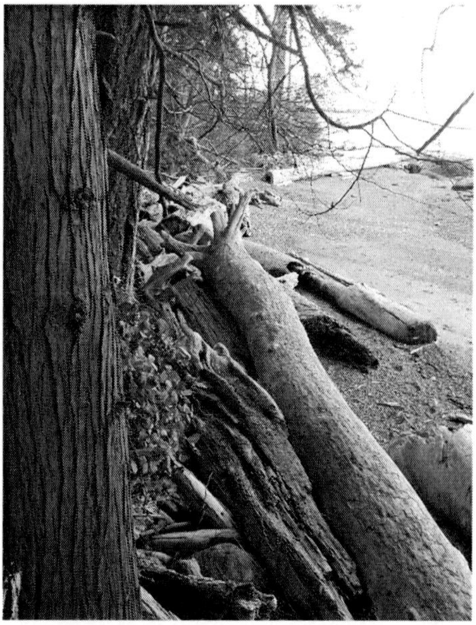

Russell Beach is located in the park. There are three accesses to the beach, all of which are from East Point Road, 1 km from the junction at Winter Cove Road. (#3 on the map)

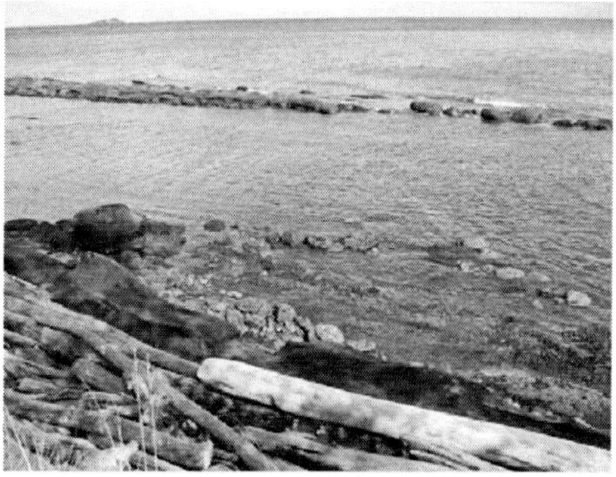

The beach provides for good swimming. It is covered in driftwood and the continuous string of rock shelves can be explored for *lele* (a long time) at low tide. The beach is a great place to see seals, sea lions, otters and tidal marine life.

Saturna Beach

In the 1870's, a settler immigrated to Canada from England. A decade later, he purchased some land on a bay on Saturna. At that time, he became the first permanent white settler on the Island.

On the beach surrounding the bay, the settler built a house out of rough lumber. Because he was afraid that Indians might attack his property, he built holes into his home, through which he could fire a gun if necessary.

Unfortunately, only one year later, he was forced to put his waterfront property up for sale, due to health reasons. As a result, it was sold to the famous explorer.

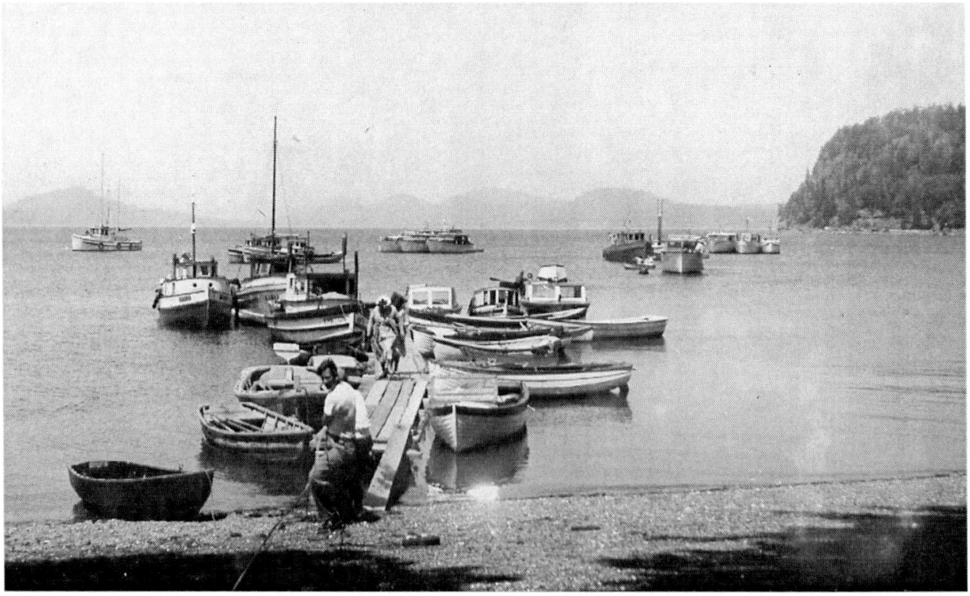

Saturna Beach in 1951 – Jim & Lorraine Campbell

Saturna Beach is located on the southwest side of Saturna. Originally the site of the annual *Canada Day Lamb Barbeque*, the beach has always been a popular destination for residents and visitors.

The beach is accessible from the end of Trueworthy Road. (#11 on the map) If you launch a boat from the beach, you can travel south around Croker Point, and then past a little bay where the Indian sheep farmer lived out his life.

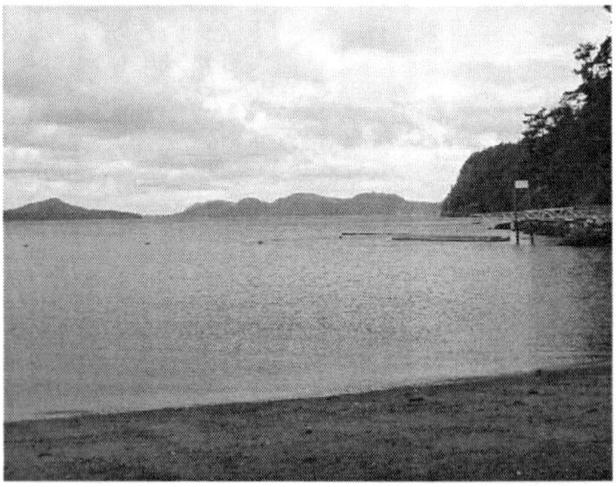

Saturna Beach as it appears today

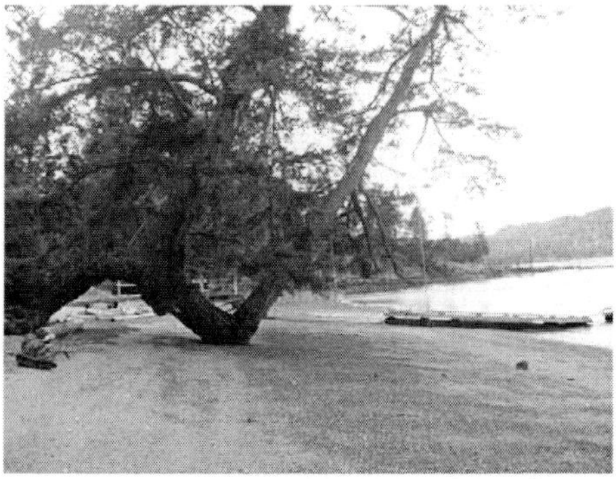

From the little bay, which is known locally as *Billy`s Bay*, you can continue east along the shoreline as far as Narvaez Bay. Alternatively, you can travel north to Payne Point.

Taylor Point

In the 1890's, a settler and his family emigrated from England to Saturna. The family settled on a bay called *Potato Bay*. Isolated by steep cliffs, the family learned to become self-sufficient.

There was a small stone quarry on the property, which had been started by the famous explorer. The settler used sandstone from the quarry to build a two-storey home for his family.

The settler was an inventor. He had a machine shop in which he built his own stationary threshing machine and hay baler. He could also turn four-cylinder engines into two-cylinder engines. His wife, who looked like a tall Scottish gypsy, baked wonderful cakes.

The couple lived happily in their stone home for many years. Unfortunately, in the 1930`s, the roof of the home caught fire and the house was destroyed. Nevertheless, the settler continued to live in the bunkhouse.

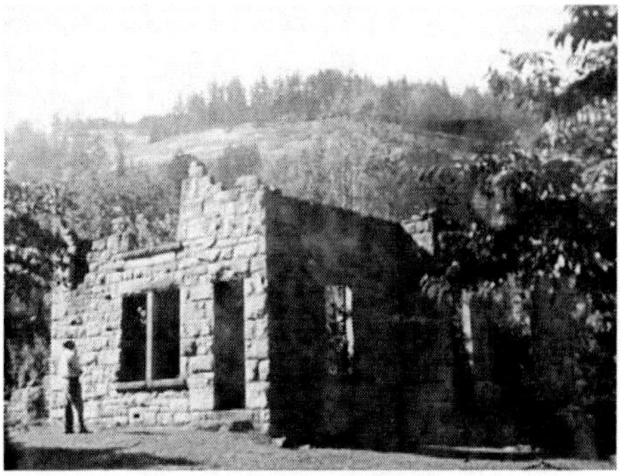

Remains of the house on Taylor Point, 1946
Jim & Lorraine Campbell

Taylor Point is located on the southeast side of Saturna. It was named after this family. The ruins of their stone house can still be seen there today.

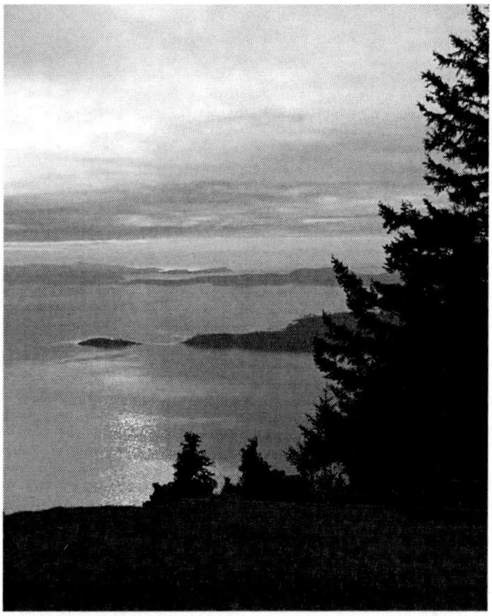

The 8 km trail to Taylor Point starts at the top of Mount Warburton Pike and runs east along Brown Ridge. (#10 on the map) It provides for one of the most incredible hikes in all the Gulf Islands, with phenomenal views of the Pender Islands and of Washington State.

Beneath the peak, the slopes of Brown Ridge are significant habitat for falcons, eagles and feral goats. There are numerous goat trails on the ridge. The large, feral goats that inhabit the area are descendants of domestic goats that were kept by some prominent English settlers around the turn of the century.

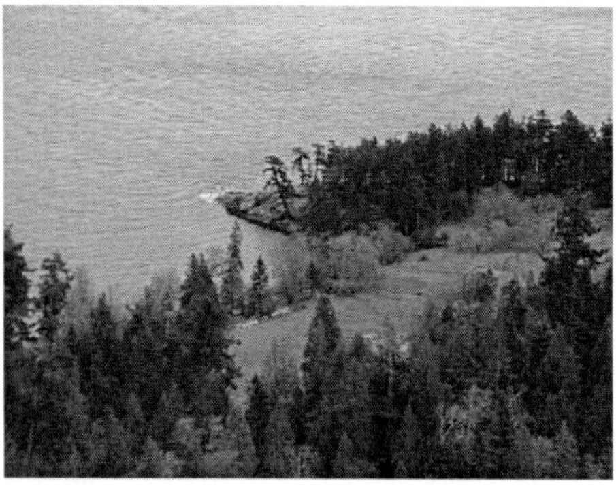

The old growth forest of Douglas-Fir, Arbutus and Garry Oak on Taylor Point sits on one of the longest, continuous stretches of protected shoreline in the southern Gulf Islands.

At the end of the ridge, the otherwise moderately difficult trail to the point becomes much more strenuous as it runs along Taylor Creek.

Thomson Community Park

When the woman who inherited the southwest side of Saturna was a young girl in the 1930's, her father invested in the development of a resort on Saturna Beach. The resort was called the *Saturna Beach Resort*.

Initially, three summer cottages were built at the resort, all of which had windows that opened like the windows on a tugboat.

Within a couple of years, three more cottages were added, as well as a cookhouse that was set above ground on cedar posts.

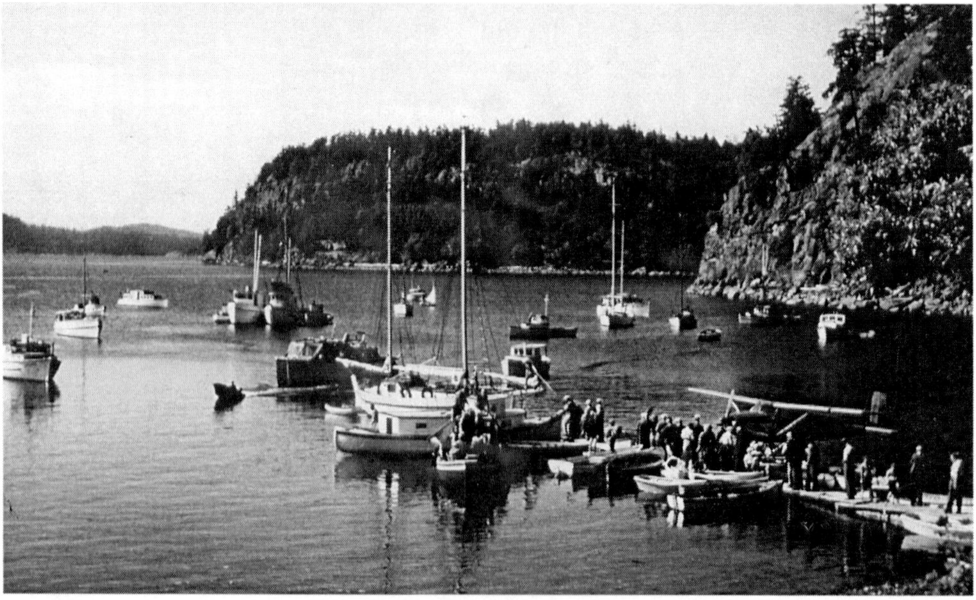

Thomson Community Park in 1954 – Jim & Lorraine Campbell

When the vineyard was established beside the beach in the 1990`s, plans were made to convert the family's resort into a park. Although the cottages were moved off the beach, the cookhouse was left behind. Unfortunately, when the park was finally developed, the cookhouse was demolished.

Thomson Community Park is named after this family, who still use one of the resort cottages as their office.

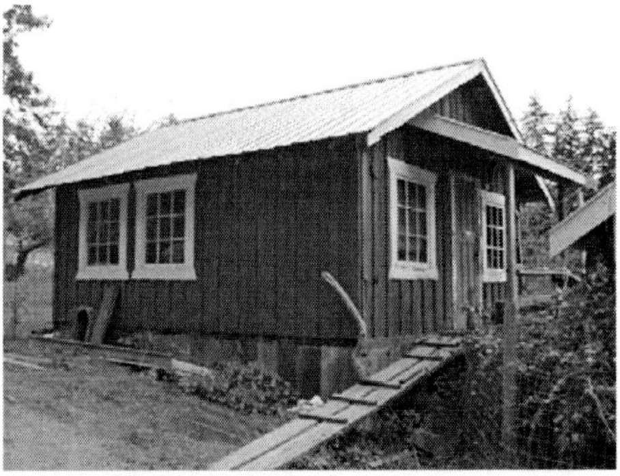

The park provides for a beachfront swimming area and there are facilities for picnics if you want to stay awhile.

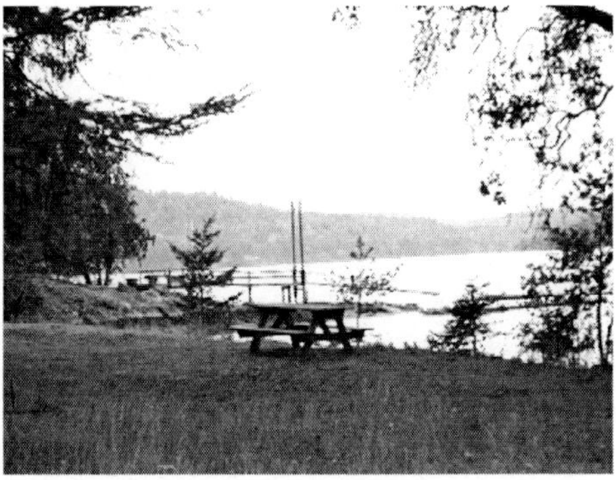

A strenuous 4 km trail follows the shoreline, eastward, from the park. The trail passes *Murder Point*, which made history in the 1860's when Indians killed a settler and his daughter there. The park is accessible from Trueworthy Road. (#11 on the map)

Tumbo Island

At the turn of the century, a German recluse, known locally as 'Jack The Ripper', was living on a little island.

During an evening storm, a visitor sought shelter on the island. The recluse warned the visitor to keep away. When the visitor began to argue, the recluse retrieved a gun from his cabin and fired it at him. In self-defense, the visitor fired back through the darkness, and then fled.

The worried visitor reported the incident to the Justice of the Peace on Mayne Island. When a constable rowed to the scene of the crime to investigate, he found Jack The Ripper dead on his doorstep.

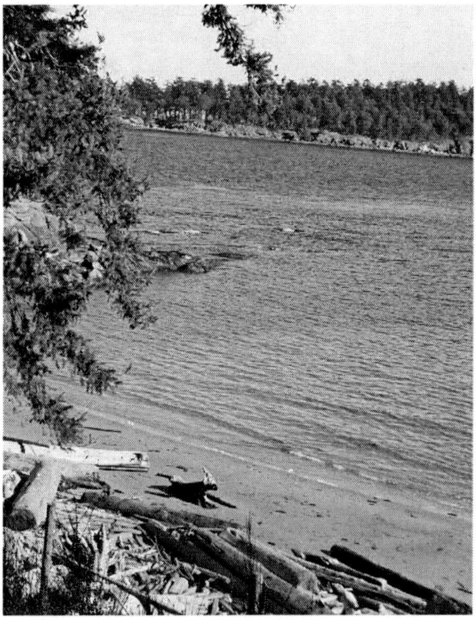

Tumbo Island is located off the northeast side of Saturna. Acquired in the 1990's for inclusion in the Gulf Islands National Park Reserve, it is a day-use area that can only be visited by small boat.

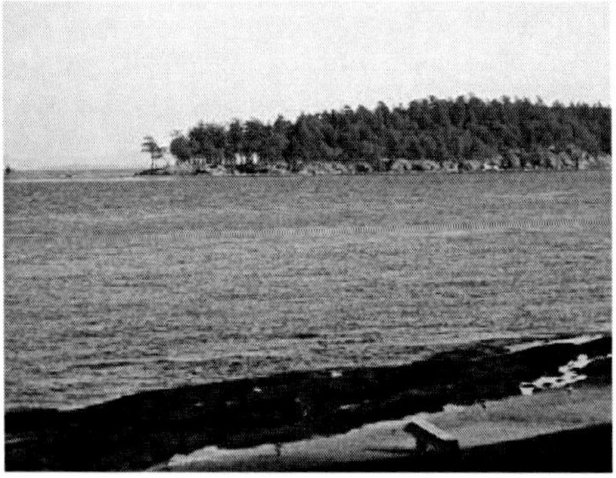

A short trail system through old growth Douglas-Fir and Garry Oak meadows provides for exploration of the island. However, keep in mind that the dock on the island is privately owned and the house is often inhabited. (#9 on the map)

Veruna Bay

Veruna Bay is located on the northwest side of Saturna. It provides for a sandy swimming beach.

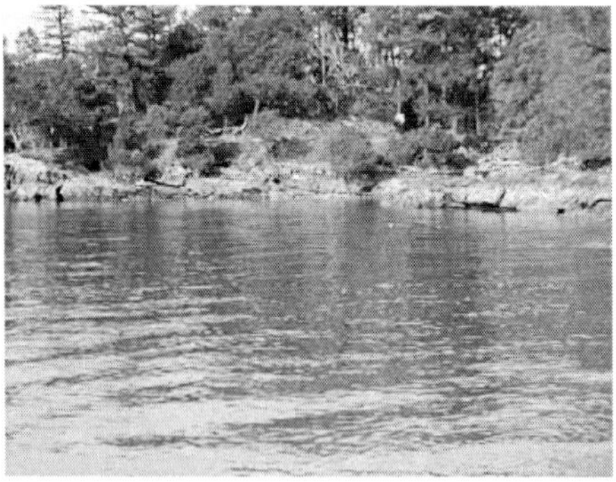

If you put a boat in the bay, you can travel south to the *King Islets* and around the shoreline of Lyall Harbour. The beach is accessible by way of an unmarked road at the end of Church Bay Road. (#13 on the map)

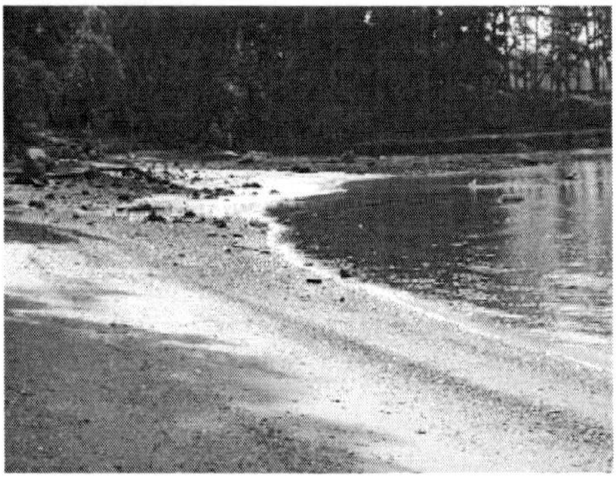

Winter Cove Provincial Marine Park

Like his older brothers, **the Postman** received a small income from England. In the late 1890's, he purchased some land on a cove on the northwest side of Saturna. There, he started a family.

His children were cut off from the other Islanders because there was no road into the cove. The only place they could walk was over a very rough trail to the lighthouse on East Point.

The children learned to row in the cove by the time they were four years old. However, because the water was very cold, they did not learn to swim until much later.

Once they learned how to swim, they would spend hours making rafts. Sometimes, they would trade apples from their orchard with the Indians, in exchange for old, leaky canoes. Then, they would patch them with tar and put sails on them.

The children earned extra money by salvaging logs. They would take a launch into the Strait, corral the logs, and then wrestle them down the beach. Then, they would pull the logs into the cove by hand, through a narrow passage. At that time, the passage was called *Canoe Passage*, but it was later renamed *Boat Passage*.

In the late 1970`s, a portion of the property at the cove became *Winter Cove Provincial Marine Park*.

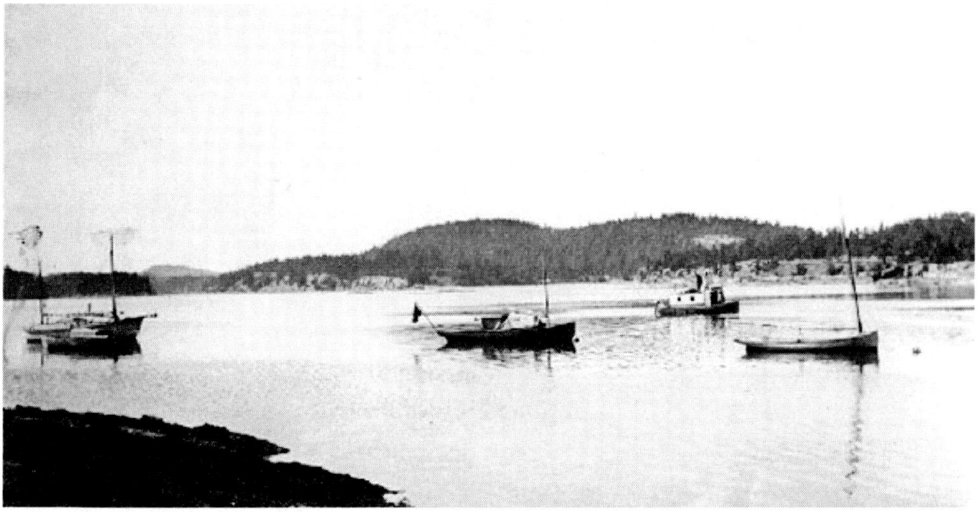

Winter Cove in the early 1900's - BC Archives NA-41821

The site of the *Canada Day Lamb Barbeque*, Winter Cove Park is now a beautiful recreational park that provides for a beachfront swimming area and a boat launch. There is a baseball diamond and facilities for picnics if you want to stay awhile.

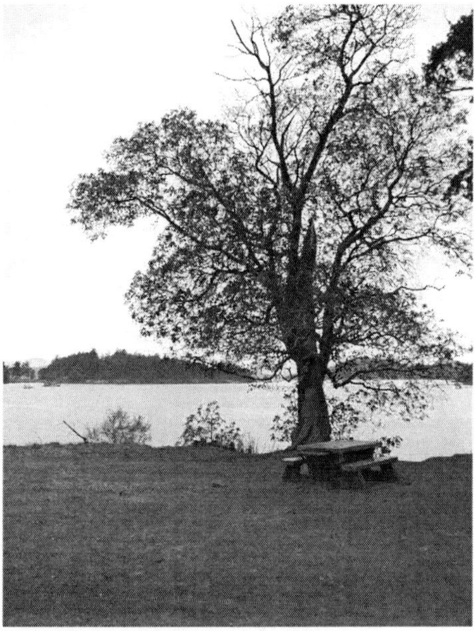

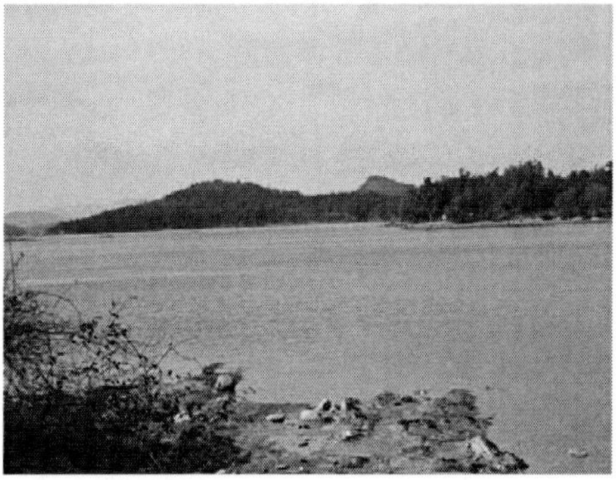

Winter Cove as it appears today

Winter Cove is located in the park. It is a nature-lover's paradise, where seals, sea lions and myriad birds can be seen.

The beach consists of sandstone, shale and midden. There are areas for swimming and it is a good vantage point for spotting whales during the summer. You can access the beach by way of Winter Cove Road. (#1 on the map)

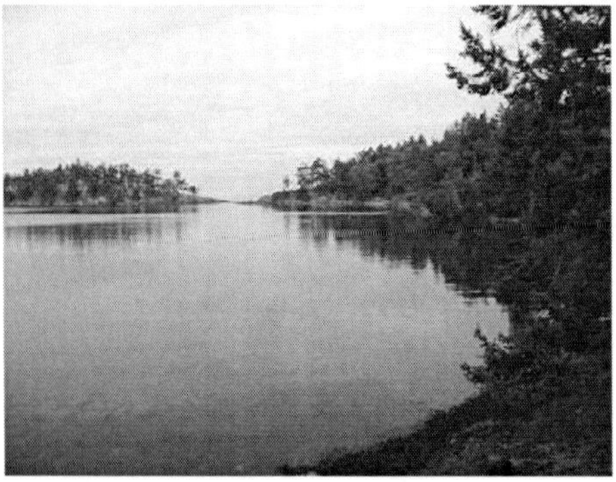

If you launch a boat from the cove, you can navigate through a fascinating maze of islands and waterways that exist between Saturna and Mayne Islands. However, it is shallow and the west entrance is partially blocked by reefs.

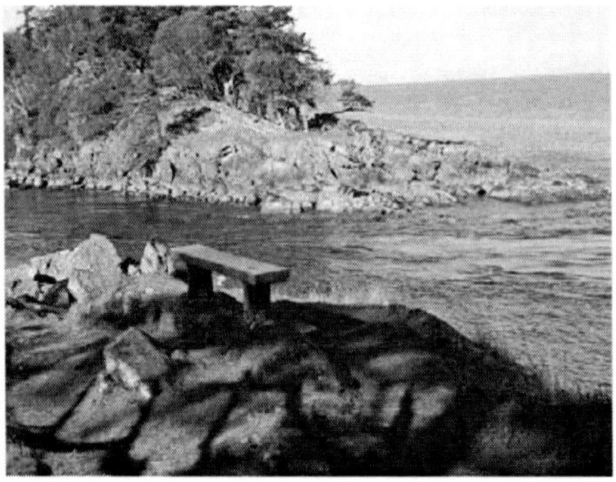

An easy, 1.5 km trail through the park leads to Boat Passage, which separates Winter Point on Saturna Island from Ralph Grey Point on Samuel Island.

The *skookumchuck* (strong currents) that rush through the passage can run up to 7 knots at certain times of the year, creating whitewater excitement for experienced kayakers. Keep in mind that Samuel Island is privately owned and has been designated as a `no access` area.

Pender Islands

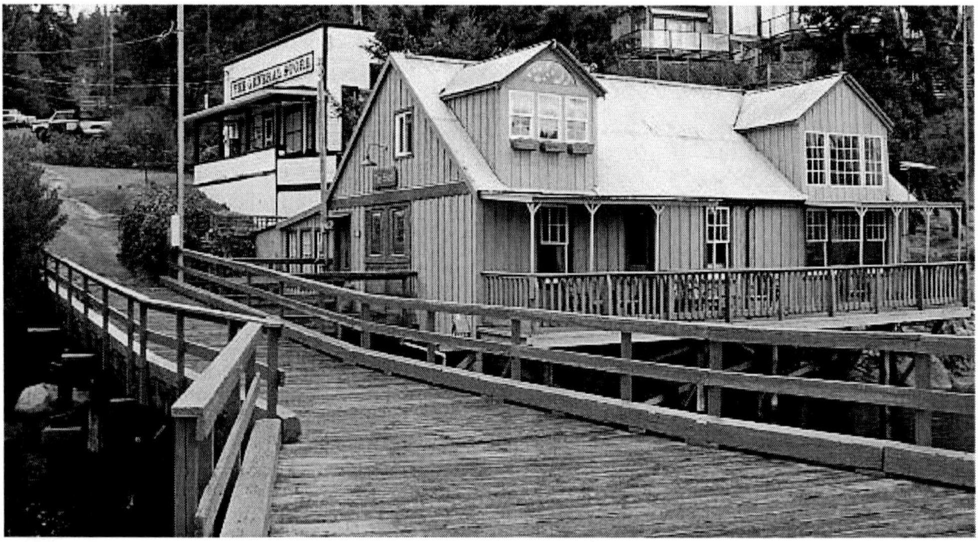

Port Washington Wharf

It was in the mid-1880's when an Englishman, named Washington Grimmer, purchased a herd of cattle from one of the southern Gulf Islands...

In a one-day cattle drive, Washington single-handedly drove his herd of cattle across the Island and hauled them onto the deck of a schooner by their horns. When the schooner reached the bay near his home, he lowered the cattle into the water and towed each one of them ashore in the darkness.

Washington Grimmer was born in the 1850's and emigrated from England to Canada with his family. In the 1880's, he crawled out of the window of a ship with his gun and dog, and set out for the Pender Islands.

The ambitious Washington Grimmer was an ardent builder, having constructed several homes on North Pender. With the help of his brother-in-law, he built the road that connects the original two wharves.

In the early 1890's, Washington became **the Postman** for the Pender Islands, operating the post office from a home he had built there. He was eventually made Justice of the Peace.

Years later, his eldest son had this to say about him:

"...being of the restless type, he always found lots to do – a quick, wiry little man with a quick temper which, like a storm in a teapot, was over in minutes."

Neptune Grimmer

Things to Know

Pender is a pristine island. At 34 sq km, it is one of the largest of the southern Gulf Islands. While numerous beaches and dark forests are its most distinguishing characteristics, the spectacular festivals and events put on by the residents give Pender Island its unique charm.

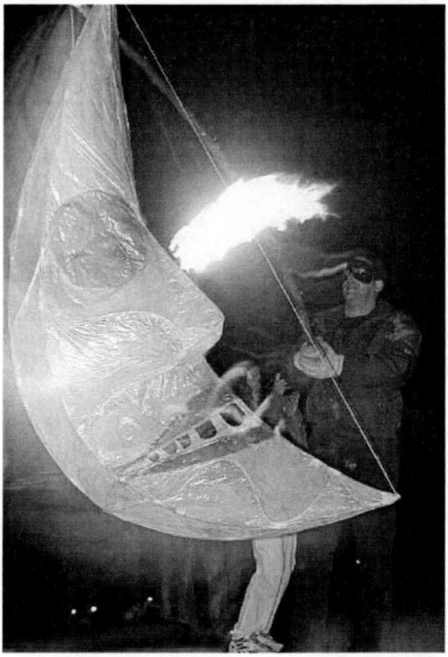

Pender Island is separated by a canal into two, small islands known as *North Pender* and *South Pender*. North Pender provides most of the services and facilities. South Pender is much more *illahee* (rural).

The two islands are, together, locally referred to as *the Penders* and a friendly rivalry has always existed between them. Because of the nationalities of the people who originally settled there, some of the settlers in the late 1800's referred to North and South Pender as *Little Scotland* and *Little England*.

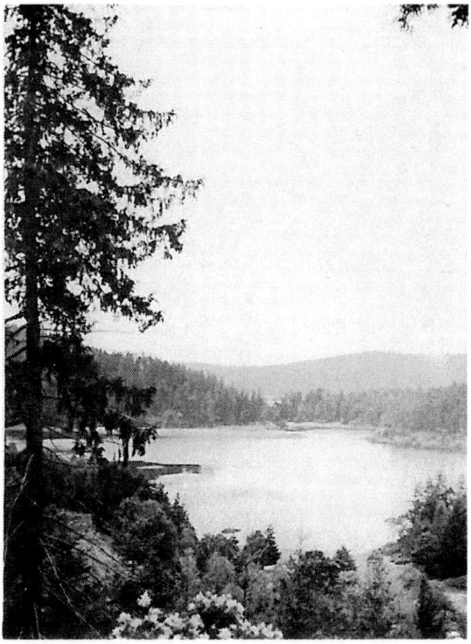

North and South Pender in 1946
Pender Islands Museum

Pender is the second most populous of the southern Gulf Islands. Its population consists mainly of young *tillikums* (families), retirees and business professionals.

Most of the 2,200 permanent residents live on North Pender. During the tourist season, the population doubles to around 4,000.

North Pender Island Wharves

In 1890, the first wharf was built, on the northwest side of North Pender. It accommodated ships coming through the waterway called *Swanson Channel*. The port was named *Port Washington*, in honor of **the Postman**.

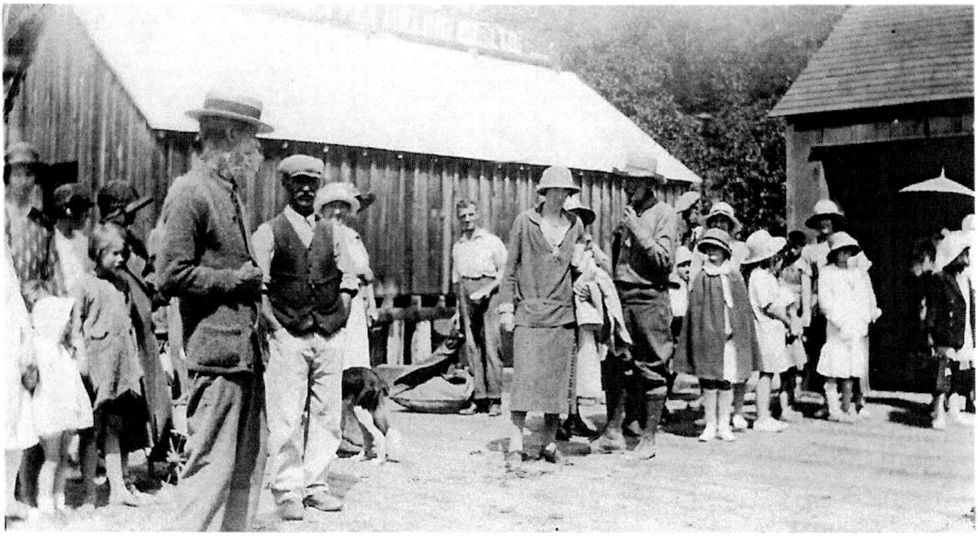

Port Washington Wharf in 1925 – Pender Islands Museum

At the turn of the century, another wharf was built, in a bay called *Hope Bay*. Because it was located on the opposite side of North Pender, a rivalry began between the largely English community of Port Washington and the Scottish community of Hope Bay.

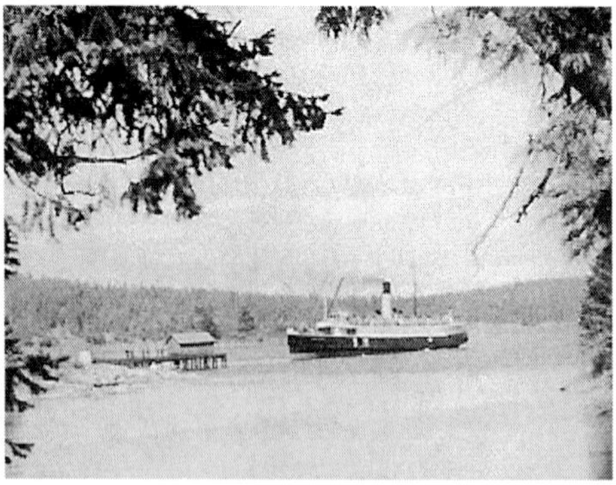

Hope Bay wharf in 1946
Pender Islands Museum

In the early 1950's, the ship named *Princess Elaine* was introduced to the waters surrounding the Gulf Islands. The Port Washington wharf was the only wharf in the outer Gulf Islands that could accommodate it.

Today, the Port Washington wharf is used to transport schoolchildren to neighboring schools, and by sea planes traveling between Pender and *Big Smoke* (Vancouver).

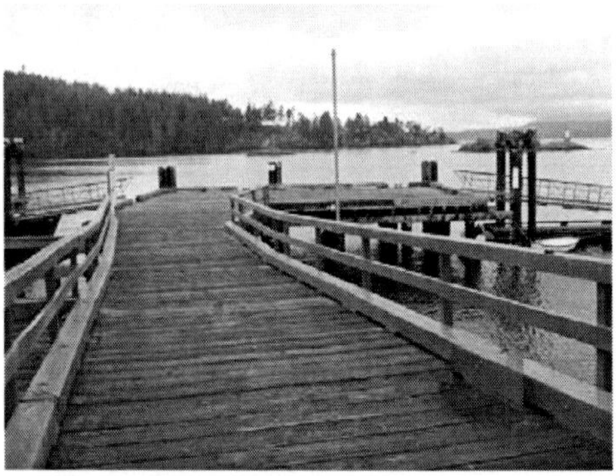

At the Hope Bay wharf, freighters can often be seen waiting their turn to proceed to larger ports of call throughout the Islands.

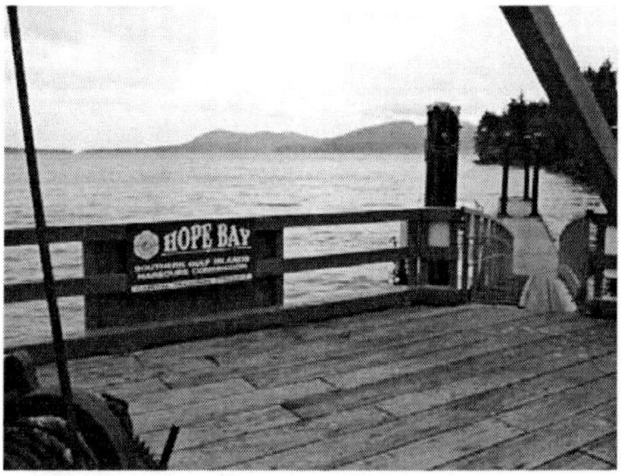

Pender Islands Post Office

Initially, **the Postman** would row to Mayne Island to collect the mail. When the Port Washington wharf was built in the 1890's, a steamer ship began delivering it directly to the wharf.

That same year, **the Postman** built a small cabin on his farm nearby and converted part of the porch into a mailroom, from which he provided postal service. The cabin was enlarged at the turn of the century. Today, it is a private residence on an old orchard.

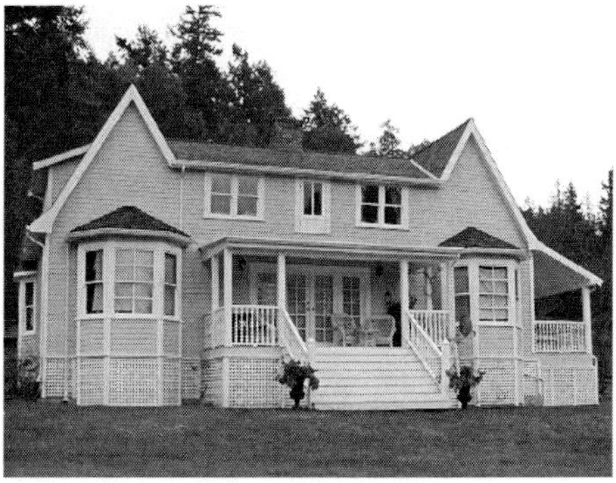

A year or so after **the Postman** accepted his postal duties, the post office was moved to a small building at the head of the Hope Bay wharf. The mail came in by way of an overland trail and the settlers would stand and wait at a little counter for their envelopes and parcels to be dispatched.

A few years later, the first store on the Penders was built near the Hope Bay wharf. Called *Corbett's Store,* the small frame building soon became the home of the *Pender Island Post Office*. The address was simply 'Pender Island'.

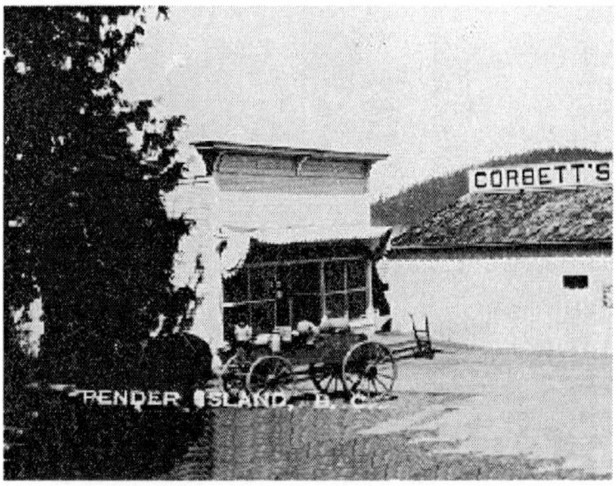

Pender Island Post Office in 1933
Hope Bay Rising Holdings Ltd.

In 1910, another store was built, at the head of the first wharf. It was called the *General Store* and the *Port Washington Post Office* was established there. Its address was 'Port Washington'.

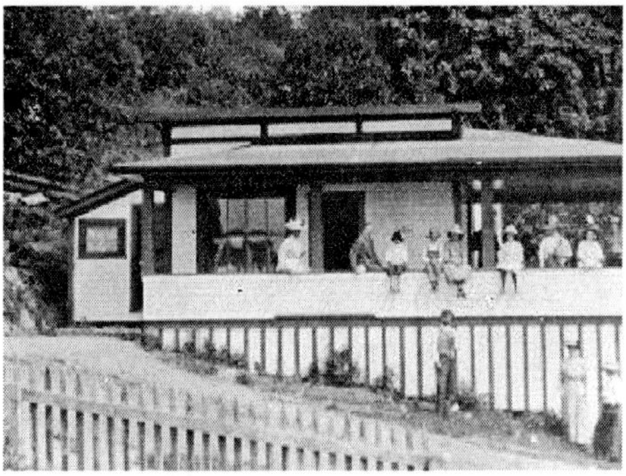

Port Washington Post Office, early 1900's
BC Archives D-08531

Soon, Corbett's Store at Hope Bay was moved into a new building that had been constructed nearby. The Pender Island Post Office was then relocated to a large area at the back of the new building. Each time the store changed hands the new owners continued to use **the Postman's** original post office box in the post office.

Much later, in the 1970's, the two post offices were consolidated as the *Pender Islands Post Office* and were moved into a mall in the center of North Pender. Within a decade, both stores had closed.

A few years prior to this writing, the store at Hope Bay was restored. The buildings are now being operated as offices, a gift store and a café.

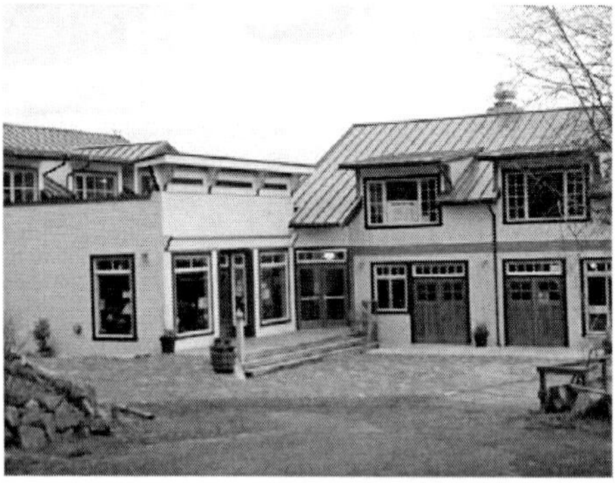

Old Pender Island Post Office as it appears today

Although the General Store at Port Washington changed owners several times, it was home to the Port Washington Post Office for over 70 years. At the time of this writing, it was also being restored.

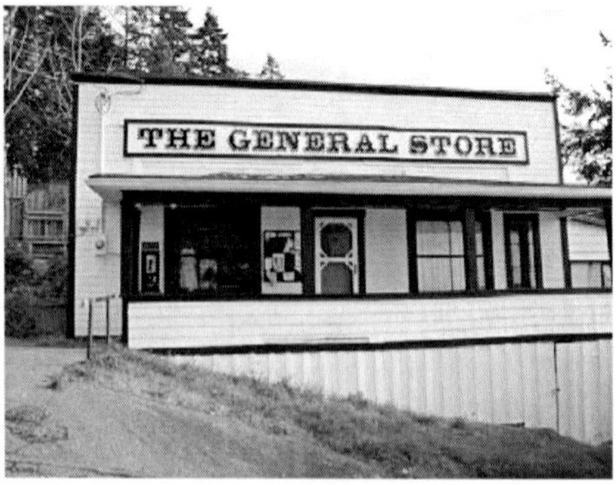

Old Port Washington Post Office as it appears today

Today, the Pender Islands Post Office sits behind the mall to which it had been moved in the 1970's. It serves both North and South Pender.

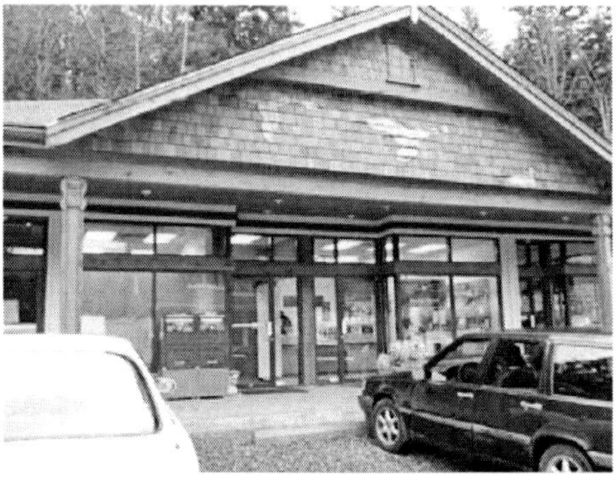

Pender Islands Community Hall

The first community hall to be built on North Pender was constructed in the 1880's, on land owned by the man who would later become **the Postman**. The hall sat midway between Port Washington and Hope Bay.

In the year 1910, a second community hall was built, beside Corbett's Store at Hope Bay. It was called the *Hope Bay Community Hall*. Unfortunately, the hall was built on uneven ground, which caused its post foundation to become unstable.

Two years later, the builder of the General Store leased some of his land for a third community hall, called the *Port Washington Community Hall*. It replaced the first hall in that community, which had been disposed of at the turn of the century.

By 1912, there were two halls in operation on North Pender; the Port Washington Community Hall and the Hope Bay Community Hall.

The Port Washington hall was initially a square box. It had a flat roof that was later replaced with a peaked roof. Because it had no electricity or indoor plumbing, water had to be brought in to the hall and gas lanterns were hung from the ceiling for light.

For a while, the Port Washington hall was used as a school and for holding church services. A year after it was built, roller-skating was introduced to it and, soon, the floor became so uneven that dancing proved impossible and a new floor had to be laid.

In the 1930's, some residents stayed up until midnight planning the Islands' first fall fair. It was hosted at the Hope Bay Community Hall and its fair grounds.

By the 1960's, the post foundation supporting the Hope Bay hall had deteriorated, causing it to be razed by fire. Subsequently, it was torn down and the Port Washington hall became the social center for the Penders.

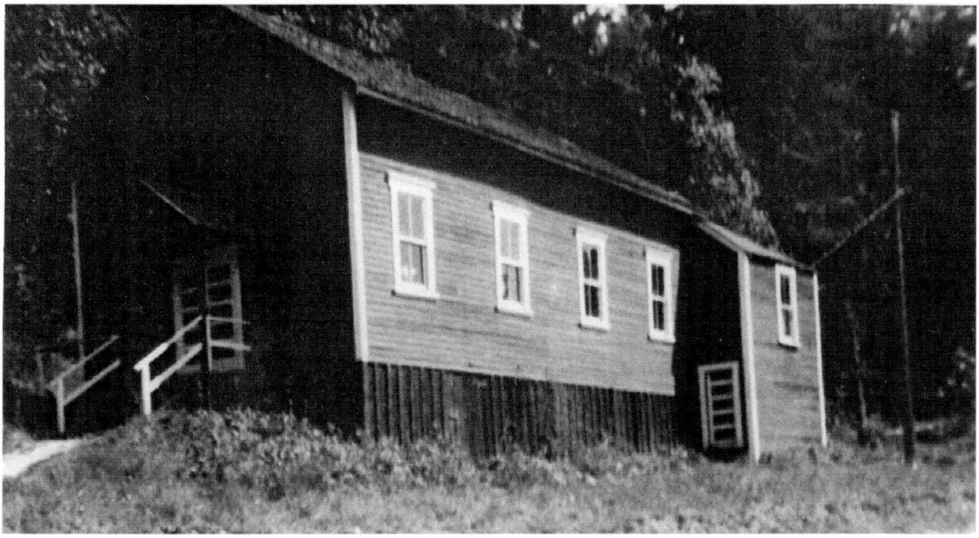

Port Washington Community Hall in 1963 - Pender Islands Museum

Unfortunately, a decade later, the Port Washington hall was also razed by fire. When its remains were torn down, its assets were transferred to a school that had just been built in the center of the Island. The plans for the school had included a hall. It was the fourth hall to be built on the Penders.

Recently, a fifth community hall was built on North Pender, on Bedwell Harbour Road. Under the guidance of a *Tsimshian* carver, a project was undertaken by about 60 women to carve three poles that now stand at the entrance to the new hall.

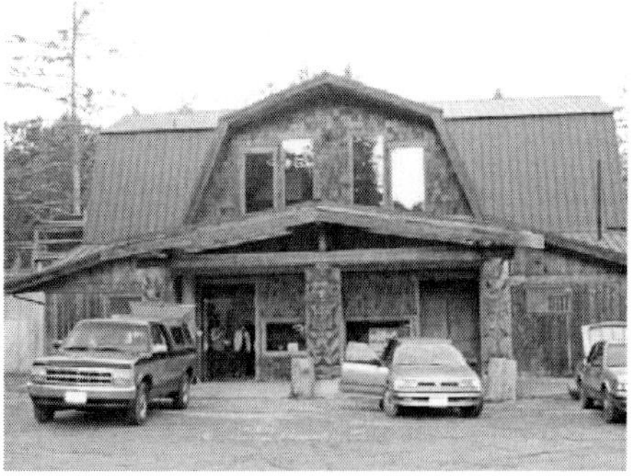

The poles, called the Women's Unity Welcome Poles, display the figures of mother bears and a bear cub.

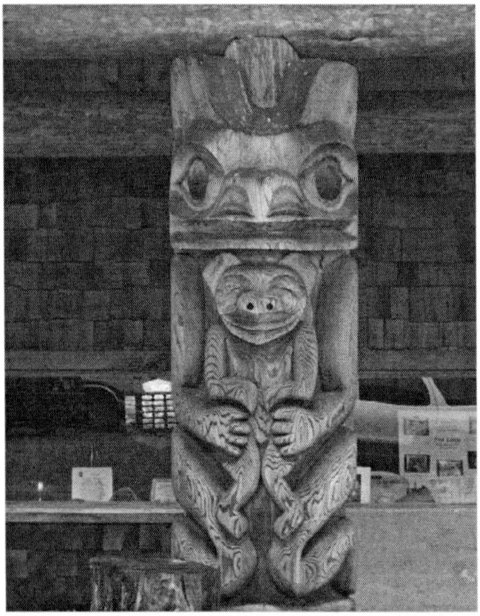

Today, the *Pender Islands Community Hall* and its fair grounds are host to the *Pender Islands Farmer's Market* and the *Pender Islands Fall Fair*.

Visitors to the Island can bring their *tillicum* (friends) to the hall and enjoy a variety of other civic functions, from musical concerts to performing arts presentations.

Driftwood Centre

In the late 1970's, a couple built a mall in the center of North Pender. In its construction, they counted and laid over 24,000 bricks by hand.

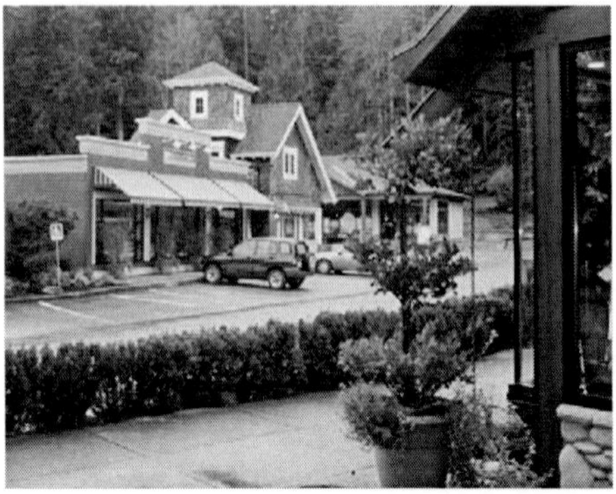

Today, the mall is called the *Driftwood Centre*, but is locally referred to as *The Drift*. Located on Bedwell Harbour Road, it is home to a variety of businesses.

At the time of this writing, the businesses included a liquor store, drugstore, laundromat, bank and bakery, as well as a grocery store and gift stores. The post office is also located there.

You can gas up your *chikchik* (wagon) at the *Driftwood Auto Centre*, which is located in the Driftwood Centre. It also provides for bicycle and scooter rentals for touring around the Penders.

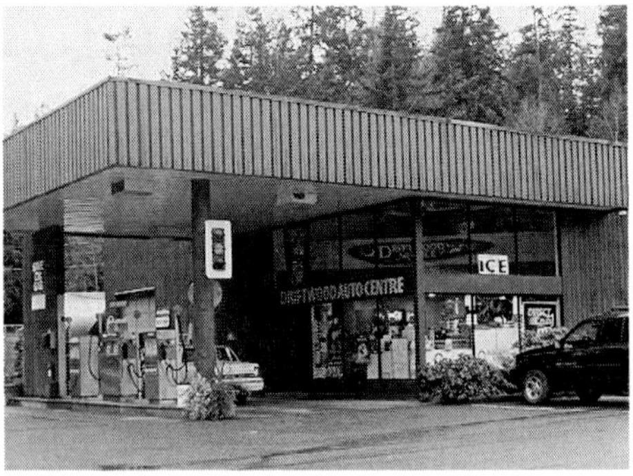

Southridge Farms Country Store

The *Southridge Farms Country Store* provides for fresh produce, groceries, coffee and pastries. It is located on Port Washington Road.

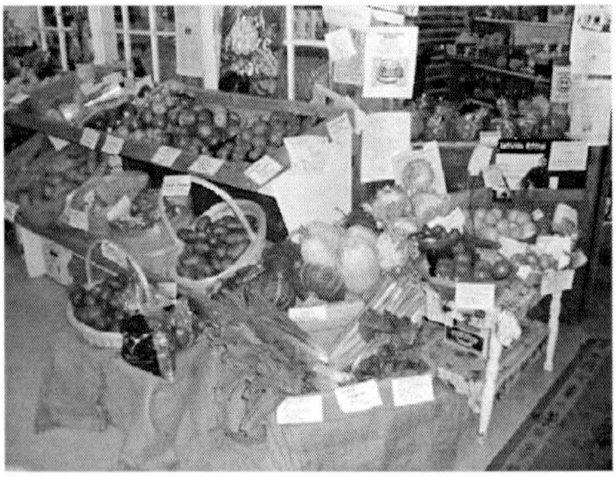

Magic Lake Market

The *Magic Lake Market* supplies the surrounding community with groceries and movie rentals. It is located on Schooner Way.

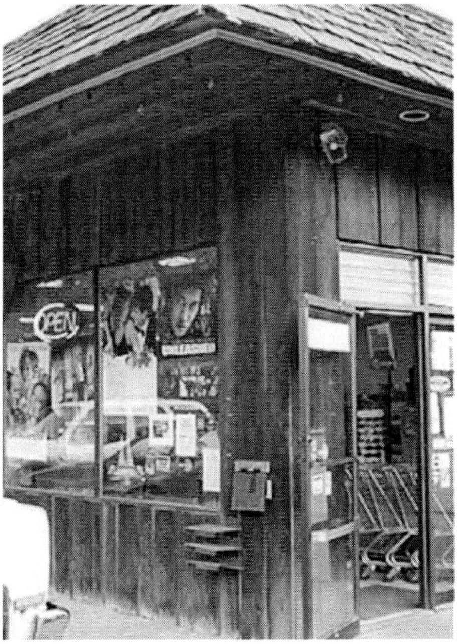

Pender Island Golf & Country Club

In the 1930's, the son of **the Postman** owned a sheep pasture in a valley. One day, he and his siblings decided to develop it into a golf course.

Over time, six people purchased the land so they could improve the course. They formed a golf club and worked hard at the tees. They set up the holes, cutting the greens with a push-type lawnmower.

Initially, the golfers had to climb down a ladder at the sixth hole. Fortunately, the club members eventually built steps there.

On the pasture was a small two-room cabin, which the club members converted into a clubhouse. Much later, in the 1980's, a new clubhouse was built.

Today, the *Pender Island Golf and Country Club* has over 350 members. The challenging 9-hole RCGA and CLGA rated course has several different tee areas and plays as an 18-hole par 68 for men and par 69 for women. The *New Year's Golf Tournament* is an event held at the golf and country club each year.

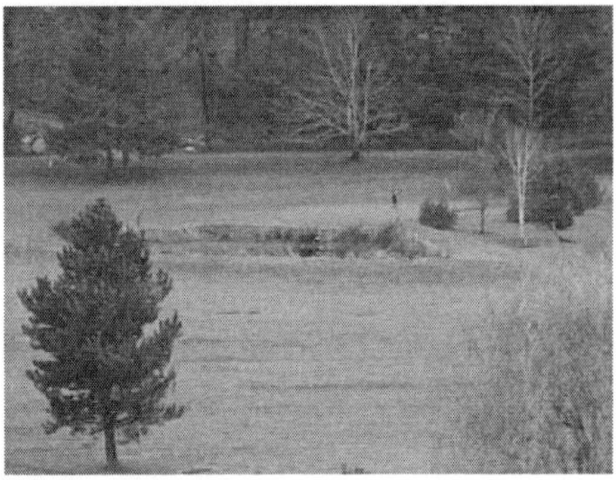

Open year-round, the course provides for a well-equipped golf shop. Power carts, pull carts and golf clubs are available for rent. Volunteers recently contributed over 6,000 hours constructing a network of golf cart paths out of driftwood. The course is located on Shoal Road.

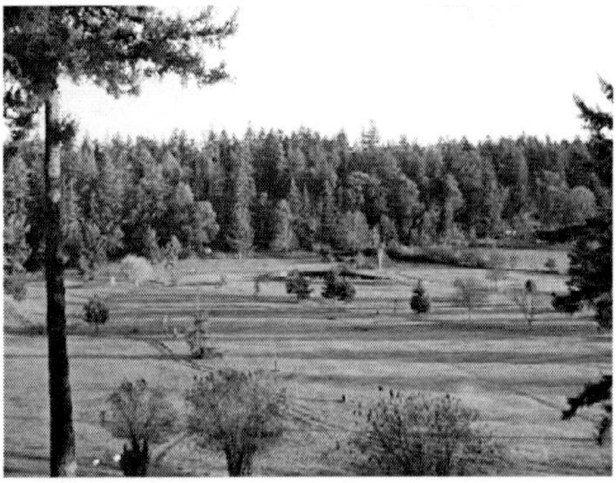

Golf Island Disc Park

In the 1980's, a few residents of the Penders laid out a special golf course near the center of the Island. Three years later, the *British Columbia Provincial Disc Golf Tournament* was held at the course.

Today, the *Golf Island Disc Park* is the only golf park of its kind in the Gulf Islands, where 'frisbee golf' has become a popular, year-round sport.

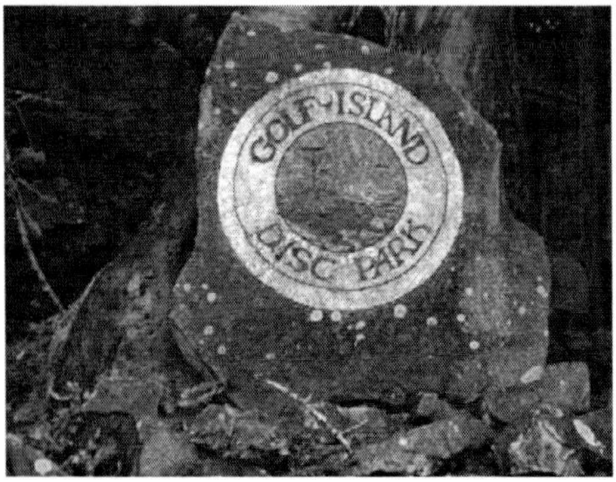

Rated as one of the top five in North America, the frisbee golf course is set up with various hoops and obstacles. Par on the front nine is 27 and par on the back nine is 29. Use of the course is free, but players are required to bring their own frisbees.

Each year, the park hosts the annual *Pender Island Invitational Disc Tournament*. The tournament attracts players from the entire West Coast of North America. The park is located on Galleon Way.

Poets Cove Resort & Spa

Initially, settlers living on South Pender would row to Saturna Island for supplies. In the 1930's, the first store on South Pender was built at a harbour.

A few years later, a couple built a marina at the harbour. At the time, they were living in a building that was once a community hall. They had moved it to the harbour, and then expanded it to accommodate a cafe.

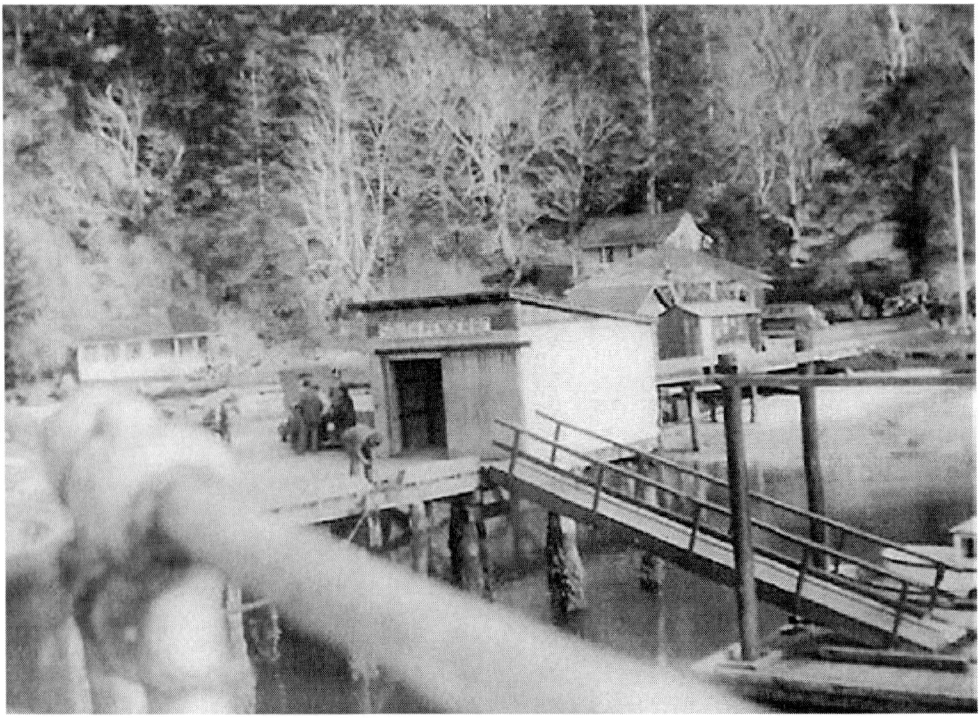

Bedwell Harbour Marina, early 1900's – Pender Islands Museum

In the year 1960, a hotel, called the *Bedwell Harbour Hotel*, was built at the harbour. The hotel was later converted into a resort called the *Bedwell Harbour Resort*.

A few years prior to this writing, new owners expanded and renamed the resort *Poet's Cove Resort and Spa*.

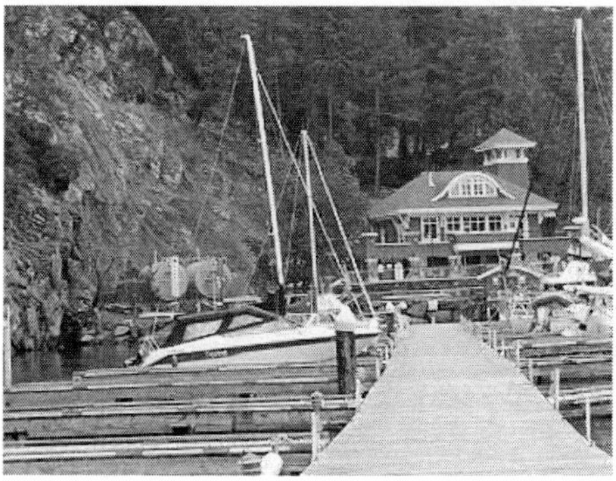

Bedwell Harbour Marina as it appears today

Today, Poet's Cove Resort is the only center on South Pender. Located on Bedwell Harbour, on the southern shore, it offers 46 rooms, villas and cottages, and provides for an activity centre, tennis courts and a swimming pool. The *Susurrus Spa* offers six treatment rooms.

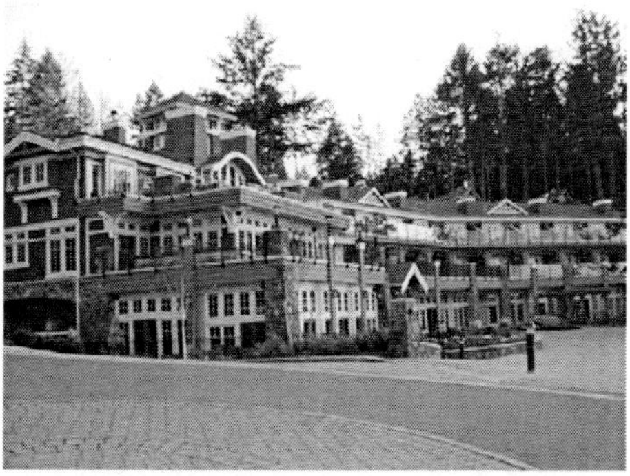

The *Bedwell Harbour Marina* at the harbour is a full-service, deep-moorage marina and boat rental. A Canada Customs point of entry is located at the marina.

Because it processes over 9,000 vessels each year, the harbour is the busiest port on the Penders. The resort and marina are located on Gowlland Point Road.

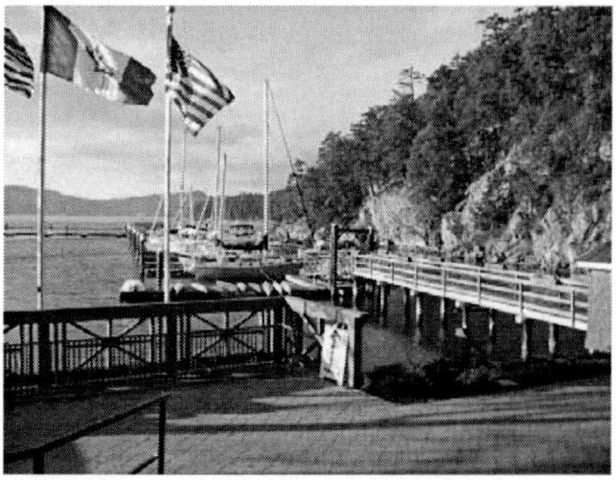

Arcadia By The Sea Lodge

In the 1940's, a lawyer purchased a 10-room, two-storey home on North Pender. The home was originally named *Mille Fleurs*.

Soon, the lawyer's wife decided to remodel the interior of the home and convert it into a guest cottage. Because a friend supplied the bedrooms with Beautyrest® mattresses, she changed the name of the home to the *Beautyrest Lodge*.

Two years later, the woman employed an agency to find guests for her lodge, and then opened it for business.

Eventually, she added six more cottages, and hired an off-island crew to build a separate building with a dining room and lounge. Subsequently, the lodge became one of the most popular resorts in all the Gulf Islands.

After 27 successful years, the woman retired and the lodge was sold. New owners changed the name to the *Otter Bay Lodge*.

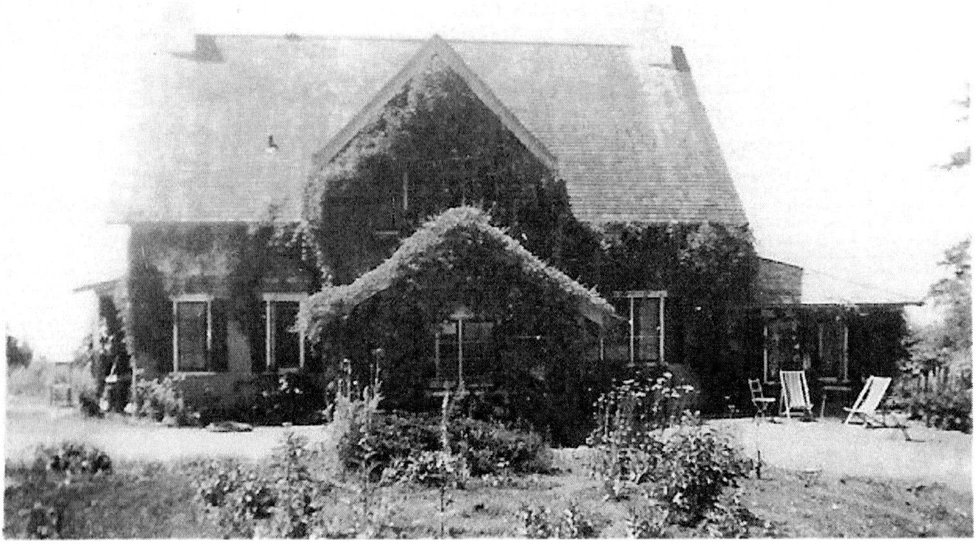

Arcadia By The Sea in 1955 - Pender Islands Museum

In the 1960's, the lodge was renamed the *Pender Lodge*. It boasted a licensed lounge and dining room, as well as sleeping and housekeeping cottages. There was also a swimming pool and tennis courts on the property.

Today, the lodge is called *Arcadia By The Sea*. It is located on MacKinnon Road, on the northwest shore of North Pender.

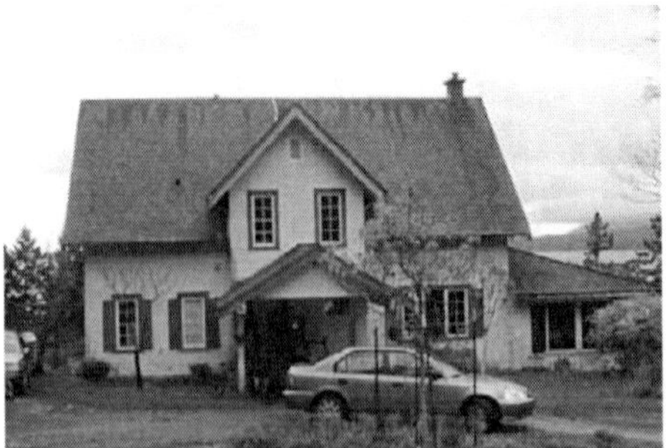

Arcadia By The Sea as it appears today

Corbett House B&B

At the turn of the century, the settler who would eventually open Corbett's Store, the first store on the Penders, moved to the Island with his family.

The following year, he purchased some land on the northeast side of North Pender. There, he established a farm, on which he built a house.

Several years later, the settler's house was converted into a bed and breakfast called the *Corbett House Bed and Breakfast*. The B&B is located on Corbett Road.

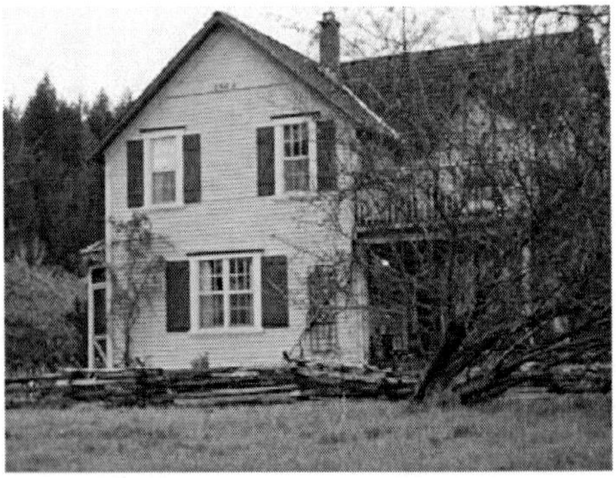

Port Browning Marina Resort

Just before the outbreak of World War I, a settler arranged for a home to be built near a harbour on North Pender.

In the 1920's, he built three cabins on the property, and he and his wife converted them into a resort. Because there were large Maple trees on the property, they called the resort *The Maples*.

The couple served meals to all of their guests and, over time, the Maples became one of North Pender's most popular resorts.

The resort operated for more than 40 years before closing in the 1970's. The home and one of the cabins can still be seen from Browning Harbour today.

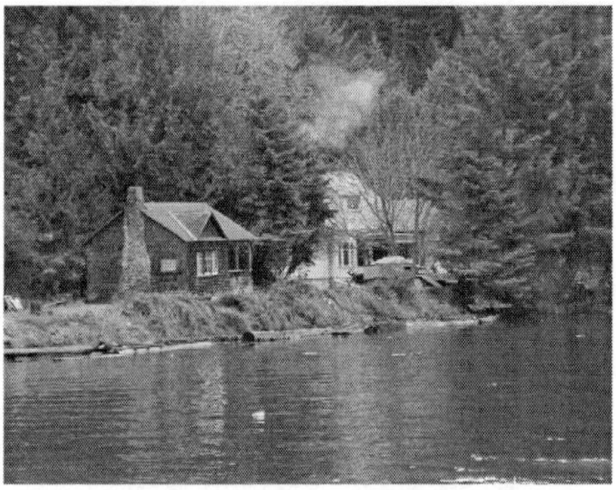

The year-round *Port Browning Marina Resort* offers self-contained cabins near the old resort on Browning Harbour. It also offers camping for tents, trailers and campervans. A tennis court and swimming pool are available.

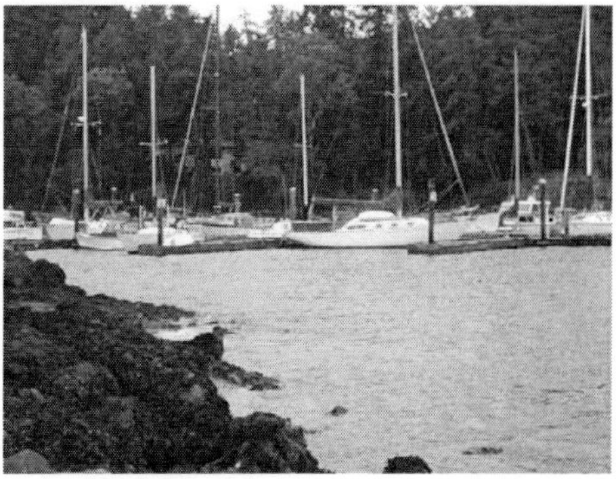

The *Port Browning Marina* provides for temporary boat anchorage at the harbour. The resort and marina are located on Hamilton Road.

Pender Islands Sights & Shops

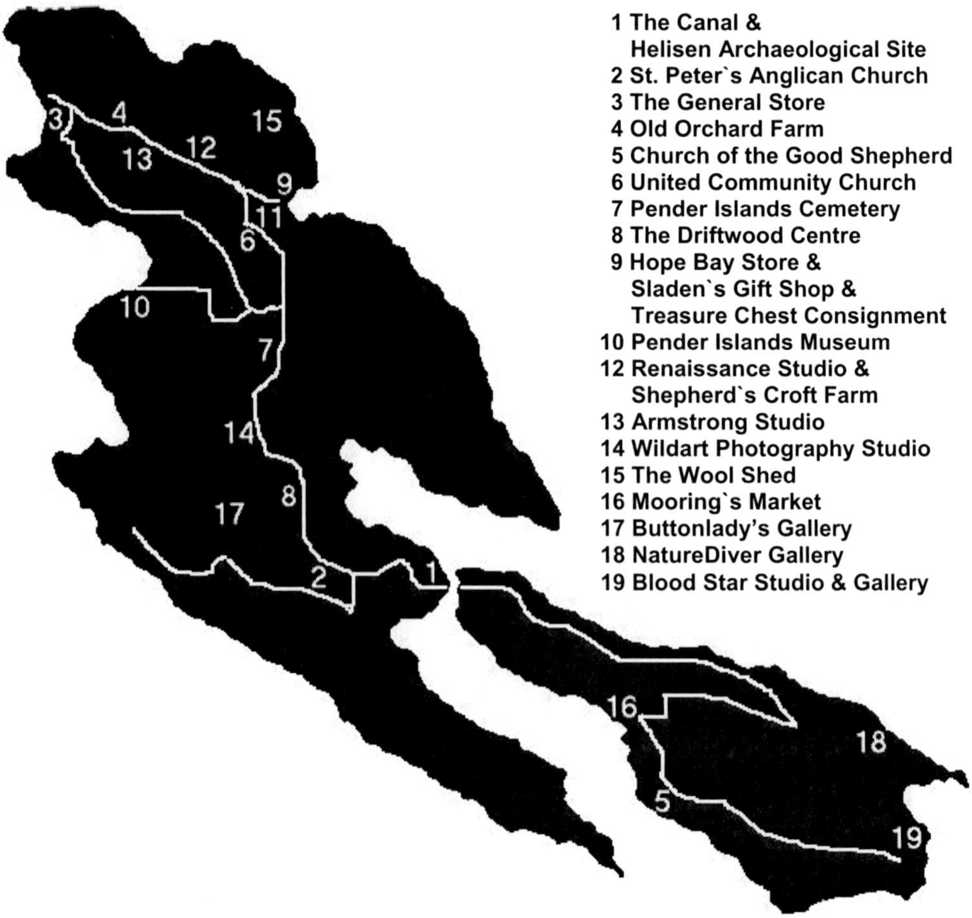

1 The Canal & Helisen Archaeological Site
2 St. Peter`s Anglican Church
3 The General Store
4 Old Orchard Farm
5 Church of the Good Shepherd
6 United Community Church
7 Pender Islands Cemetery
8 The Driftwood Centre
9 Hope Bay Store & Sladen`s Gift Shop & Treasure Chest Consignment
10 Pender Islands Museum
12 Renaissance Studio & Shepherd`s Croft Farm
13 Armstrong Studio
14 Wildart Photography Studio
15 The Wool Shed
16 Mooring`s Market
17 Buttonlady's Gallery
18 NatureDiver Gallery
19 Blood Star Studio & Gallery

Things to See

The Pender Islands are scenic getaways with a variety of areas to explore. Many people come to Pender to partake in the events or go for a hike in the forest.

North Pender consists of four major routes. Port Washington Road runs east and west, connecting the two wharves. Bedwell Harbour Road runs north and south, bisecting the Island, and then splits off at Schooner Way, which connects several minor roads along the south end of the Island.

South Otter Bay Road turns into Otter Bay Road, which connects Bedwell Harbour Road to the ferry terminal.

South Pender, which consists of only one major route, is connected to North Pender via Canal Road. It runs east and west along the north end of the Island. Canal Road turns into Spalding Road, and then into Gowlland Point Road, which runs along the south end of the Island.

The Canal

Initially, a strip of land, called *Indian Portage*, joined North and South Pender Islands. At that time, the Portage was a meeting place for settlers living on Saturna and South Pender Islands. The area made history when Indians shot two settlers there in the 1860's.

Whenever settlers wanted to travel between Bedwell Harbour and Browning Harbour, they would carry their boats across the Portage, in order to avoid having to make the dangerous voyage around South Pender.

At the turn of the century, a petition was circulated around the Pender Islands requesting that a canal be dredged, to enable the S.S. *Iroquois* to make a speedier passage around the Islands. The canal that was eventually dredged is self-scouring.

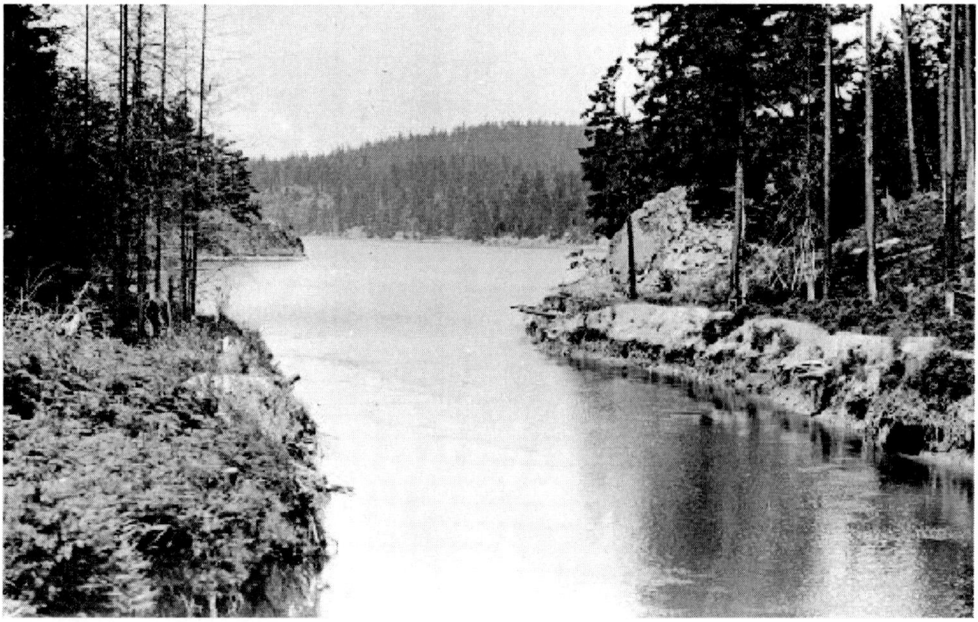

The canal separating North and South Pender Islands, early 1900's - BC Archives G-06190

Much later, in the year 1950, residents requested that a bridge be built across the canal. However, reportedly, the Federal Government disclaimed any responsibility for the blasting that took place when the canal was dredged.

Eventually, the government accepted responsibility for the work that was done and a single-lane bridge was built five years later, reuniting North and South Pender. A marching band entertained the many dignitaries who attended the official opening.

The bridge, which links the two Islands at the two harbours, made Vancouver Island more accessible. This caused traffic traveling between the Penders and Vancouver Island to double.

In the 1970's, a monument was erected to commemorate the events that had unfolded at the site over the previous one hundred years.

Today, the canal, which is now twice its original width, can be crossed by way of the bridge on Canal Road. (#1 on the map)

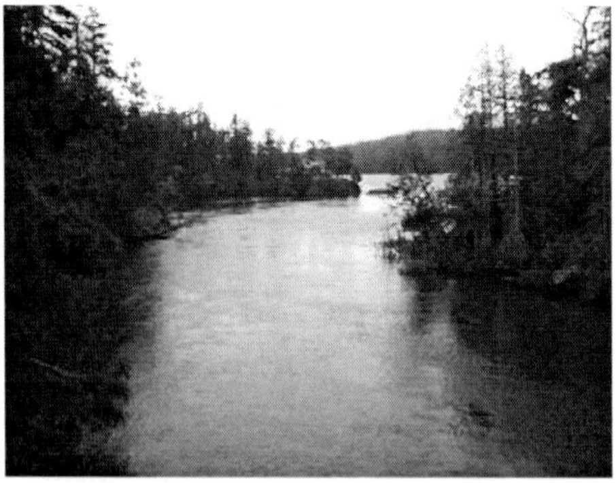

The canal as it appears today

Helisen Archeological Site

The midden and surrounding areas of Bedwell Harbour are a burial grounds for the *Tsawout* and *Tseycum* First Nations, who lived in the area seasonally. When the canal was dredged at the turn of the century, several artifacts left by the Indians were unearthed.

As vessels traveled through the canal, erosion began to damage the remains of the area. As a result, it was designated a Provincial Heritage Site.

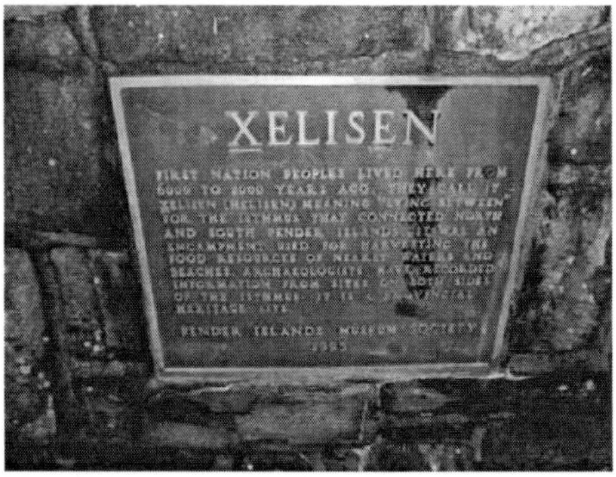

Today, *Helisen Archeological Site* is one of the largest archeological excavations in all the Gulf Islands. Excavations of the site have resulted in the discovery of thousands of artifacts, some of which are on display at the Pender Islands Public Library.

A monument was recently erected at the site, commemorating the First Nations. The site can be accessed by way of Canal Road. (#1 on the map)

Hope Bay Stores

Initially, the people of North Pender ordered their provisions and other goods by mail order, which were brought by boat to one of the two wharves.

When Corbett's Store opened at Hope Bay at the turn of the century, it served local residents, as well as settlers from neighboring Saturna and Mayne Islands. It also provided a second home for the post office.

The storekeeper asked all the ladies on the island to make up grocery lists indicating their favorite brands of goods. They ordered long, black-beaded hatpins for their wide-brimmed hats, high-button shoes, as well as wool cashmere and pure silk stockings. The men generally shopped for gunpowder and buckshot. The supplies were brought in to the store by the S.S. *Iroquois*.

Corbett's Store became very successful, eventually expanding into hardware and farm supplies. Before the onset of World War I, a new store with two small warehouses was built. A few years later, the two warehouses were replaced with a two-storey structure.

In the 1920's, the store was modernized with an electric plant, refrigerator and ice cream cabinet. It was then further enlarged at the back.

When the store was sold in the 1950's, it held claim to being the oldest, established, Gulf Islands general store to have operated under the same management for at least four decades. On the firm's monthly accounts were many names of customers who had frequented the store when it first opened.

The new owners changed the name of the store to *Smith Brothers*. Later, it was shortened to *Smith's* and was then changed to the *Hope Bay Store*.

In the 1960's, the Hope Bay Store ceased to operate as a grocery store and became home to various arts and crafts stores. It closed its doors in the 1980's.

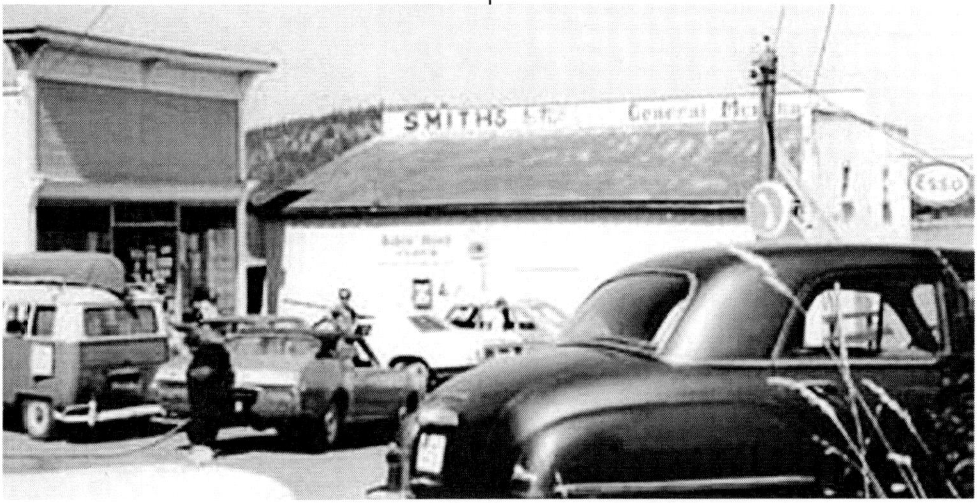

Hope Bay Stores in the 1970's – Hope Bay Rising Holdings Ltd.

A few years prior to this writing, the original buildings at the Hope Bay Store were razed in an early morning fire. The property was partially restored, and then purchased in a foreclosure sale by a cooperative of Islanders who completed the restoration.

The new two-storey complex, which is located at the end of Port Washington Road, houses a variety of businesses. (#9 on the map) The renovation project was recently nominated for a Commercial Building Award, which recognized it for its exceptional quality.

The original owners of the store still conduct business near the new stores as *R.S.W. Corbett and Son*. Their company is one of the oldest firms still doing business in the Gulf Islands.

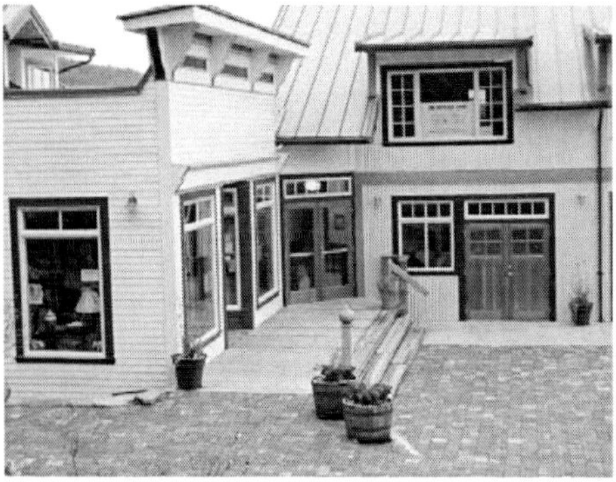

Shepherd's Croft Farm

Shepherd's Croft Farm is a unique roadside stand with a number of oddities on display. It is located on Port Washington Road. (#12 on the map)

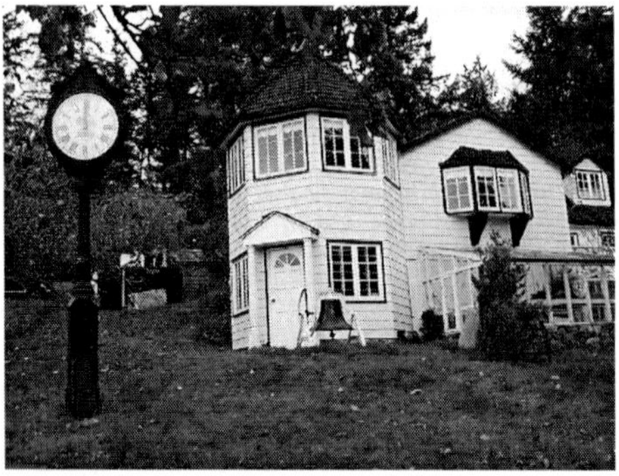

United Community Church

In the 1890's, the work of the Presbyterian Church began on North Pender. Services were held in the community hall, and a set of used Sankey hymnbooks and an organ were donated.

A missionary, who had accepted the task of pioneering the work, made the first set of slatted benches. He also built a rowboat to provide transportation to and from the services.

At the turn of the century, the first ordained minister was appointed and a gas-powered boat was built for his use.

That same year, a very prominent settler donated some land for a church and the *Pender Island Presbyterian Church* was soon built on a hill overlooking Hope Bay. In the 1920's, a Manse was built below the church for use as the Reverend's residence.

Four years later, the Presbyterian Church merged into the United Church of Canada and the church building became known as the *United Community Church*.

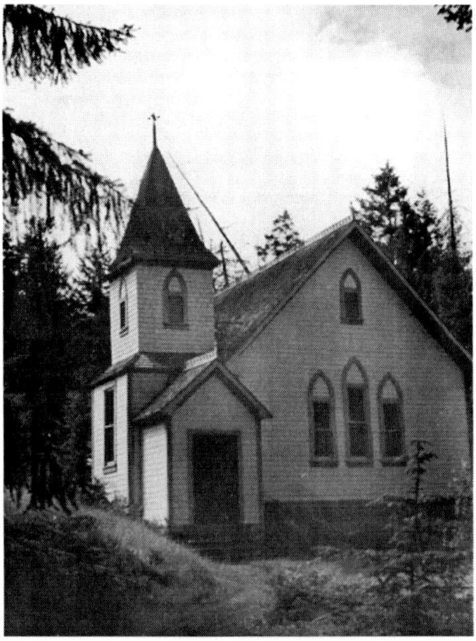

United Community Church in 1946
Pender Islands Museum

In the late 1980's, when the Roman Catholics had no venue in which to hold church services on the Penders, the United Community Church building was used as a location for Catholic services.

Today, the United Community Church is the oldest church on the Penders. Located on Bedwell Harbour Road, it operates as a non-denominational church, while Catholic services are now held in a house in Magic Lake Estates. (#6 on the map)

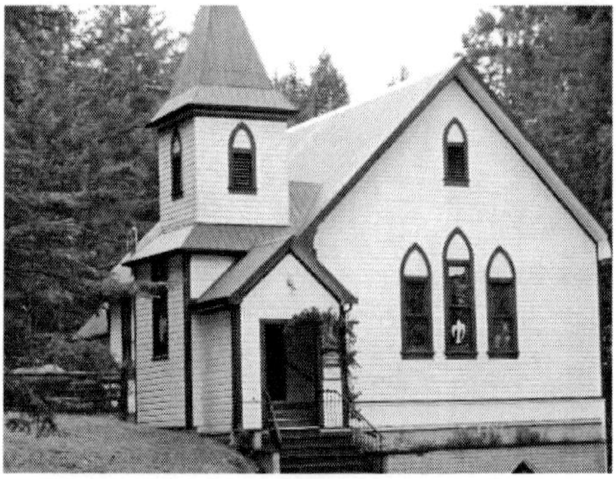

United Community Church as it appears today

Pender Islands Cemetery

At the turn of the century, a prominent settler donated some land for the development of an Island cemetery. Maintenance of the cemetery was a community responsibility.

Because there was no church on the Island at the time, funeral services were always held at one of the settlers' homes. A horse-drawn wagon would then travel to the cemetery and friends would prepare the grave.

Much later, in the 1950's, wrought iron gates were donated to the cemetery. In the 1960's, two residents donated some land so the cemetery could be enlarged.

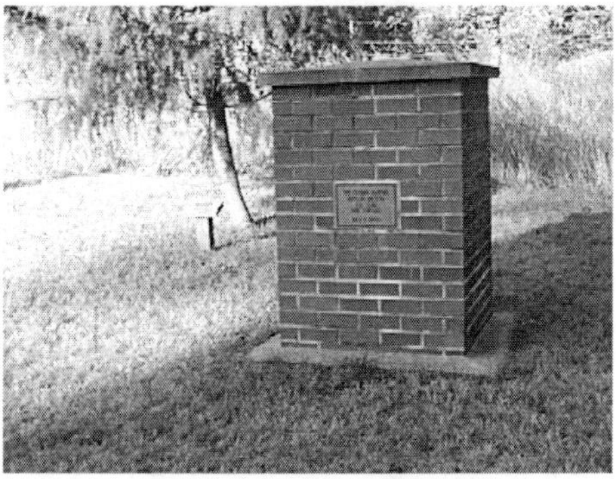

Recently, the Pender Islands' Museum Society donated a 100-year time capsule to the cemetery. It had been started at the turn of the century by a settler who lived on Hope Bay. The cemetery is located on Browning Harbour Road. (#7 on the map)

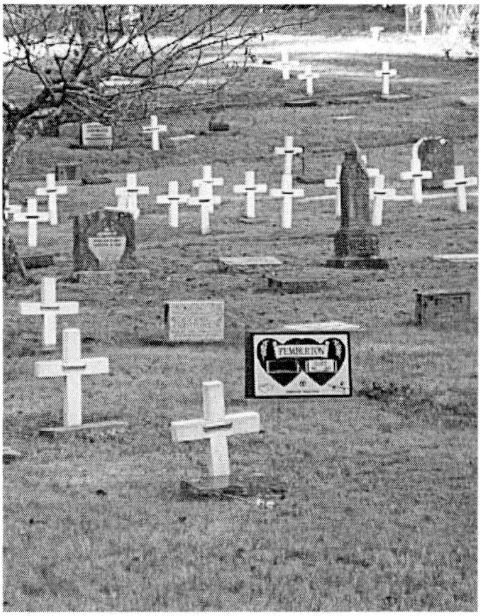

Old Orchard Farm

At the turn of the century, the settler who would later operate the General Store purchased the farm from which **the Postman** had provided postal services. The settler called the farm *Sunny Side Ranch*.

Over the years, the settler and his wife made many changes to the single-gable cabin on the old farm. They substantially enlarged it, and then added a veranda and bay windows to it.

Although it had an abundance of exterior doors, they never removed them. As a result, it is difficult for guests to determine which door to enter through, even today.

The couple created a floor-to-ceiling collage of calendars, greeting cards, magazine clippings and photographs in the hall and in the study.

At one end of the living room, they used oil paints to paint a large landscape. Beneath the chair rails, at the opposite end of the room, they painted a floral scene.

Eventually, the space that had been used as a mailroom by **the Postman** was converted into a dining room.

Throughout the orchard, the settler installed an elaborate irrigation system of water pipes.

Later, he opened a tennis court on the lawn and the first tennis club was formed there. It served as the site of many inter-Island tennis matches during the 1920's.

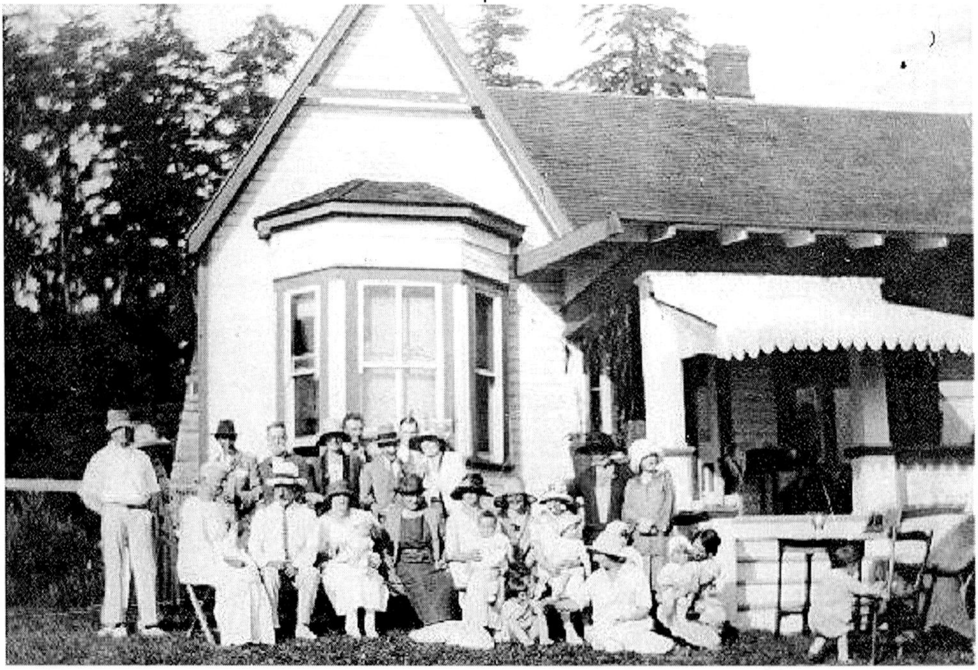

Old Orchard Farm in 1925 - BC Archives C-07017

In the late 1930's, new owners covered all the walls with plywood, concealing the collages and paintings. Then, they added a second storey as an apartment, which they rented to numerous tenants through the years.

Much later, in the 1970's, the property was sold again and renamed *Old Orchard Farm*. Recently, when the new owners began restoring the old home, they discovered the artwork that had been boarded up by the previous owners.

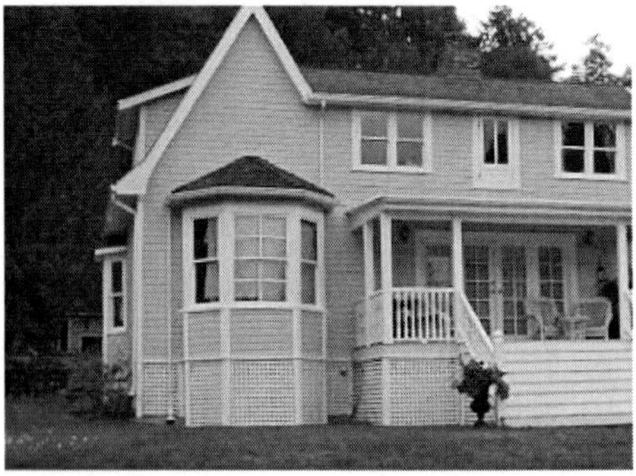

Old Orchard Farm as it appears today

Today, the meticulously restored Old Orchard Farm is a private residence on Port Washington Road. (#4 on the map) The house, which is nearly five times the size of the original building, can be seen through one of the finest ancient orchards on the Penders. The orchard is still producing over 40 varieties of apples, pears and plums.

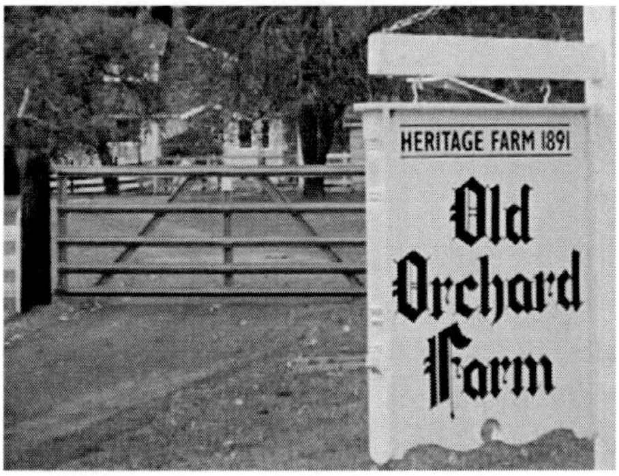

St. Peter's Anglican Church

Before the first church was built on North Pender, **the Postman** would row to Mayne Island to attend church services. Sometimes, his own home was used as a place of worship. Later, the Port Washington hall was used for holding church services.

Just before the outbreak of World War I, the owner of the General Store donated some land for a church. The 50-person church was called *St. Peter's Anglican Church* and **the Postman** was instrumental in the building of it.

Several items were donated to the church, including an antique silver chalice, a patent from England and an Italian marble font.

In the 1920's, a cottage was built behind the church so the visiting clergy had a place in which to live during their visits. It was later renovated to provide a vestry for a resident Vicar.

During the 1940's, a Reverend served both St. Peter's Church and a church on South Pender. When his successor drowned in a storm shortly after starting parish work, a carved Oak lectern and a prayer desk were placed in the church, as memorials to both Reverends.

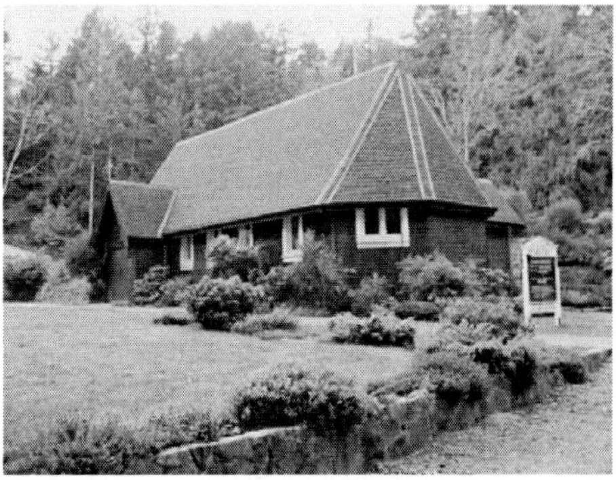

Originally, St. Peter's Anglican Church was located at Port Washington. However, a decade ago, it was moved to a more central location on Canal Road, where it now sits beside a hall called *Parish Hall*. (#2 on the map)

Pender Islands Museum

In the 1890's, a family immigrated to Canada from Scotland. At the turn of the century, they purchased some land on a bay on North Pender. There, they established a farm.

Soon, the family built a cabin for their friends to vacation in. Their friends enjoyed it so much that the family decided to develop the property into a resort. They called it *Roesland Resort*.

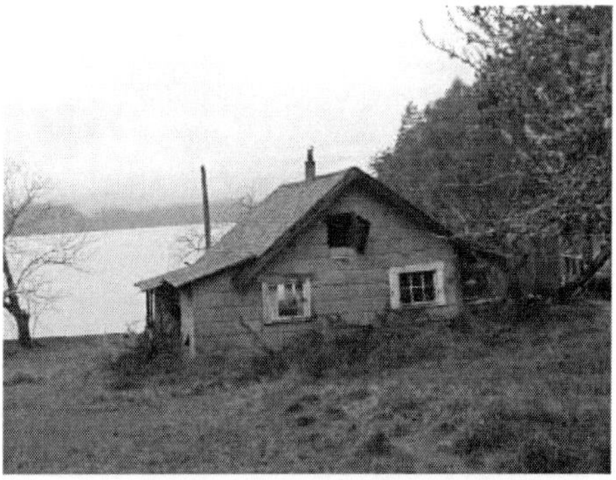

Each winter, the family added more cabins to the resort. Because the cabins only included the basic of necessities, their guests brought their own bedding and dishes, and carried their own water.

By the 1920's, a son had taken over the resort. He built a general store on the property, for the use of his guests. He also maintained a gas station on nearby Roe Islet.

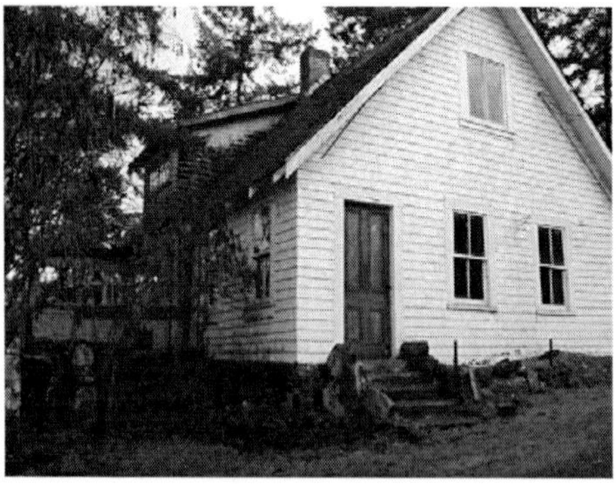

By the 1950's, there were 17 cabins at Roesland Resort, each with its own bed, kitchen and outhouse. For those who could secure a reservation, it was one of the most popular vacation destinations in the southern Gulf Islands.

The property was sold to new owners in the 1970's, who continued to run it as a resort, but built their own home there.

In the 1990's, the resort was closed, after operating for over 70 years. Many of the regulars had been third and fourth generation guests. When the land was purchased for use as a park, the owners were granted a life-long tenancy.

Recently, the Pender Islands Museum Society restored the family's house, and then converted it into an historical museum. In the year prior to this writing, the *Pender Islands Museum* opened on South Otter Bay Road. (#10 on the map)

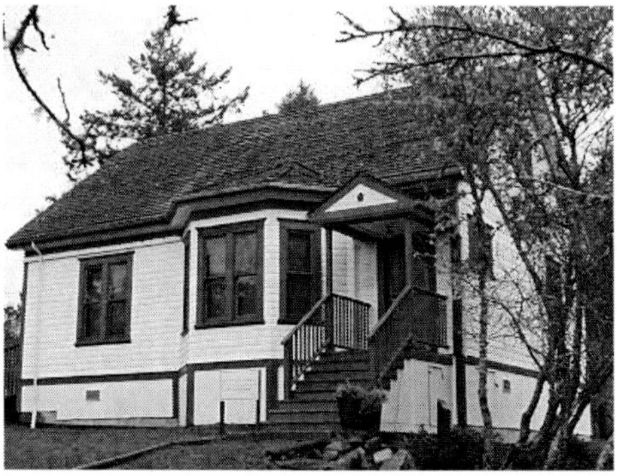

The General Store

When the General Store opened at Port Washington, it became the social center for the community and also the home of the post office.

The builder of the store was its first proprietor. Reportedly, he had no experience as a storekeeper, but because he was a generous man, the store thrived.

One day, an evaporated milk salesman offered the storekeeper a discount on case lots. Although he had little hope of selling them, the storekeeper ordered 50 cases. For a while thereafter, every time an Indian would arrive at Port Washington from Galiano Island, he would leave with a can of milk.

Over the years, the store changed owners several times. Between the 1940's and 60's, a very small library operated from the store.

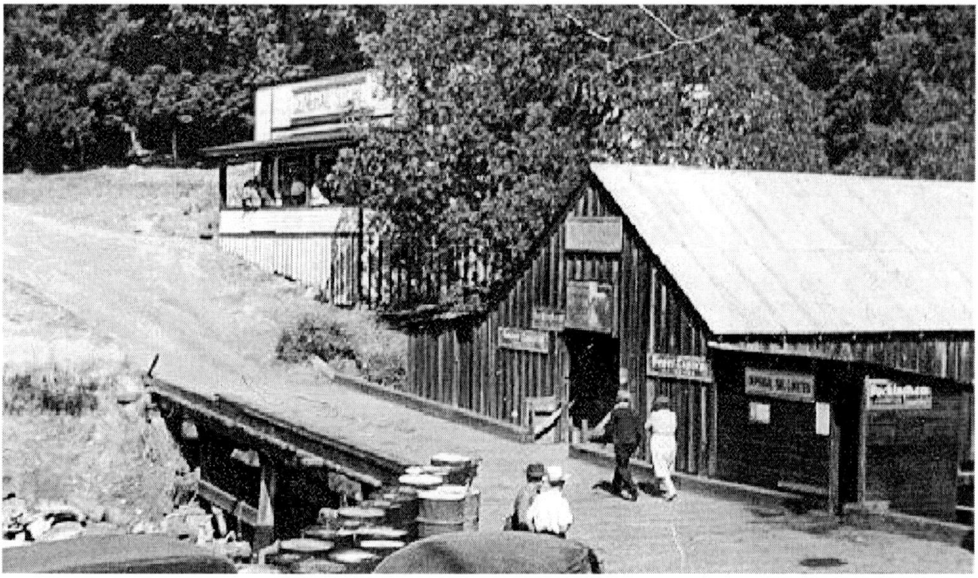

The General Store in 1947 - BC Archives I-20737

When the store changed hands in the 1970's, the new owners ran it primarily as a grocery store.

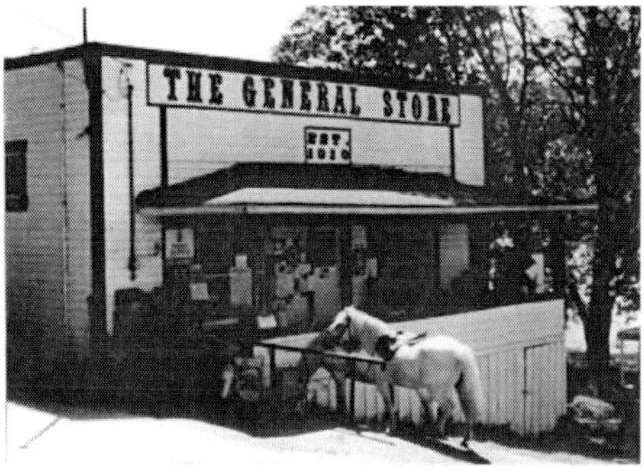

The General Store in the 1970's
Pender Islands Museum

A decade after the post office was re-located, the store closed, having been continuously operated as a grocery store for over 75 years. It then operated for several more years as a retail outlet for local artists.

In the year prior to this writing, the community put it in Trust, using the strongest legal protection that exists for a heritage building. Then, they began to restore it. The store is located at the end of Bridges Road. (#3 on the map)

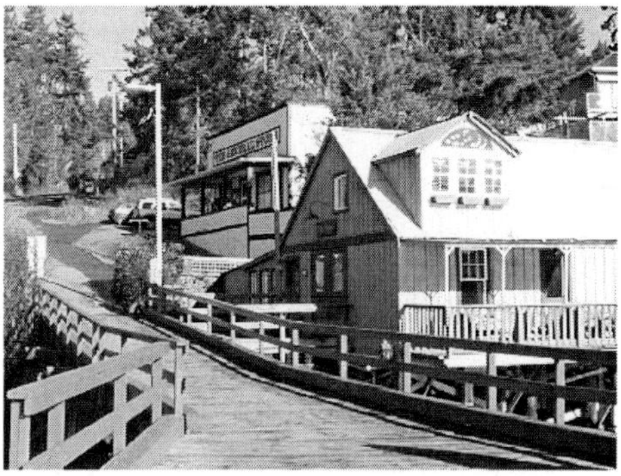

The General Store as it appears today

Church of the Good Shepherd

In the 1930's, a Reverend gave the fittings from a log chapel on Saturna Island to be used in the construction of a church on South Pender.

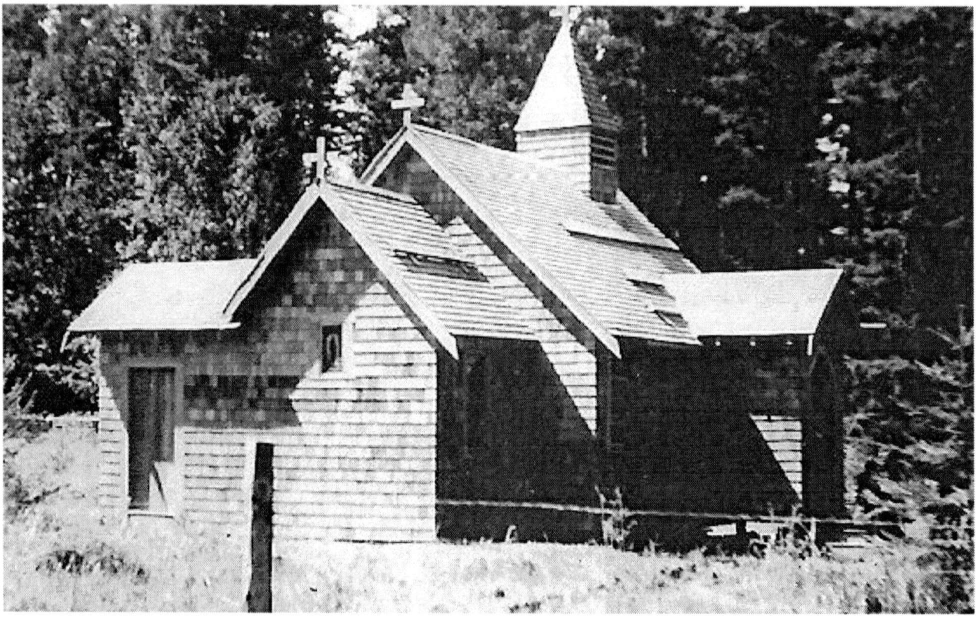

Church of the Good Shepherd, early 1900's - Pender Islands Museum

An English woman who owned the land on which the church was built donated a substantial amount of money to its construction.

The following year, the *Church of The Good Shepherd* was opened. Several items were donated to the church, including the altar and altar cloth, some furniture, the tower bell, the baptismal font and a stained glass window.

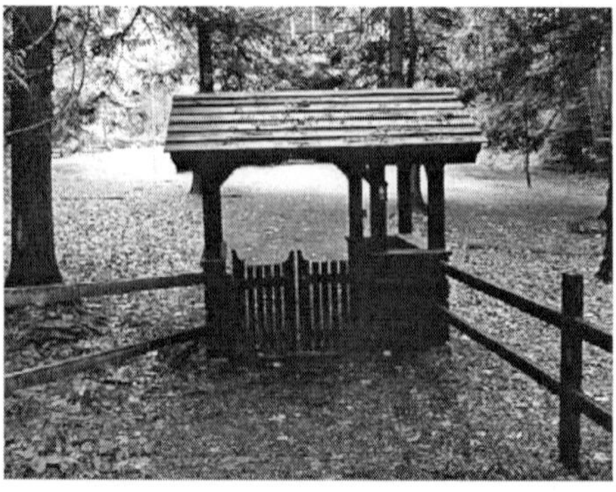

To commemorate the coronation of King George VI, an Oak tree was planted on the church grounds. At the front of the grounds was erected a *lych* gate, in memory of an early settler and his wife.

Today, the lych gate provides for a traditional English entrance to the church, which is located on Gowlland Point Road. (#5 on the map)

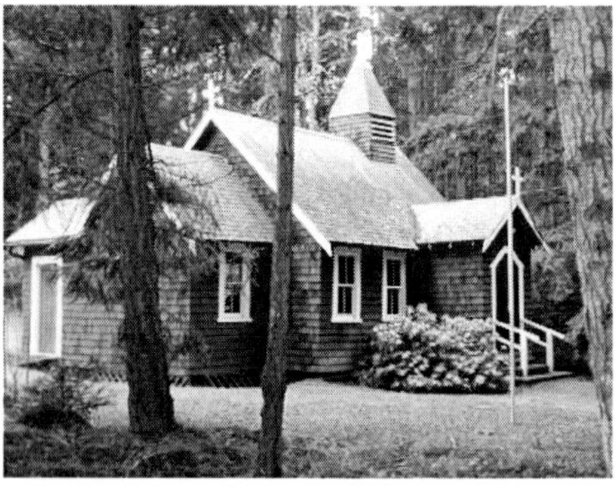

Church of the Good Shepherd as it appears today

Places to Shop

In the 1960's, a group of artists on the Pender Islands began gathering together to sketch and paint. Soon, they were organizing workshops at the Royal Canadian Legion hall and exhibitions at the Port Washington hall. For a while, they made their home in the old school at Hope Bay.

One of the first art shows held by the group was at the Legion hall. Another show was held at the golf course. Yet another was held in the 1970's, at the old community hall.

Today, there are several art galleries, shops and studios situated along Port Washington Road. Known locally as *Gallery Row*, the stretch of roadway provides visitors to the Penders the opportunity to pick up a *potlatch* (gift) for someone special. Watch for road signs and the chance to meet an artist working in their studio.

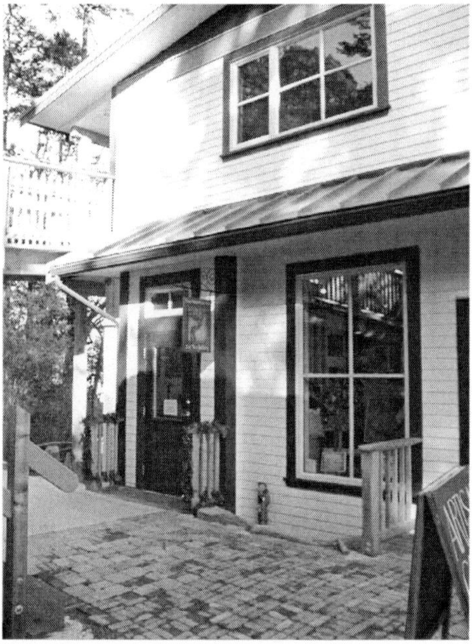

Recently, the Pender Islands Artisan Cooperative opened a gallery to make it possible for the variety of fine artisans on the Penders to display their works. Located at the Hope Bay Stores on Port Washington Road, the gallery is called the *Red Tree Gallery*.

Gwen's Fine Art

Gwen's Fine Art is located on North Pender, at the Driftwood Centre. It offers fine Native art and gifts. (#8 on the map)

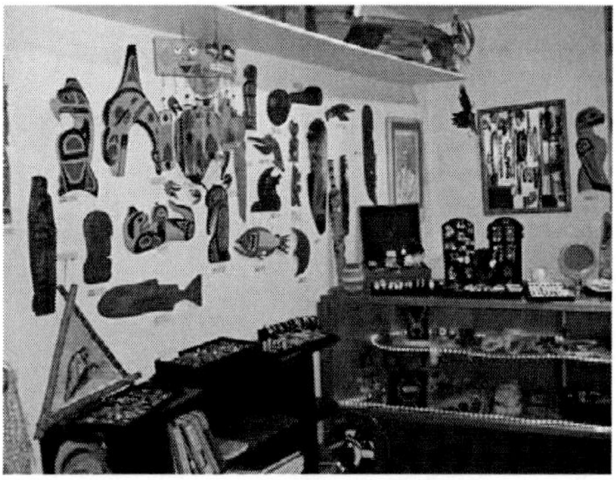

Casual Pender - Unique Gifts

Casual Pender – Unique Gifts provides for an enticing variety of gifts, clothing and jewelry. It is located on North Pender, at the Driftwood Centre. (#8 on the map)

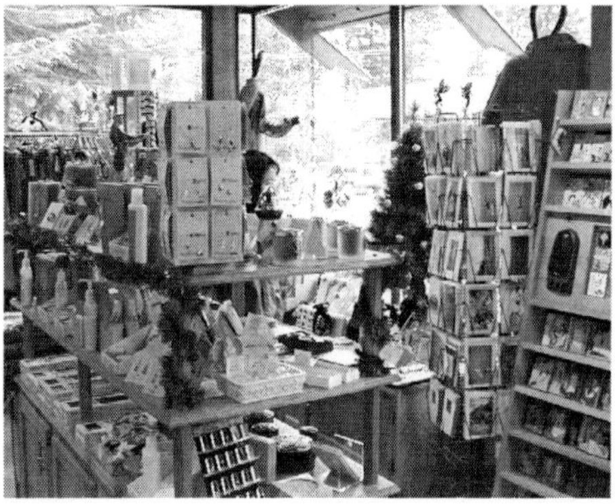

Benevolent Beast Studio Gallery

The *Benevolent Beast Studio* offers paintings, mixed media and sculpture. It is located on North Pender, on Bedwell Harbour Road. (#14 on the map)

Talisman Books & Gallery Ltd.

Talisman Books and Gallery is a fine bookstore gallery, which offers a wide selection of new and used books, as well as quality glass and pottery created by local artisans. It is located on North Pender, at the Driftwood Centre. (#8 on the map)

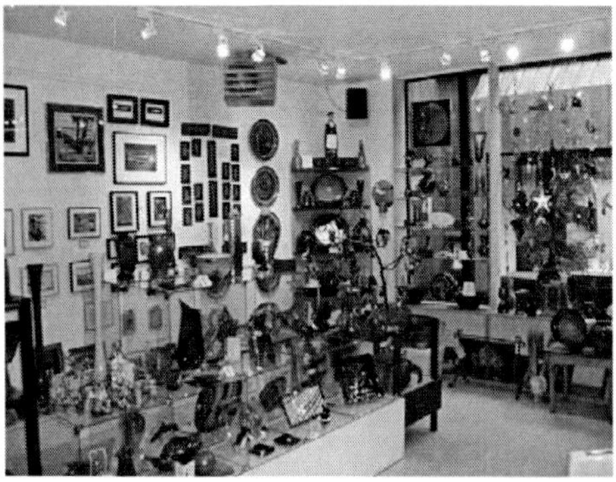

The Goldsmith

The Goldsmith is a jewelry store that specializes in custom goldsmithing, diamonds, gemstones, knives and repairs. It is located on North Pender, at the Hope Bay Stores. (#9 on the map)

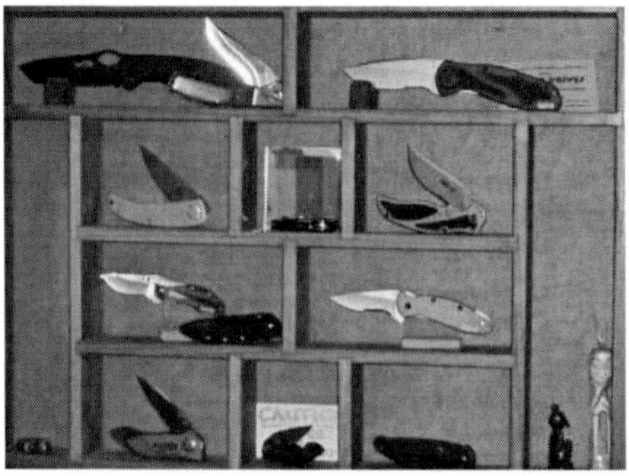

The Wool Shed

In the 1920's, a settler bought a small house on a bay. To supplement his income, he and his family built three cottages on the property and opened his house to guests.

The family called their resort the *Welcome Bay Inn*. They supplied their guests with home-cooked meals, which they served in their dining room.

The resort closed at the onset of World War II, after which the Royal Canadian Legion used one of the guest cottages as their meeting place for a while.

Today, the property is called *Welcome Bay Farm* and a descendant of the settler still resides there.

The owners of the farm raise goats and sheep on the property. They also run a studio called *The Wool Shed,* in which they shear, spin and hand-dye wool. The farm and studio are located on North Pender, on Clam Bay Road. (#15 on the map)

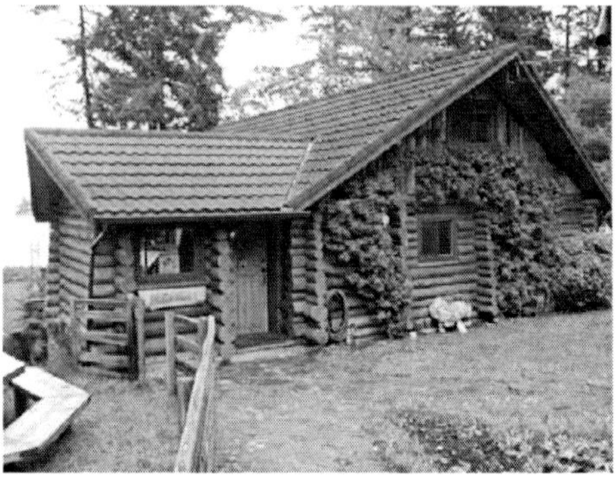

Renaissance Studio

The *Renaissance Studio* is an art gallery that offers art and antiques, as well as renowned custom, hand-made jewelry. It is located on North Pender, on Port Washington Road. (#12 on the map)

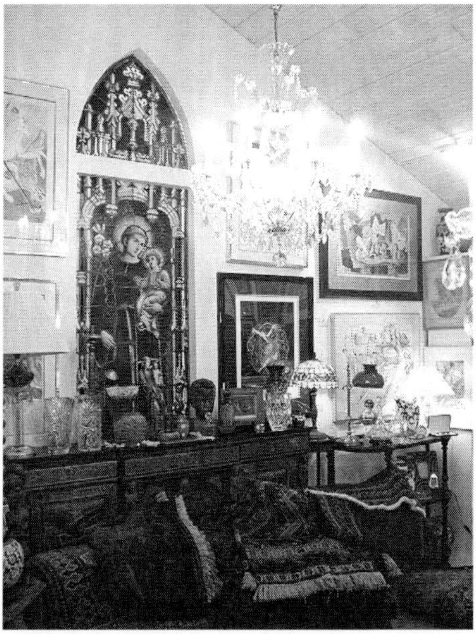

Pender Treasures Consignment & Gift

Pender Treasures Consignment and Gift is located on North Pender, at the Hope Bay Stores. The store offers local crafts, body care, clothing, books and gifts. (#9 on the map)

Mooring's Market

Mooring's Market is located on South Pender, at Poet's Cove Resort. (#16 on the map) It provides for gifts, as well as specialty coffees, ice cream and sandwiches.

NatureDiver Gallery

The *NatureDiver Gallery* offers photographs of wildlife, including underwater scenes. It is located on South Pender, on Boundary Pass Drive. (#18 on the map)

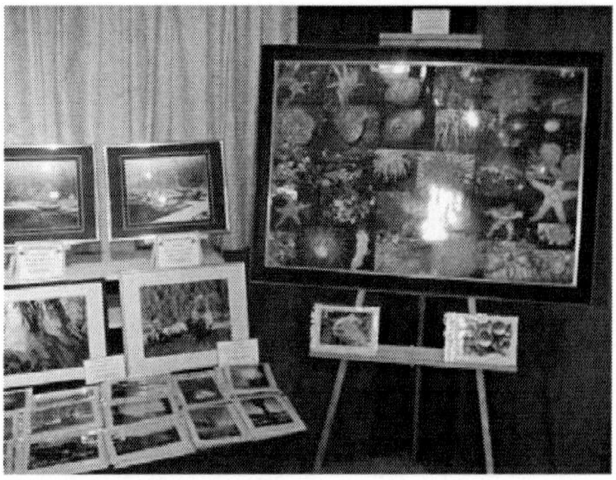

Armstrong Studio

The *Armstrong Studio* provides for oil and watercolor paintings. It is located on North Pender, on Otter Bay Road. (#13 on the map)

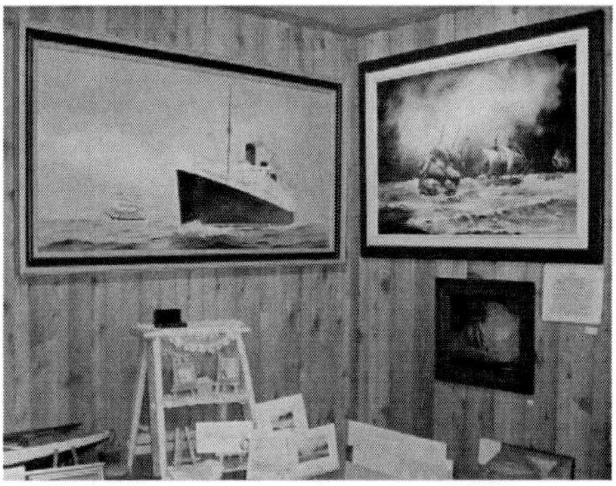

Buttonlady's Gallery

The *Buttonlady's Gallery* offers handmade ceramic buttons, embellishments and original art. It is located on Frigate Road in Magic Lake Estates. (#17 on the map)

Blood Star Studio & Gallery

The *Blood Star Studio and Gallery* provides for drawings and folk art. It is located on South Pender, on Jennens Road. (#19 on the map)

Wildart Photography Gallery

The *Wildart Photography Gallery* offers a selection of over 8,000 images, specializing in hard-to-access wilderness areas of British Columbia. The gallery is located on North Pender, on Bedwell Harbour Road. (#14 on the map)

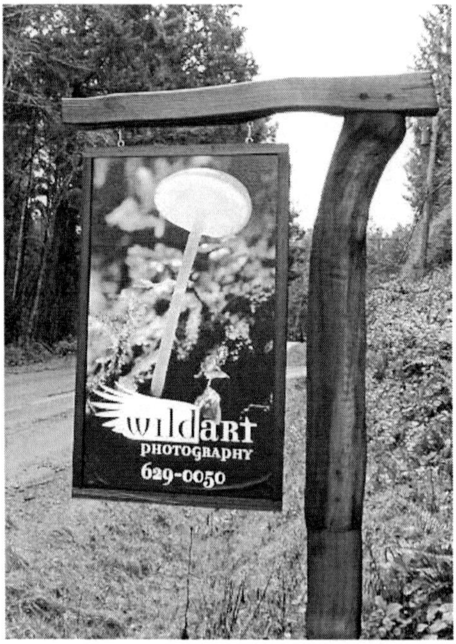

Sladen's Gift Shop

Sladen's Gift Shop is located on North Pender, at the Hope Bay Stores. It offers fine home decor. (#9 on the map)

Events to Attend

Before the turn of the century, evening entertainment on the Pender Islands was organized in a local hall or school. Later, an organist formed the Pender Island Choral Society, which put on some outstanding concerts.

Each summer, one or two public picnics were held, usually on Victoria Day or on Dominion Day. At the picnics, races were run, sports were played and good food was eaten.

Whether it is an annual event, such as the *Garden Party* or the *Fall Fair*, or a special event, such as a music festival or play, there is always something to take in on the Penders today.

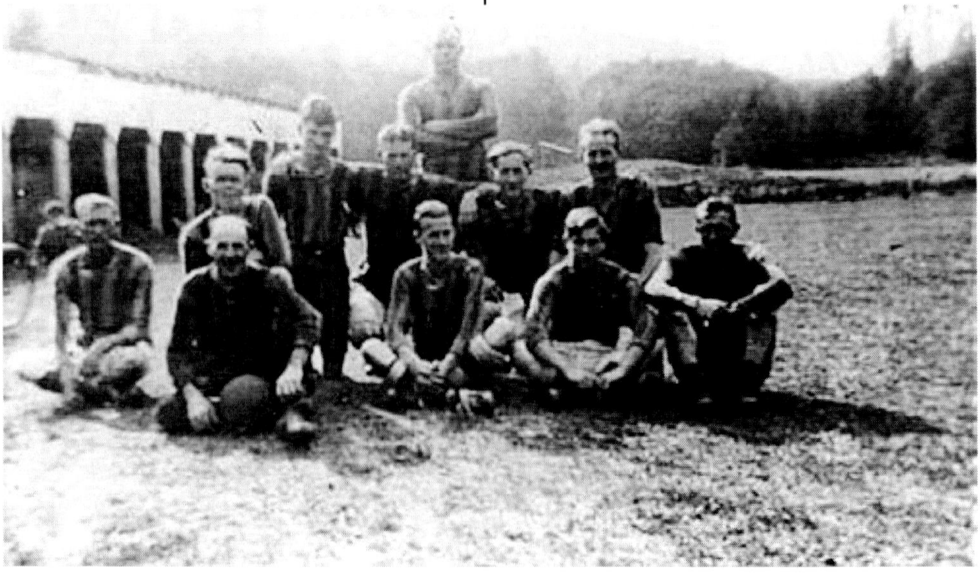

Pender Islands' Soccer Team in 1932 - Salt Spring Archives 56

The Pender Island Lions Club has been active for over 30 years and a few years prior to this writing, the Pender Island Volunteer Firefighter's Association was formed. Both organizations host a variety of events throughout the year.

Easter Celebrations

The annual *Easter Egg Hunt* is an event that is held every Easter at the Port Browning Marina. Children scatter across the field in search of hundreds of tiny chocolate Easter Eggs hidden in the rocks and grass.

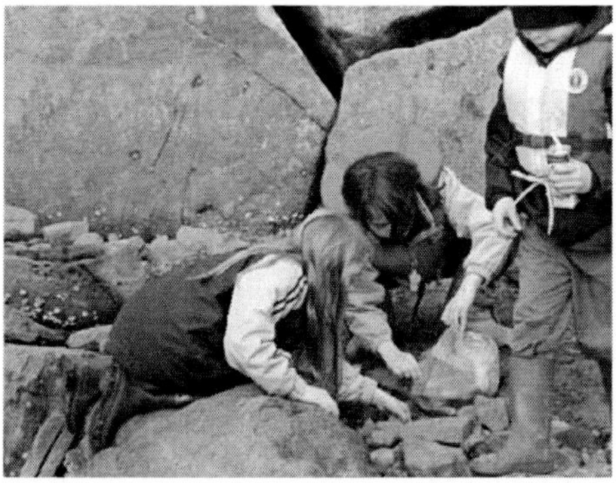

The *South Pender Easter Art Walk* is an annual event that has been taking place at Easter since the late 1990's. Look for the yellow balloons to guide you around the studios and galleries on South Pender.

Pender Island Health & Wellness Fair

The *Wellness Fair* is an annual event that takes place in May at the Pender Islands Hall. It provides for therapies and products for creating a healthy mind, body and spirit. Demonstrations include Tai Chi, Qi Gong and crystal bowls. There are also door prizes.

Pender Islands Farmer's Market

The *Pender Island Farmer's Market*, which runs every Saturday, from May to October, is held at both the Pender Islands Hall and the Driftwood Centre. The market provides for a cornucopia of fresh produce from local farmers, as well as art from local artists and craftspeople.

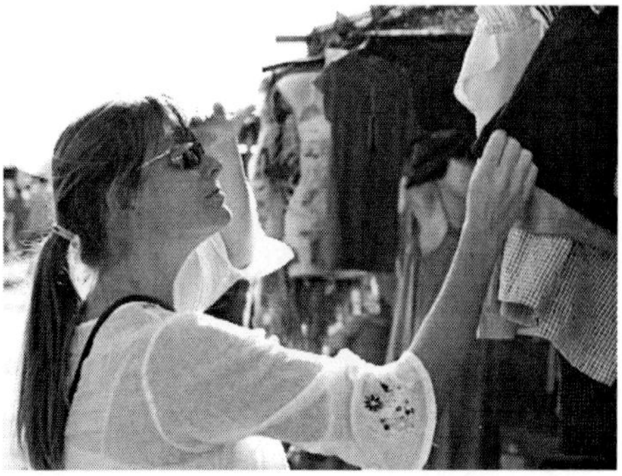

Pender Invitational Disc Tournament

On the last weekend in May, the annual *Pender Island Invitational Disc Tournament* attracts almost 100 participants of frisbee golf from all over the West Coast. The tournament takes place at the Golf Island Disc Park. Use of the course is free, but players are required to bring their own frisbees.

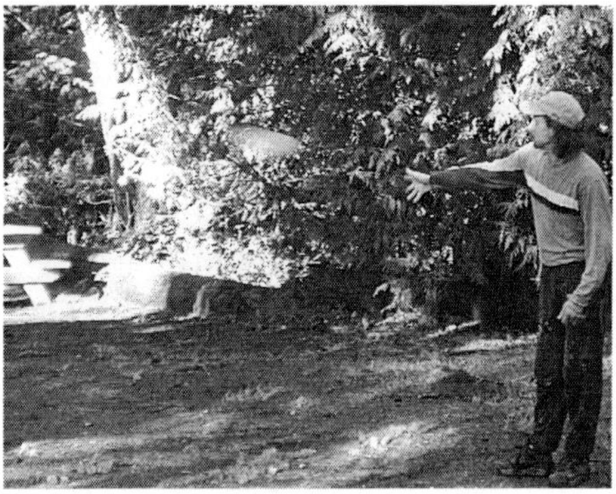

Canada Day Celebration

Canada Day Celebrations are held each year on July 1 at the Pender Islands Hall. There is food, events and a variety of festivities.

Art Off The Fence Show

Art Off The Fence is an outdoor art show and sale that has been taking place since the 1990's. The event is held in July on South Pender Island.

Pender Islands Art Show

The *Pender Islands Art Show* is an annual event, which has been taking place since the 1970's. Today, there are over 30 artists displaying drawings, fabric art and collages, as well as watercolors, oils and acrylics.

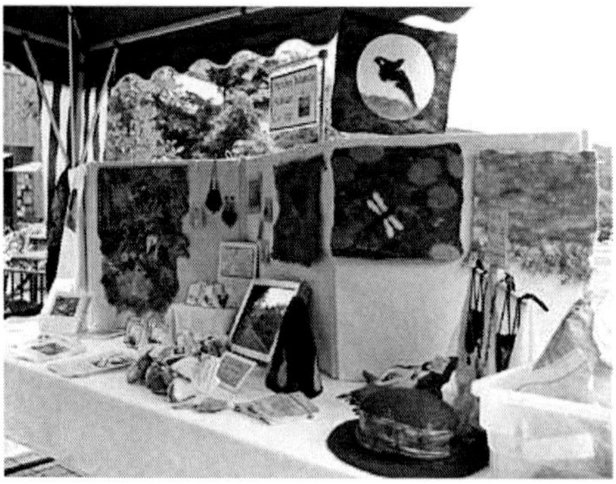

Garden Party

St. Peter's Guild grew out of a Women's Auxiliary that included many pioneer women from Port Washington.

In the early 1930's, the Guild started hosting a fair to raise funds for the Columbia Coast Mission, the Salvation Army and other causes. Reportedly, the fair was always held at a private residence, in their garden. Thereafter, it became known as the *Garden Party*.

Today, the Garden Party provides for games and prizes, as well as a flea market. It is held each year in July, at the Parish Hall beside St. Peter's Anglican Church.

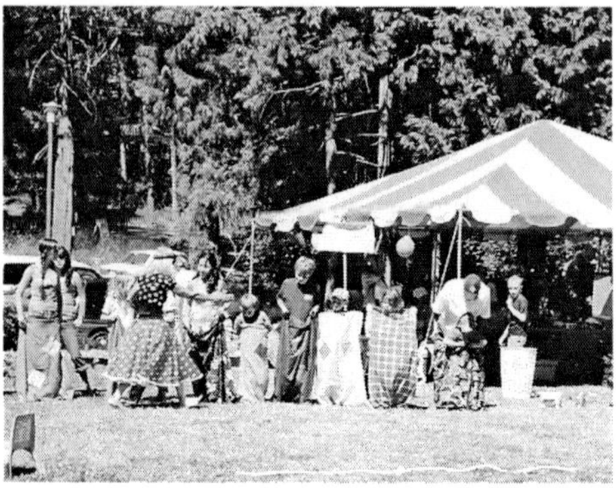

Yacht Club Regatta

The annual *Yacht Club Regatta* takes place in *Navy Channel* and *Plumper Sound*, the waters bounded by Mayne, Saturna and the Pender Islands. During the event, an estimated 600 sailors occupy Port Browning Marina for a full week in August.

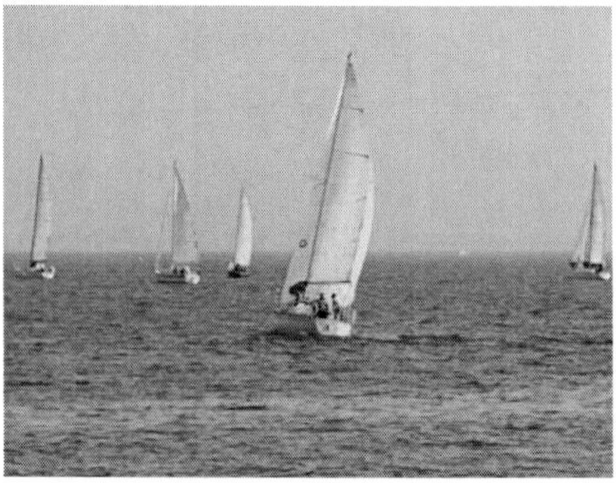

Officially known as *RIPS Canadian Race Week*, the regatta is fashioned after the highly successful Whidbey Island Race Week, in Washington State, and is open to all types of sailboats. The event includes daily racing and prizes, as well as barbecues, beer gardens, a dance and other activities.

Pender Islands Fall Fair

The first *Pender Islands Fall Fair* was held during the depression of the 1930's at the Hope Bay Hall.

In an effort to encourage them to plant vegetables to enter in the fair, the Farmers' Institute gave seeds to all the children living on the Island. Then, they came to the children's homes to inspect their gardens.

Initially, the sponsoring community groups had to borrow folding tables for the fair and haul them across the Island for each and every event, including the evening dance, which was a highlight.

In the first year of the fall fair, a settler's son won first prize for his entry. He took a vacation with his winnings.

Another year, a woman decided to enter a cake decorated like the Union Jack, which was the national flag at the time. When she discovered that she had run out of blue food coloring, she used ink, instead. The cake won first prize.

The fall fair was terminated at the onset of World War II and was not re-introduced until the 1960's.

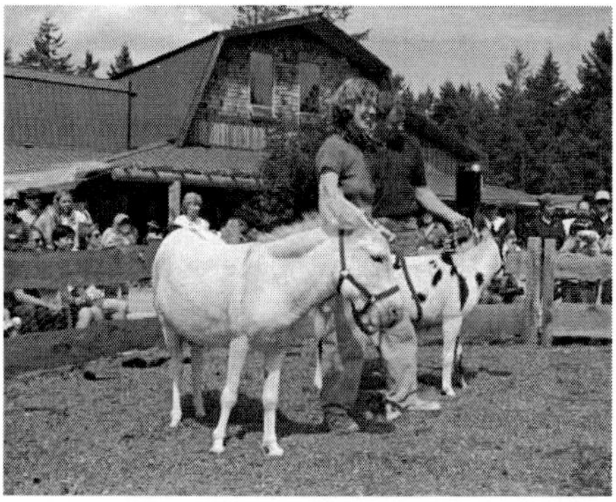

Today, the Pender Islands Fall Fair takes place in August at the Pender Islands Hall. There are 1,000 exhibits entered each year, in a variety of categories. Judging takes place in numerous events and there is live entertainment.

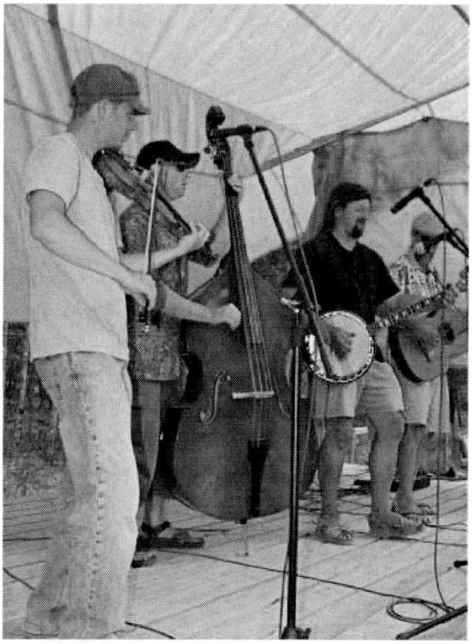

Halloween Howl

The *Halloween Howl* is held at Halloween at the Pender Islands Hall. It provides for a dance, games and prizes for the best costume. There is also a fireworks display.

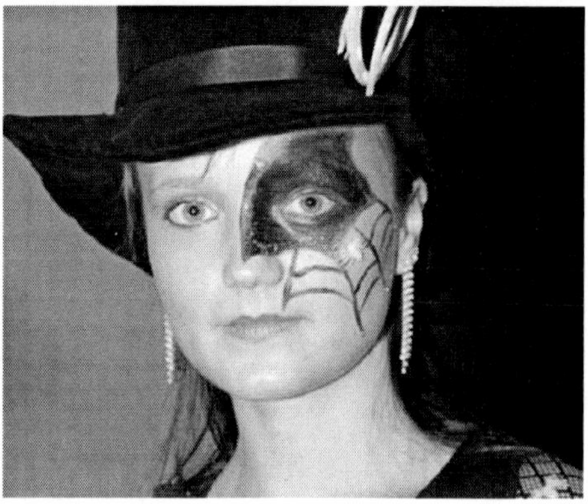

Christmas Celebrations

In the 1940's, a prominent Englishman moved to the Penders from the mainland. In the year 1960, he and his wife decided to solicit donations for CARE Canada. For every donation, he placed a Christmas light on a tall Fir tree that was growing in their garden. He called it *The Tree of Light*.

The first year, the couple raised just over one hundred dollars from donations. However, each year, the amount grew higher until, by the 1970's, they had raised thousands of dollars for CARE Canada.

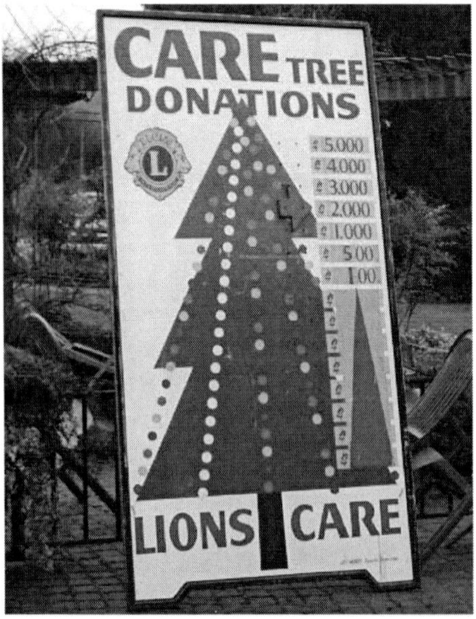

Eventually, the Pender Island Lions Club took over the project from the man, who was 89 years old at the time. By the 1990's, it was estimated that The Lions Club had donated over $140,000.

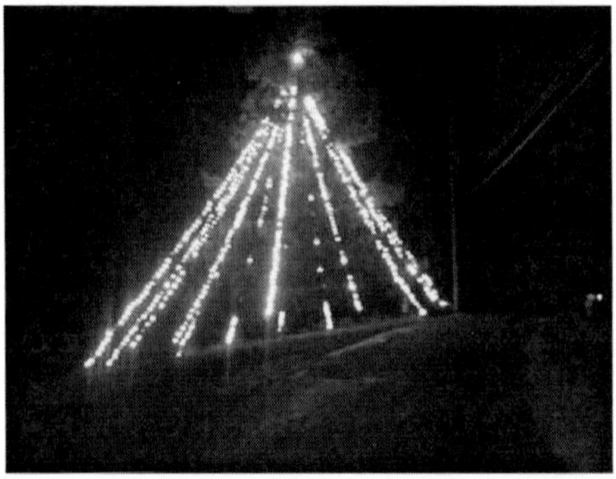

The Tree of Light, which is now known as the *CARE Tree*, has been moved more than once since the inception of the project. It now shines throughout the Christmas season on Bridges Road.

While the CARE Tree shines, the Bellingham Central Lions Club, in Washington State, continue the Christmas season by loading a *Christmas Ship* with toys and gifts, and then sending it to the Penders.

Known locally as the *Santa Ship*, the Christmas Ship is greeted at the Port Washington wharf, and then Santa and his 'helpers' distribute gifts to the kids.

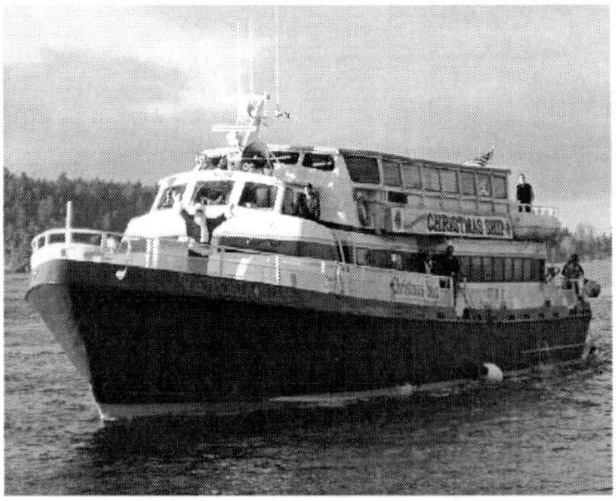

Residents of the Penders also celebrate the Christmas season with a craft fair held at the Pender Islands Hall. The fair includes a silent auction and raffle.

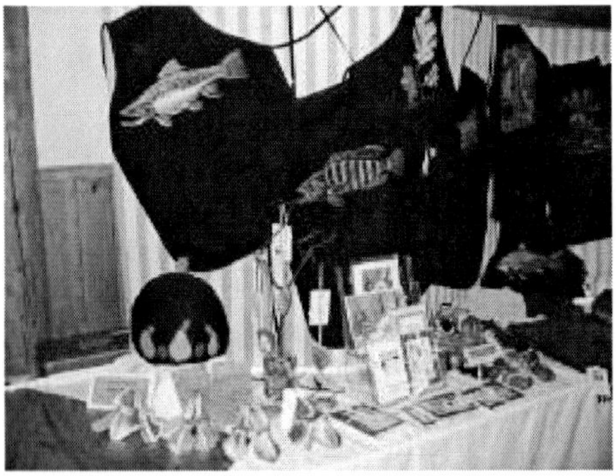

The season is completed with carols sung by the Otter Bay Symphony Orchestra and Choral Society. The event takes place on Christmas Eve at Hyashi Cove.

New Year's Celebrations

The *Magic Lake Lantern Festival* is a spectacular theatrical production that is held on New Year's Eve at Magic Lake, in Magic Lake Estates. It is put on by the Three On The Tree theatre production company.

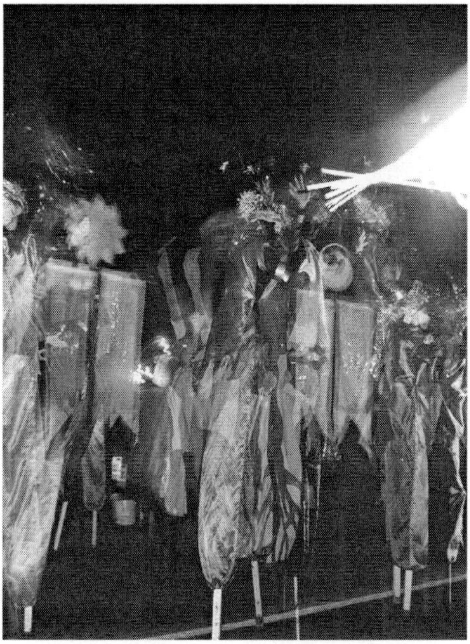

Spectators carry lit sparklers around the lake during the events, which include fire spinners, stilt walkers and a lantern ballet on the lake.

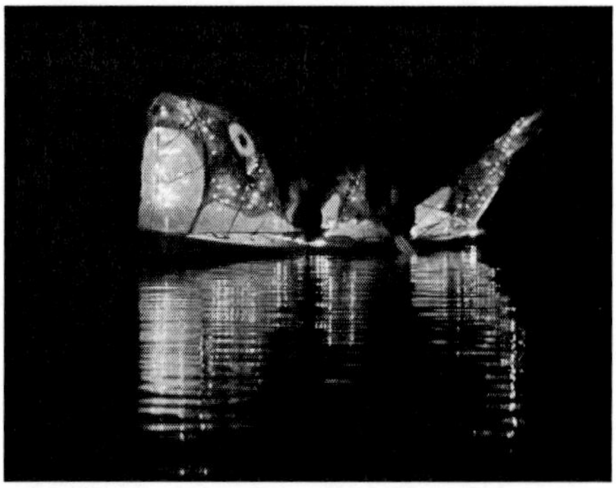

The lantern festival is followed by a Masquerade Ball, which is held at the Pender Islands Hall. Live entertainment is provided.

On New Year's Day, residents of the Penders choose between golfing in the *New Year's Golf Tournament* and swimming at the annual *Polar Bear Swim* at Hamilton Beach. Spectators are welcome.

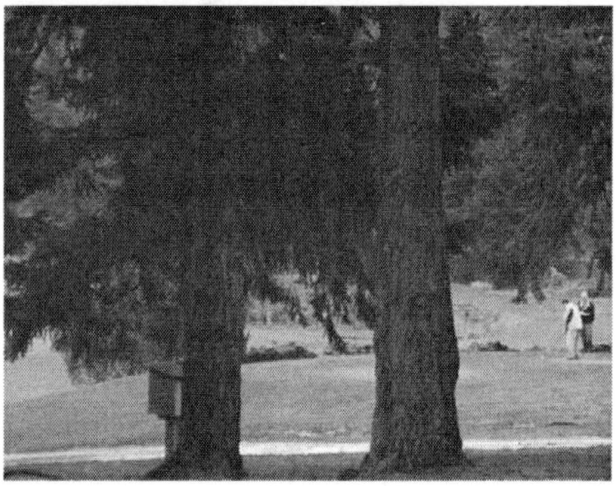

Pender Islands Parks & Beaches

1 Susan Point
2 Davidson Bay
3 Bricky Bay
4 Welcome Bay
5 Mt. Elizabeth Pk
6 George Hill Pk
7 Grimmer Bay
8 James Point
9 Hyashi Cove
10 Irene Bay
11 Roesland Pk & Roe Lk
12 Shingle Bay Pk
13 Panda Bay
14 Thieves Bay Pk
15 Boat Nook
16 Prior Centennial Pk
17 Oak Bluffs
18 Wallace Point
19 Medicine Beach
20 Danny Martin Pk
22 Mt. Menzies Pk
23 Mt Norman Regional Pk
24 Cedar Creek
25 Little Bay
26 Teece Point
27 Gowlland Point
28 Drummond Bay
29 Beaumont Marine Pk
30 Enchanted Forest
31 Abbott Hill Pk & Magic Lk
32 Lilias Spalding Pk
33 Mortimer Spit Pk
34 Fawn Creek Pk
35 Lively Peak Pk
36 Hope Bay
37 Hamilton Beach

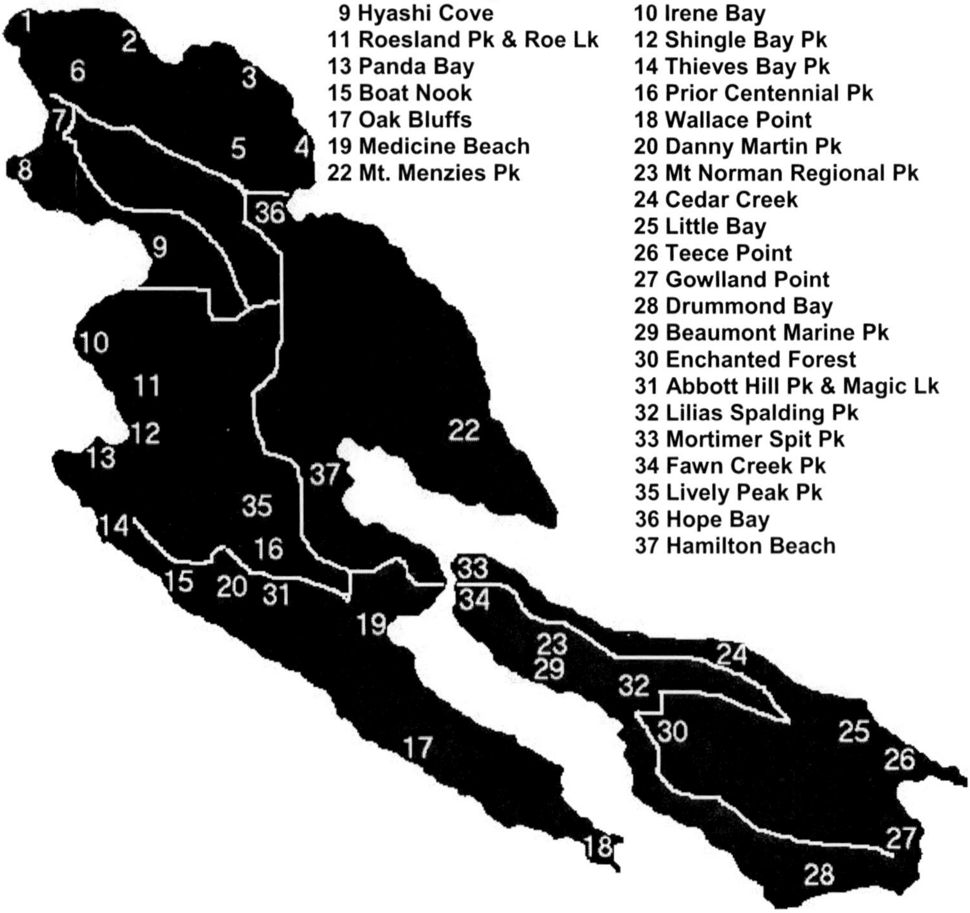

Parks & Beaches to Explore

In the 18th century, a Spanish mariner named North and South Pender Islands, *Sayas* and *San Eusbio*.

One hundred years later, the English commissioned the ship, HMS *Plumper*, to survey the waters around the southern Gulf Islands. The ship's Second Master renamed the Pender Islands after the Captain of the ship.

Ironically, several years later, a descendant of this same Captain was washed ashore on South Pender during a storm one Christmas Eve.

Today, the Pender Islands are well known for their numerous bays and coves, which are ideal for boat moorage. The protected bays and shallow waters make it easy to find a cove to anchor in for the *poolakle* (night).

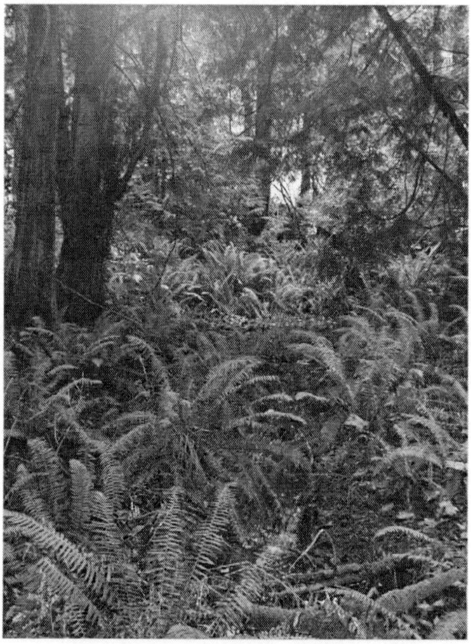

A portion of the land on the Penders is protected within the Gulf Islands National Park Reserve. In addition, there are numerous smaller parks outside the reserve.

The trails range from seashore-access, walking trails to forest hikes, so you might want to invest in a pair of *waffle stompers* (hiking shoes). As well as ensuring that nothing is left on the trails, hikers should take as much of their *iktas* (belongings) as possible off the Island.

Abbott Hill Park

In the 1960's, daily ferry service from Vancouver Island brought land speculators to the Penders.

When it was completed in the 1970's, *Magic Lake Estates*, on the west side of North Pender, was the largest planned subdivision in all of Canada. Originally called *Gulf Garden Estates*, it was heavily marketed in the cities. Soon, most of the lots were sold and newcomers began to build summer cabins and retirement homes there.

Abbott Hill Park is named after the surveyor who purchased the land that is now the Magic Lake Estates development.

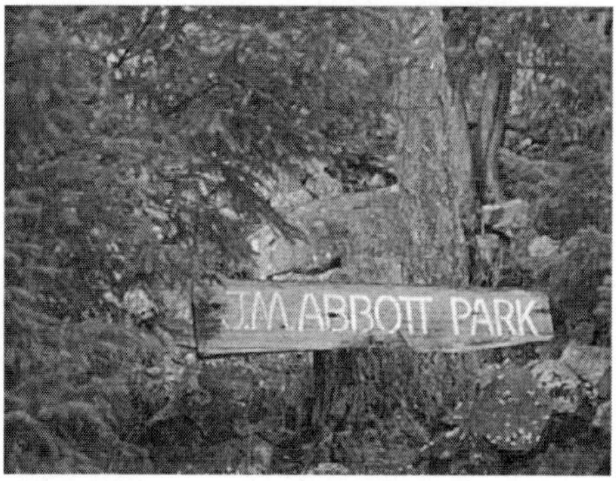

The steep trail through the park is accessible by way of Spyglass Road, in Magic Lake Estates. (#31 on the map)

Boat Nook

Boat Nook is located on the west side of North Pender, in Magic Lake Estates. The beach is accessible by way of steps off Schooner Way. (#15 on the map)

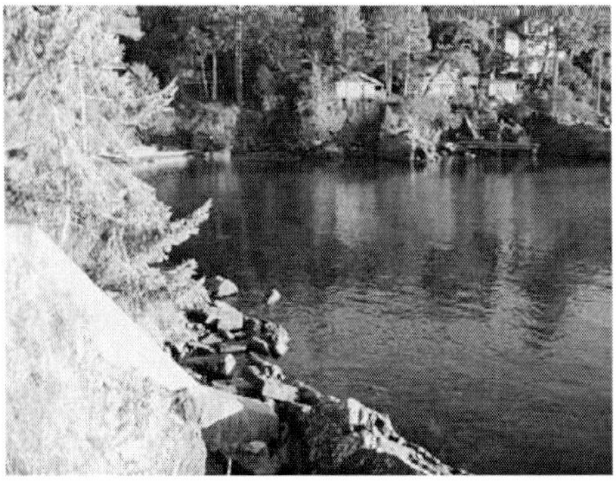

Bricky Bay

Shortly before the outbreak of World War I, the Coast Shale Company purchased some land on a bay. There, they constructed a brick factory with grinders, mixers and ovens. Then, they laid narrow track rails that led through a tunnel to a shale pit.

Before it shut down and was demolished in the 1920's, the plant, which employed about 75 men, was producing up to 300,000 bricks every day. The bricks were then shipped from a wharf in the bay.

Originally named *Colston Cove*, Bricky Bay is located on the northeast side of North Pender. The sandy beach at the bay is strewn with bricks that are the remains of the brickworks.

The beach is accessible by way of steps at the end of Armadale Road. There are two other beach accesses along the road, just north of the bay. (#3 on the map)

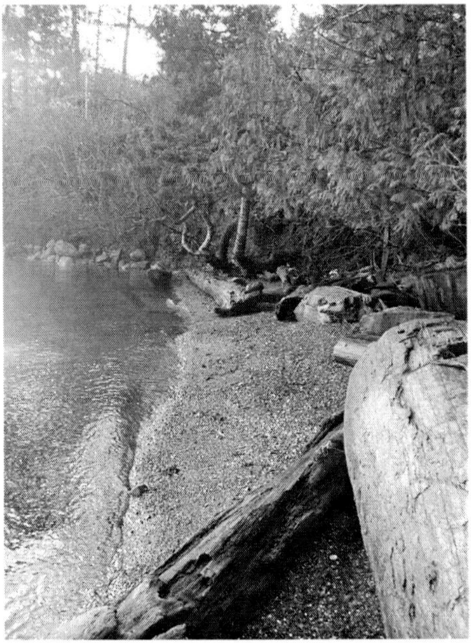

Canned Cod Bay

At the turn of the century, a settler owned a farm on a bay. He called his farm *Southlands*.

The settler made periodic trips to the U.S. to smuggle back cases of canned goods. The police had been suspicious of the smuggler for a while, but could not catch him.

One day, he arrived home with a load of cans. He carried them from his boat and hid them in some thick Alder trees. Then, he began falling the Alder trees over the cans to hide them.

As he was falling the trees, the police arrived to search his property for smuggled cans. As they searched, he continued falling trees. They searched everywhere, except under the falling trees and, as a result, he was never caught.

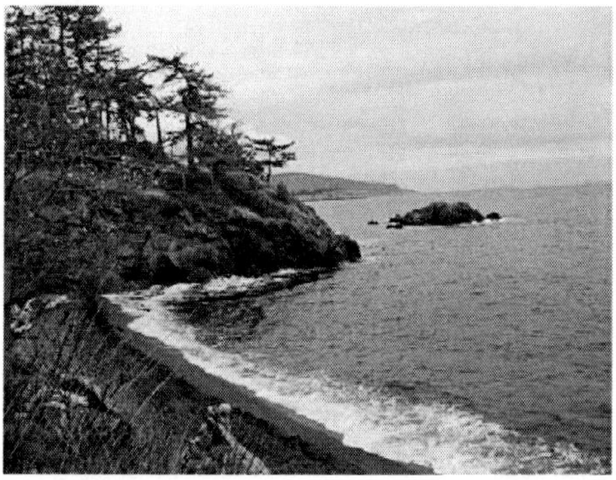

Canned Cod Bay is located on the southern tip of South Pender. It provides for great views of the San Juan Islands, the Strait of Juan de Fuca and Mount Baker, in Washington State. It is also a great place to spot whales.

The beautiful pebbled beach on the bay is lined with driftwood. At low tide, you can explore shallow caverns that have been carved out by the tides. The beach is accessible by way of Gowlland Point Road. (#27 on the map)

Cedar Creek

Shortly after the turn of the century, two brothers emigrated from England and became apprentice farmers in a valley called the *Spalding Valley*.

The following year, they purchased some property from a settler who owned a ranch on South Pender. They called the property *Cedar Creek.*

Soon, the brothers constructed a cabin on their property. It had a fireplace and chimney, which they built out of granite that had been hauled over from Saturna Island.

When one of the brothers was killed in World War I, the property was passed to the surviving brother's son.

The cabin, which can be seen from Canal Road, is reported to be the oldest log cabin still in use on the Penders today. A descendent of the brothers still owns the property.

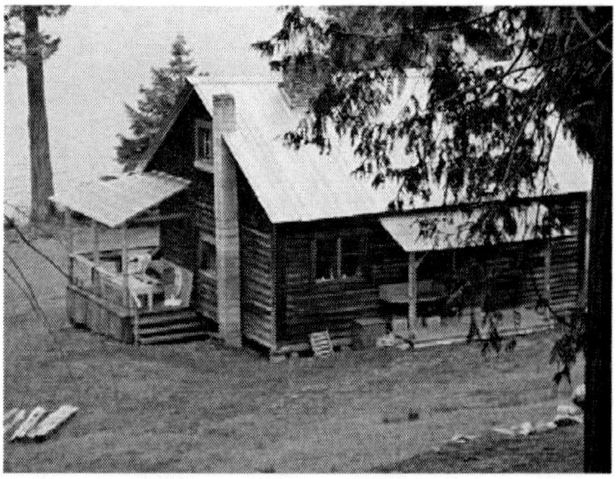

Cedar Creek is located on the south end of South Pender. It provides for a sandy beach that is accessible by way of steps off William Walker Road. (#24 on the map)

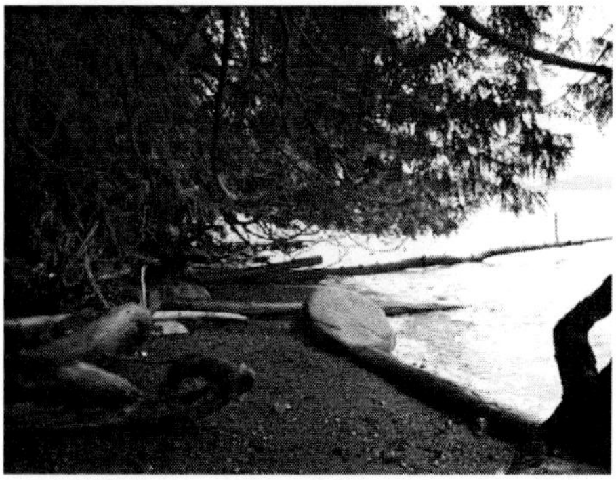

Danny Martin Park

Danny Martin Park is located on the west side of North Pender, in Magic Lake Estates.

The park is a recreational area that provides for a playground and baseball diamond. There are also facilities for picnics if you want to stay awhile. The park is accessible by way of Schooner Way. (#20 on the map)

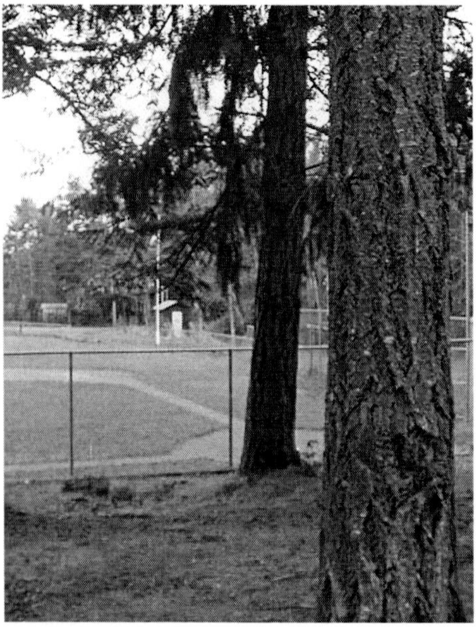

Davidson Bay

In the 1890's, **the Postman** sold some of his land on a bay to a Scottish settler who was known for his rowing ability.

When he needed lumber to build his home, the Scotsman rowed to Vancouver Island with his sons, and then walked the 30 km to Victoria to purchase it. Then, they towed it back to their property on a homemade raft.

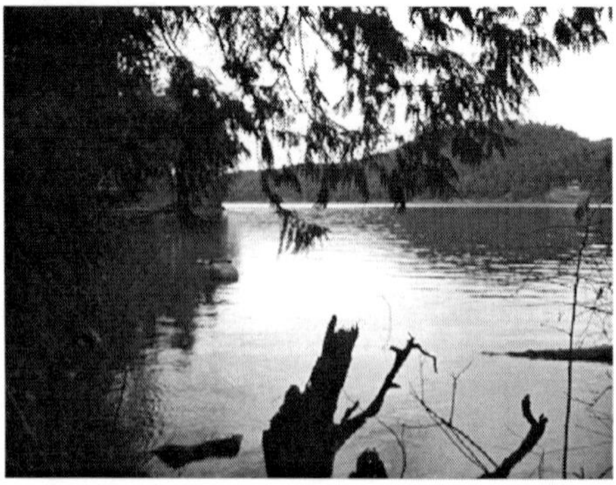

Davidson Bay is located at the north end of North Pender. Although it was named after this settler, it is known locally as *Clam Bay*.

The pebbled beach at the bay is accessible by way of a stunning 1.5 km trail of moderate difficulty. The trail to the beach is called the *Found Road Trail*. It leads through lush forest of dense Douglas-Fir and Western Red Cedar, and passes through five ecological zones. The trail is accessible by way of Clam Bay Road. (#2 on the map)

Drummond Bay

Drummond Bay is located on the southern tip of South Pender. At low tide, you can walk along the beach looking at the Sea Stars. There are also good views of Mount Baker in Washington State.

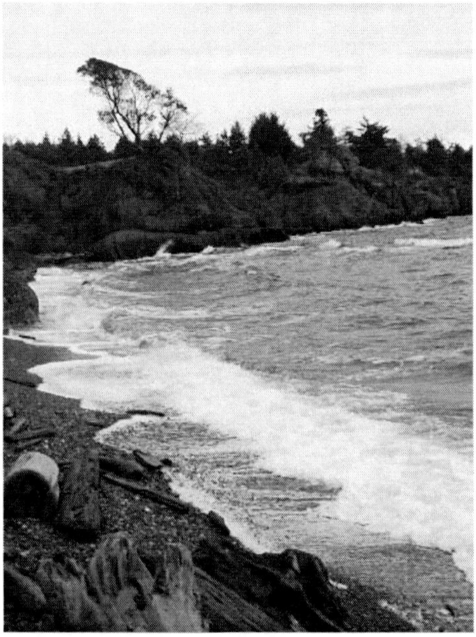

There are two beach accesses on Drummond Bay. A small, rocky beach, which surrounds some reefs, is accessible at low tide by way of Higgs Road.

Another access is by way of steps at the end of Craddock Road, which lead to a pebbled beach off Tilly Point. Originally named Bilk Point, Tilly Point is known for its eerie, underwater caverns, which are covered with anemones. They provide for great scuba diving at a depth of up to 9 m. (#28 on the map)

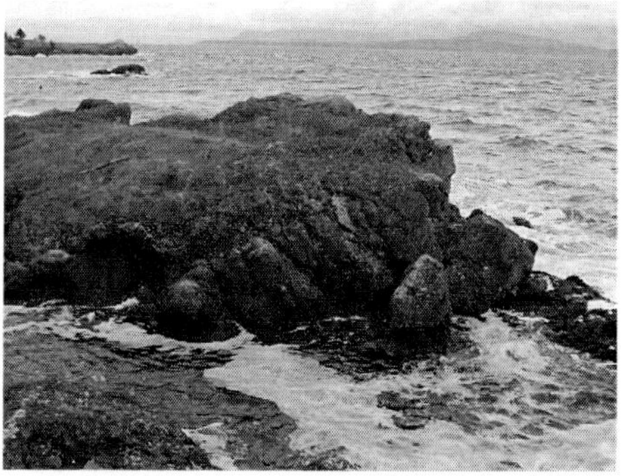

Enchanted Forest Park

The *Enchanted Forest Park* is a beautiful wetland on the west side of South Pender. The easy 2 km interpretive trail that winds through the park leads to a seasonal waterfall. It can be accessed at the end of Spalding Road. (#30 on the map)

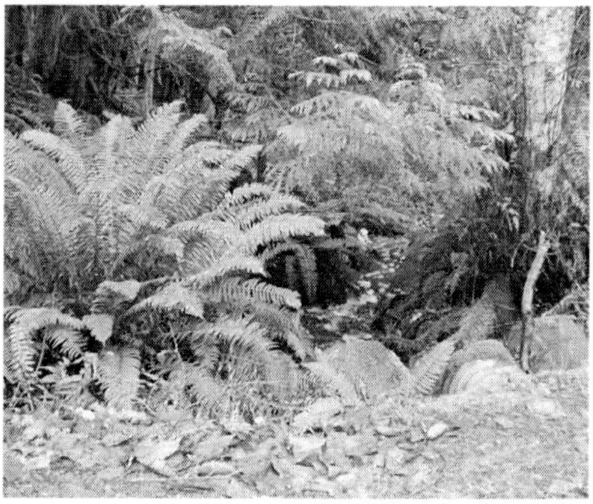

Fawn Creek Park

Fawn Creek Park is set in a mature forest of large, spectacular Western Red Cedar and Douglas-Fir, on the northwest tip of South Pender.

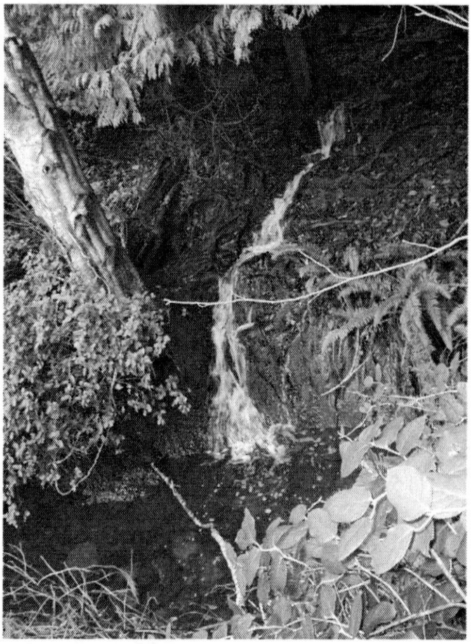

Fawn Creek is a seasonal creek that flows through the park and into the ocean. The trail through the park is accessible by way of steps off Ainslie Point Road. (#34 on the map)

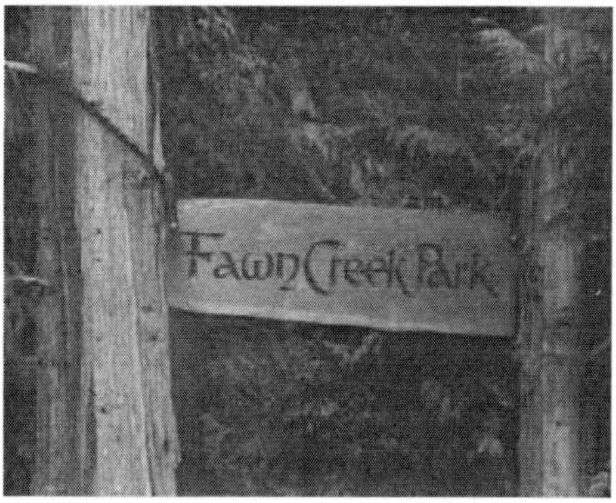

George Hill Park

George Hill Park, on the northern tip of North Pender, provides for a forest hike to two viewpoints. The challenging 2 km trail is accessible from the corner of Walden Road and Ogden Road. (#6 on the map)

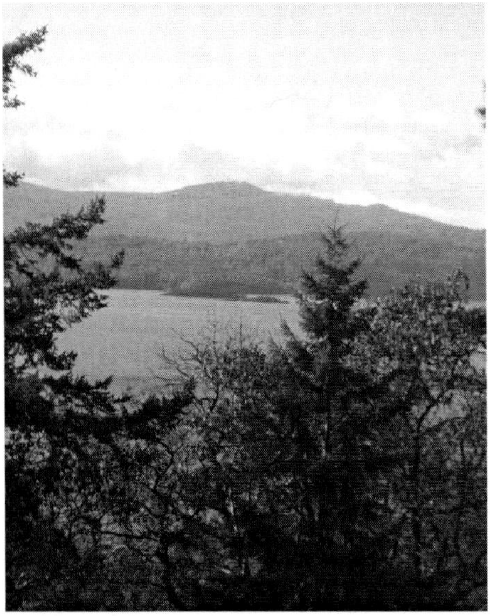

Grimmer Bay

In the 1880's, the settler who would later become **the Postman** settled in what is now called the *Grimmer Valley*. There, he built a four-room farmhouse.

Because he found entering the bay near his home dangerous, the settler sometimes left his rowboat on a nearby island and swam to shore, instead. Walking up from the beach was also difficult. By the time he found the trail that led to his home, he had often used up a box of matches to light his way. Nevertheless, he soon brought his young bride to live in his home.

The couple's oldest child was the first white child born on the Penders. When his wife went into labor with their second child, they launched a boat to see a midwife on Mayne Island. However, before they reached their destination, his wife delivered their baby in the boat.

In the early 1890's, **the Postman** built a small cabin, only to sell it a few years later and move deeper into the valley where he developed a dairy farm.

When his sons started entering his Jersey cows in all the major fairs in the province, his cattle became famous all over British Columbia.

Shortly before the outbreak of World War I, he divided his farm among his children. Then, he enlarged his home and turned it into a guesthouse.

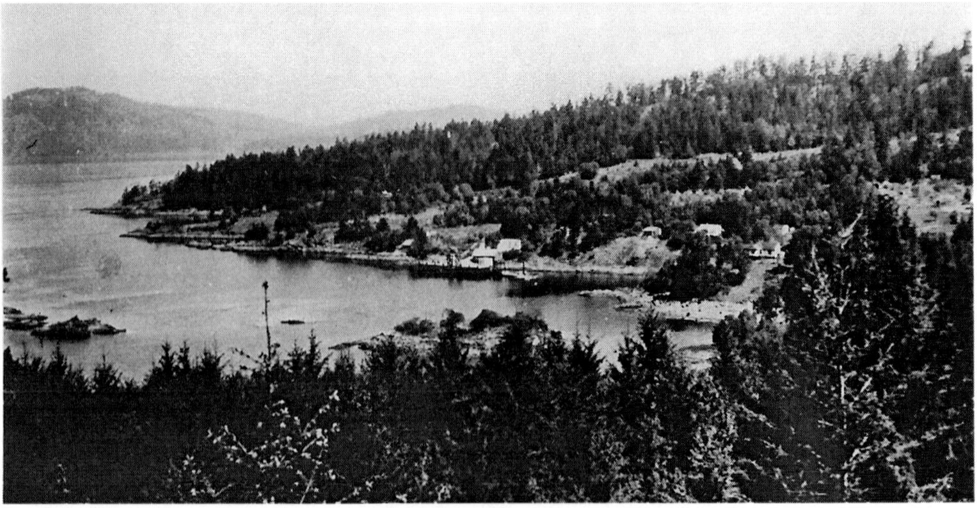

Grimmer Bay, early 1900's – Pender Islands Museum

Grimmer Bay was named after **the Postman**, whose 1920's retirement home still stands overlooking the bay.

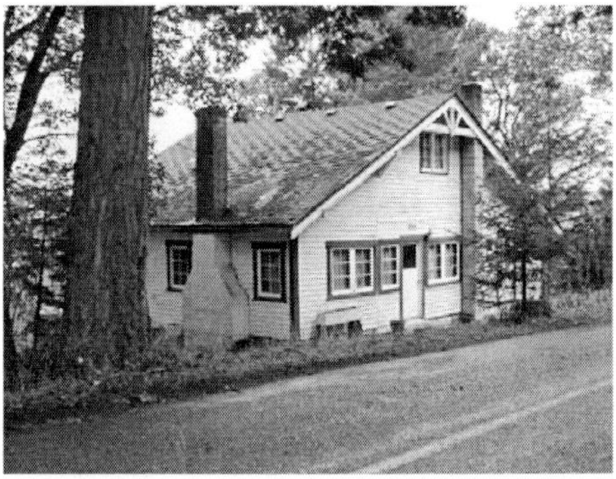

The bay is located on the northwest side of North Pender. The sandy beach on the bay is accessible from Bridges Road. (#7 on the map)

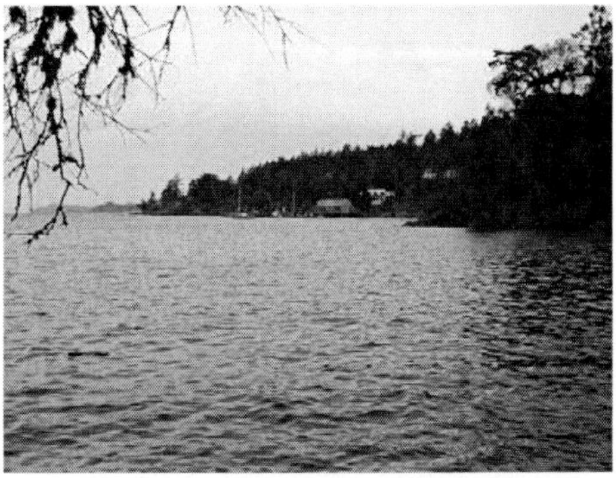

Grimmer Bay as it appears today

If you launch a boat from the Port Washington wharf, which extends into the bay, you can travel south to Mouat Point. The shoreline between Mouat Point and Stanley Point is quite captivating.

From there, you can continue all the way to Wallace Point. However, keep in mind that Swanson Channel can be dangerous and there are only a few places to pull out around Oaks Bluff.

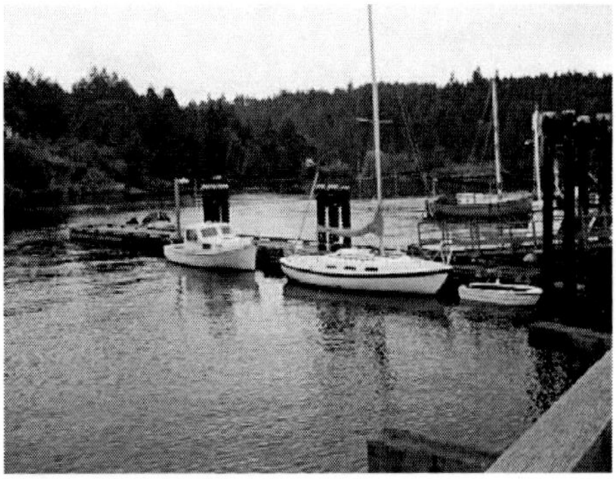

Hamilton Beach

In the 1880's, a Scottish stonecutter was carving gravestones on Vancouver Island for the Mortimer Monumental Works Company.

At that time, the company was also quarrying at the harbour on North Pender. Because they liked his work, they sent the settler to the harbour to help with the quarrying.

Soon, the stonecutter purchased some land at the head of the harbour. There, he built a log cabin where he and his family vacationed.

Three years later, his younger brother emigrated from Scotland and moved into a small frame house on the stonecutter's property. At the turn of the century, when the stonecutter brought his family to live in the house full-time, his younger brother built another home nearby.

Whenever there was mail to be picked up at the South Pender Post Office, one of the brothers would raise a flag on his property. Some of the other settlers would walk a long way just to see if the flag had been raised. If it had, they would then walk the rest of the way through the bush to pick up their mail.

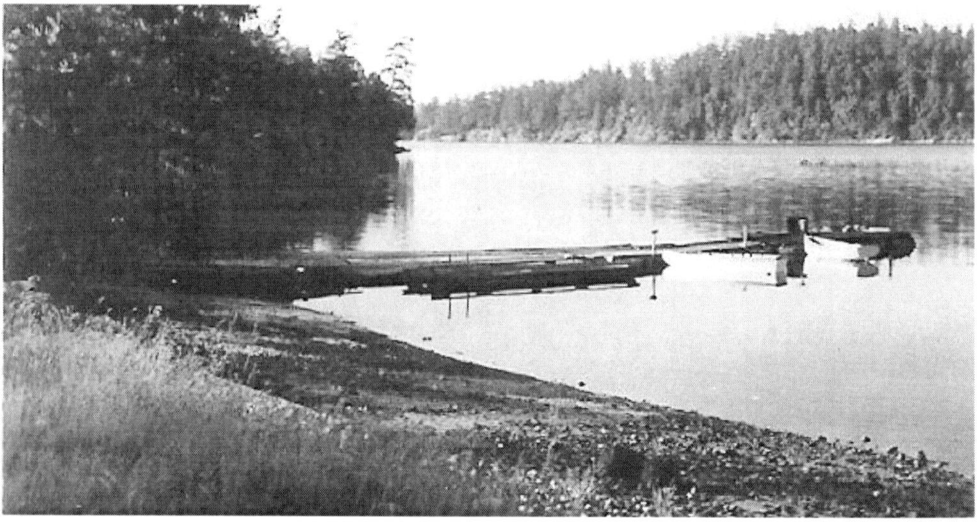

Hamilton Beach in the 1920's - Pender Islands Museum

Hamilton Beach, at the head of Browning Harbour, is named after these two brothers who, in the year 1890, also brought the first horse to the Penders.

The beach is accessible by way of Hamilton Road and is a good place for a *soak* (swim). It also provides for a wharf that is accessible off Razor Point Road. (#37 on the map)

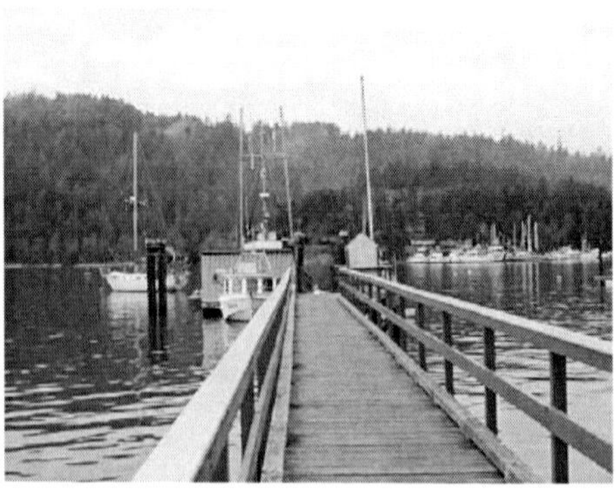

The Port Browning Marina at the harbour offers temporary boat anchorage and there are facilities for picnics if you and your boat want to stay awhile.

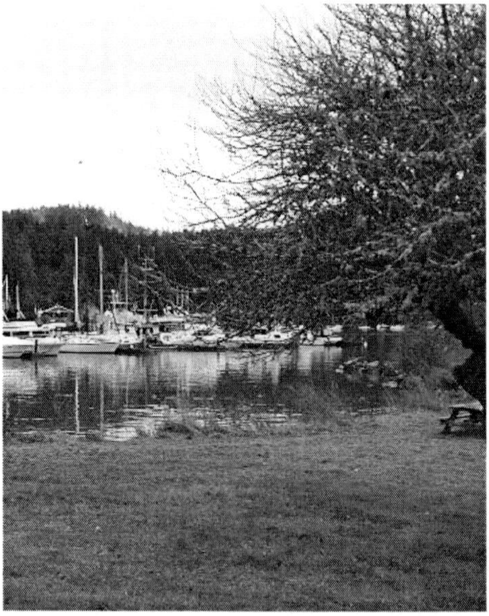

If you launch a boat from the beach, you can travel south to Mortimer Spit. At certain times, you can pass through the canal and on to Peter Cove. However, because the canal is only 12 m wide and *skookumchuck* (strong currents) run up to 4 knots, it should only be navigated at slack water.

Alternatively, you can travel south to Razor Point, and then head north to Bricky Bay. However, tides there run up to 3 knots.

Hope Bay

In the 1870's, two settlers purchased the entire northern half of North Pender, and then built a cattle fence that spanned the width of the Island.

On his portion of the land, one of the settlers built one of the first homes on the Penders. Unfortunately, a wounded buck killed him, while he was on a hunting trip. Subsequently, his brother inherited the property and lived in the home until the 1890's.

The brother's home was a little log cabin with a window on each side. The walls were built out of round Fir logs and the roof was made of split Cedar shakes. The ceiling was so low that visitors had to lower their heads to move around.

There was a stone fireplace at one end of the cabin. Behind it, was a chimney that was built out of square, coal-oil cans. Above it, stretched a steel rod from which a kettle could be hung. Across the end of the cabin was a lean-to shed that was built out of poles and split Cedar.

Hope Bay was named after this brother, who was famous for his home-baked bread, which he would set out in the sun to rise.

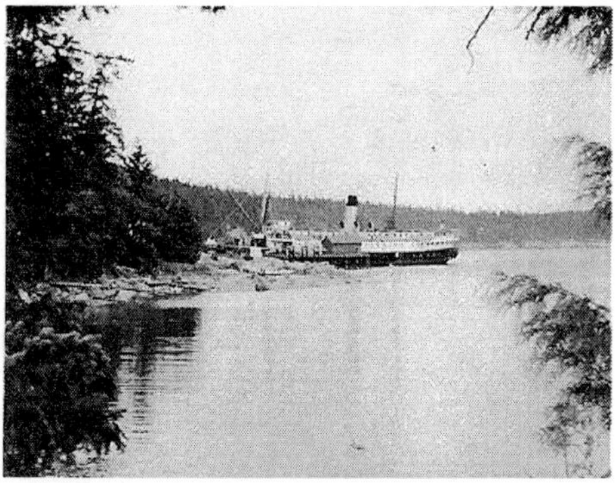

Hope Bay in 1946 - Pender Islands Museum

The bay is located on the east side of North Pender. The rocky beach on the bay is accessible by way of Port Washington Road. (#36 on the map) If you launch a boat from the government wharf, you can travel north to Bricky Bay. However, keep in mind that tides run up to 3 knots.

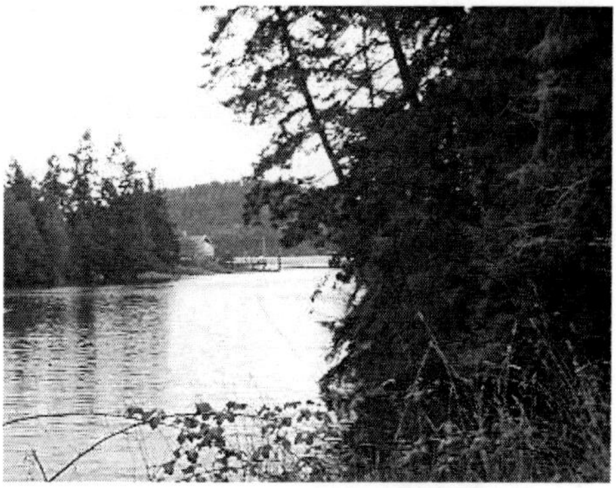

Hope Bay as it appears today

Alternatively, you can travel across Navy Channel to Mayne Island, and then on to Saturna Island, through a fascinating maze of islands and waterways.

Hyashi Cove

In the late 1920's, a retired Japanese-Canadian sea Captain started a herring saltery and fish processing plant in a cove.

Over time, the Captain brought other Japanese families to the cove. Subsequently, he became the boss of a Japanese camp that was established there.

The saltery operated a fleet of seiners that fished in the Channel. At night, the fishing fleet displayed a spectacle of lights, while it traveled through the water.

The saltery employed a large number of men, of various nationalities, who had a reputation for singing while they worked. As they sang, they packed the fish in cases, salting the fish heavily to escape paying a salt tax. Then, they sold them to countries in the Orient.

At the onset of World War II, when the Japanese-Canadian families were taken from their homes on the Penders, the saltery was taken over by The London Packers. Unfortunately, the plant burned down in the 1950's.

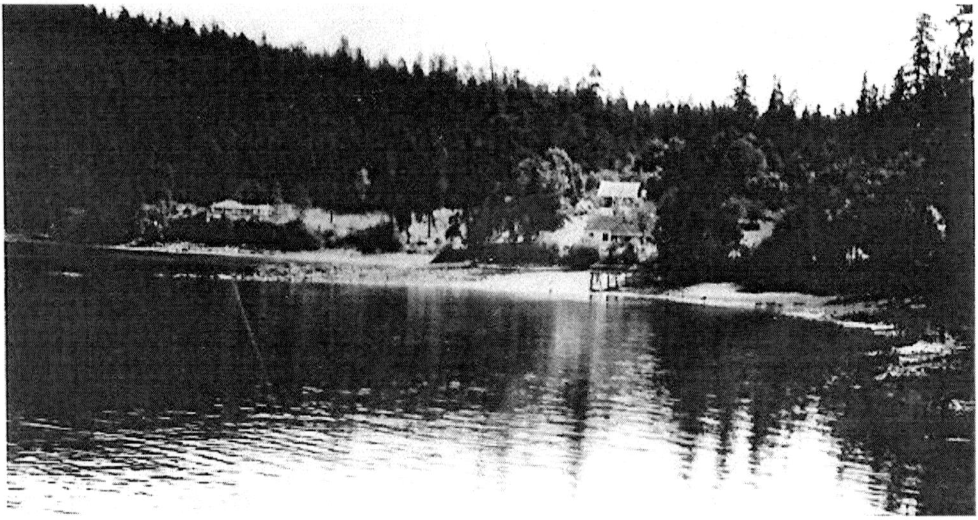

Hyashi Cove in 1946 – Pender Islands Museum

Hyashi Cove was named after this Japanese-Canadian sea Captain. Some remains of the saltery he ran can still be seen there.

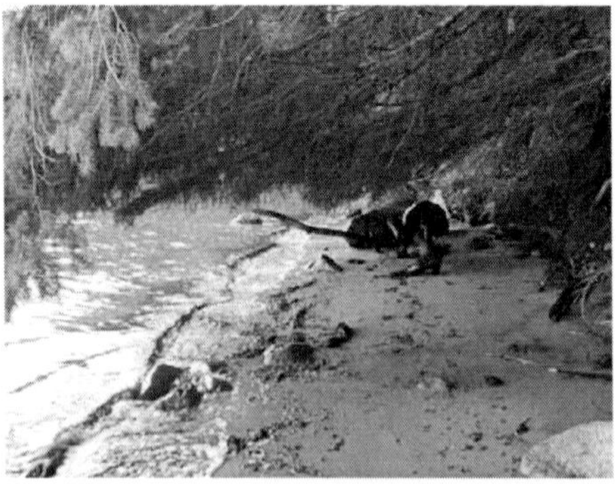

The cove sits within a larger body of water, called *Otter Bay*, on the northwest side of North Pender. The cove provides for the finest sandy beach on the Penders. It is accessible by way of steep steps off Niagara Road, which provide for a seasonal waterfall. (#9 on the map)

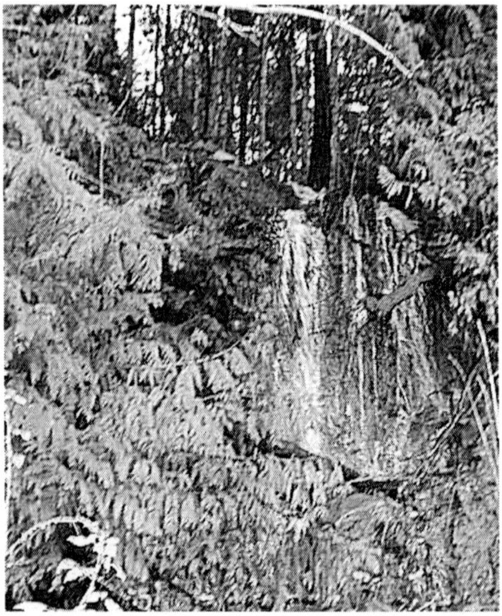

The *Otter Bay Marina* at the cove provides for temporary boat anchorage. If you launch a boat from the marina, you can travel south along a fascinating shoreline to Mouat Point. From there, you can continue all the way to Wallace Point. However, there are few places to pull out around Oaks Bluff.

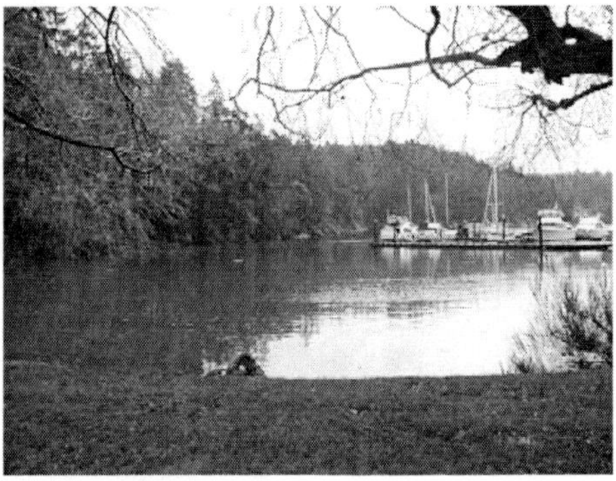

Irene Bay

Irene Bay, on the west side of North Pender, provides for a sandy beach that is accessible from Irene Bay Road. (#10 on the map)

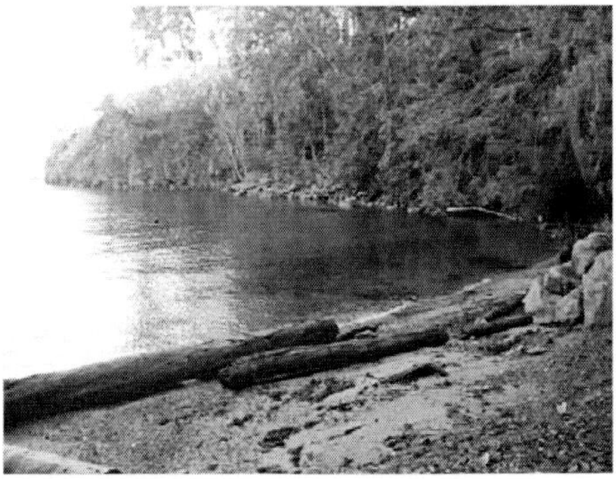

James Point

During World War I, a sea Captain purchased some property that was called *Waterlea*. He gave to his daughter.

His daughter's husband was the first real estate agent to reside on the Penders. In their home, he would provide free room and board to prospective clients who came to the Island to view properties.

The Captain's daughter soon became accustomed to providing for her husband's clients. So she converted their home into a resort, taking in guests in the summer.

The resort had several rowboats, a tennis court and a pavilion that extended out over the water. Whenever the couple's children wanted to prevent the guests from using these facilities, they would wait until low tide, and then suggest to the guests that they have a picnic on a nearby island. As a result, the guests would become stranded on the island when the tide came back in.

During the 1930's, the Canadian Pacific Railway steamers would pass by the resort. Sometimes, one of them would stop so guests could disembark. The guests would crowd onto one side of the ship and a rope ladder would be let down.

The family lived at Waterlea until the 1940's. The home can still be seen sitting on a point today.

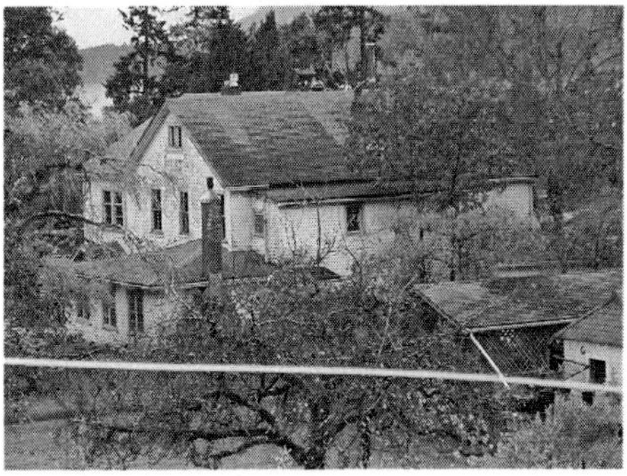

James Point is located on the west side of North Pender. It has an ecologically sensitive sandy beach that is accessible by way of steps off the end of MacKinnon Road. (#8 on the map)

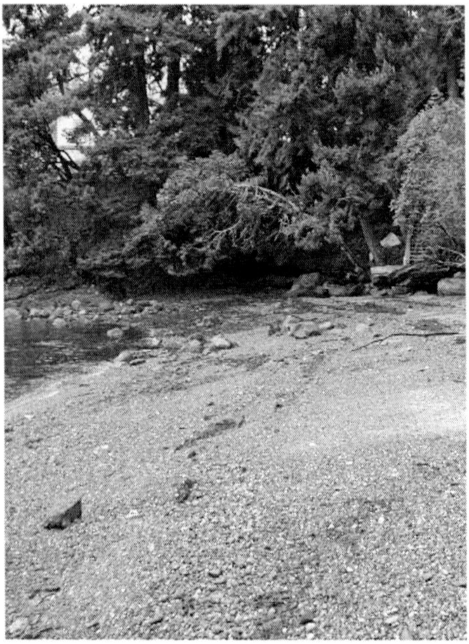

Lilias Spalding Heritage Park

In the 1880's, an Englishman purchased some land in a valley where he established a farm. He was the very first permanent settler on South Pender.

Initially, the settler lived in a log cabin, which he built on a site now known as *Ingos Corner*.

In the late 1880's, he hired a builder to construct a three-bedroom frame home that had three fireplaces. The house also had a large verandah that overlooked his farm. That same year, he brought his new wife to live in his home.

His wife was a good shot and would shoot at the deer if they ate the crops. She baked bread, and made butter, cottage cheese and preserves. When the grapes were ripe, she made wine. Whenever a pig was slaughtered, she rendered the lard, and cured hams and bacon.

The settler owned a library of 2,000 books. While he read, wrote poetry and sketched, his wife spun wool, which she then dyed by hand.

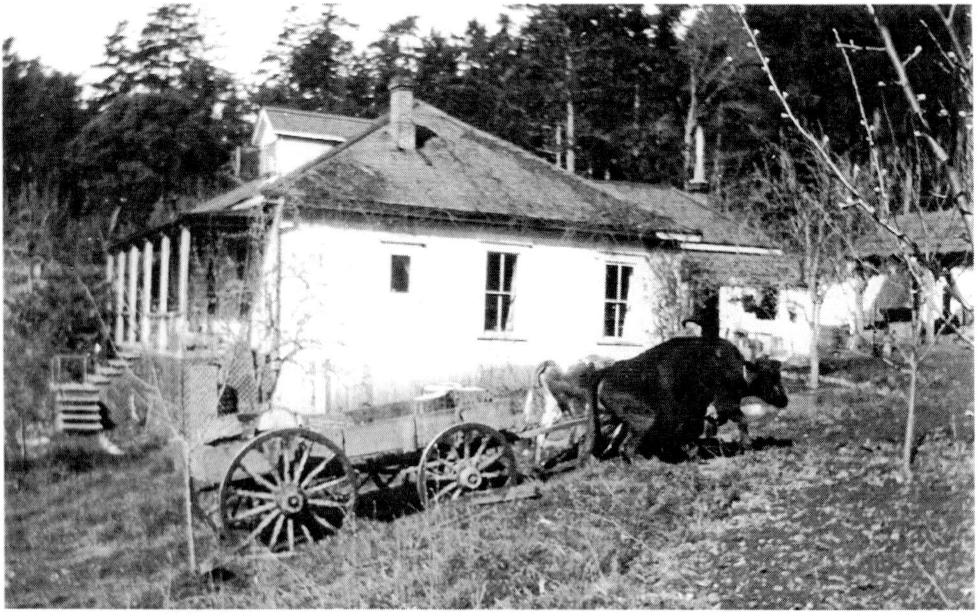

Home of the South Pender Postmistress in 1908 – David Spalding

At the turn of the century, a wharf was built in Bedwell Harbour. When the S.S. *Iroquois* began sailing through the Gulf Islands, the delivery of mail began once a week to the new wharf.

At that time, the settler's wife became the Postmistress for South Pender, sorting the mail at the end of the wharf.

Shortly thereafter, the crew of the HMS *Egeria* landed on the bay to study the tides. To carry out their duties, they built a small hut at the head of the wharf. When the crew departed three years later, the couple fell heir to the little building and converted it into the *South Pender Post Office*.

The delivery of mail to the post office developed into a weekly social event. The Postmistress would drive her horse and buggy from the farm to the post office, along a dangerous wagon road.

If the mail was late, the woman would often wait until after midnight for it to arrive. When the residents of South Pender turned up to discuss current events, she would serve them tea and cake.

In the 1930's, the little hut from which she performed her postal duties was removed from the wharf. Although her farm was sold a few years later, she continued to provide postal services to South Pender until her death in the 1950's.

Lilias Spalding Heritage Park was named after this pioneer woman, whose weaving loom can still be seen today at the Pender Islands Museum.

The old farm is known locally as 'The Ranch'. A short trail through Lilias Spalding Park leads to the remains of one of the buildings on The Ranch.

The ruts, which are reported to have been left in the field by the settler's wagon, can still be seen there. The trail through the park is accessible from Castle Road. (#32 on the map)

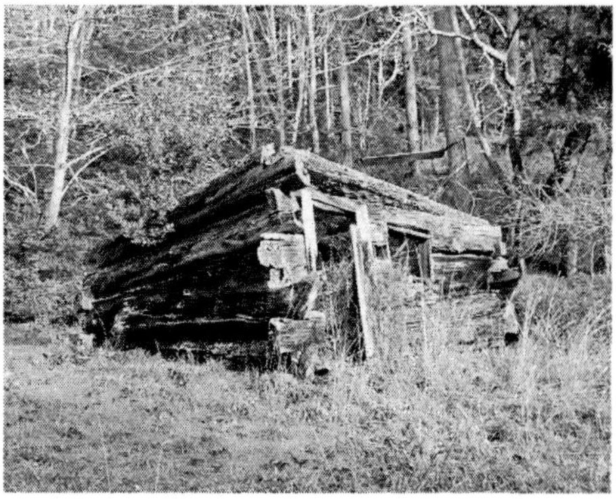

There is a steeper trail to the park, which is accessible from up the road. It leads to *Spalding Hill*, which provides for great views and beautiful rock faces, and is one of the best places in the Gulf Islands to see Turkey Vultures and Bald Eagles.

Little Bay

In the late 1880's, the first permanent Penderite was married on a Saturna Island ranch. His bride, who would later become the Postmistress for South Pender, wore a white satin dress that was custom-made in London.

After the wedding, the couple began their honeymoon by sailing home to South Pender in a war canoe. The father of the bride had hired two Indians to paddle it. Upon landing in a bay, they made their way through the woods to their new home.

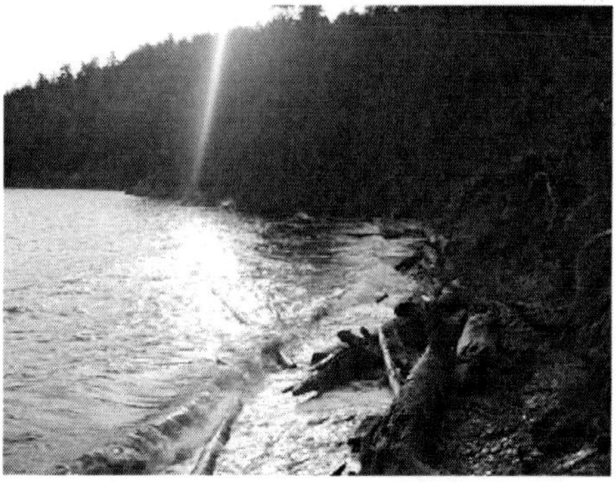

Little Bay, on the northeast side of South Pender, provides for views of Mount Warburton Pike on Saturna Island. The rocky beach on the bay is accessible by way of two flights of steep steps off Ancia Road. (#25 on the map)

Lively Peak Park

Lively Peak Park is located in the center of North Pender, in Magic Lake Estates. The park is accessible by way of a rough, steep trail off Ketch Road, which leads to a lovely viewpoint. (#35 on the map)

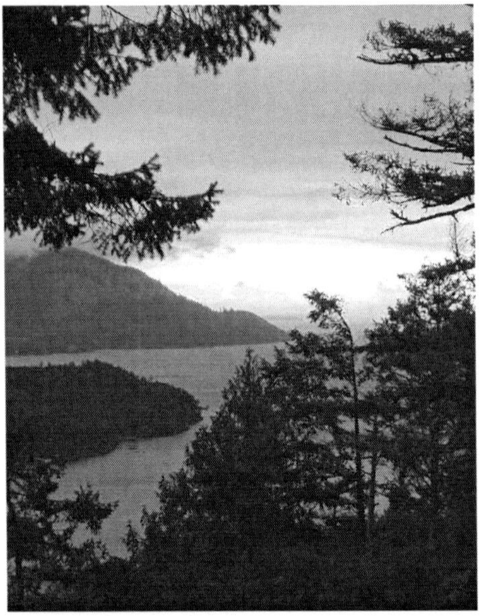

Magic Lake

Much of the population of the Pender Islands is concentrated around its most popular swimming hole. Originally named *Dead Cow Slough*, it is officially named *Pender Lake*, but is known locally as *Magic Lake*.

Magic Lake is located on the southwest side of North Pender, in Magic Lake Estates. It is accessible by way of Pirates Road. (#31 on the map) You can launch a boat in the lake and there are facilities for picnics along the shore if you want to stay awhile.

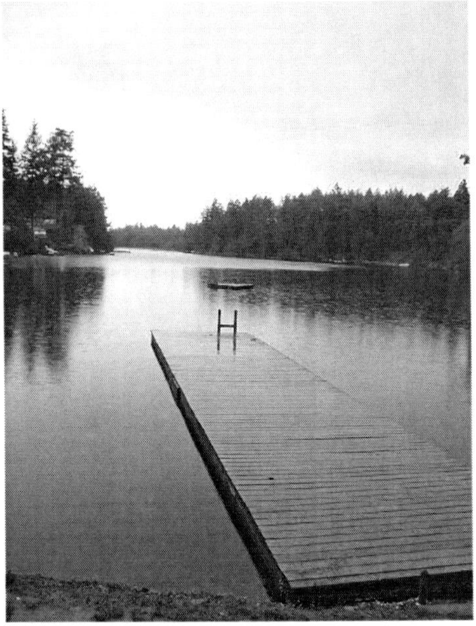

Medicine Beach

Medicine Beach is located at the north end of Bedwell Harbour. It contains low shell midden from the site of an ancient Coast Salish Indian settlement. The Pender Island Conservancy Association recently purchased the land as a wildlife sanctuary.

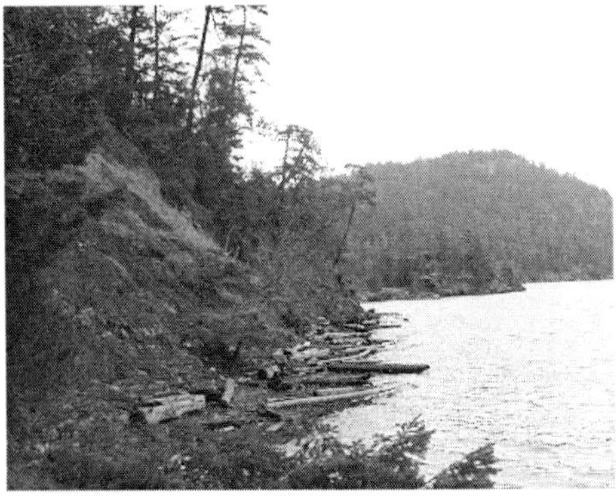

Two rare species of plants grow in this ecological reserve, which is now protected as one of the few remaining wetlands in the southern Gulf Islands. Great Blue Herons and Kingfishers are plentiful there, and there is also the occasional Osprey sighting.

There are three accesses to Medicine Beach; one is off Schooner Way and two are off Wallace Road. (#19 on the map) However, the beach is closed to the harvesting of scallops, mussels, oysters and clams.

Mortimer Spit Park

In the 1880's, the company who owned a quarry at the harbour on North Pender produced some of the stone that was used to build the tower of Holy Trinity Cathedral on the mainland.

Eventually, the company vacated the area and, when the canal was dredged between North and South Pender at the turn of the century, the dredging started at the site of the abandoned quarry.

Mortimer Spit is a sandbar on the most westerly tip of South Pender. Named after the company who owned the quarry, it provides for one of the best swimming and clam digging beaches on the Penders.

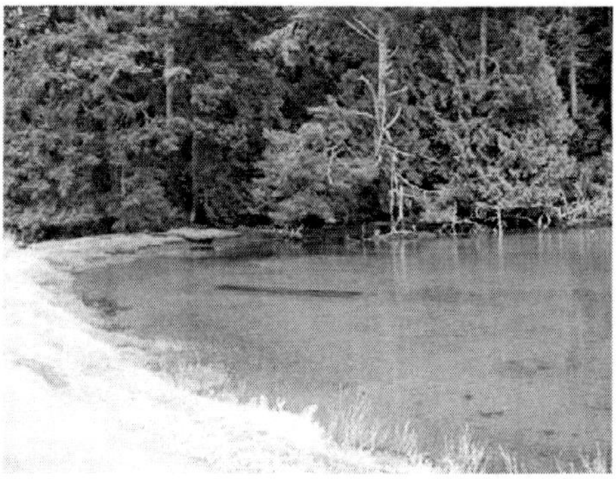

The spit sits in *Mortimer Spit Park*, which provides for views of Shark Cove. The spit and park are accessible by way of Canal Road. (#33 on the map)

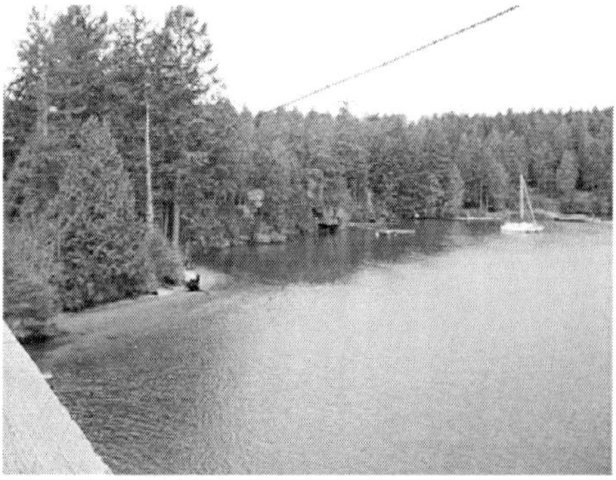

Mount Menzies Park

In the 1890's, **the Postman** ran an ad for a farm hand to help him farm his land. The settler who filled the position worked on the farm for three years. Later, he leased and then purchased his own farm, in a valley.

The settler bred award-winning poultry on his farm, which he initially called the *Nob Hill Poultry Farm*, but later renamed the *Valley Home Farm.* Later, when he won second prize for his Ayrshire bull at the Victoria Fair, the showing of cattle from around the Penders began.

The settler entered animals at all the major fairs in the provinces. All of his cattle were on the Record of Performance Test. The first few cows of that breed ever to pass the test in Canada were from his herd.

Soon, the settler purchased two Jersey cows and a bull, establishing a fine Jersey herd that also won numerous prizes. One year, he won first prize for the most milk and butterfat produced by a single cow in two days.

Mount Menzies was named after this settler, who lived on his farm for over 70 years. Originally named *Bald Cone*, the mountain is a 120 m peak on the east side of North Pender, which provides for great views of Mayne and Saturna Islands.

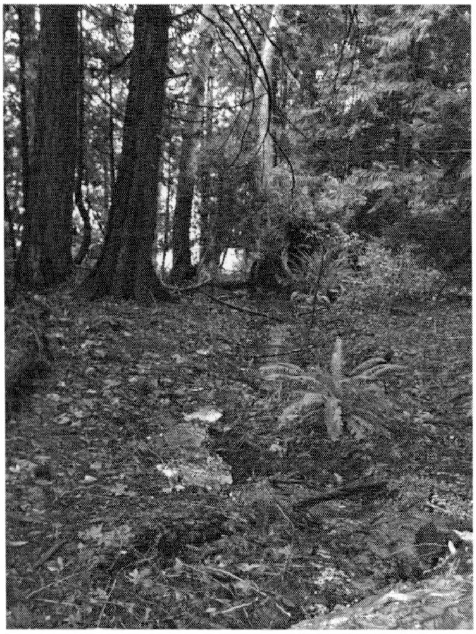

The peak sits in *Mount Menzies Park*, which is part of the Gulf Islands National Park Reserve. The park provides for 2 km of moderately difficult trails through beautiful, dense Western Red Cedar and Douglas-Fir. (#22 on the map)

Mount Norman Regional Park & Beaumont Provincial Marine Park

At the turn of the century, a settler wanted to transport a log house from Saturna Island to South Pender. So he arranged with a Captain to dismantle it, transport it, and then reassemble it. The Captain completed the task in less than two days. He later purchased the property.

Beaumont Provincial Marine Park was named after this Captain, who donated a portion of the land for its use. Established in the 1960's, it is one of the most popular marine parks in the outer Gulf Islands and is one of the best places to see Garry Oak trees.

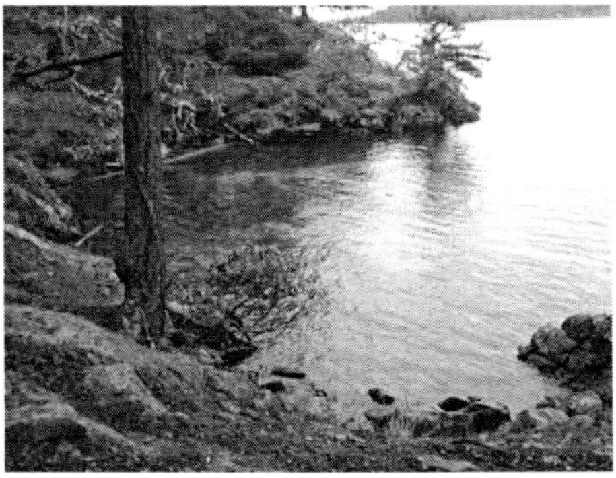

Beaumont Marine Park sits on Bedwell Harbour, which contains shell midden from a Coast Salish Indian *rancherie* (village). You can access the park by boat or from the edge of *Mount Norman Regional Park*. (#29 on the map)

Mount Norman Regional Park is connected to Beaumont Park. Acquired in the 1980's, it was the first regional park established in all the Gulf Islands.

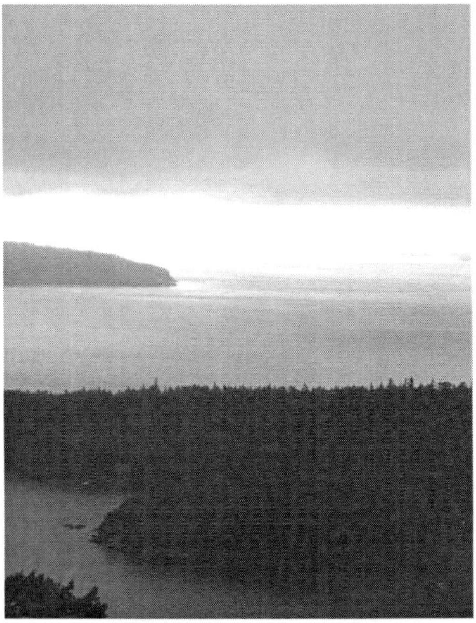

The moderately difficult trail through Mount Norman Park can be accessed from Ainslie Point Road. (#34 on the map) A longer, but more beautiful, trail can be accessed from Canal Road. (#23 on the map)

The two trails lead through second-growth forest to the top of *Mount Norman* and provide for one of the most beautiful hikes in all the Gulf Islands.

At 260 m, the mountain is the highest peak on the Penders and provides for incredible views of Vancouver Island and the San Juan Islands. From the summit, you can continue south to Beaumont Marine Park.

Oaks Bluff

Around the turn of the century, a Scottish stonecutter and his neighbor built a large fence on North Pender. The fence enclosed a bluff that was used for raising sheep at the time.

Several times a year, the settlers would hold a sheep run, herding the sheep from the bluff to the end of a point. The women and children would row to the end of the point to prepare a picnic lunch for when the men arrived.

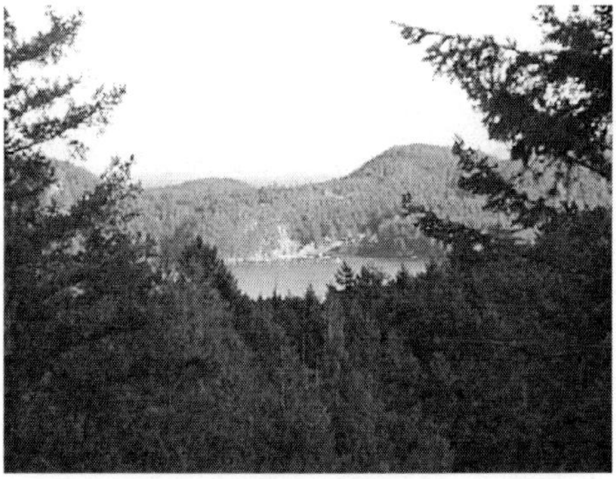

Oaks Bluff, at the south end of North Pender, overlooks Swanson Channel. Known locally as *The Oaks*, it is accessible by way of a steep trail on Pirates Road. The trail provides for spectacular panoramic views of Bedwell Harbour and Swanson Channel. (#17 on the map)

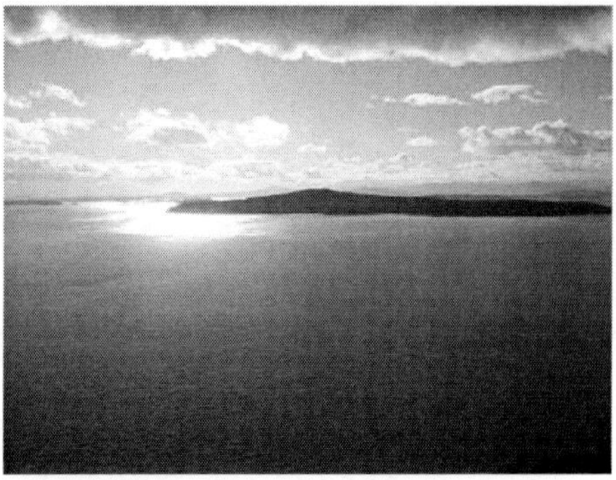

Panda Bay

Panda Bay is located on the west side of North Pender, in Magic Lake Estates. A trail off Harpoon Road leads to steps down to a sandy beach. (#13 on the map)

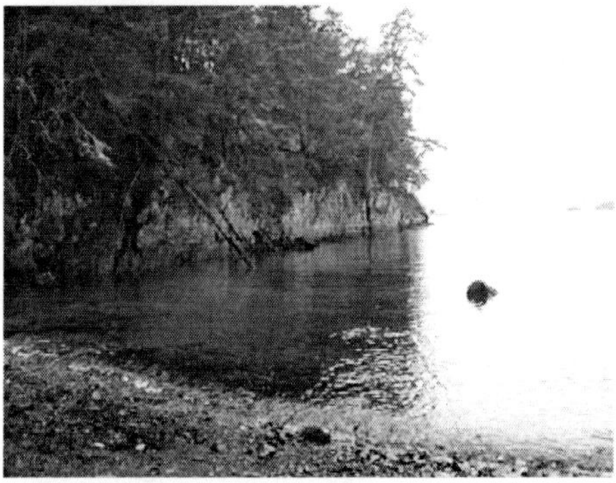

Prior Centennial Provincial Park

Set in the shade of a dense forest, *Prior Centennial Provincial Park* is located on the south end of North Pender. It is part of the Gulf Islands National Park Reserve.

There is a steep, 1 km trail through the park, which is called *Heart Trail*. Heart Trail connects to a network of other trails and is accessible by way of Ketch Road, in Magic Lake Estates. (#16 on the map)

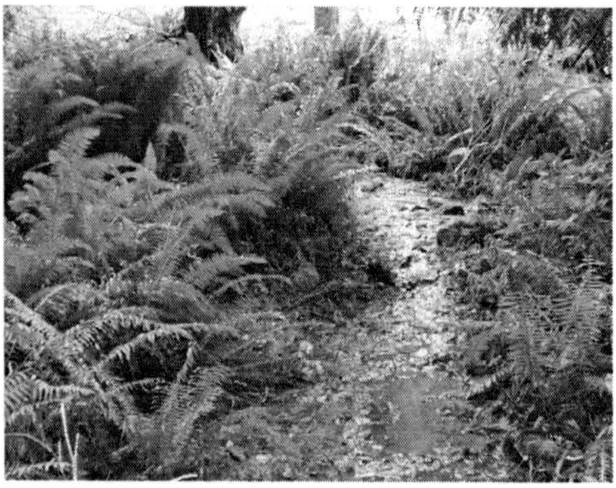

Roesland Park

When the Scottish family that established the Roesland Resort first settled on North Pender, they purchased the community hall that had been constructed on **the Postman`s** land, as well as an outbuilding that had originally been used as a school. Then, they moved the two buildings together to make themselves a home.

Roe Lake was named after this family. Located on the west side of North Pender, it is one of the only natural, freshwater lakes in the Gulf Islands and provides for secluded swimming.

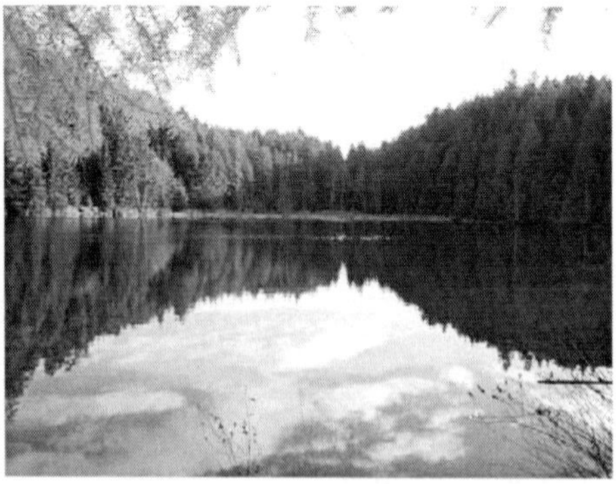

The easy 2 km trail to the lake wanders through second-growth forest. Walking south along the trail leads to the trail junction. At the junction, the trail to the left encircles the lake in a clockwise direction. The trail is accessible by way of Shingle Bay Road.

The lake sits in *Roesland Park*, which is dense with Western Red Cedar and Douglas-Fir, and contains a highly sensitive ecosystem.

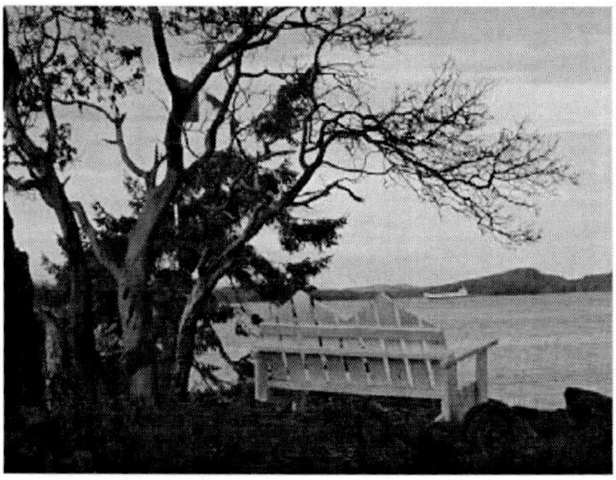

Established in the 1990's, Roesland Park is now protected as part of the Gulf Islands National Park Reserve. The family was granted a life-long tenancy on the property.

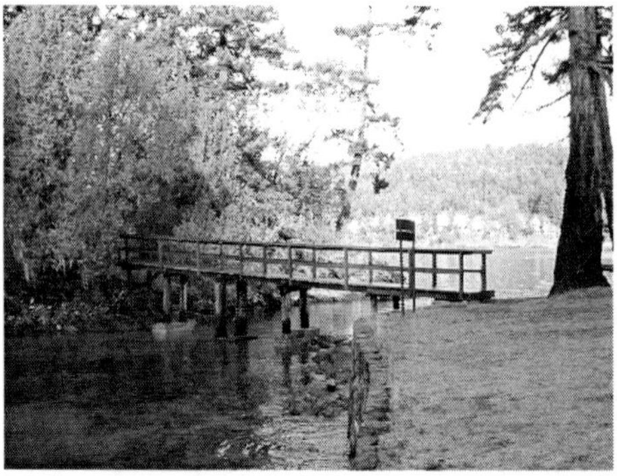

The easy 600 m trail through the park leads to a footbridge that extends to *Roe Islet*. The islet is a good place to see Arbutus trees. The trail is accessible by way of South Otter Bay Road. (#11 on the map)

Shingle Bay Park

At the turn of the century, two brothers purchased a portable sawmill and began to cut boards and shingles out of a fine stand of Western Red Cedar that grew behind a bay. Then, they built a scow and established the first mill ever to exist on the Pender Islands.

The brothers used a steam launch, called *Pearl*, to transport the lumber from the bay. It was the first powerboat ever used on the Penders.

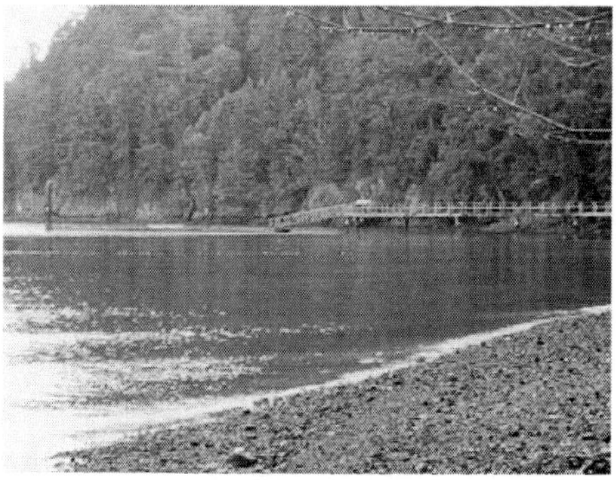

Shingle Bay is located on the west side of North Pender. It sits in *Shingle Bay Park*. The shady family park provides for playgrounds and there are facilities for picnics if you want to stay awhile.

The park and beach are accessible either from Galleon Way or by way of trails on Masthead Crescent and Yardarm Road. (#12 on the map)

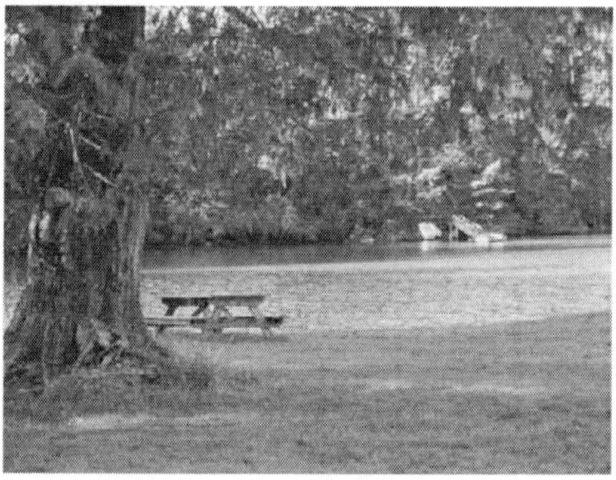

Susan Point

Susan Point, on the northern tip of North Pender, provides for a short trail that is accessible from Walden Road. (#1 on the map) The trail heads toward steps that lead down to a pebbled beach.

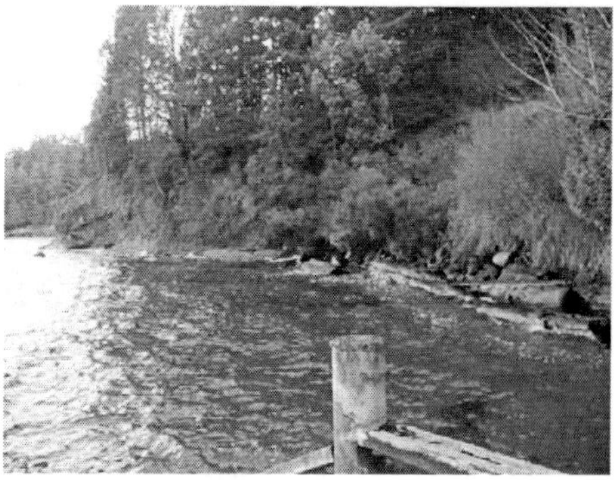

Teece Point

In the 1930's, The Ranch on South Pender was sold to a married couple who turned it into a thriving poultry business. Later, they sold the business to their son-in-law, but continued to live there as managers, running a herd of fine beef cattle.

Teece Point was named after this couple. Originally named *Blunden Point*, it is the most easterly tip of South Pender.

A short trail near the end of Boundary Pass Drive leads to steps that descend to the beach on the point. (#26 on the map) At low tide, you can walk to a small, rocky islet.

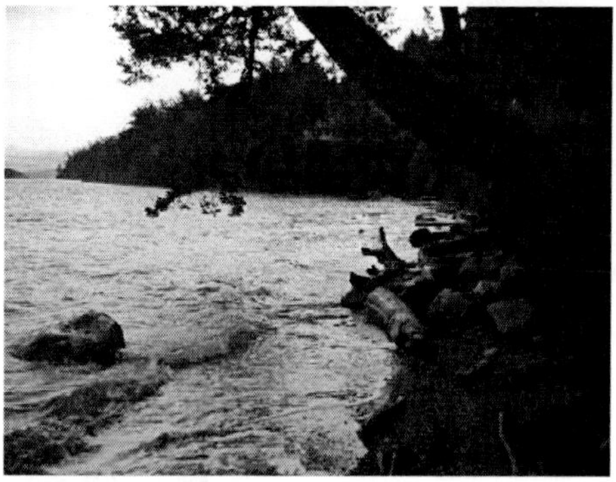

Thieves Bay Park

Around the turn of the century, the provincial police learned that two sheep rustlers were killing and salting down sheep on a bay. So the police rounded up a posse of settlers, gave them guns and ammunition and swore them in as special constables. Then, they all rowed to the bay to arrest the sheep rustlers.

When the posse arrived at the bay, they apprehended the two criminals and handcuffed them. After the settlers rowed home, the policeman removed the handcuffs from the prisoners and made them do the rowing to the *gaol* (jail) on Mayne Island.

Unfortunately, when they arrived on Mayne, the policeman made the mistake of getting out of the boat first and his prisoners seized the opportunity to push the boat away from the shore. Then, they quickly paddled into the Pass and were never seen again.

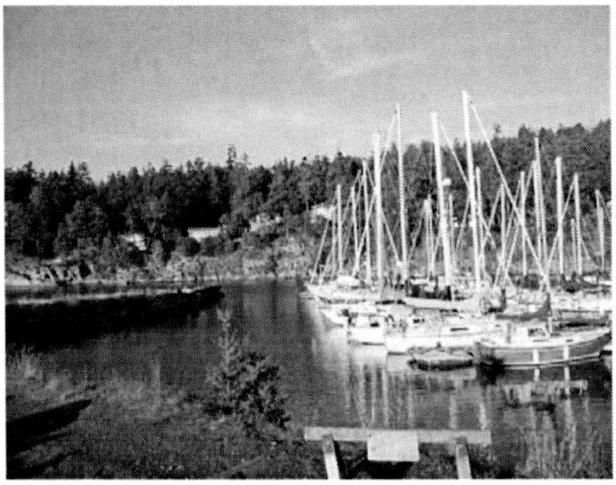

Thieves Bay is located on the west side of North Pender. It provides for a sandy beach and marina.

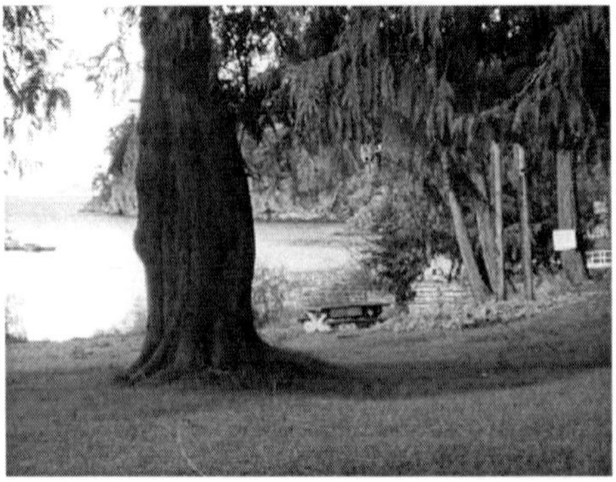

The bay sits in *Thieves Bay Park*. The recreational park provides for playgrounds and there are facilities for picnics if you want to stay awhile. The park and beach are accessible by way of two trails off Anchor Way. (#14 on the map)

Wallace Point

During Prohibition, a point on North Pender became a favorite rendezvous site for liquor runners. They would take shelter on the point whenever they transferred their illegal cargo to boats traveling across the U.S. border.

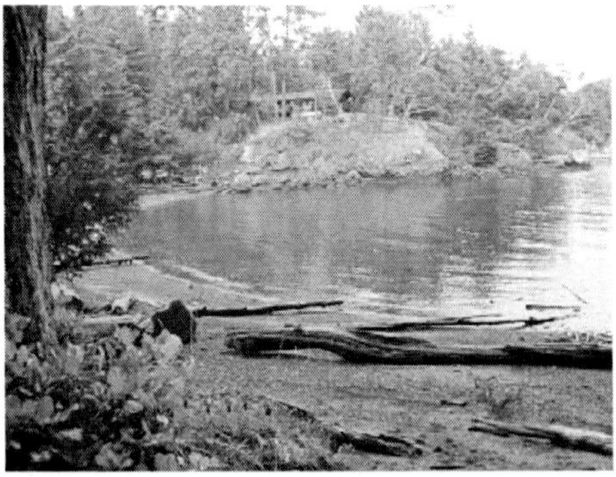

Wallace Point is the southernmost tip of North Pender. There are three sandy beaches at the end of this very lovely point. (#18 on the map) The beaches are accessible by way of Trincoma Place, Bedwell Drive and Plumper Way.

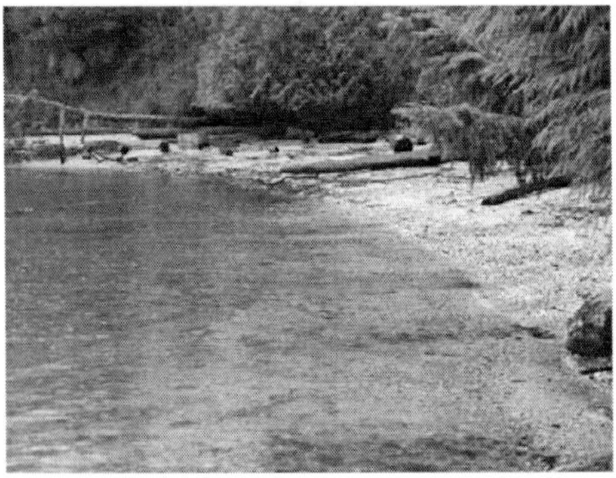

Welcome Bay

Welcome Bay is located on the northeast side of North Pender. It provides for views of tiny Fane Island. A trail off Clam Bay Road leads to steps down to a pebbled beach on the bay. (#4 on the map)

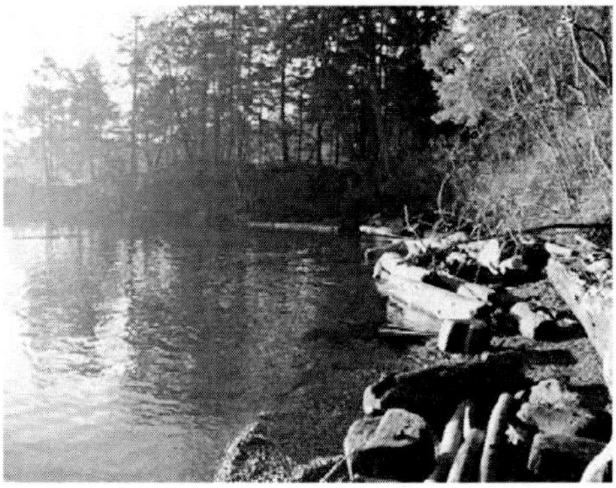

Galiano Island

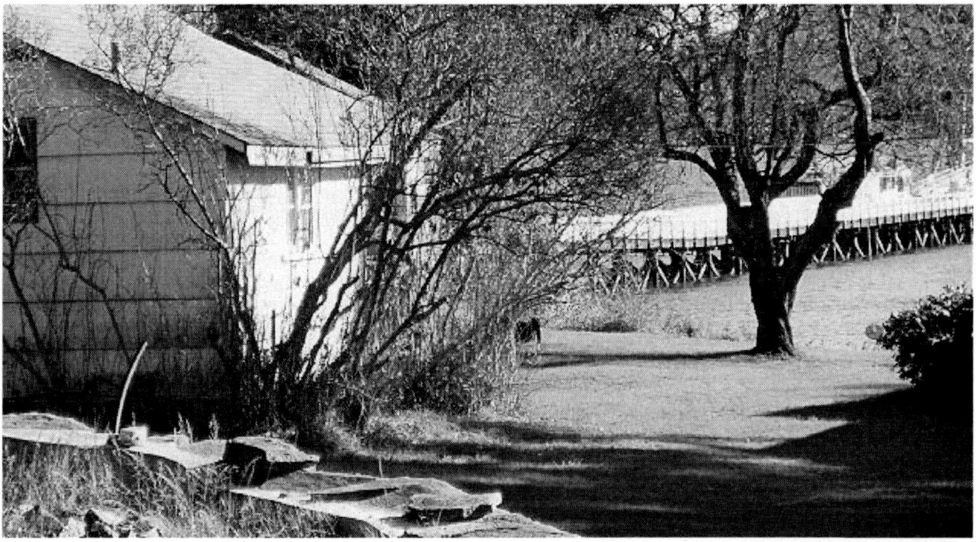
Sturdies Bay Wharf

It was in 1901 that an Englishman, named Stanley Page, came to Galiano Island and was given a portion of his father's land...

Stanley Page was born in the 1880's and emigrated with his family, from England to Canada. At the turn of the century, they moved to Galiano Island.

In the year 1910, Stanley's mother passed away, leaving him and his siblings to be raised by his father, alone. Two years later, Stanley built a home on his portion of the property and brought his bride to live there with him.

In the 1920's, Mr. Stanley Page became **the Postman** for South Galiano. Using a horse and a boat, he moved a little building onto his ranch. It was from there that he operated the post office.

In the 1940's, he became Galliano's only taxi driver. After 30 years of service, he retired at age 89, as the oldest taxi driver in all of Canada. He and his wife had lived on the same property for 60 years.

Later, when speaking about how his father had felt about delivering the mail during his youth, one of his sons had this to say about him:

"Dad was much happier working his farm, or building local houses and bridges."
Kenneth Page

Things to Know

Galiano is a friendly island. At 57 sq km, it is the second largest of the southern Gulf Islands. While shell beaches and endless forest drives are its most distinguishing characteristics, the lively, spirited people give Galiano Island its unique charm.

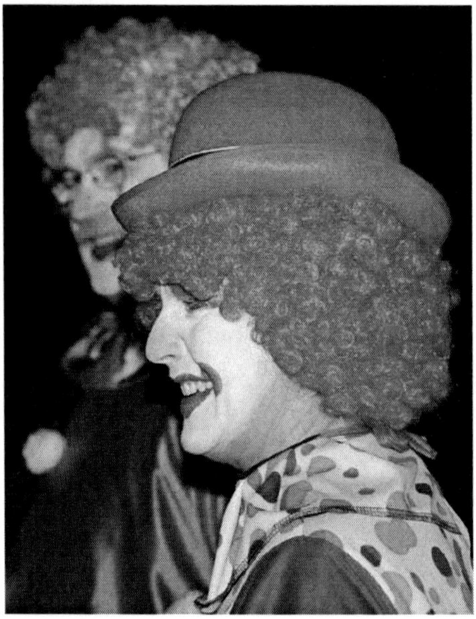

Called *The Jewel of the Strait of Georgia*, Galiano holds claim to having one of the largest provincial parks in all the Gulf Islands. Almost 75 percent of Galiano falls within a tree farm license held by British Columbia's forestry giant.

Galiano has a population of just over 1,000 permanent residents, a large percentage of which are over 55 years of age and retired.

Most of the residents live at the south end, where most of the services and facilities are located. During the tourist season, the population swells to around 4,000.

Sturdies Bay

Residential development began on South Galiano in the 1860's, along the waterway that is officially called *Active Passage*, but was then known locally as *Plumper Pass*. The community that developed was named *Sturdies Bay*, in honor of a family who settled there.

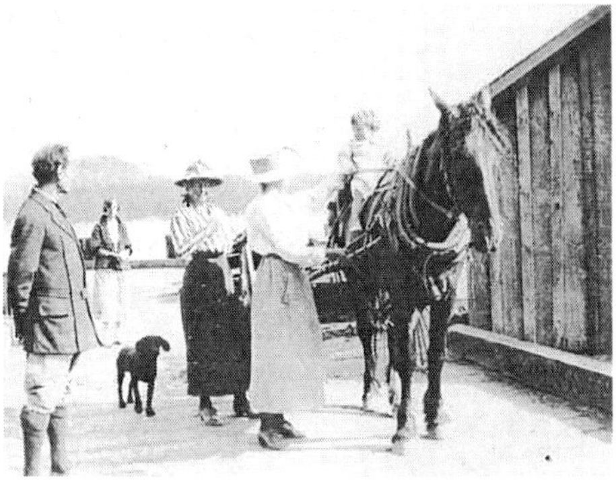

Early settlers on Galiano
Galiano Archives 2004026505

Over the next 60 years, the community at the north end of the Island also began to develop.

By the 1920ès, North Galiano had become one of the most prosperous communities in all the Gulf Islands, growing to several thousand people during the fishing season.

In the late 1940's, South Galiano acquired its own power company. However, because of the tree farm that exists between the north and south ends of the Island, power was not extended to North Galiano until the 1960's.

By then, the communities on South Galiano had become more populous than those on North Galiano.

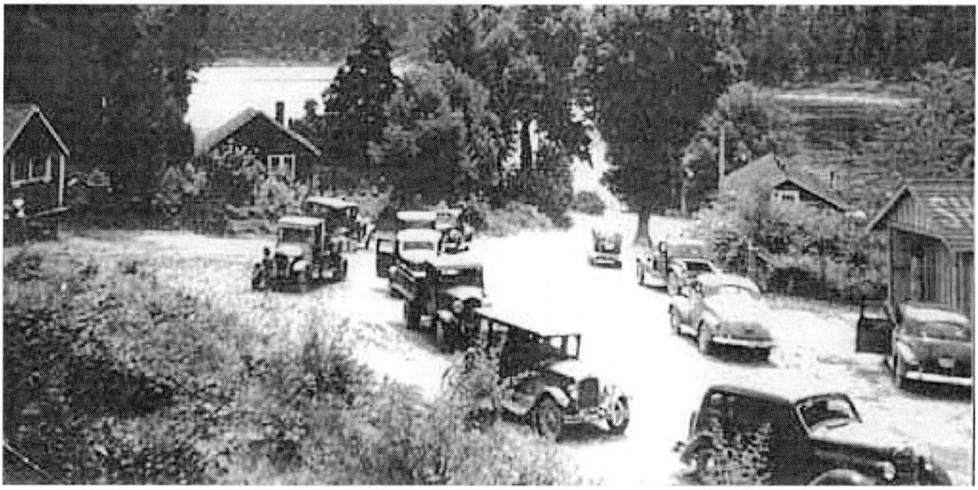

Sturdies Bay in the 1940's – Galiano Archives 2004026512

In the 1970's, South Galiano experienced a population explosion. However, when the last cannery on North Galiano closed, only about a dozen families lived there.

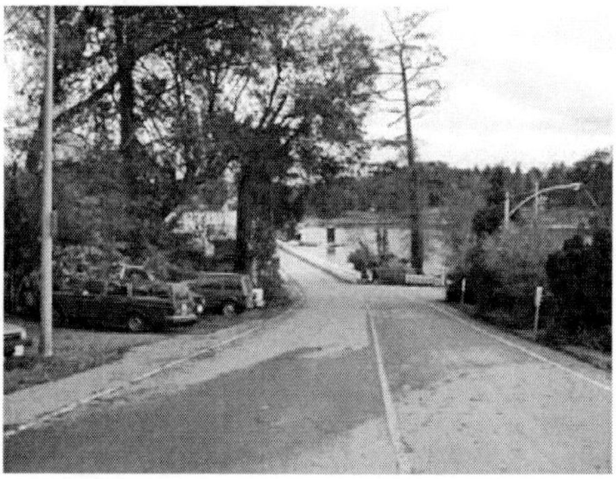

Sturdies Bay as it appears today

Today, Sturdies Bay, on South Galiano, is 'downtown' to the Island residents. It is a seaside village where the residents and businesses co-exist.

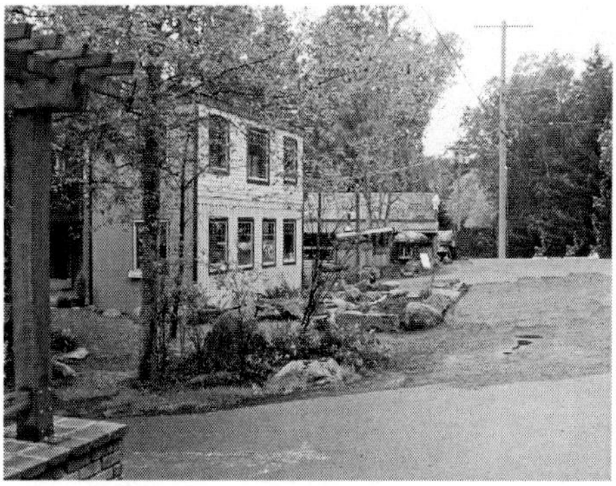

Sturdies Bay Wharf

At the turn of the century, a wharf was built at Sturdies Bay. The wharf accommodated ships coming through Active Pass.

There was no railing along the sides of the wharf at that time. Unfortunately, one day, a team of horses, which was pulling a wagonload of bricks, bolted, and then fell overboard and drowned.

Later, in the 1950's, a new wharf was built, to accommodate the ship named *Princess Elaine*. It was built beside the original wharf so the piles could be driven deeper into the ocean floor.

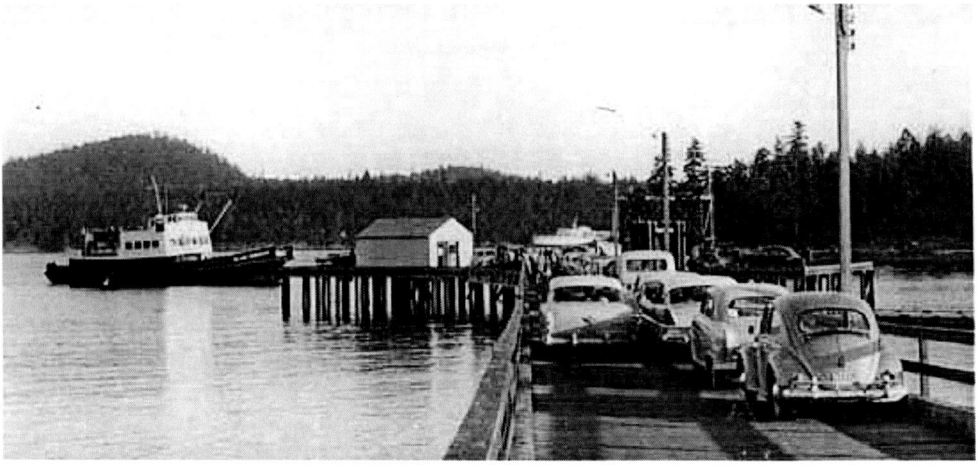

Sturdies Bay wharf in the late 1950's - Galiano Archives 2004026519

A decade later, a ferry linking the mainland to neighboring Salt Spring Island was introduced, making Galiano more accessible to Vancouver Island and the mainland.

Today, British Columbia Ferry Services uses the land at Sturdies Bay to operate scheduled ferry services from both the mainland and Vancouver Island.

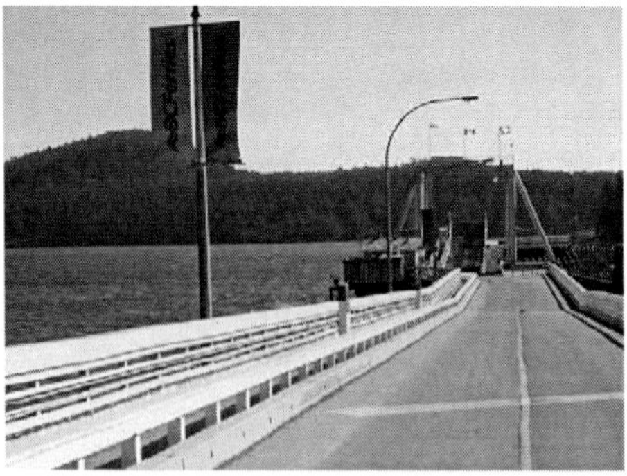

Sturdies Bay wharf as it appears today

Galiano Island Post Office

Before the turn of the century, steamer ships delivered the mail to Salt Spring Island, and then it was delivered to neighboring Mayne Island.

The first *North Galiano Post Office* was operated from a house near a bay on North Galiano.

Once a month, an Indian, who called himself 'Captain Peatson', would row to Salt Spring in a canoe and pick up the mail addressed to 'North Galiano'. Later, when steamers began to dock in the bay, the mail was retrieved from the crew.

Initially, residents of South Galiano would row to Mayne Island to collect their mail. By the turn of the century, a steamer ship began to deliver mail once a week to the Sturdies Bay wharf.

Soon, the *South Galiano Post Office* began to operate from various homes at the south end.

At that time, there was only a cow trail running between the north and south ends of the Island.

If a settler on South Galiano had a package to send to North Galiano, he would use an axe to pin instructions to a tree at the south end of the trail and the next settler on route to North Galiano would carry the instructions on foot or by horseback.

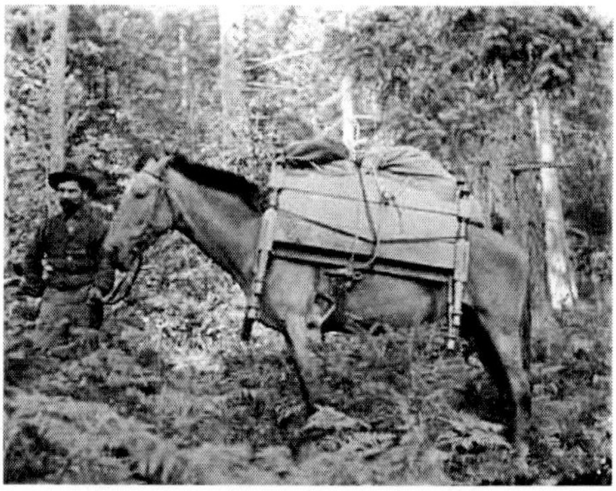

Pack horse at the turn of the century
Galiano Archives M005

By the early 1920`s, mail had ceased to be delivered to North Galiano by steamer. It was simply transferred there once a week from South Galiano. Much later, the house that served as the first North Galiano Post Office was demolished, along with some priceless letters.

In the late 1920's, postal service for South Galiano was transferred to **the Postman** who performed his duties from a little, shingled, post office building on his ranch.

Shortly thereafter, the Royal Canadian Legion decided that a war veteran should fill the position. So **the Postman** lost the post.

Today, the little post office building that was used by **the Postman** still stands in a backyard on Georgeson Bay Road.

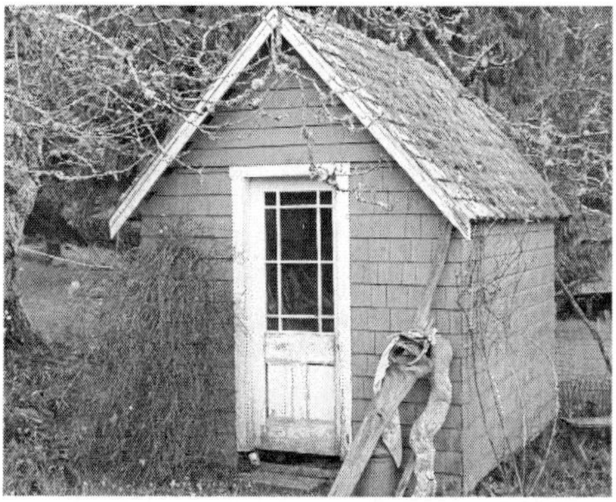

Soon, the South Galiano Post Office was moved again, to a house that was located about 5 km from the wharf. It was the fifth building to which it had been moved.

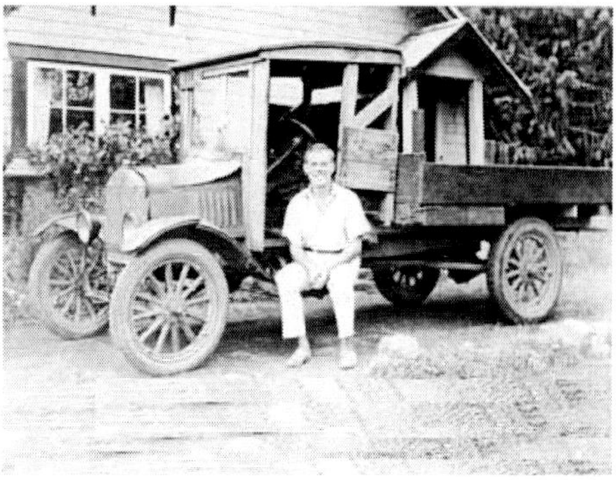

South Galiano Post Office, in the 1930's
Galiano Archives 2004020037

The house had originally been a barn. Postal services were performed from a room on the right-hand side of the house. It was entered by way of a little door.

The house served as the fifth post office for several years. It was eventually passed down to a descendant and still stands on Georgeson Bay Road today.

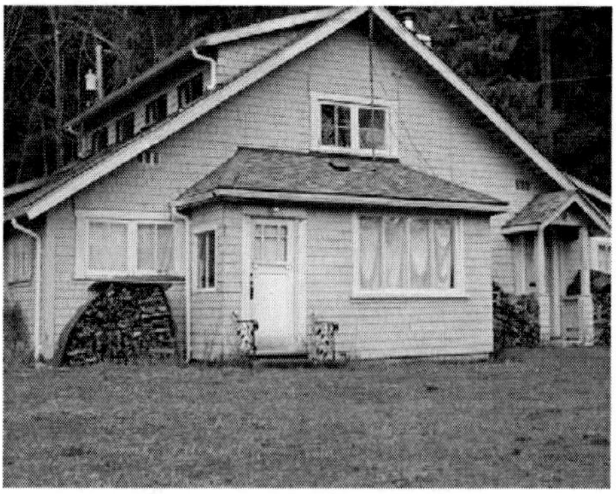

Old South Galiano Post Office
as it appears today

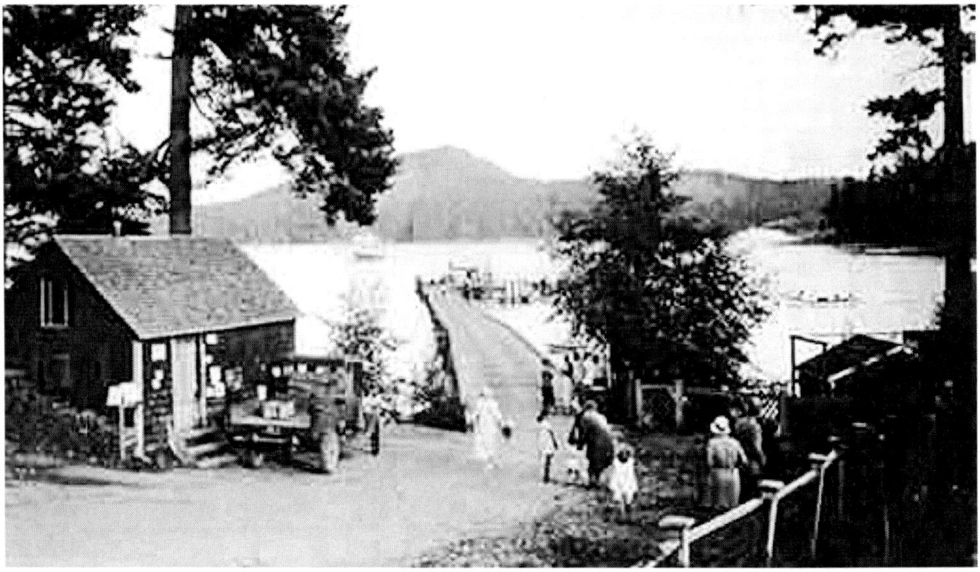

Sorting office at the Sturdies Bay wharf in the 1930's - Galiano Archives M309

In the 1930's, a small building was set up at the Sturdies Bay wharf, for use as a mail sorting office.

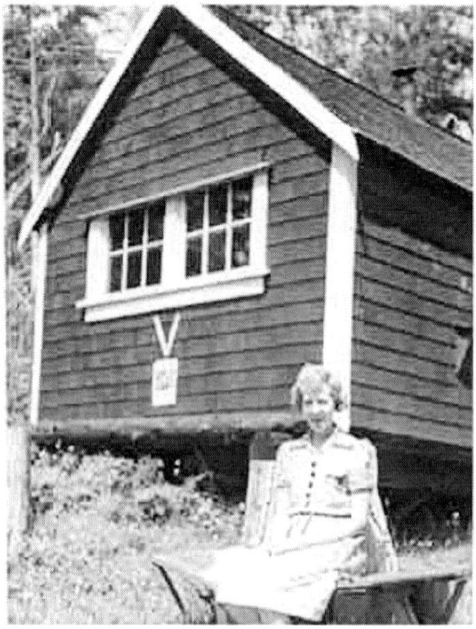

Sorting Office in the 1940's
Donald New 2004020078

The sorting office building was opened an hour before the mail was due to arrive and the settlers would stand and wait at a counter for their envelopes and parcels to be dispatched.

One day, after 15 years of sitting at the wharf, the sorting office building vanished. It was eventually located on another road, where a road crew had moved it.

The following day, it was moved near Sturdies Bay Road, where it remained for two years.

In the 1960's, the government built a little post office out of bricks at Sturdies Bay. It operated until the 1990`s when it was sold. The post office was then moved further north, to a market.

Today, the little brick building at Sturdies Bay operates as an antique and gift store, and the *Galiano Island Post Office* sits in a storefront across the road.

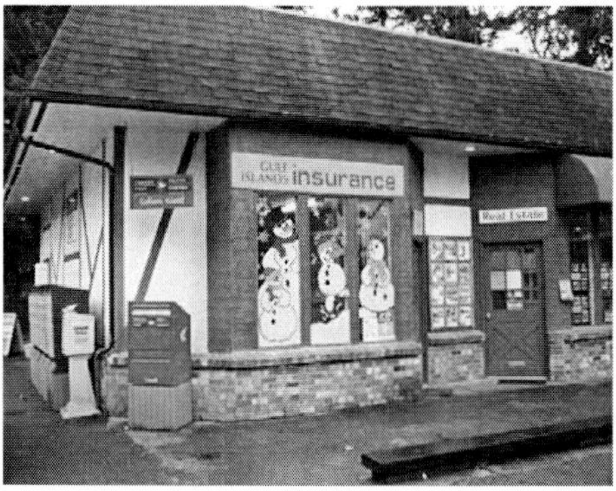

North Galiano Community Hall

During World War I, a log schoolhouse was built on North Galiano. It was called the *North-End School.*

In the 1920's, the owner of a marine shop built a frame building beside the log schoolhouse. It was called the *North Galiano School*. For the most part, it replaced the log schoolhouse, maintaining an enrollment of about 24 students.

When the Retreat Cove School closed in the late 1930's, the schoolchildren were transferred to the North Galiano School. Their parents rented a cabin for the students to live in while they attended school there.

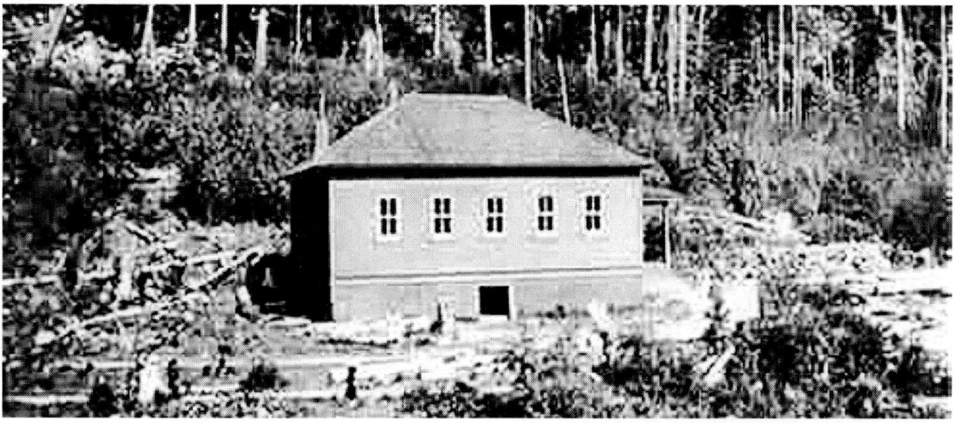

North Galiano Community Hall in the 1930's - Galiano Archives M204

A decade later, the North Galiano School had four additional windows added to provide more light. In order for them to fit, they had to be placed in a staggered formation between the existing windows. This gave the building a unique characteristic.

When the North Galiano School closed in the 1950's, the schoolchildren were transferred to a school on South Galiano. In the 1970's, the North Galiano School became the home of the *North Galiano Community Hall*.

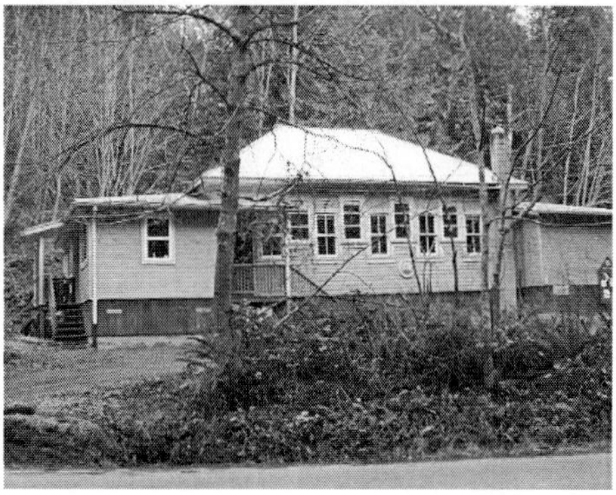

North Galiano Hall as it appears today

Today, the North Galiano Community Hall is host to many events, including the annual *Canada Day Jamboree*. It is located on Porlier Pass Road.

Galiano Community Hall

In the 1920's, **the Postman** donated some land for the building of a community hall on South Galiano. Upon completion, it was called the *Galiano Community Hall*.

The hall had a closed porch with a gable. There was a lean-to kitchen with a wood stove at one end and two dressing rooms at the back.

A big steel drum between the windows generated heat. Light was provided by old Coleman mantle lanterns that hung off the walls and from the ceiling.

The official opening of the community hall was a celebration. Special guests received a royal welcome at the wharf as they arrived by boat.

In the 1930`s, the hall was enlarged so that, during the winter, it could accommodate badminton matches and other events. Later, in the 1960`s, heaters were installed in the hall, followed by indoor plumbing.

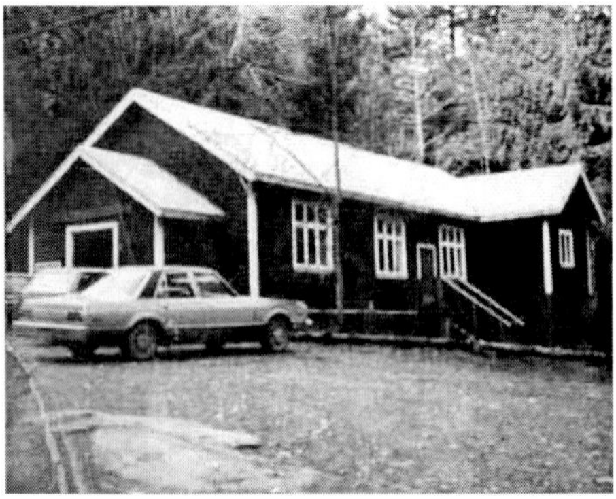

Galiano Community Hall in the 1970's
Galiano Archives M103

Today, the Galiano Community Hall serves as a venue for various events. It is located on Sturdies Bay Road.

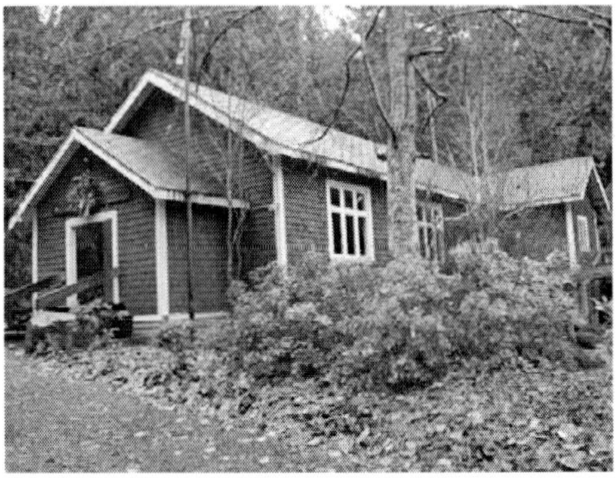

Galiano Community Hall as it appears today

Daystar Market

In the 1980`s, a painter moved to Galiano where he and his partner spent a week painting a large mural of a garden on the side of a mobile market. Later, the market housed the post office.

Today, the market is called the *Daystar Market*. It provides for fresh organic and conventional produce, specialty, health and grocery items, as well as movie rentals. It is located on Georgeson Bay Road.

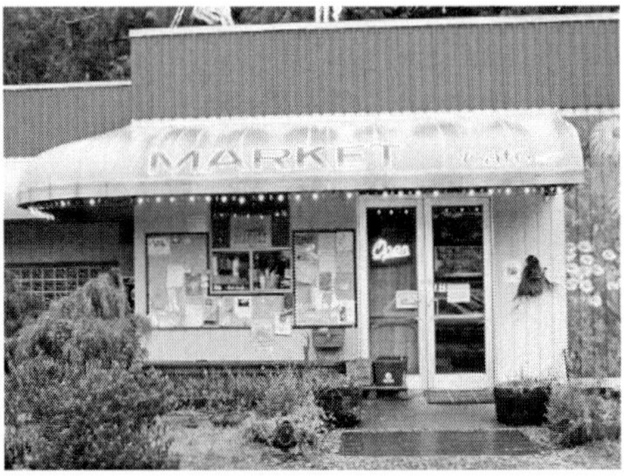

The Corner Store

In the 1970's, a general store was built in a central location on South Galiano.

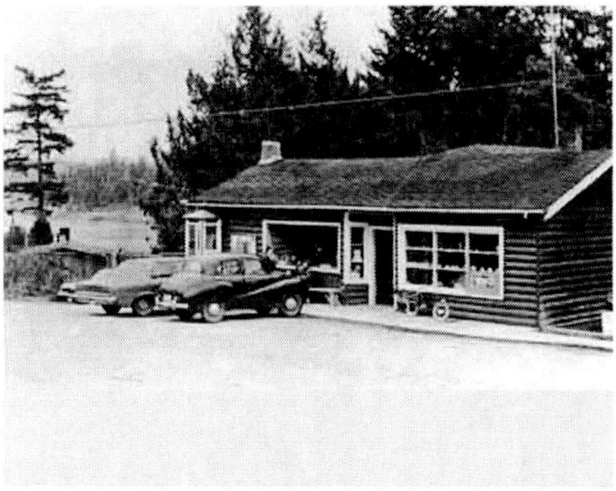

Corner Store, 1970's Galiano Archives M065

Today, the store is called *The Corner Store*. It operates as a grocery, liquor and drug store. Located on Georgeson Bay Road, it also provides for movie rentals.

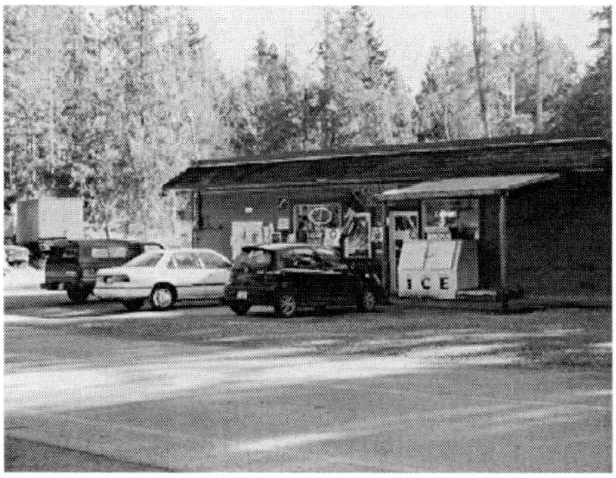

Corner Store as it appears today

Galiano Garage & Groceries

During World War I, it was not unusual to meet what appeared to be a driverless horse and wagon, only to find that the driver was resting on the floor of the wagon, while his horse navigated his way down the road.

At that time, a horse-drawn carriage with a coachman's box was often seen driving down the Island roads. The carriage was called a 'Victoria'. The settler who owned it had it shipped from England, where it had been driven on London's Rotton Row.

In the 1920's, gasoline-powered engines were introduced to Galiano. Within a few years, there were five Model 'T' Fords being driven around the Island. They put an end to the sight of the Victoria on the road.

Today, you can gas up your *chikchik* (wagon) at *Galiano Garage and Groceries*. In addition to gasoline, you can also purchase groceries and rent movies there. The station is located at Sturdies Bay.

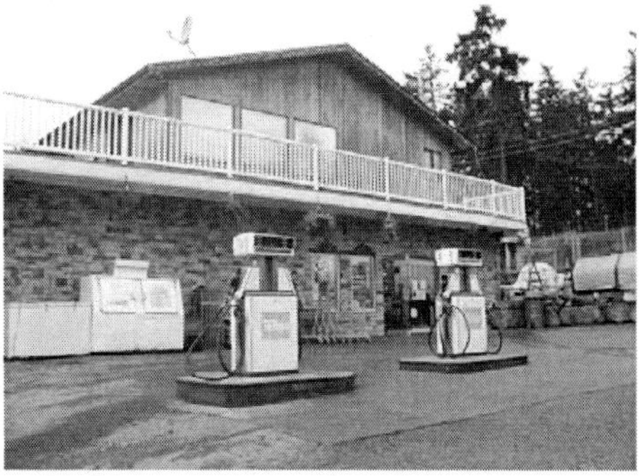

Galiano Island Skate Park

Recently, a skate park was built on Galiano. An old B.M.X. racetrack was used in the construction. The cement finishers who constructed the park stayed awake all night because the cement refused to harden.

Galiano Island Skate Park is located in Galiano Lions Park on Burrill Road. To help pay for the park, a music CD, called 'The Galiano Collection', was recorded by the Island's top musicians.

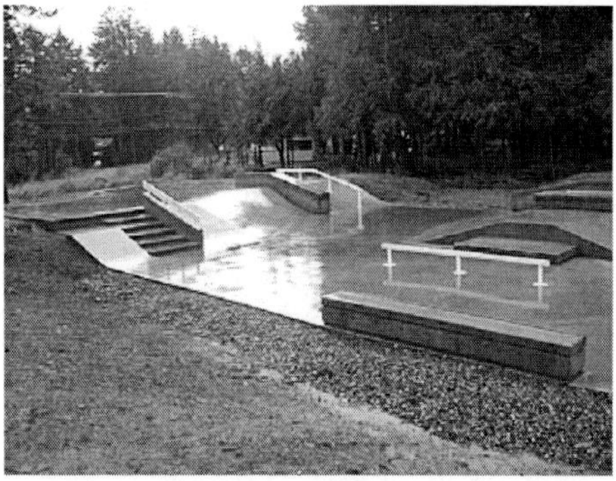

Galiano Island Golf & Country Club

Just before the onset of World War I, the settler who drove the horse-drawn Victoria carriage built a house on his farm. The house had a square roof.

In the late 1930's, the house was used as a clubhouse for the first Galiano golf club. A decade later, it was traded for a Jersey cow, and then dismantled.

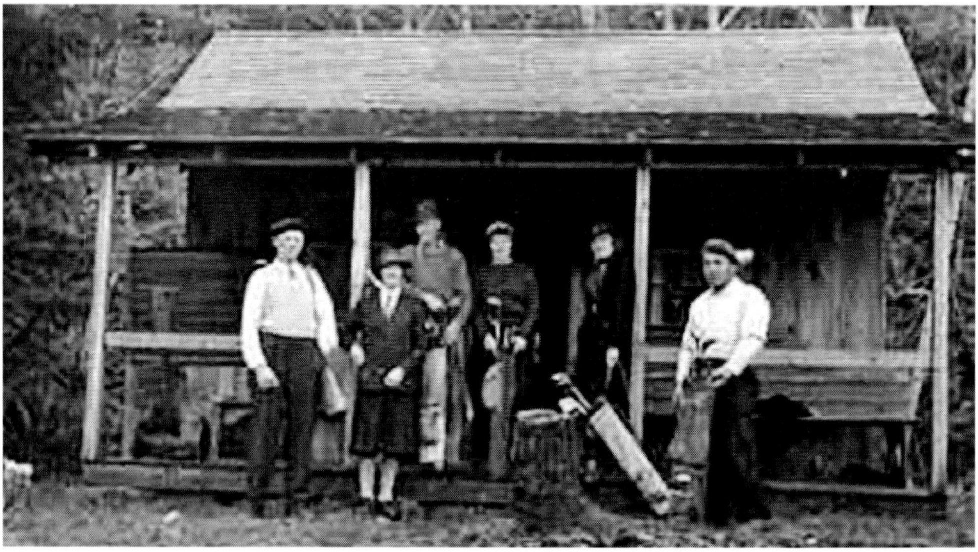

Golf Clubhouse in 1940 – Galiano Archives 2004020057

Today, the farm is the site of the *Galiano Island Golf and Country Club*. It offers a challenging 9-hole golf course that features unique sandstone tee markers. Carts and golf clubs are available for rent at the club, which is located on St. Andrews Drive.

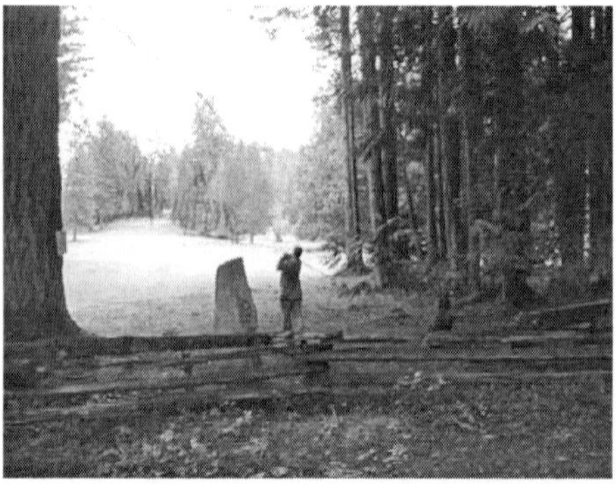

First Nations Reserve

Initially, an Indian village that belonged to the *Penelakut* Band resided on a point on North Galiano, called Virago Point. The small *rancherie* (village) was named *xínepsem* (caught by the neck). It consisted of a few permanent houses, which were occupied mainly in the summer for gathering food.

Today, the Penelakut First Nation accounts for about 13 percent of the entire *Hul'qumi'num* Indian population. The land on Virago Point is still owned by the band and permission must be attained prior to hiking it.

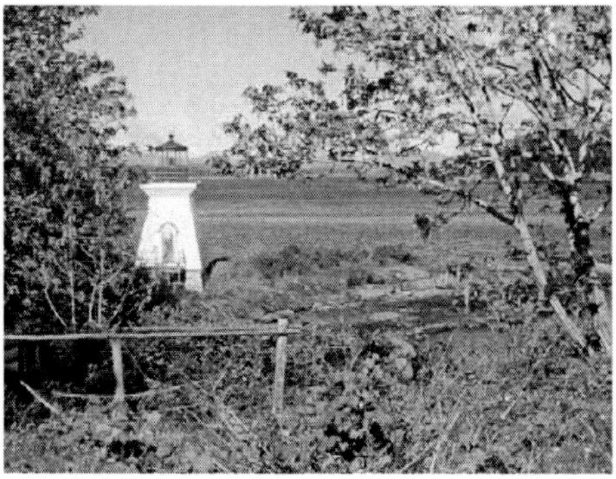

Galiano Island Bank

The *Galiano Island Bank* might never be built. However, at the time of this writing, there were Automated Teller Machines (ATM's) at the Montague Marina Grocery, the Corner Store, Galiano Garage and Groceries, and the Hummingbird Inn Pub.

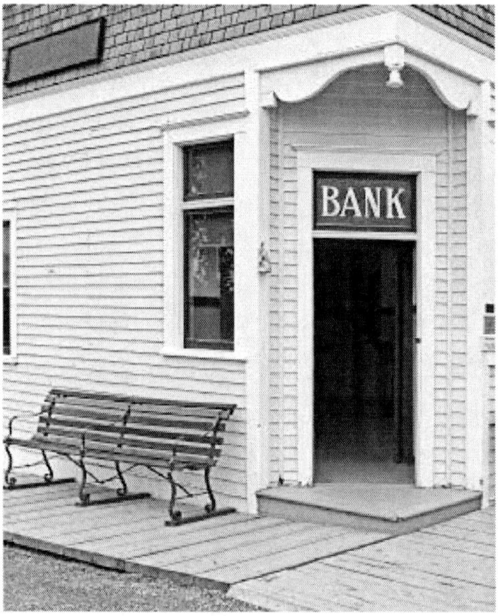

Not the Galiano Island Bank

Active Pass Caboose Cottage

In the 1970's, a turn-of-the-century Canadian Pacific Railway caboose was barged to Galiano from the mainland. She was then restored and converted into a cottage, complete with a miniature train station.

Today, the caboose is a cottage rental, called the *Active Pass Caboose*. It is located on South Galiano, on Mary Anne Road.

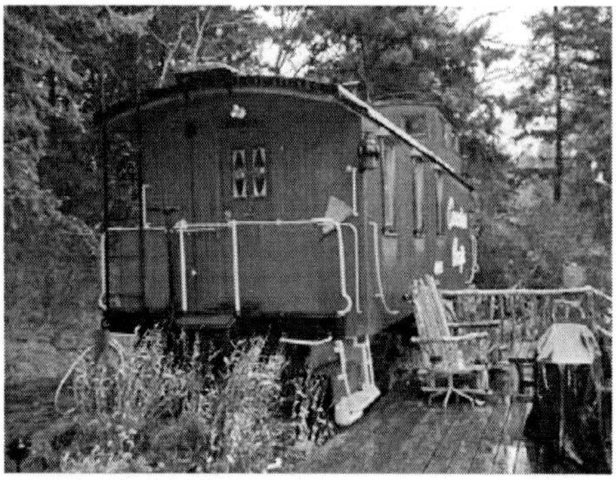

Bellhouse Inn

At the turn of the century, a settler wearing a Stetson hat came to Galiano, where he purchased a farm called *Active Pass Stock Ranch*. On the farm was a little log home, which he enlarged to accommodate his growing family.

In the 1920's, his son took over the house and farm. With the help of his stepmother, he converted the house into a nine-bedroom lodge, called the *Farmhouse Inn*.

The lodge had a main dining room. To polish the dining room floor, it became the custom for one person to sit on a pair of old long johns, while the other family members spun them around.

Guests of the lodge arrived by steamer and were brought from the wharf to the lodge in a converted fishing boat. When there was no vacancy at the Inn, they were put up on a point, in tents that had wooden floors and walls.

The guests were free to explore the farm and often helped with the haying. The son would use his steam launch to take them on errands to the wharf or to the other Islands.

A few years after it opened, the lodge caught fire. The son ran through the building in search of people who might need rescuing. When he found no one inside, he seized a vase on his way out. It was the only item that was saved from the fire. Subsequently, the Inn was destroyed and a new building had to be constructed.

The new home had more bedrooms, and a larger kitchen and dining room. It had its own power plant and was the first home on Galiano ever to receive electricity.

For many decades, the son and his own family operated the Inn. Their boats, the *Betsy Prig* and the *Betsy*, took guests to and from the wharf.

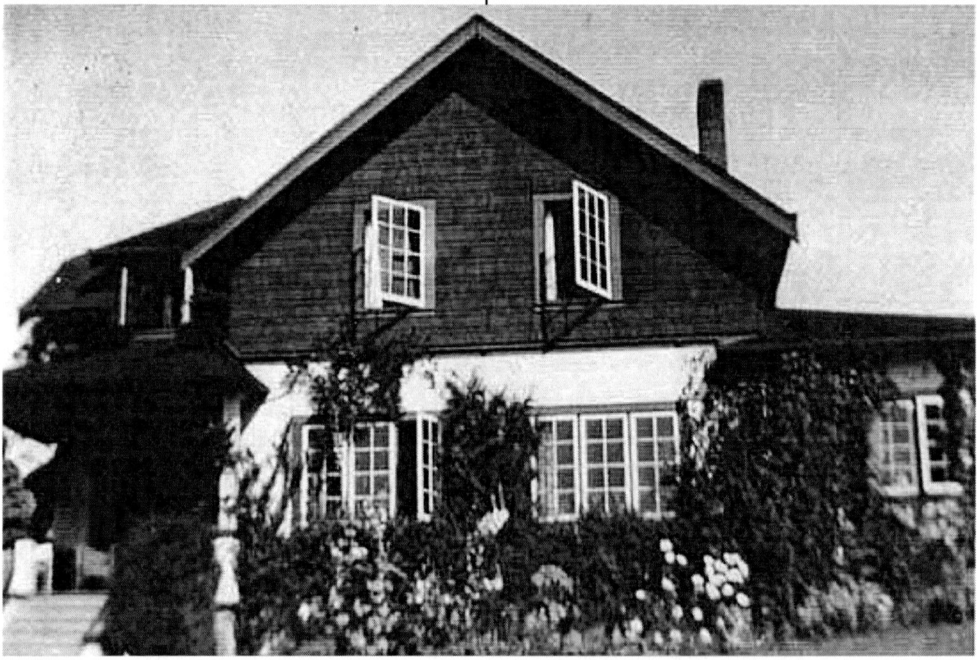

The Bellhouse Inn in the 1950's - Galiano Archives 2004026107

The property was sold in the 1960's. The new owners used the house as their private residence.

In the 1990's, a couple purchased the property and renovated it. Then, they reopened it as the *Bellhouse Inn*.

Today, the Bellhouse Inn is operated as a bed and breakfast. The B&B is located on the southern shore of South Galiano, on Bellhouse Road.

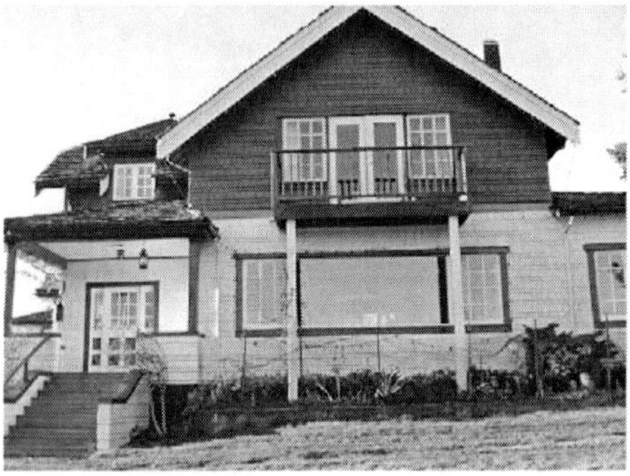

The Bellhouse Inn as it appears today

Galiano Inn & Spa

In the 1920's, an English family built a large, Elizabethan-style house at Sturdies Bay. They called it *Dunromin*.

A decade later, an English seaman purchased the home and ran it as a resort. He renamed it *Greenways*.

The resort served as the location for many parties, prospering until the end of World War II when new owners subdivided and sold the property. At that time, it was renamed the *Galiano Lodge*.

The main floor of the lodge consisted of a large living room. It led off a spacious entrance that had a wide Oak staircase. On the second floor were eight bedrooms, as well as a large bathroom with an extra large bathtub.

The grounds, which had extensive rockwork, had been designed to simulate an English courtyard. There was also a riding stable and a tennis court.

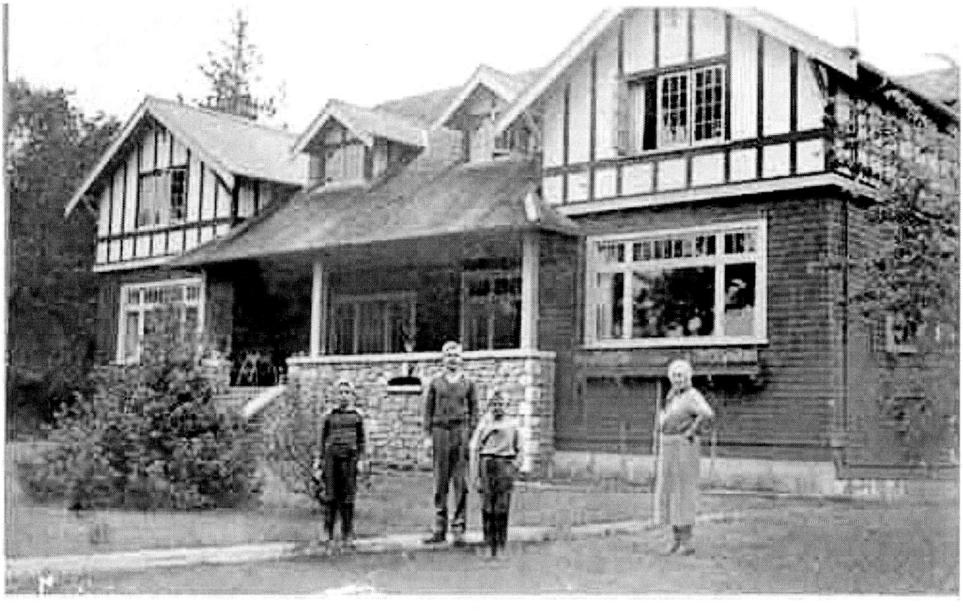

Galiano Inn & Spa in the 1930's - Galiano Archives 2004021043

Because the main attraction to the lodge was the fishing, the owners built a wharf and float in the bay. Then, they purchased four small boats with gear and rented them to guests by the hour.

In the 1950's, the Galiano Lodge was destroyed by fire, leaving only the brick steps and stone verandah standing. The owners built a single-storied house on the same site and continued to operate it as a resort into the 1960's. Subsequent owners added more rooms to the building.

Today, the Galiano Lodge is known as the *Galiano Inn*. It offers guest rooms, as well as a meeting room with seating for 40 people. Situated at Sturdies Bay, the Mediterranean-style Inn features the *Madrona Del Mar Spa and Wellness Retreat*. The Inn is located on Madrona Road.

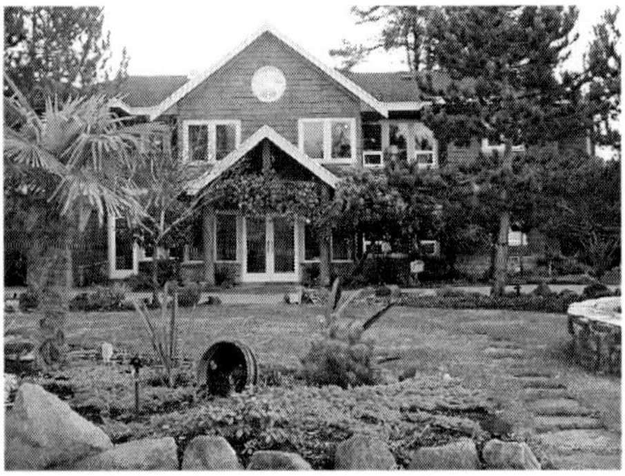

Captain's Quarters Cottage

In the year 1890, a sea Captain emigrated from England to Galiano. A few years later, he established a farm on a bay on North Galiano. Initially, a simple lean-to with an earth floor served as the family's home.

The following year, the Captain and his son built a log home with dovetailed corners. Because he worked off-Island, he hired a live-in governess for his children. She educated them in a lean-to classroom that was attached to the back of the log house.

Later, the Captain's son inherited the property. He lived in the home for the rest of his life. The building was then left in an abandoned state for several decades, during which time much of the interior rotted away.

In the 1980's, another sea Captain purchased the property. One hundred years after the house was originally built, he began to restore it.

Today, the log home is operated as a cottage rental called the *Captain's Quarters*. It is located on North Galiano, on McCoskrie Road.

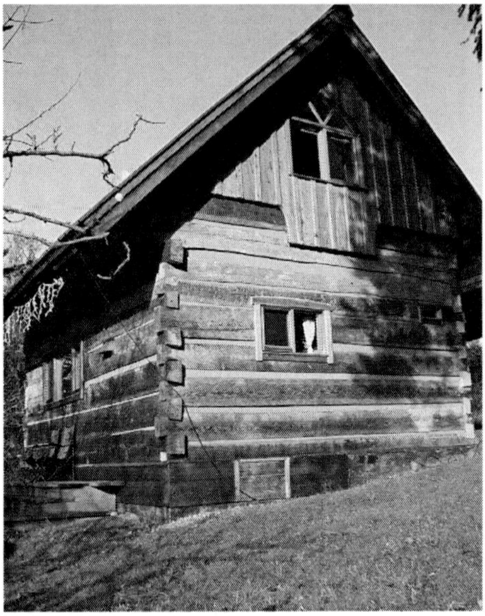

Galiano Island Sights & Shops

1 Thistledown Antiques
3 Galiano Art Gallery
5 Galiano Island Books
7 St. Margaret`s Church
9 Murcheson's House
11 Porlier Pass Light Station
12 Cedar Grove Pottery & Maria DeVicque Glassworks & Bill Boyd Ceramics
16 Cooked Goose Studio

2 Art & Soul Craft Gallery
4 Grand Central Emporium
6 Ixchel Craft Shop
8 Mary Anne Point Light
10 Ixchel Craft Shop & Montague Marina Gifts
13 Galiano Island Cemetery
14 Insight Art Gallery
15 Schoenfeld Custom Knives

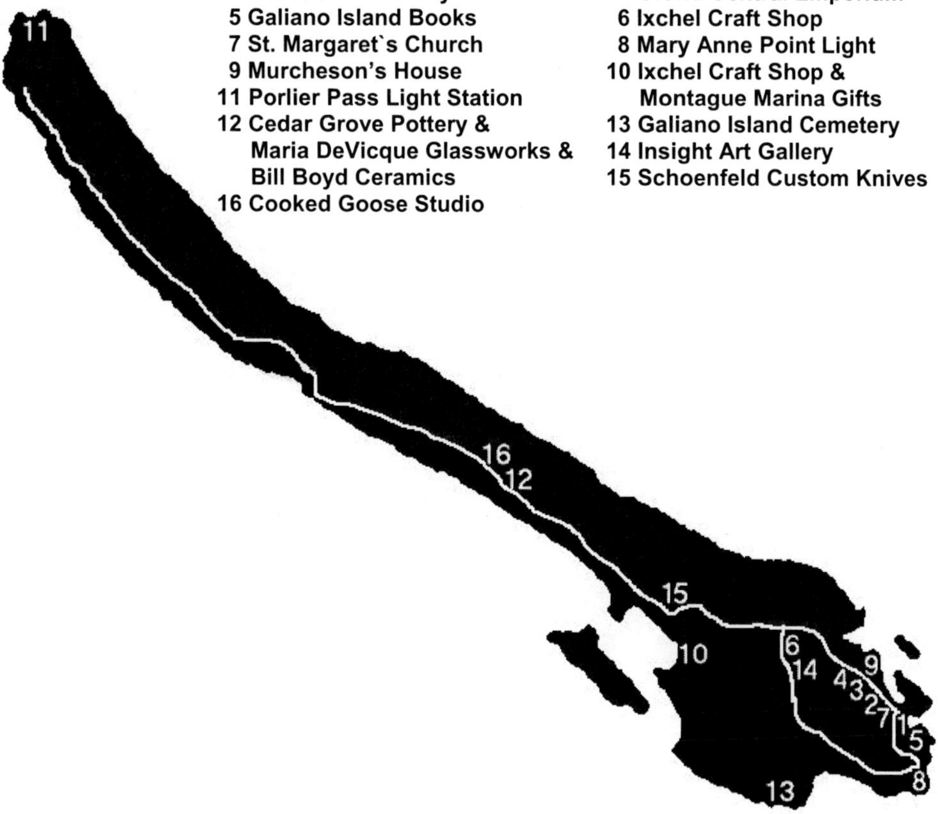

Things to See

Galiano Island is a peaceful getaway with numerous areas to explore. Many people come to Galiano simply to camp near the beach, drive through the park or sail out to the lighthouse.

There are only two major routes on Galiano. Porlier Pass Road runs the length of the Island, bisecting it. It connects to Sturdies Bay Road, which leads to the ferry terminal. Sturdies Bay Road turns into Georgeson Bay Road, then into Bluff Road, and then into Burrill Road, circumventing the southern tip of the Island.

St. Margaret of Scotland Church

Initially, Catholic church services were held in a little shed on a South Galiano bay, where a fisherman had previously mended and dried his fish nets. Later, they were held in an old schoolhouse that sat near that same bay. At that time, Galiano was part of the parish of the church on Mayne Island.

During World War I, a woman donated some waterfront property on the bay and a Mission Room was opened there. The altar, organ, lectern, prayer desk and silver communion vessels were all donations. At least once, a baptism was performed in the kitchen sink in a nearby home.

Shortly thereafter, monthly services on North Galiano began at the Retreat Cove and North Galiano schools. Eventually, the Mission Room was purchased by the Island's undertaker, who made it his home.

In the 1950's, a settler donated some land up the hill for the building of a proper church. A number of projects were undertaken to raise money for its construction, including the first *Galiano Art Show*.

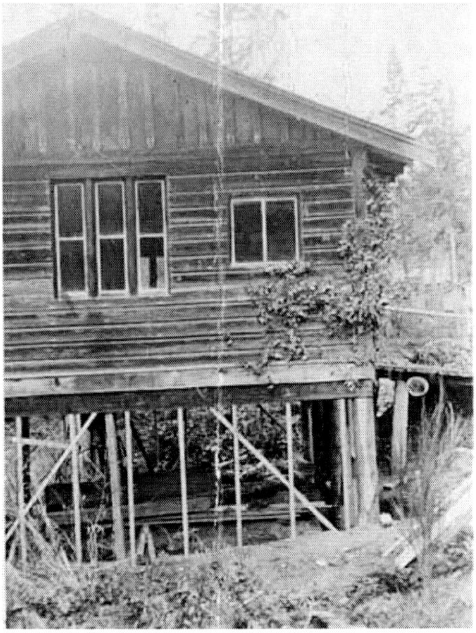

Mission Room in the 1950's
Galiano Archives 2004026171

Upon its completion, the church was called the *Church of St. Margaret, Queen of Scotland*. A larger-than-life painting of The Crucifixion was hung above the altar. A stained glass window was placed in the rear of the church, in memory of a Reverend who drowned shortly after his appointment to the Gulf Islands' Parish.

For many years thereafter, the owner of a store at Sturdies Bay would stop at the church with his family, on his way to the Saturday night dance. He would light the oil stove in the church so it would be warm for the morning service.

Today, St. Margaret of Scotland Church is the only church on Galiano. It is located on Burrill Road. (#7 on the map)

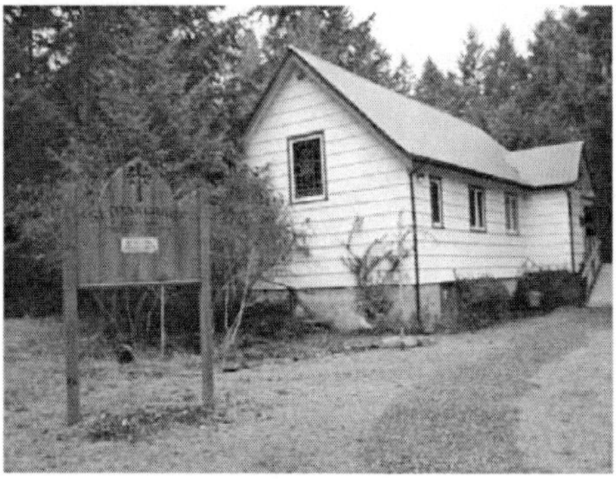

Galiano Island Cemetery

Before the 1860`s, Indians buried their dead high in the trees on South Galiano, on a point that is now called Collinson Point. Later, the point became the private burial ground of a very prominent settler.

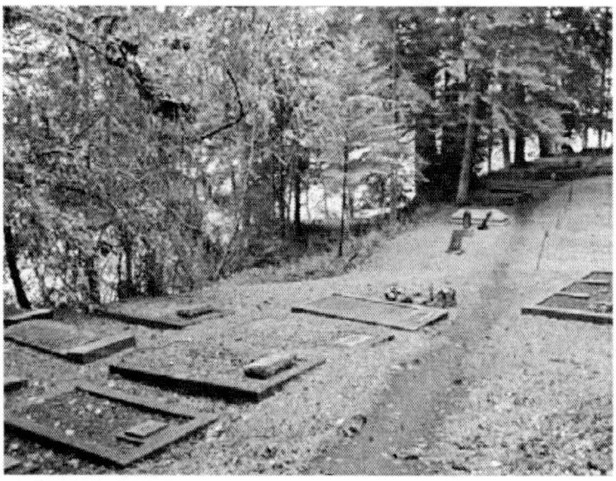

In the 1920`s, the settler donated the land to be used as the Island's cemetery. He placed two conditions on his donation; that there be no charge for burial of a resident of Galiano and that plots would be reserved there for his own family.

The local undertaker cleared most of the property, which is still surrounded by huge Arbutus and Douglas-Fir trees today. The *lych* gate and the fence seen along one side were both donations.

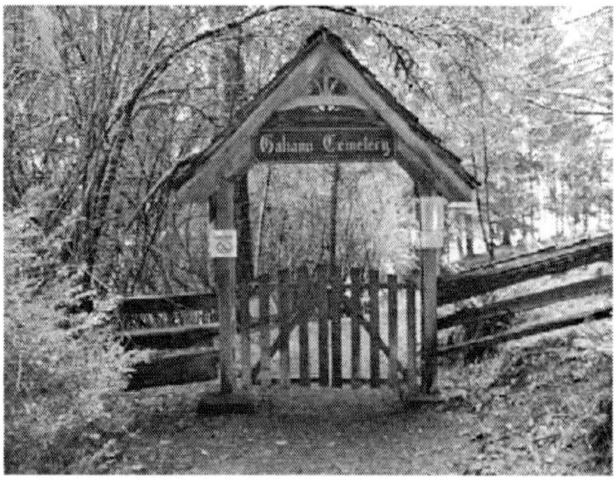

The cemetery is accessible from what was once called *Dead End Road*, but was later renamed *Cemetery Road*. (#18 on the map)

Porlier Pass Light Station

Prior to the turn of the century, the passage at the north end of Galiano was called *Cowichan Gap*, but was known locally as *The Gap*. It was later renamed *Porlier Pass*.

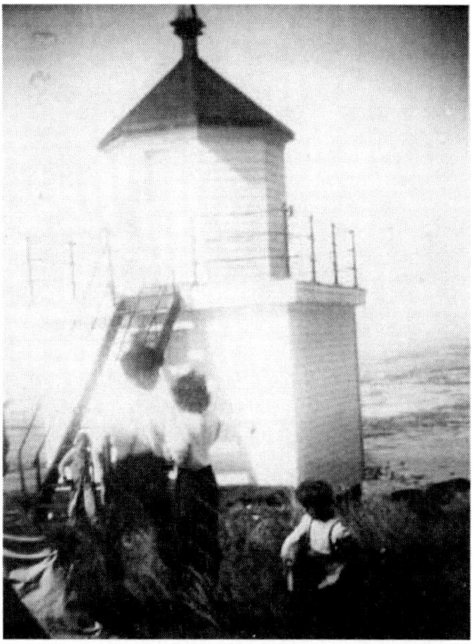

Race Point Tower at the Porlier Pass Light Station, 1950's - Galiano Archives 2004026354

At the turn of the century, construction of a major light station began at the Pass. It was called the *Porlier Pass Light Station* and it overlooked what is now known as *Lighthouse Bay*.

There were two beacon towers at the light station. One beacon sat on Race Point and the other sat on Virago Point. Ships navigated the waters by lining up the lights in both towers.

The first light keeper was a sailor known locally as 'Sticks'. In the morning, he would fill the brass coal oil lamps in each tower, and then trim the wicks and polish the chimneys. At dusk, he would light the lamps so they would burn through the night.

Whenever the weather was foggy, he would beat an old tin can to indicate to the boats where the Pass was.

The light keeper served the light station for 40 years. The wicks were in operation in the beacon towers until he retired in the 1940's.

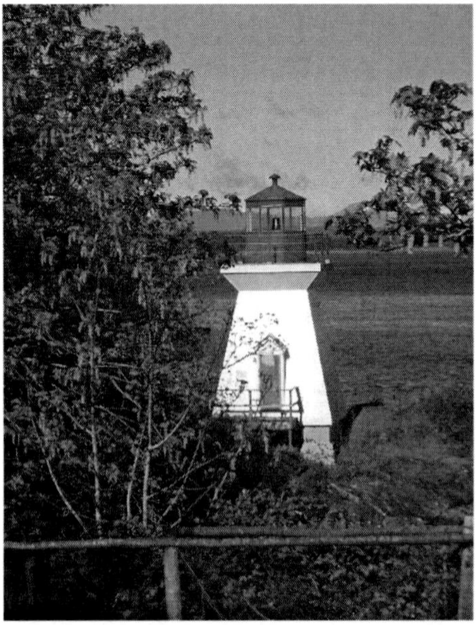

The tower on Race Point was recently removed and replaced with an automated beacon. However, the tower on Virago Point is still standing on the First Nations reserve and can be seen from Dionisio Point Provincial Park. (#11 on the map)

Mary Anne Point Light

In the 1880's, the English seaman who would later own the Galiano Lodge purchased some property on South Galiano. The property sat on a point called Mary Anne Point. There, he began to build a waterfront home.

At the turn of the century, the seaman moved to England, and then returned after World War I with his fiancé. In the 1920`s, he exchanged the property for property owned by his brother. Thereafter, his brother owned the home on the point.

The windows in the home faced a light that sat on the point. It was called the *Mary Anne Point Light*. Fuelled by carbide, it guided the ships through the Pass.

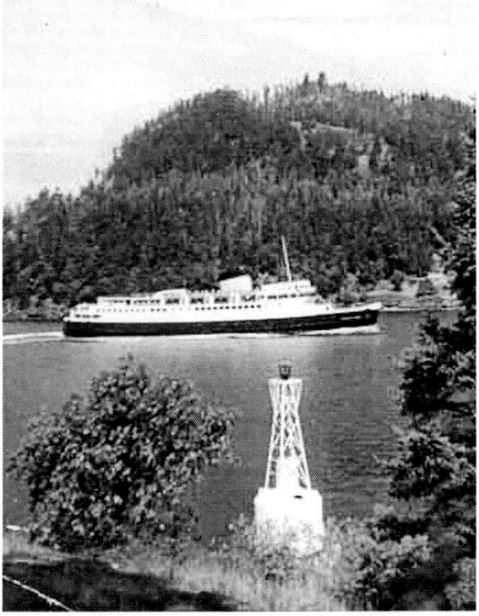

Mary Anne Point Light, mid 1900's
Galiano Archives M297

A seaside trail led over flat rock and grass, down to the waters in the Pass, and then through the woods and down the hill to the house and the light.

A garden of wildflowers grew among the rocks, behind which visitors could see the ships sailing through the rough waters.

In the 1950`s, the Mary Anne Point Light was dumped into the sea and the property was sold to a descendant for one dollar.

Today, a new light stands on the point. It can be seen from the ferries as they travel through the Pass between Vancouver Island and the mainland.

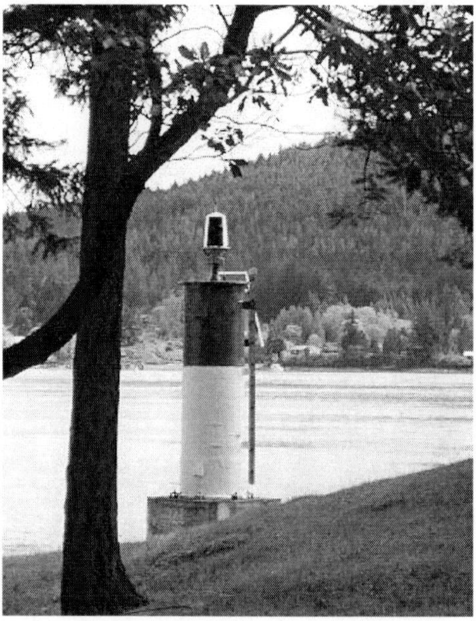

Mary Anne Point Light as it appears today

The 120-year old home that once belonged to the seaman still stands nearby. The house was first enlarged in the 1920's. Subsequent owners have made numerous modifications to it. (#8 on the map)

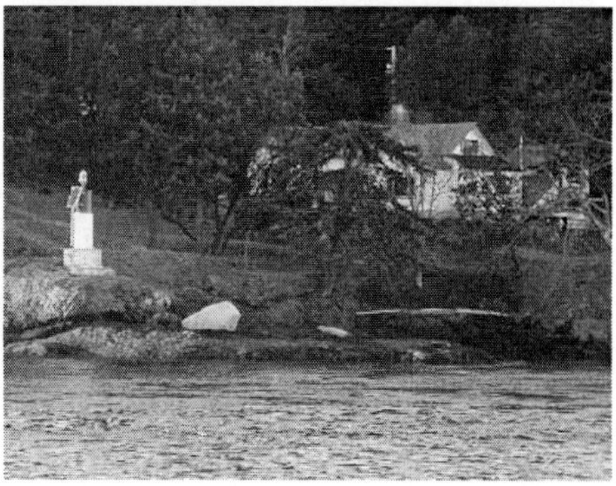

The Oldest House on Galiano

In the 1880's, a Scotsman came to South Galiano and purchased some land on Sturdies Bay. There, he established a farm on which he built a square-timbered home.

The Scotsman's eldest son was the first white child to grow up on Galiano. When the son drowned at the turn of the century, his younger brother inherited the family farm.

The young brother eventually married and became the father of seven children, which earned him the nickname 'Father Finlay'.

Later, he became a roads foreman for Galiano and many of the roads on the Island were staked out under his supervision.

Today, the Galiano Island Golf Course sits on part of the family's old farm. Their 125-year old home can still be seen from Sturdies Bay Road. It is the oldest house on Galiano. (#9 on the map)

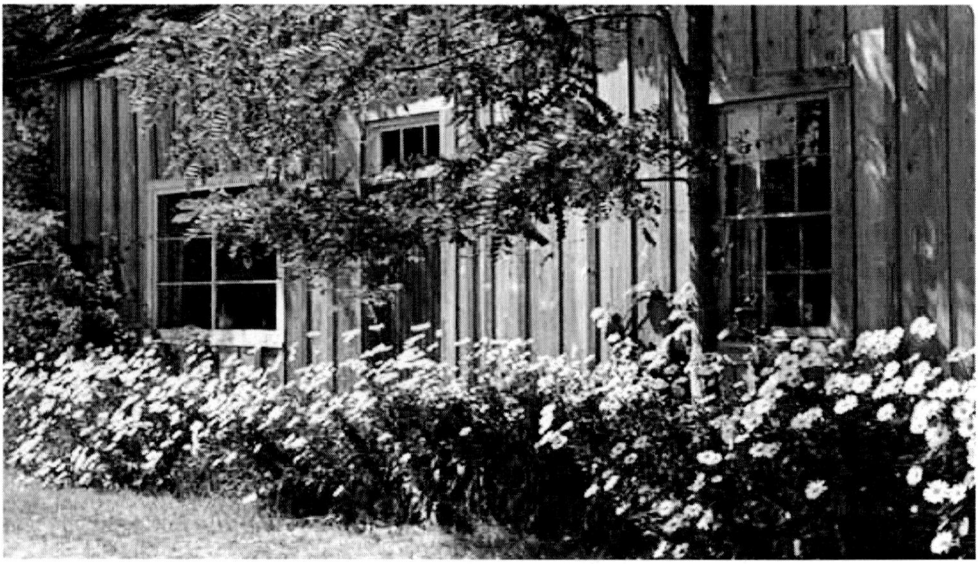

Oldest house on Galiano, in the 1960's – Galiano Archives 2004026157

A single-storey kitchen addition was constructed just before the outbreak of World War I. The outside chimney was constructed much later, around the 1950's. However, the house is still very much the way it was at the turn of the century.

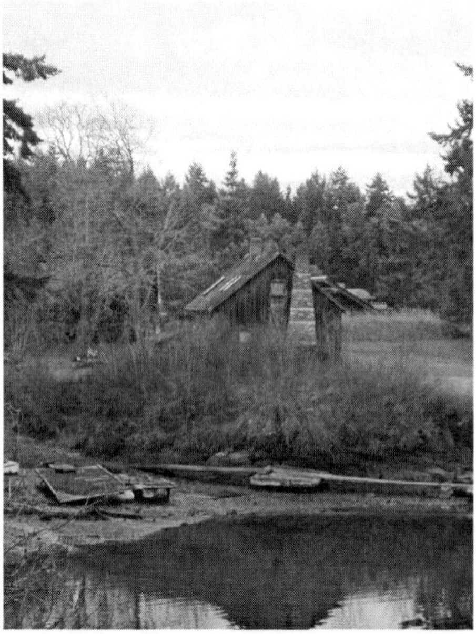

Places to Shop

In the 1920's, a grocery store was built at the head of the Sturdies Bay wharf. The store changed owners twice, eventually becoming *Heryet's Store*.

In the 1930's, the store was sold to a witty Irishman, who became its new storekeeper. Later, he turned the store over to his son.

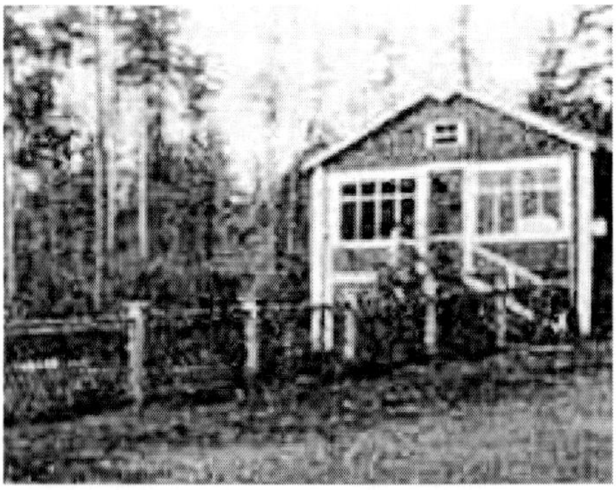

Heryet`s Store in the 1920's
Galiano Archives 2004017021b

In the 1950's, the Irishman's son purchased and enlarged a building that housed a coffee shop just up the road. Then, he moved the store there. A decade later, he incorporated the business as *Bambrick's Stores Ltd.*

In addition to a grocery department, the new store now contained a coffee bar and butcher shop on the main floor and a hardware department on the lower floor.

In the year 1970, a fire destroyed the store. The sound of exploding paint cans could be heard from far away. All that remained was the chimney.

Today, shops, studios and art galleries provide visitors to Galiano Island the opportunity to pick up a *potlatch* (gift) for themselves or for *tillicum* (friends). Galiano is home to many fine artists, writers and artisans.

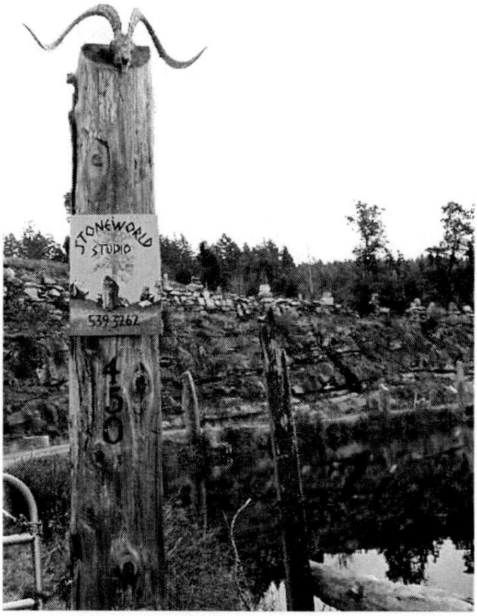

Many art studios keep extended hours during the self-guided *Galiano Art Studio Tour*, which allows visitors to see the work of artisans in their studios during the summer.

A Studio Tour map, which is published by the Trincomali Community Arts Council, displays the locations of the participating studios. Watch for road signs and the chance to meet an artist working in their studio.

Schoenfeld Custom Knives

Schoenfeld Custom Knives is a studio that offers knives, utensils and pens created by a master knife maker. The studio is located near Montague Harbour, on Clanton Road. (#15 on the map)

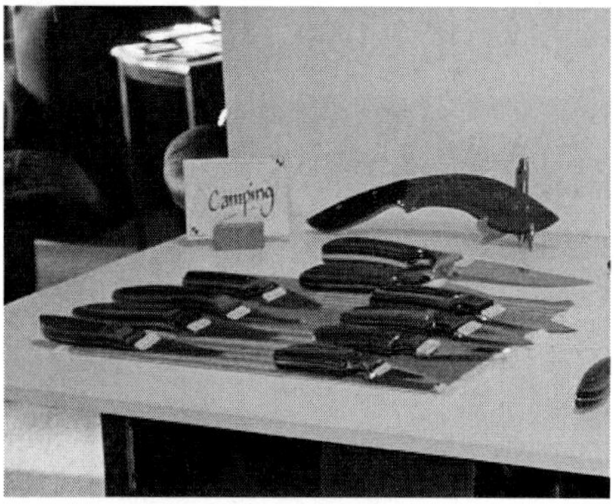

Grand Central Emporium

In the 1890's, an Englishman immigrated to Canada. Three years later, he came to Galiano and purchased some property on a bay near the Pass. There, he established a farm. Later, his older brother moved to the Island and helped him run his farm.

Because settlers initially had to row to Mayne Island for supplies, the brothers were forever lending merchandise to their neighbors. So, at the turn of the century, the older brother built a store near the water. He called it *Burrill Bros. Store.*

Three years later, he built a larger store on the same property and the first store was then used as a shed. While he ran the farm, the younger brother tended to the store.

The store became a gathering place for the Islanders and, for many years, it had the only telephone on the Island. The brothers hung a Swiss cowbell over the door, which their customers rang for service.

Initially, the brothers used a sled pulled by a team of oxen to deliver large orders around the valley. Later, they purchased an old rheumatic horse to serve that purpose, which they hoisted up with a block and tackle each morning.

Eventually, they added a post office, library and gas pumps to the store. They also added an apartment above the building, which they rented out.

In the 1940's, the brothers sold their store. Subsequent owners dragged it further north, and then added a false front to it. The building has changed owners many times over the years.

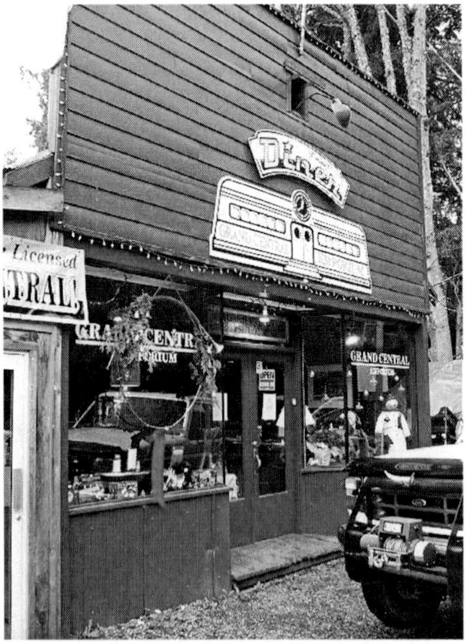

Today, the building is the home of the *Grand Central Emporium* gift store. Known locally as the *Old Burrill Store*, it is located at Sturdies Bay on Sturdies Bay Road. (#4 on the map)

Art & Soul Craft Gallery

The *Art & Soul Craft Gallery* provides for artwork, jewelry, candles, soaps, gifts and clothing. It is located in a small mall at Sturdies Bay. (#2 on the map)

Cedar Grove Pottery

Cedar Grove Pottery, on Porlier Pass Road, is a studio that offers raku, stoneware and sculptures produced by local artists. (#12 on the map)

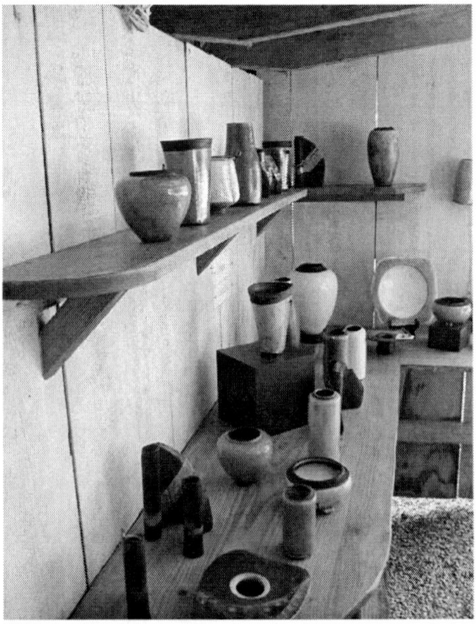

Galiano Art Gallery

The *Galiano Art Gallery* offers unique and original works by regional artists. In the year prior to this writing, it moved into a newly built complex at Sturdies Bay on Sturdies Bay Road. (#3 on the map)

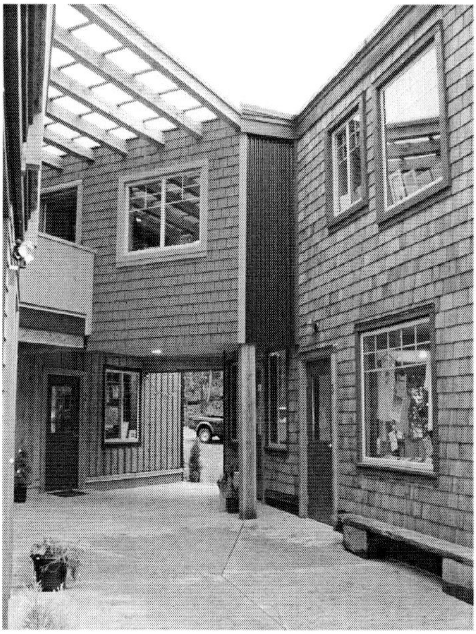

Ixchel Craft Shops

Formerly a taco stand, the *Ixchel Craft Shop* opened for business in the year 1990, on Georgeson Bay Road. It offers artwork, stained glass, soaps, chimes, pottery and jewelry made by local artists. (#6 on the map) A second seasonal outlet is located at the Montague Harbour Marina on Montague Park Road. (#10 on the map)

Bill Boyd Ceramics

In the year 1970, an artist began making pottery in Sweden. Today, he lives and works on Galiano, using four different porcelain and stoneware clays from the Pacific Northwest.

The artist's studio is called *Bill Boyd Ceramics*. Located on Porlier Pass Road, it offers hand-made pottery that is fired in electric and gas kilns. (#12 on the map)

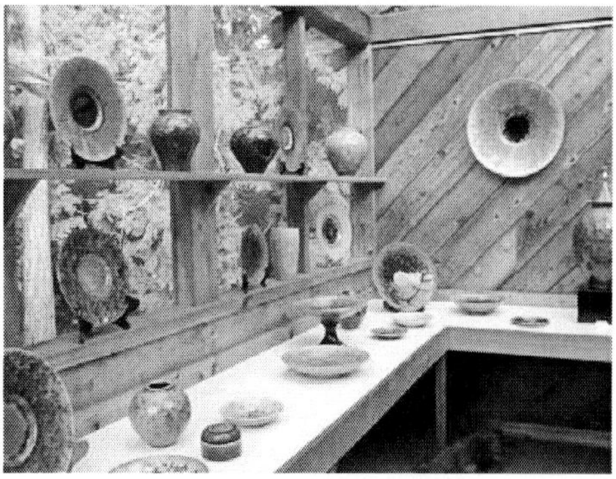

Maria DeVicque Glassworks

Maria DeVicque Glassworks is a charming studio on Porlier Pass Road. It offers fine glassware. (#12 on the map)

Thistledown Old & Odd Antiques

Located in a building that was once the home of the post office, *Thistledown Old and Odd Antiques* offers pottery, jewelry and handcrafted items by local artists. It is located at Sturdies Bay on Madrona Road. (#1 on the map)

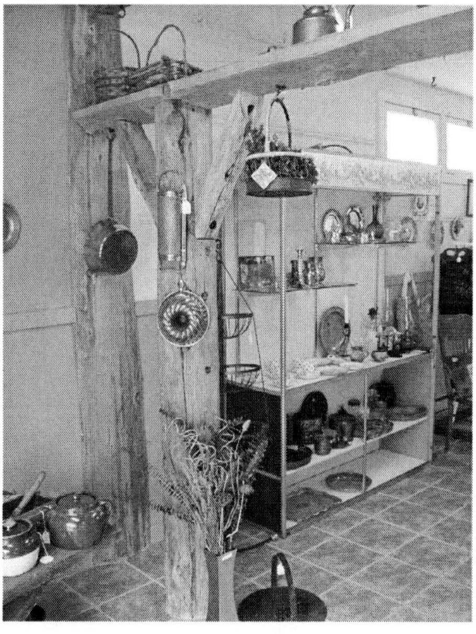

Insight Art Gallery

In the year prior to this writing, the *Insight Art Gallery* opened on South Galiano. It features a collection of works by local artists, with displays in glass, sculpture, painting, ceramics, mosaics and textiles. The gallery is located on Georgeson Bay Road. (#14 on the map)

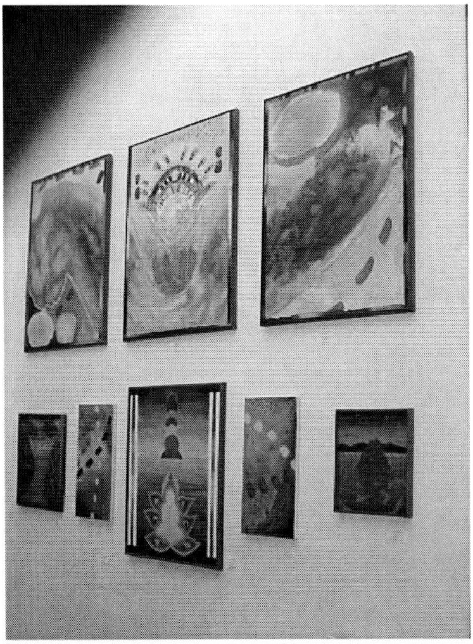

Galiano Island Books

Galiano Island Books is an impressive bookstore at Sturdies Bay, which offers over 15,000 titles. It also carries art supplies. The bookstore is located on Madrona Road. (#5 on the map)

Events to Attend

Early settlers celebrated Queen Victoria's birthday by holding events in the month of May, such as foot and potato sack races. They called the holiday 'May Day'. A popular event held during the festivities was the Maypole Dance, which was performed by Galiano Island schoolchildren.

Whether it is an annual event, such as the *Galiano Wine Festival* or the *Canada Day Jamboree*, or a special event, such as a music festival or play, there is always something to take in on Galiano Island.

The Galiano Island Lions Club has been active for over 30 years. Together with the Galiano Island Volunteer Firefighter's Association, they host a variety of events throughout the year.

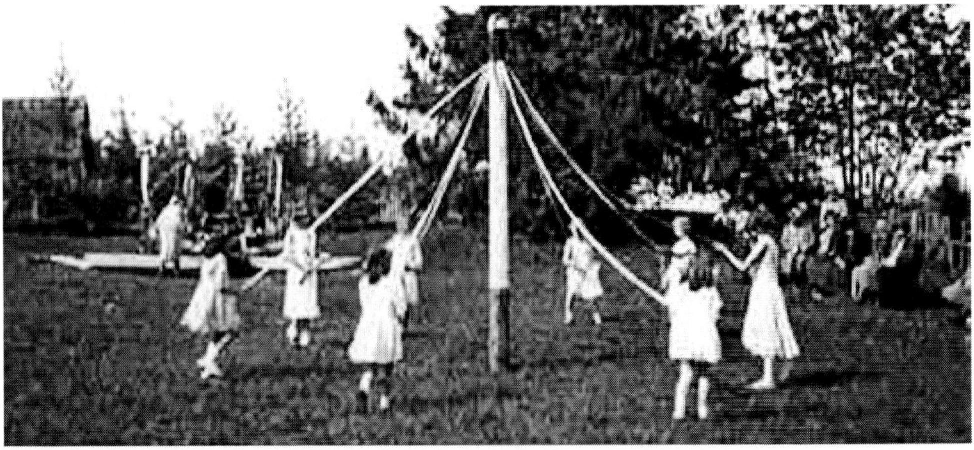

Maypole Dancing in 1929 - Galiano Archives M176

Modern Antiques Sale

The *Modern Antiques Sale* is an annual event that is held in April, at the North Galiano Community Hall on Porlier Pass Road.

Seafood Dinner & Dance

The all-you-can-eat *Seafood Dinner* is held each year at the Galiano Island Lions Club on Burrill Road. The annual seafood buffet includes dancing, raffles, auctions and door prizes.

Galiano Fun Triathlon

A few years prior to this writing, two women started an event, called the *Galiano Fun Triathlon*. The triathlon takes place each May, in Montague Harbour Park on Montague Park Road. It involves kayaking, cycling and running.

Well over 100 people participate in the event. One year, a 76-year old competitor took place in the triathlon. He had not ridden a bicycle in almost 60 years.

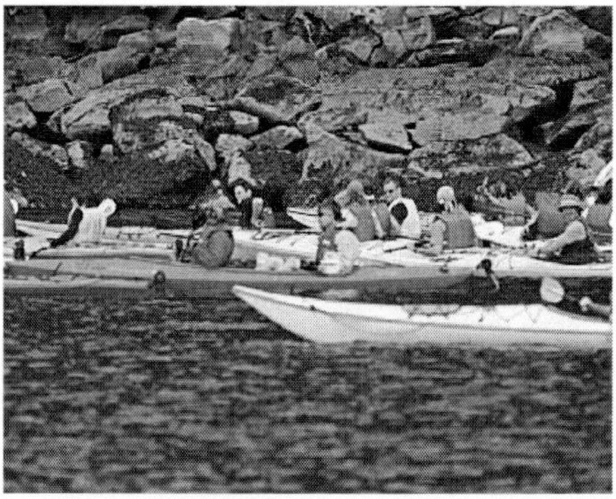

Saturday Market

The *Saturday Market* is held every Saturday from June to September. It features locally produced art and crafts, foods and fresh produce. The market is held at the Galiano Island Lions Club on Burrill Road.

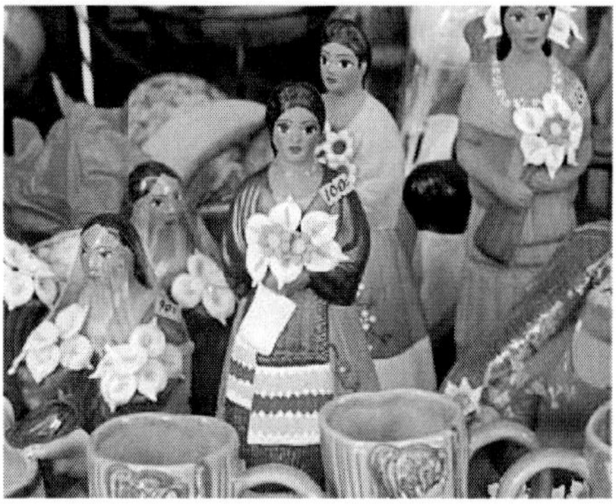

Canada Day Jamboree

The *Canada Day Jamboree* is held each year on July 1, at the North Galiano Community Hall on Porlier Pass Road. It provides for a colorful parade and fair.

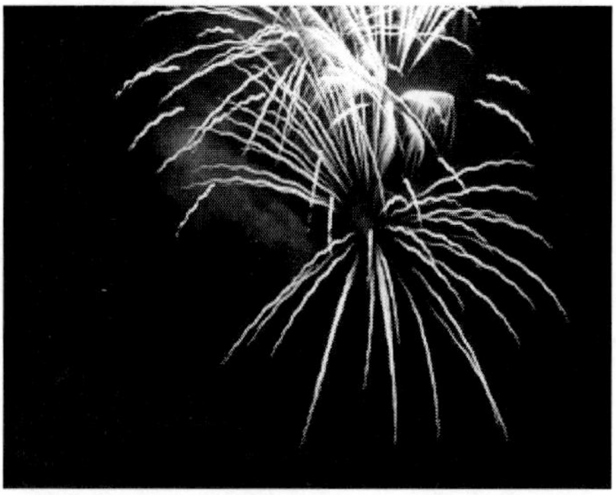

Galiano Art Show

At the turn of the century, a school-aged boy moved with his family from Mayne Island to Galiano.

The boy loved to draw. As he grew older, he learned how to paint. He would make paints by grinding color out of berry juice and earth pigments. Sometimes, he would buy paints from the brothers who ran the Burrill Bros. Store at Sturdies Bay.

At the turn of the century, the budding artist and his family moved to the mainland where he became a well-known painter.

Much later, in the 1940s, the painter returned to Galiano and built a home and studio, where he spent summers with his own family. Shortly thereafter, he sponsored the first *Galiano Art Show*.

It was at his studio that he painted an interpretation of The Crucifixion. It was hung in St. Margaret's Church, where a memorial service was held for him after his death in the 1960's.

Today, the Galiano Art Show is hosted by the Artists Guild of Galiano. The event is held each year in July.

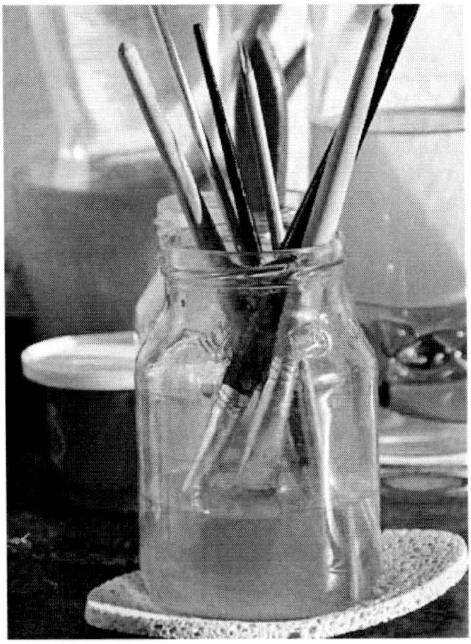

Galiano Fiesta

The Galiano Fiesta is an annual event that provides for a barbecue, beverage garden, craft booths, games and exhibits. A feature of the event is the Gumboot Toss. There is also a colorful parade.

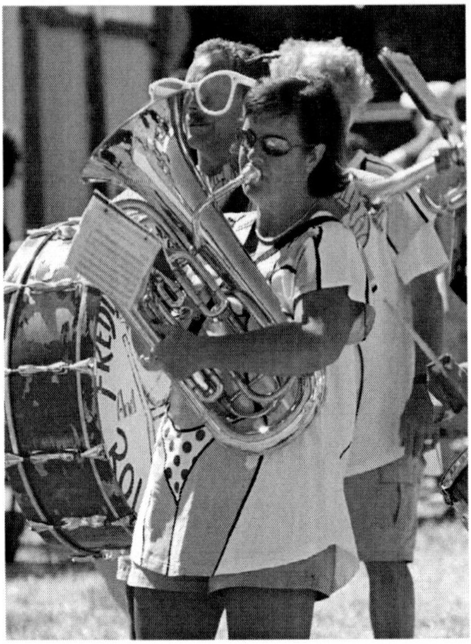

Sponsored by the Galiano Island Lions Club, the Galiano Festival takes place on July 31, in Galiano Lions Park on Burrill Road.

Galiano Wine Festival

The *Galiano Wine Festival* is an annual event held in August. The event allows visitors to the Island to sample wines from around the world. The festival, which is held in Galiano Lions Park on Burrill Road, provides for music, great food and other activities.

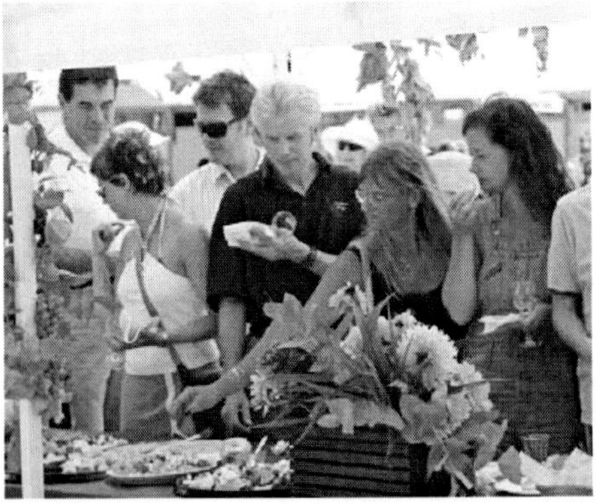

Roddy Wilson Tournament

The annual, memorial *Roddy Wilson Slow Pitch Tournament* is held in the fall, in Galiano Lions Park on Burrill Road.

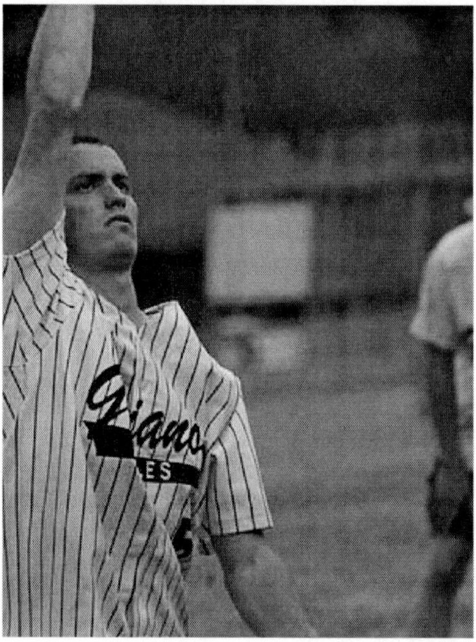

Halloween Howl

The annual *Halloween Howl* is held at Halloween. It provides for games, as well as prizes for the best costume. A fireworks display is also provided, in Galiano Lions Park on Burrill Road.

Christmas Celebrations

Every Christmas Eve during World War I, the light keeper at Porlier Pass would make two huge Christmas puddings. He would tie them in large pillowcases and boil them all day in an old fashioned, copper wash-boiler. Then, he would make two big jugs of brown sugar sauce to pour over them.

When the puddings were ready, he would row out to the Indian reserve and serve up his pudding on a platter to each Indian family. Then, he would serve it to the Japanese-Canadians.

Today, residents of Galiano start the Christmas season off with a Christmas craft fair and market.

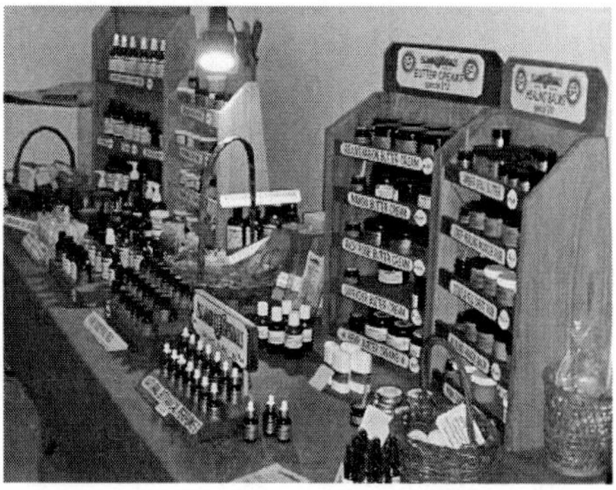

The season continues as the Bellingham Central Lions Club, in Washington State, loads the *Christmas Ship* with toys and gifts, and sends it to Galiano.

Known locally as the *Santa Ship*, the ship is greeted at Montague Harbour, and then Santa and his 'helpers' distribute gifts to the kids.

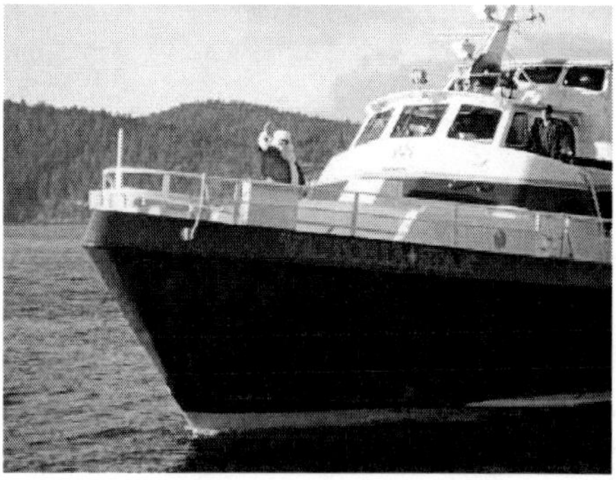

Galiano Island
Parks & Beaches

1 Dionisio Point Prov. Park
2 Spanish Hills
3 Spotlight Cove
4 Shaw's Landing
5 Bodega Ridge
6 Retreat Cove
7 Pebble Beach
8 Garner Road Beach
9 Montague Harbour Prov. Park
10 Cook Cove
11 Morning Beach
12 Cain Peninsula & Whaler Bay
14 Bellhouse Prov. Park
15 Twiss Road Beach
16 Matthews Point Reg. Park
17 Galiano Bluffs Park
18 Georgeson Bay
19 Mount Galiano

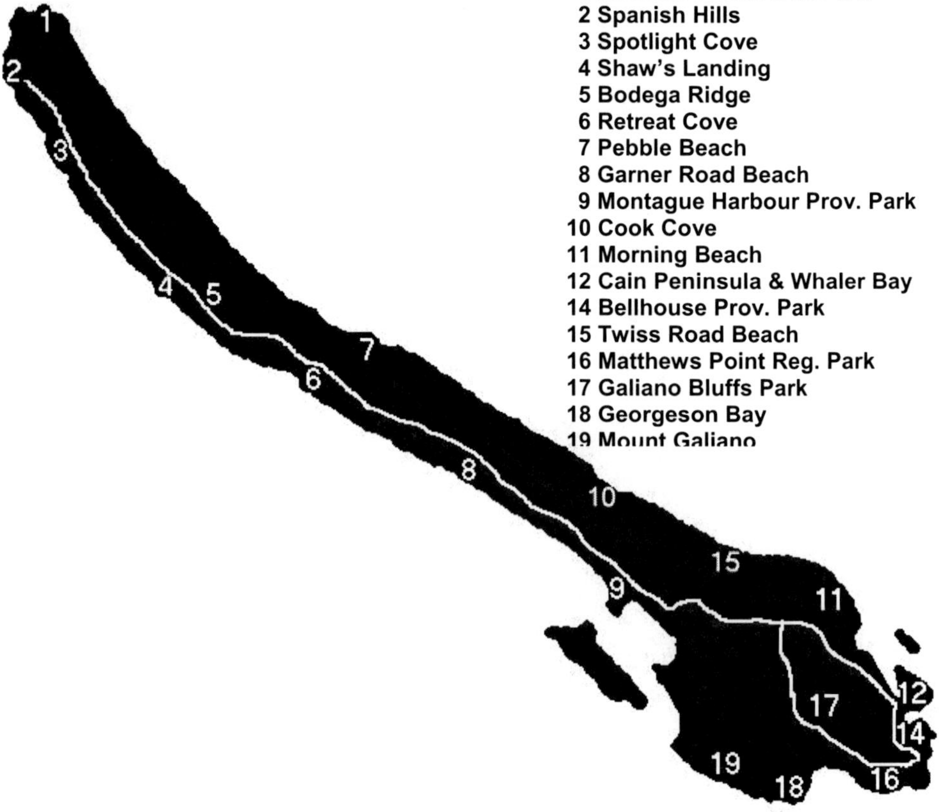

Parks & Beaches to Explore

In the 18th century, a Spanish Commander led the last Spanish exploration of the British Columbian coast. In the 19th century, an English sea Captain named Galiano Island after this Commander.

Recently, a news columnist discovered a 19th century map, which displayed another island off the coast of British Columbia, whose name was also *Galiano*. The newly discovered island was located 250 miles north of the Galiano of the southern Gulf Islands.

Ironically, the Spanish Commander had named the island of the north several years before the English had named the island of the south after him. Fortunately for southern Gulf Islanders, the Galiano of the north was renamed *Nigei* before the turn of the century.

Today, the Galiano of the south provides for plenty of limestone shoreline, and white sand and shell beaches. Its protected bays and shallow waters make it easy to find a cove to anchor in for the *poolakle* (night).

The scuba diving around Galiano is the best in all the outer Gulf Islands. Anywhere in Active Pass can be found fish, kelp beds and anemone beds. Keep in mind that much of the scenery in the Pass is at a depth of more than 30 m.

Although Galiano Island has fewer parks than most of the other Gulf Islands, it makes up for in splendor what it lacks in number. Its mature forests are dark with Western Red Cedar, Red Alder, Giant Sword-Fern and Oregon Grape, making for excellent hiking.

The trails range from seashore-access, walking trails to forest hikes, so you might want to invest in a pair of *waffle stompers* (hiking shoes).

As well as ensuring that nothing is left on the trails, hikers should take as much of their *iktas* (belongings) as possible off the Island.

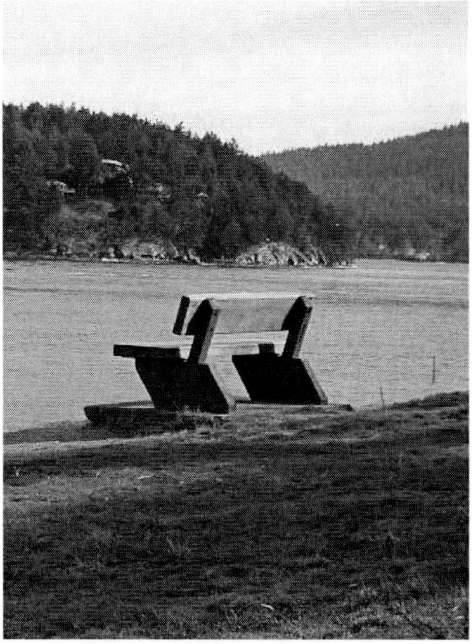

Bellhouse Provincial Park

Bellhouse Provincial Park was named after the family who originally built the Bellhouse Inn. They bequeathed the property to the province in the 1960's.

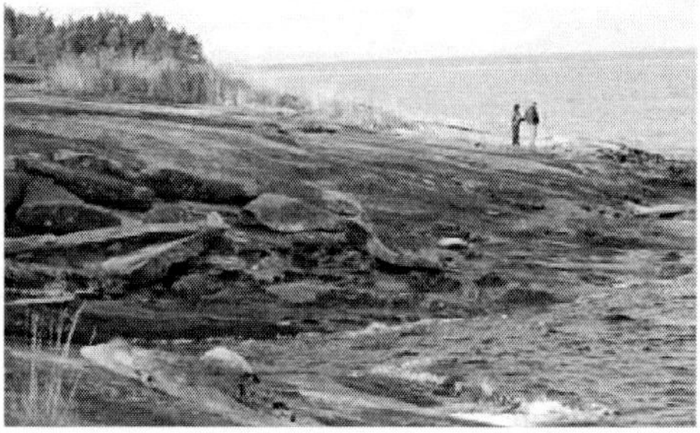

Bellhouse Park sits on a rocky peninsula, on the south side of Galiano. It slopes to the sea at the entrance to Active Pass.

The park provides for wonderful sandstone and limestone formations on the shoreline around the Pass. Whale sightings are frequent there, and Sea Lions and Harbour Seals are in abundance. There are facilities for picnics if you want to stay awhile.

Accessible from Bellhouse Road, the park is one of the most scenic in all the Gulf Islands. (#14 on the map)

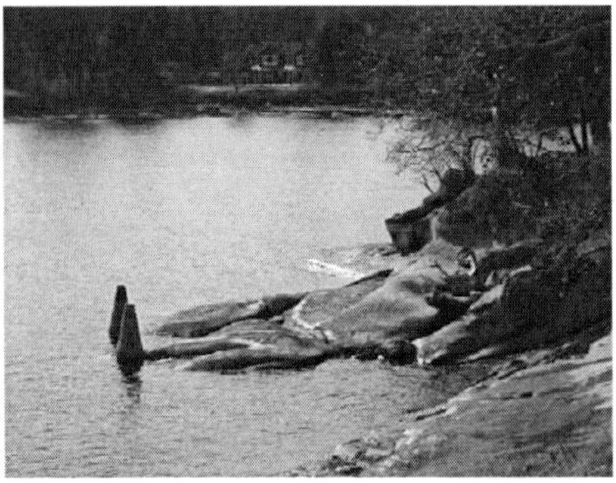

Bluffs Park

At the turn of the century, the settler who would later be seen driving a horse-drawn Victoria carriage around Galiano emigrated from England. He brought 11 Belgian people with him.

Soon, the settler purchased some land on Galiano, which was occupied by high bluffs that overlooked the Pass. There, he established a farm, called the *Valley Farm*.

In the year 1910, his daughter became the first white child born on Galiano. Later, when one of his Belgian helpers went into labor, he delivered her baby, with the help of a first aid book that was written in Spanish.

In the 1920`s, the settler returned to Europe to live. After World War II, he and his wife sold the bluffs to the Galiano Island Development Association. The land was then passed to the Galiano Club and a park was opened there.

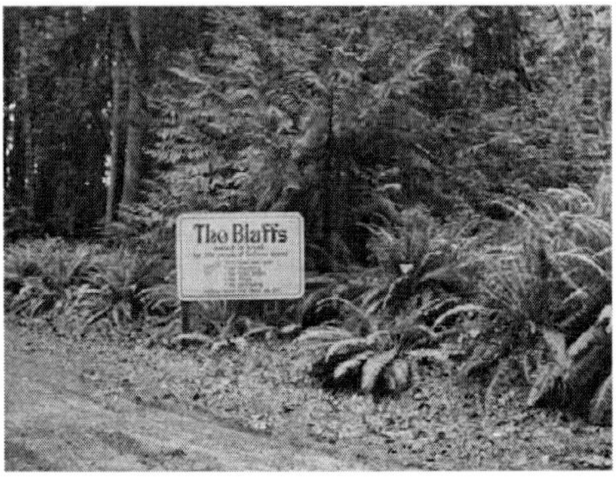

Bluffs Park sits in a beautiful, dark, old-growth forest on the southwest side of Galiano. There are 4 km of easy trails that wander through the park.

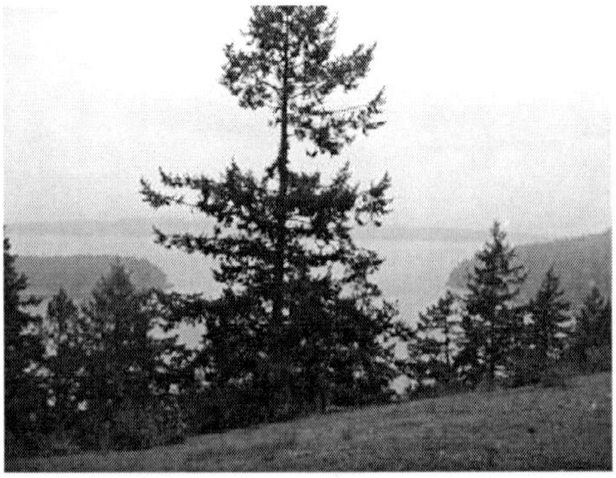

The trails lead to a ridge that provides for views across the Pass and down the Channel. They are accessible by way of Bluff Road, which is dotted with some of the largest Western Red Cedar trees in all the Gulf Islands. (#17 on the map)

Bodega Ridge Provincial Park

Bodega Ridge Provincial Park is located on the northwest side of Galiano. Within the park boundaries, a 4 km long ridge, called *Bodega Ridge*, rises 328 m above sea level. Below the ridge, can be seen Bald Eagles, Peregrine Falcons and Turkey Vultures.

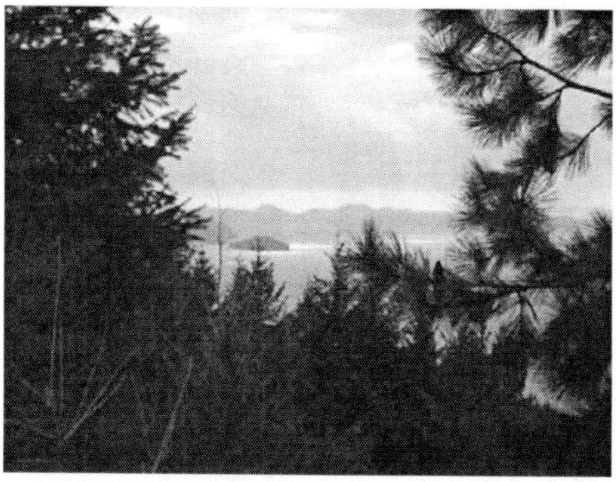

The easy trail along the ridge loops through a rare coastal habitat of Douglas-Fir and Garry Oak, and is one of the best places to see the Hairy Manzanita shrub.

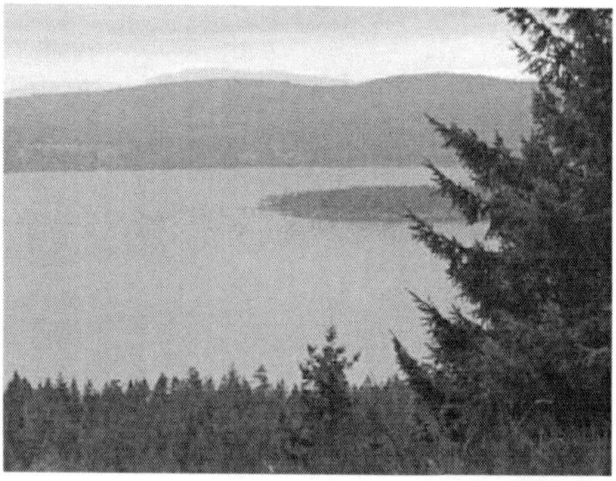

A viewpoint, called *Lover`s Leap*, provides for a spectacular panoramic view of Salt Spring and Vancouver Islands. The trail is accessible from the end of Cottage Way. (#5 on the map)

Cain Peninsula

In the early 1920's, a man emigrated from Ireland to Canada. When he had borrowed enough money to purchase Gossip Island, off the southeast side of Galiano, he moved his family there.

Although they had no experience living in the bush, the family initially lived in a tent. There was no water on the Island so the man rowed to Galiano every day to fetch water from a spring. Later, **the Postman** helped him dig a well and build a log cabin on his property.

Soon, the man decided to start a resort. So he built some self-contained cottages on the property, each on its own bay.

In the late 1920's, he started a hotel on what his family called Hotel Point. He called it the *Gossip Island Hotel.* It had 13 bedrooms, a large dining room and a sitting room with a fireplace. It hosted many dances.

The man pioneered the use of propane as fuel for the hotel and, until it became too expensive, the family used it to cook, heat water and run the lights. The toilets ran on saltwater from the ocean.

In the 1930's, **the Postman** built a summer house on the point. It was built hexagonally out of Cedar and had a Cedar shake roof. He also built a turnstile at the entrance to the hotel.

At the beginning of World War II, the hotel was closed down and partially dismantled.

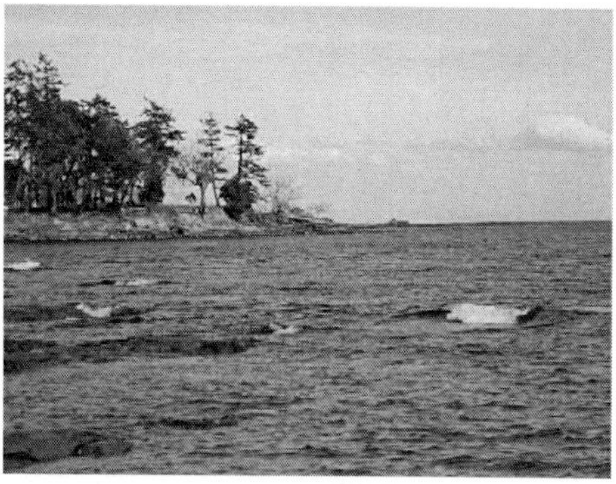

Gossip Island can be seen from the *Cain Peninsula*. Located on the southeast side of Galiano, the peninsula provides protection to an adjacent bay from the winds blowing in from the Georgia Strait.

The rocky beach on the Cain Peninsula is dotted with large pieces of driftwood and provides for interesting sandstone formations. Keep in mind that the beach is closed to the harvesting of scallops, mussels, oysters and clams.

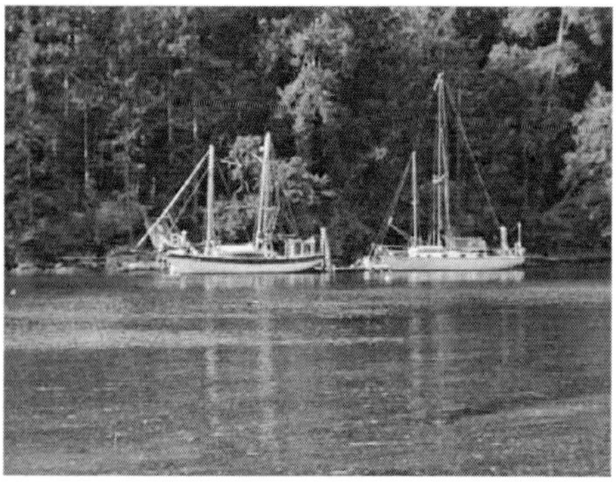

If you launch a boat from the peninsula, you can travel around Gossip Island and the coves nearby. The peninsula is accessible from the end of Cain Road. (#12 on the map)

Centennial Community Park

Centennial Community Park is a small recreational park located on the school grounds on Gardner Road. It provides for a baseball diamond, tennis courts and playgrounds.

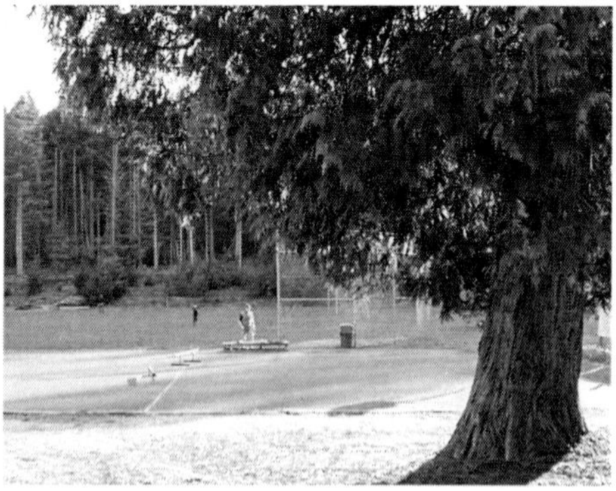

Cook Cove

Around the turn of the century, a settler and his wife purchased some land near a cove. There, they established a farm that had a fine orchard.

The settler was a fisherman. His wife was a midwife who liked to read Western magazines.

Cook Cove was named after this happy couple. It provides for a sandy beach on the southeast side of Galiano. There are two accesses to the beach, both of which are on Sticks Allison Road. (#10 on the map)

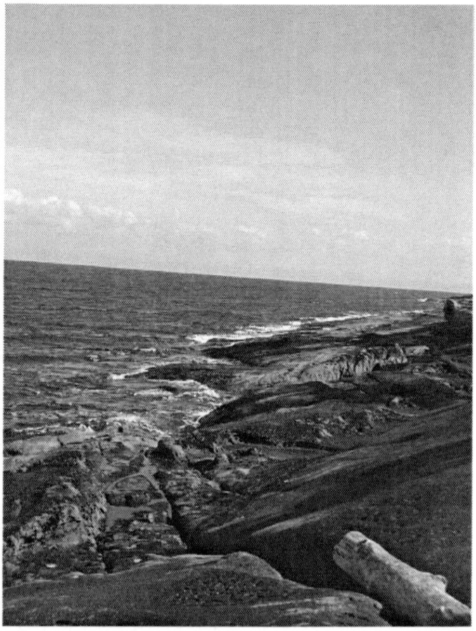

Dionisio Point Provincial Park

In the 1860`s, a 57 m passenger steamer, called the *Del Norte*, sank in a bay. The hulk lay undiscovered for one hundred years.

Coon Bay is located off Dionisio Point, at the tip of North Galiano. The bay is one of the most beautiful bays in all the Gulf Islands. It provides for a sandy swimming beach where sculpted sandstone, rocky ledges and abundant marine life become exposed at low tide.

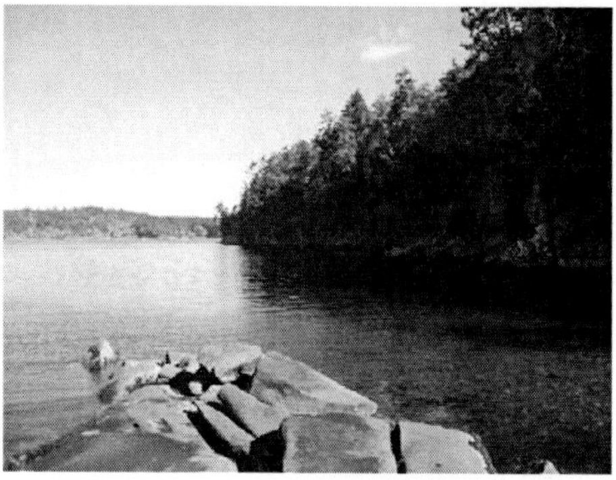

The bay sits in *Dionisio Point Provincial Park*, one of the most scenic places on the Island. It provides for views of Porlier Pass and Valdes Island.

There are 7 km of easy trails through the park. Two trails, called *Maple Bay Trail* and *Sutil Ridge Loop Trail*, provide access to mature forest in the interior of the park.

The point, which is covered with small stands of Arbutus and Garry Oak, is an excellent place to see Bald Eagles and to find Sea Stars. The easy trail around the point is called *Porlier Pass Trail*.

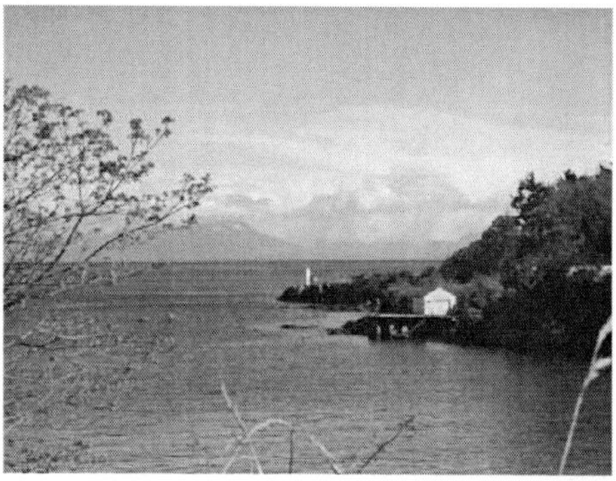

The park and beach are only accessible by water. However, there is a seasonal water taxi that transports visitors to the park, from the community of Spanish Hills on North Galiano. (#1 on the map)

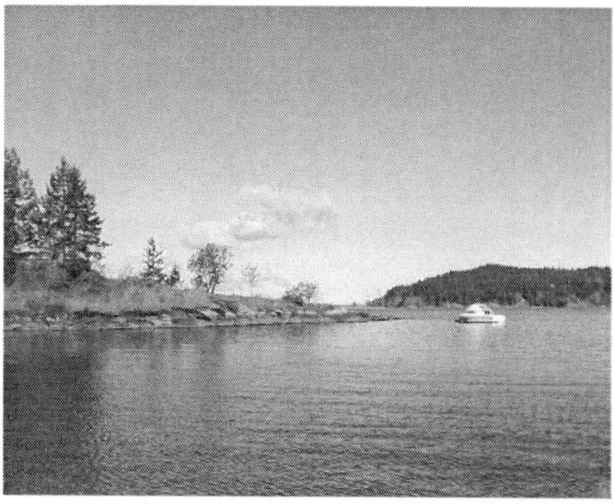

If you launch a boat from the bay, keep in mind that high seas can build in Porlier Pass. Further out from the bay, *Canoe Islet* is a favorite spot for scuba diving, where the wreck of the Del Norte exists. (#1 on the map)

Ganner Road Beach

There is a short trail on the west side of Galiano, which leads to a secluded, pebbled beach. The beach, which is accessible from the end of Ganner Road, provides for views of Wise Island and the Ballingal Islets. (#8 on the map)

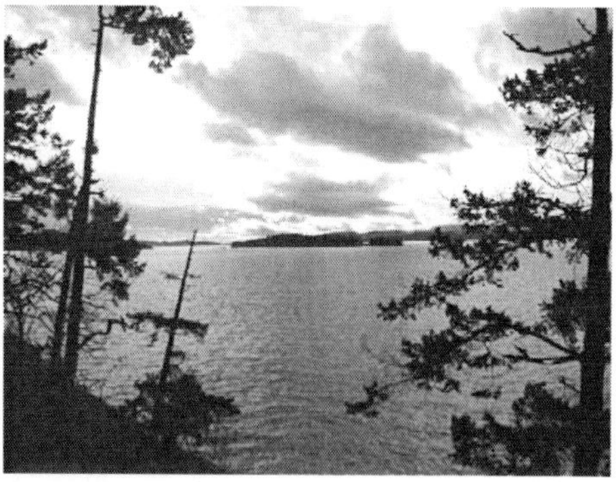

Georgeson Bay

In the 1840's, a child ran away from a Scottish school at the age of 14. He then sailed to far away lands as a cabin boy. Later, the Scotsman purchased some land surrounding a bay. There, he built a cabin on the banks of a creek.

In the 1870's, the Scotsman, who had become known locally as 'Scotty', purchased the remainder of the land around the bay. There, he established a farm and built another home.

Around that time, a tinker who lived on Mayne Island was shot to death and his cabin was looted. When a reward was posted by the police, Scotty gave evidence against an Indian called 'Indian Tom'. The Indian was later executed as a result of Scotty's testimony.

On returning home one day, Scotty found his wife lying on the floor. Indians had forced poison down her throat. Thereafter, he and his wife were in constant danger from the Indians.

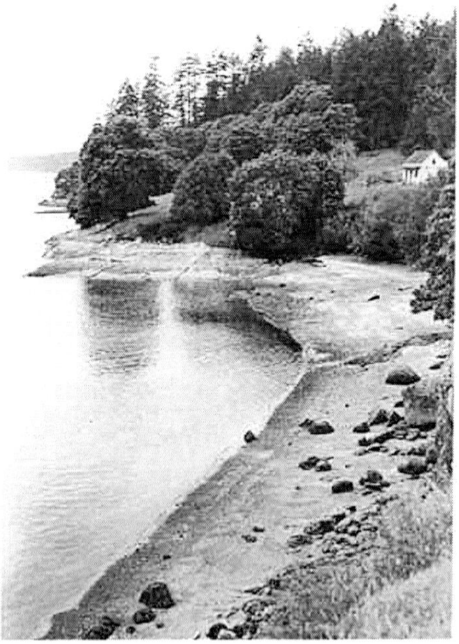

Georgeson Bay at the turn of the century
Galiano Archives MOR42

In the 1880's, Scotty moved to Mayne Island and became its first lighthouse keeper, providing service to the lighthouse for over 35 years.

In the early 1920's, his family built him a large retirement home at the head of the bay on his Galiano property. Two years later, he retired and the whole family moved into the house. It soon became known locally as the *Big House*.

Georgeson Bay was named after this Scotsman. Located on the southwest side of Galiano, it provides for a rocky beach, which is a great place to see Sea Lions. The beach is accessible by way of Active Pass Drive. (#18 on the map)

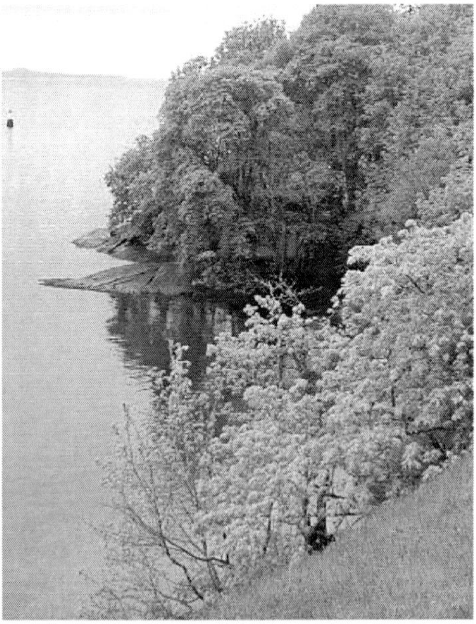

Georgeson Bay as it appears today

Matthews Point Regional Park

Matthews Point Regional Park was established only recently. It provides for a dense forest of mature Douglas-Fir, Arbutus and Garry Oak trees, as well as a stunning beachfront swimming area.

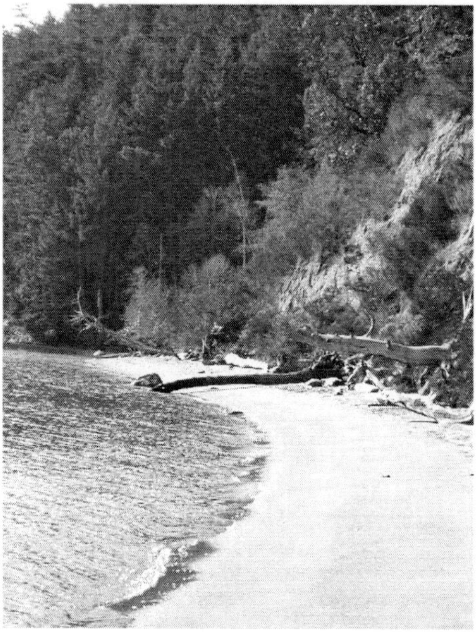

Matthews Point is located in the park. At low tide, it provides for one of the most beautiful white sand beaches in all the Gulf Islands. The rough trail through Matthews Point Park is accessible from Bluff Road. (#16 on the map)

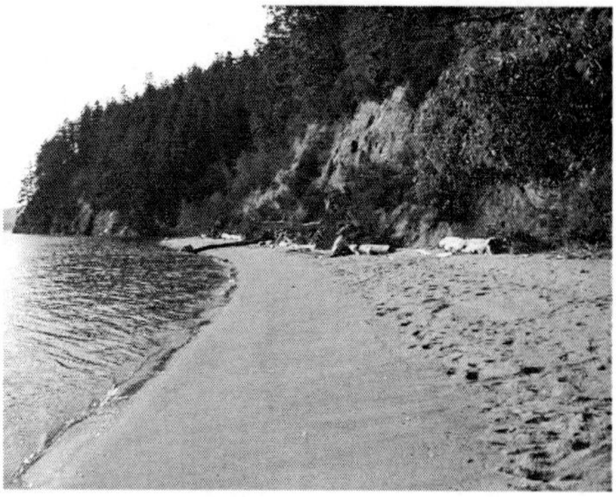

Montague Harbour Marine Park

Montague Harbour was once an ancient Coast Salish Indian village. Originally named *Stockade Harbour*, the waters made history in the 1860's, when the British captured Indians there because of attacks they had carried out on Pender and Saturna Islands.

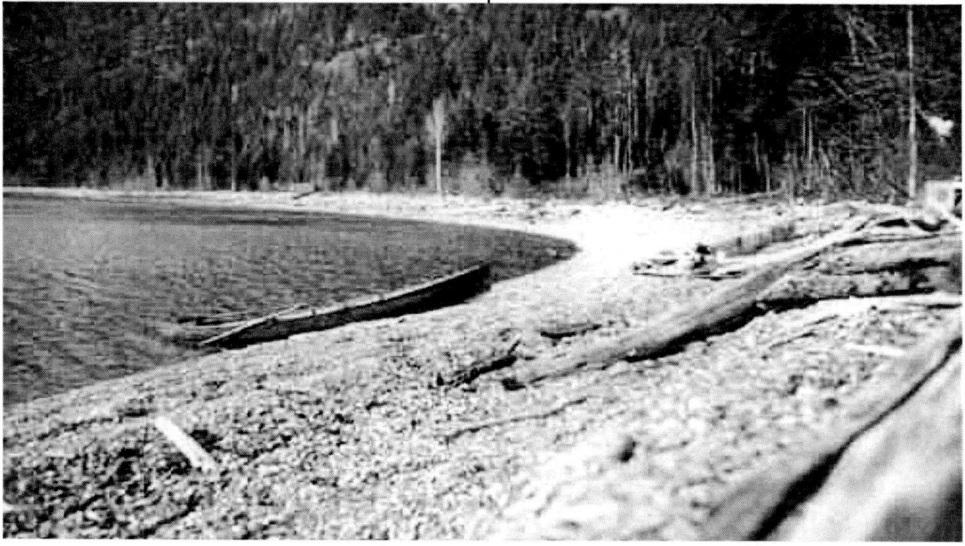

Shell Beach at the turn of the century - Galiano Archives 2004021028

One hundred years later, an end-loading wharf was built at the harbour. For the most part, it replaced the wharf at Sturdies Bay for a while. Shortly thereafter, the *Montague Harbour Marina* opened there.

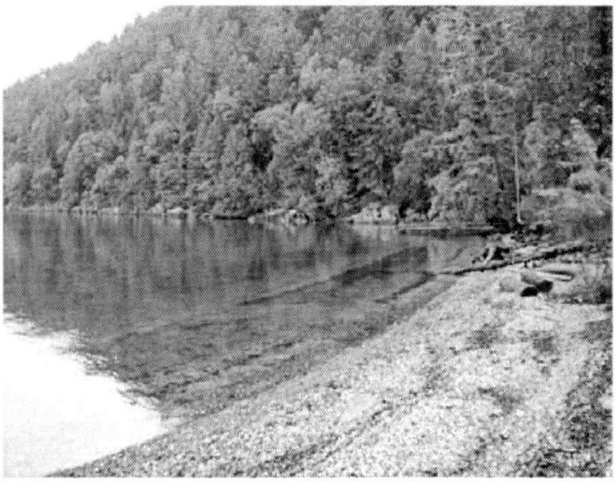

Shell Beach as it appears today

Today, Montague Harbour is one of the most popular anchorages in the Gulf Islands. Located on the southwest side of Galiano, the wharf is now used by sea planes and to transport schoolchildren to neighboring schools.

Montague Harbour Provincial Marine Park was the first marine park to be established in all of British Columbia. It provides for lovely forest trails. There are also facilities for picnics if you want to stay a while.

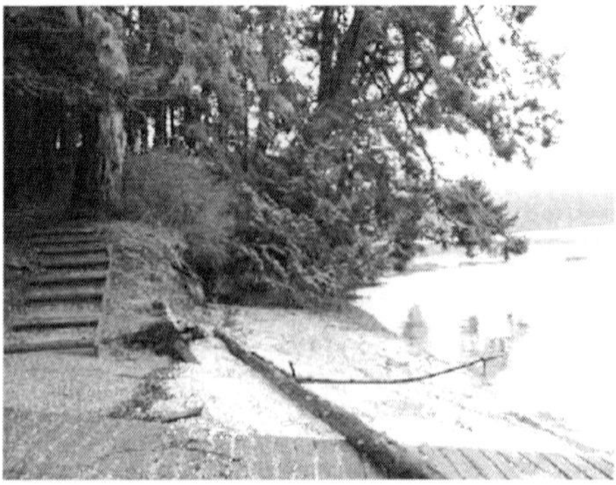

During the summer, British Columbia Parks runs an extensive schedule of free interpretive programs, which are held in the park at The Meeting Place and at The Marine Park Nature House. The park is accessible from the end of Montague Park Road. (#9 on the map)

The Gray Peninsula, which is connected to the head of the harbour, provides for a popular, white shell, swimming beach, called *Shell Beach*. Underwater excavations are regularly performed there by *Montague Mudsuckers* (archeologists).

The easy 3 km trail that follows the waters around the peninsula is a great place to find clams and to see Great Blue Herons, Kingfishers, Bald Eagles and other birds. The beach is accessible from the end of Montague Park Road. (#9 on the map)

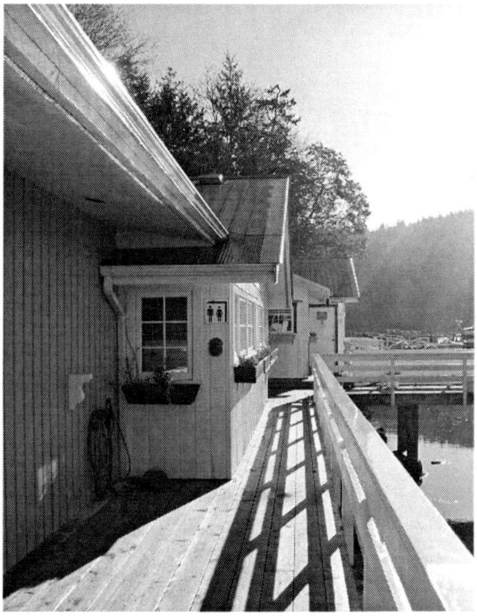

The Montague Harbour Marina offers a wide range of services for boaters. In addition to moorage, fuel and boat rentals, it carries groceries, and camping and fishing supplies. There is also a seasonal restaurant.

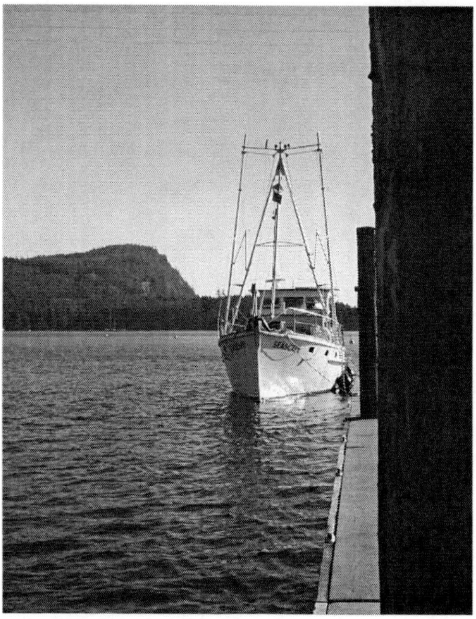

If you launch a boat from the wharf, you can circumnavigate a group of privately owned islands located in the harbour. The Ballingal Islets, at the northwest end of the group, make for an interesting destination.

Morning Beach

After World War I, an Englishman purchased some property that included Lion Islet off the southeast shore of Galiano. He called the property *Lyons*. There, he built a large home.

In the 1920's, the Englishman exchanged the property for property owned by his brother. Thereafter, his brother became the owner of Lyons.

In the year 1930, the brother leased Lyons to a family who ran it as a resort. A few years later, he returned to the property and ran it as a resort for another year, himself.

During World War II, the property was leased to the YWCA as a summer camp.

Lyons changed owners several times until the year 1950, when it was operated as a large chicken farm. A decade later, the house was torn down and a new house was built on the property

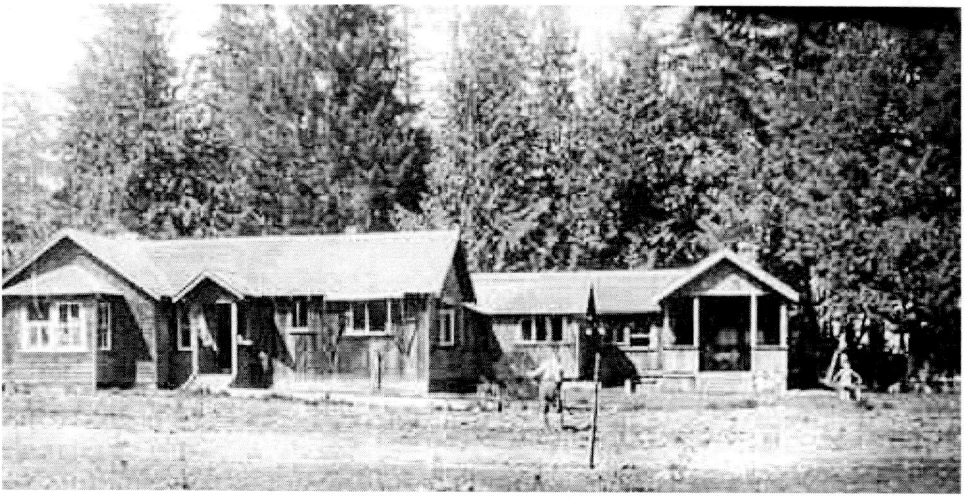

***Lyons* on Lion Islet - Galiano Archives 2004021091**

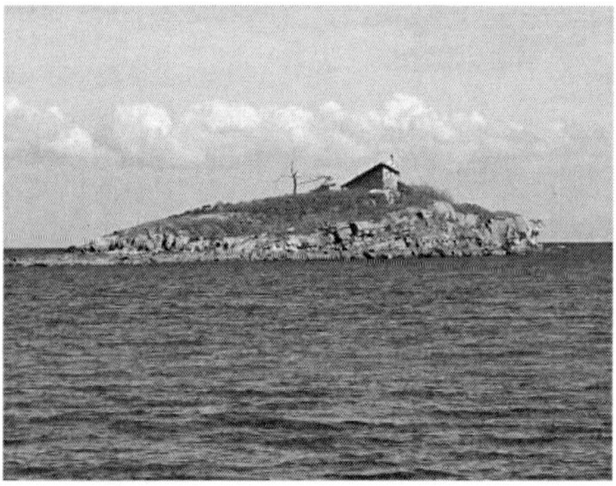

Lion Islet can be seen from Salamanca Point on the southeast side of Galiano. The pebbled beach on the point is called *Morning Beach.* It is accessible by way of a short trail on Ellis Road. (#11 on the map)

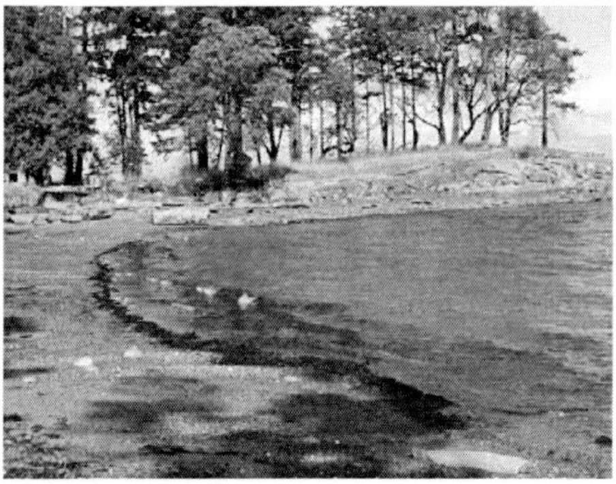

Mount Galiano Park

At 300 m, *Mount Galiano* is the highest peak on Galiano. It provides for incredible views of the Gulf Islands and of the San Juan Islands. It is also known for its forest and its spring wildflowers.

Mount Galiano is located in *Mount Galiano Park*, an ecologically sensitive, nature protection area. The 3 km trail through the park is of moderate difficulty. It is accessible from Active Pass Drive. (#19 on the map)

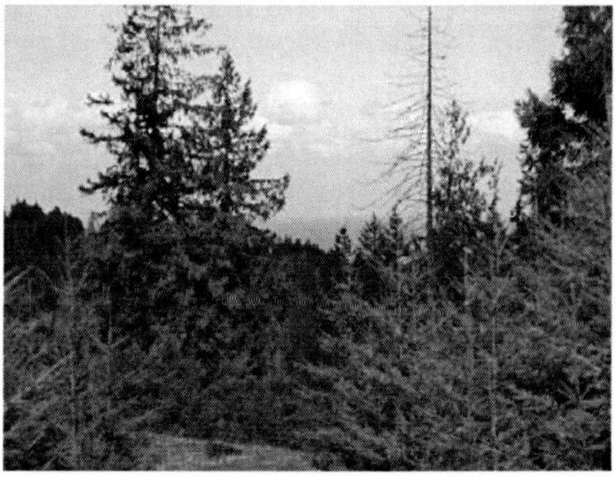

Pebble Beach Reserve

In the 1880's, a land survey of Galiano reported the existence of a large beaver dam near a bay on North Galiano. Unfortunately, over the years, the dam disappeared.

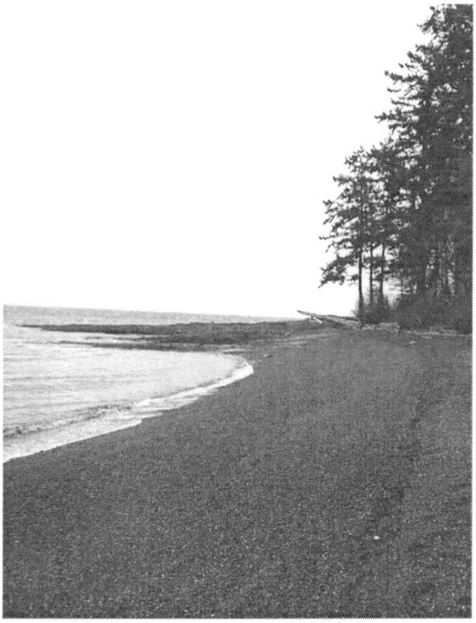

A short time ago, *Pebble Beach Reserve* was established as a protected area. It includes rare stands of mature Douglas-Fir. Only recently have the beavers returned to the area to restore the dam.

There are three main trails through the reserve, all of which are accessible from the end of McCoskrie Road. (#7 on the map)

The *Cable Bay Trail* and the *Laughlin Trail* are linked by a short interpretive trail that was set up to contrast a mature forest ecosystem. The trail travels through lands that were once a commercial forest plantation.

The *Laughlin Lake Trail* leads to *Laughlin Lake*, the largest body of water on Galiano. Because it is home to at least 55 species of resident and migratory birds, the lake provides for excellent bird watching.

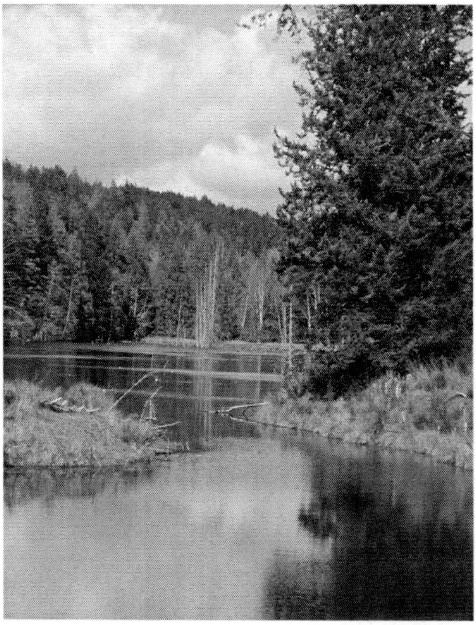

The *Pebble Beach Trail* travels through a beautiful mature forest to *Cable Bay*. It passes *Greig Creek*, *Beaver Creek* and the *Great Beaver Swamp*.

Cable Bay is well known as a place to find agates and other semi-precious stones. The beach on the bay is called *Pebble Beach*. It is a great place for a *soak* (swim).

Retreat Cove

Shortly before the outbreak of World War I, a settler immigrated to Canada from Greece. In the late 1920's, he and his wife purchased some property on a cove. There, they established a farm.

On their farm, the couple lived in a little house overlooking a Japanese-Canadian owned herring saltery where the settler worked.

In the 1930's, the settler built a log cabin for his growing family. Because he had several children, he soon became known locally as 'Papa'.

The settler raised Black Quebec mink on the farm. So his family called the farm the *Seven Sister Fur Farm*. During World War II, the mink became hard to find, so they were forced to sell them at a loss. Eventually, their farm was also sold.

At that time, the area surrounding the cove was a thriving community, with a school, fish saltery and grocery store.

One day, a party was held for all the fishermen at the Japanese owned saltery. While the fishermen were enjoying the festivities, a fire started on the dock.

The fire spread through the saltery and through all the stores, offices and homes at the cove. Ironically, the next day, news came of the Japanese attack on Pearl Harbour.

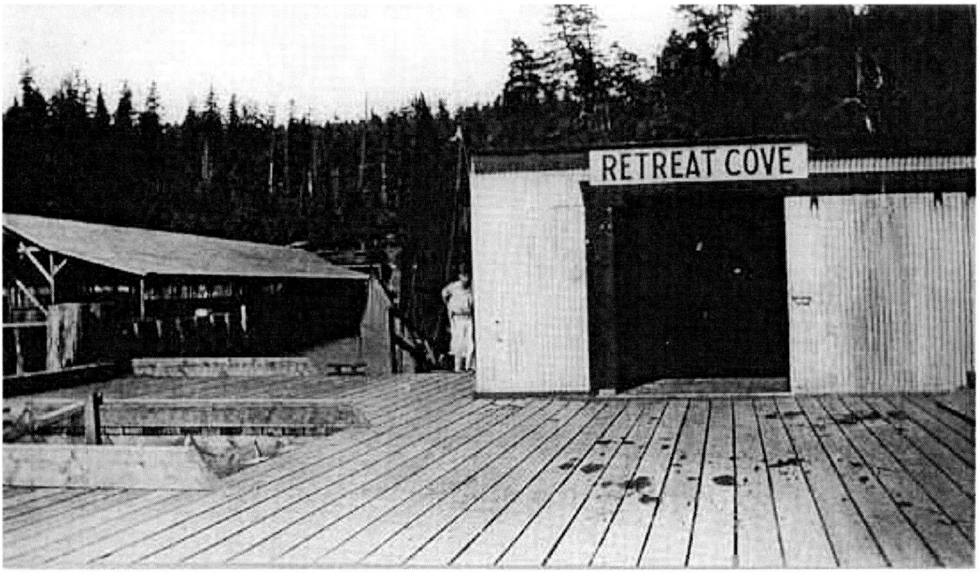

Retreat Cove wharf, early 1900's – Galiano Archives 2004026520

Retreat Cove is a beautiful cove on the northwest side of Galiano. It provides for views of Salt Spring Island. A government wharf that extends into the cove serves as a water access point.

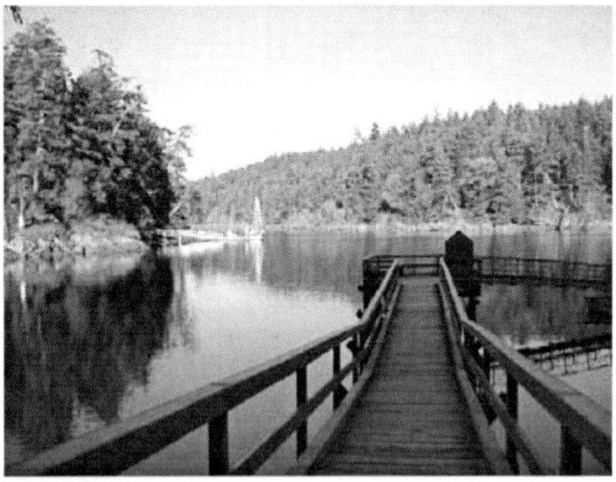

The beach on Retreat Cove provides for overhanging rocks and a cavern. It is accessible from the end of Retreat Cove Road. (#6 on the map)

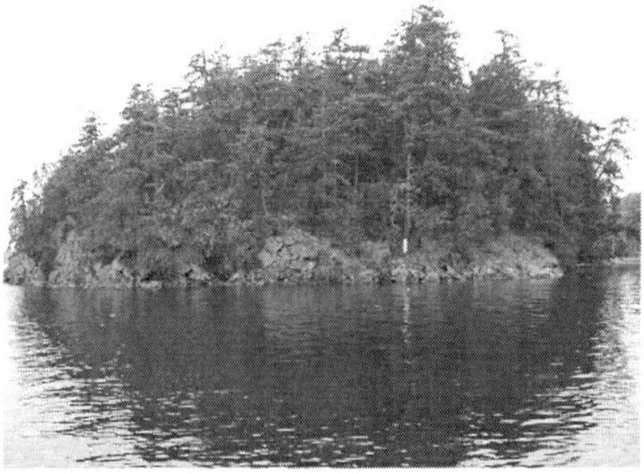

You can launch a boat from the cove and take a relaxing, quiet tour around a nearby island called *Retreat Island*. However, keep in mind that the cove is exposed to westerly winds and the waters behind the island are shallow.

Shaw's Landing

In the 1870`s, a settler emigrated from England to Galiano. At that time, he became the first man to settle on North Galiano.

Because there was no store in the community, the settler had to row to Vancouver Island for supplies. When steamers began stopping in a little bay near his home, he would row out to them, and then pick up mail and groceries from one of the crew.

Soon, he became the first person to offer postal service to the other residents of North Galiano. When he died in 1890, one of his sons took over his postal duties.

The settler's son tended to the family orchard and continued his father's postal duties. Over time, he became adept at building large model sailboats.

In the year 1912, the Postmaster General approved a request for a post office on North Galiano. It was established at the little bay near the settler's home.

Shaw's Landing was named after this family, who provided postal services to North Galiano for several decades. The beach on the little bay provides for a seasonal waterfall. It is accessible by way of Porlier Pass Drive, just south of Cook Road. (#4 on the map)

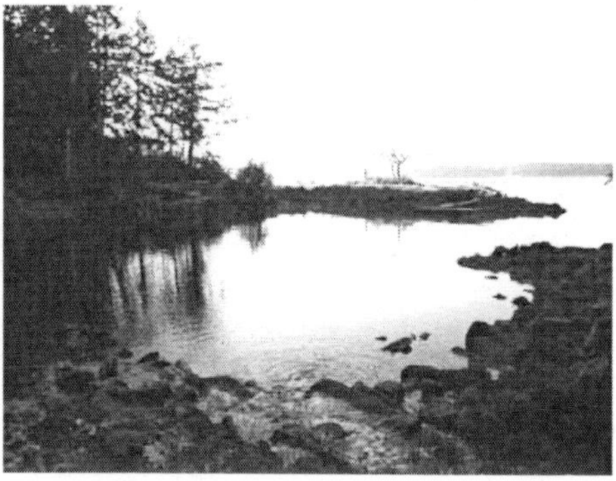

Spanish Hills

At one time, North Galiano had a sawmill, six salmon and herring canneries, and a marine shop called *Baines Motor Boat Repair Shop*. The owner of the marine shop built the North Galiano School, which was also located nearby.

In the 1940's, the post office at Shaw's Landing was moved up the Island, to a store that had been opened at the turn of the century.

The post office operated from inside the store and there were living quarters in the back. The store's new owners changed the name to *Clutterbuck's Store*.

A decade later, the store was destroyed by fire and was rebuilt. At that time, it was renamed the *North Galiano Store.*

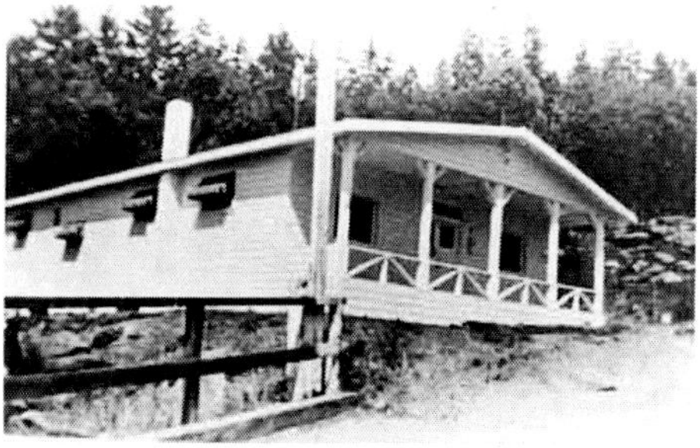

Store at Spanish Hills in the 1950's
Galiano Archives M207

The store changed owners many times. In the 1960's, it was renamed the *Spanish Hills Store*. It is now a private residence on Porlier Pass Road.

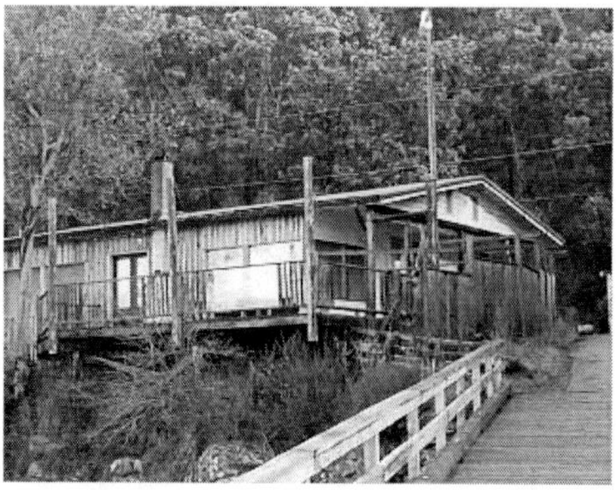

Store at Spanish Hills as it appears today

Today, the community of *Spanish Hills* provides mainly for wonderful scenery and great sports fishing. The government wharf that extends into the Channel is owned by the Department of Fisheries.

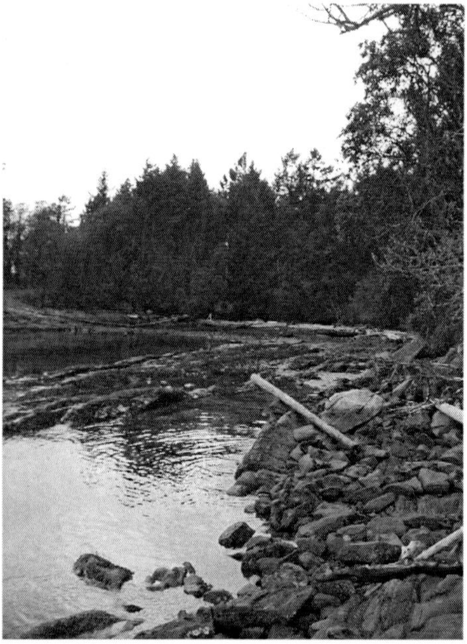

The beach at Spanish Hills is accessible by way of Porlier Pass Road. (#2 on the map) The area is a great spot for scuba diving at a depth of up to 30 m. The waters further north provide for some spectacular underwater scenery. Keep in mind that the *skookumchuck* (strong currents) there can run up to 7 knots.

Spotlight Cove

At the turn of the century, a seaman owned a small boatyard in a cove. With the help of the model sailboat builder who lived at Shaw's Landing, he transformed a 50-year old dugout canoe into a sailing vessel.

The seaman strengthened the hull of the canoe with an Oak frame and added a cabin, floorboards, decking, a 135 kg keel, three masts and two watertight bulkheads. The b woatas named the *Tilikum*.

Later, a sea Captain sailed around the world in the boat, becoming the first person ever to do so in a vessel of that size. The voyage took him three years to complete. The Tilikum can be seen today at the Maritime Museum of British Columbia.

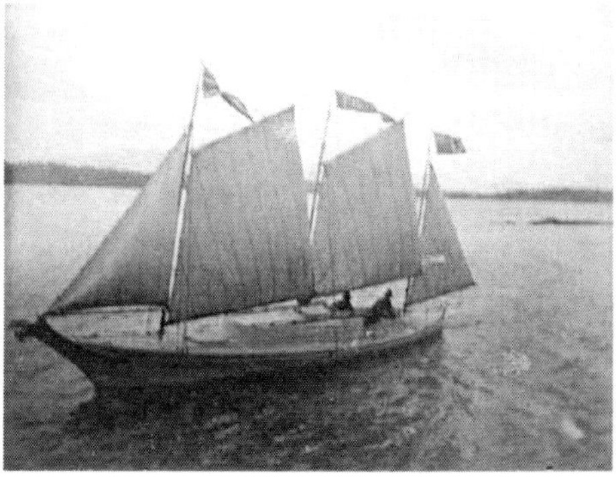

The Tilikum at the turn of the century
Galiano Archives MOR69

Spotlight Cove, on the northwest side of Galiano, provides for a long beach. The trail to the beach is accessible by way of Porlier Pass Road. (#3 on the map)

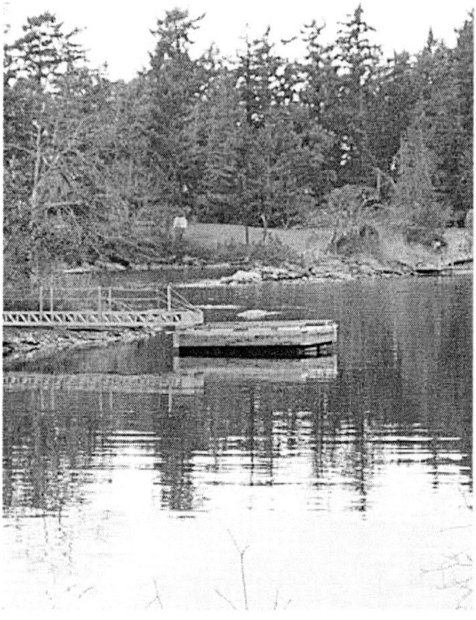

Twiss Road Beach

The beach off Twiss Road, on the southeast side of Galiano, is dotted with driftwood. It provides for views of Gossip Island to the east. (#15 on the map)

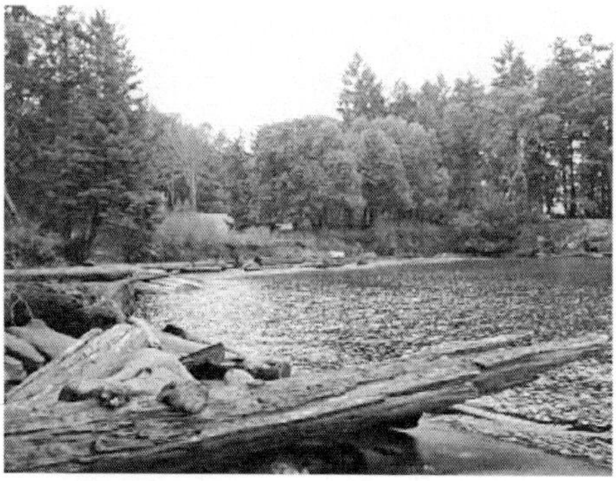

Whaler Bay

In the 1880's, a settler moved from Retreat Cove to a bay. There, he built a log cabin and started a family. Unfortunately, a few years later, his wife passed away.

When his sister emigrated from Ireland to help him raise his two baby sons, he decided to built a larger home.

The settler's new home had three large rooms on the main floor and three bedrooms upstairs, all of which were plastered on the inside. At one end of a long verandah there was a milk-cooling room. At the other end was a summer kitchen with an adjacent wood shed.

When the settler finished building the house, his sister married and moved off the Island, leaving him with a large home to maintain.

Desperate, the settler hired a housekeeper, who took care of his home and family well. Over time, he made her his second wife. Ironically, she died in childbirth shortly after the turn of the century.

At the onset of World War I, the unfortunate settler drowned while crossing from Mayne Island to Pender Island in his boat.

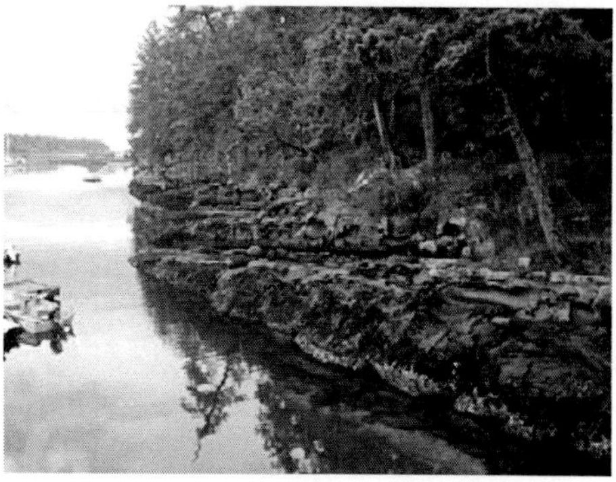

Whaler Bay is a lovely bay on the southeast side of Galiano. It can be accessed by way of Cain Road. (#12 on the map) Once an anchorage for small whaling boats, it is now used as a home for commercial fishing boats.

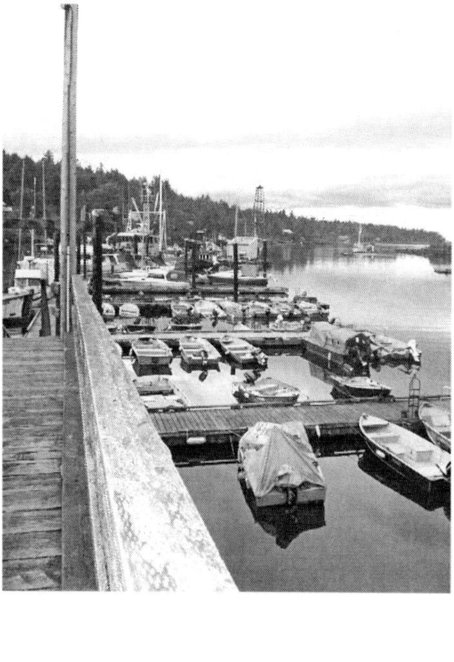

Salt Spring Island

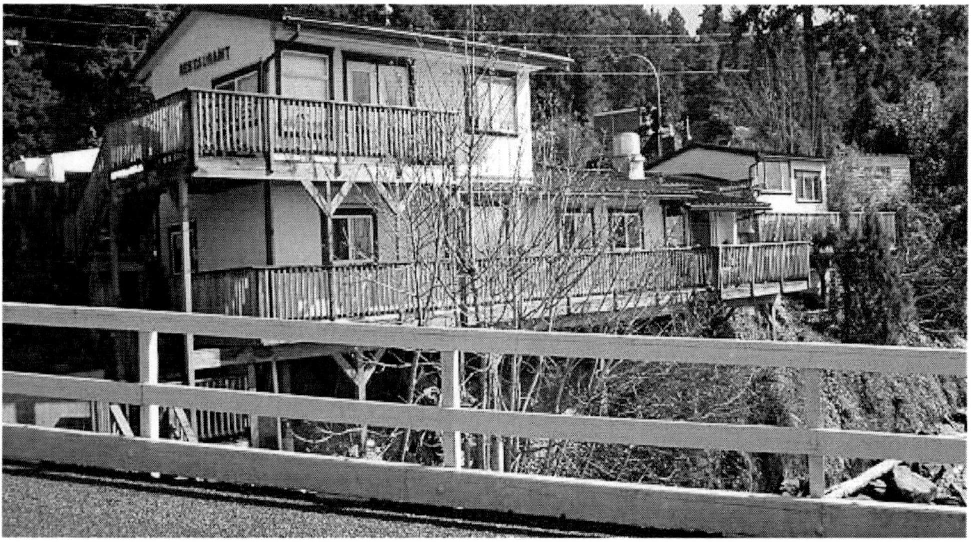

Vesuvius Bay Wharf

It was in the spring of 1861 that a Scotsman, named Jonathan Begg, was awakened by a band of Haida Indians who were stealing from his store...

With Jonathan aboard, the British Royal Navy pursued the Indians in a gunboat named the H.M.G. *Forward*. When they found the Indians camped on Vancouver Island, they fired on their camp. In the exchange of gunfire, four Indians and one crewman were killed.

Jonathan Begg was born in Scotland in the early 1800's. In 1859, he arrived penniless, in what was at that time the Colony of Vancouver Island.

Jonathan was among the first settlers to reform the land pre-emption system for the colony. He then settled in that same colony, on Salt Spring Island. There, he became **the Postman**, operating the Island's first store and post office.

The politically minded Jonathan Begg was a reporter of the news, having been Salt Spring's correspondent for the *British Colonist* newspaper. In response to his request for a post office, another newspaper said this about him:

"From Mr. J. Begg, one of the first, and most respectable of the settlers on Salt Spring Island, we are rejoiced to hear a most satisfactory account of the prospects of their happy little community."

New Westminster Times

Things to Know

Salt Spring is a bustling island. At 180 sq km, it is the largest of the southern Gulf Islands. While diverse scenery is its most distinguishing characteristic, the fact that it offers something for everyone gives Salt Spring Island its unique charm.

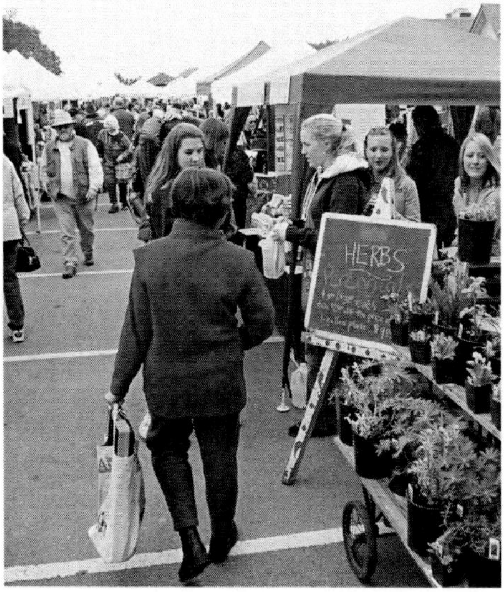

Salt Spring is the fastest growing and most populous of the southern Gulf Islands. It has a population of approximately 10,000 permanent residents, of which most are young families, retirees and business professionals.

Known as *The Art Lover's Gallery*, Salt Spring is home to the greatest collection of artists in all of Canada. During the tourist season, the population swells to around 20,000 when visitors tour the Island in search of local art.

Ganges

Urbanization of the Island began at its north end when a group of settlers arrived during the gold rush in the late 1850's. Most of these immigrants were Black men who were former slaves from the U.S. They were followed immediately by Australians and settlers of other descents.

Soon, a community called *Central Settlement* developed in an inner location at the north end. Of the 26 families that settled there, 17 were Black.

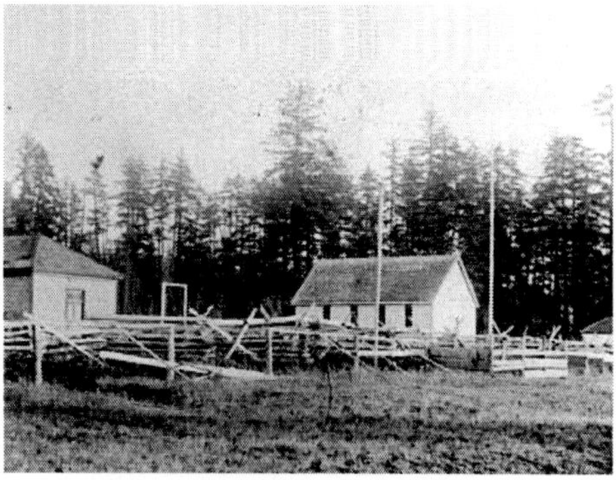

Central Settlement in the 1890`s
Salt Spring Archives 1994137031

The settlers found the winter of 1862 to be unusually severe, which resulted in a 30 percent decrease in the Island's population. Then, after the Civil War, many of the Black residents returned to the U.S. However, as more women and children arrived in the 1870's communities began to develop in each of the corners of the Island.

Some of the families who settled at the south end were *Kanakas* (people of Hawaiian descent). By that time, the Island's population had tripled and it held claim to being the first agricultural settlement in all of British Columbia.

Over the next decade, British and Irish immigrants settled on the Island and, soon, another community began to develop, near a harbour called *Ganges Harbour*. In time, the community became known as *Ganges*.

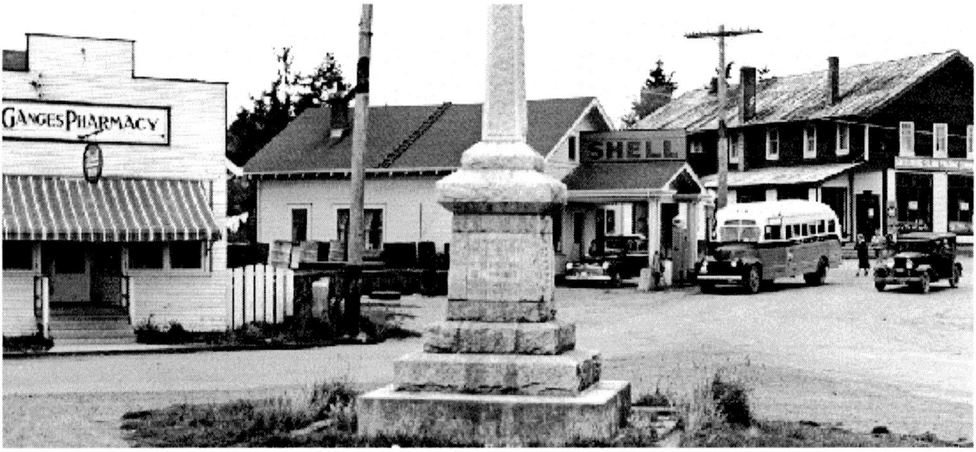

Main street through Ganges in 1948 – Salt Spring Archives CKC998162076

Today, Ganges is 'downtown' to Salt Spring Islanders. As the commercial hub of the Island, it is the largest community in all the Gulf Islands.

Ganges provides for grocery stores, restaurants, banks, art galleries, quality retail stores and other businesses. The village also provides for a marina. A visitor information centre is located in the heart of the village.

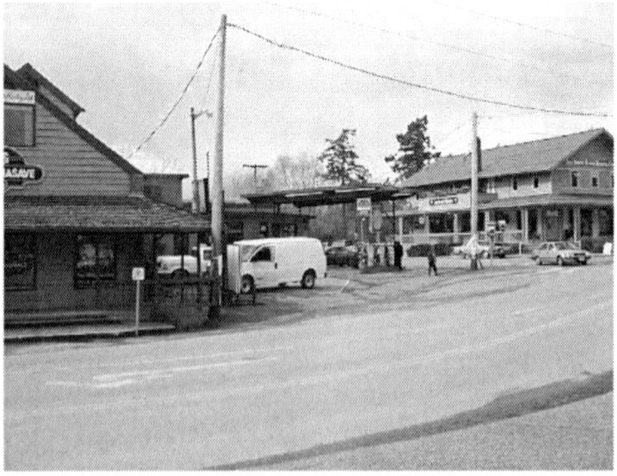

Ganges main street as it appears today

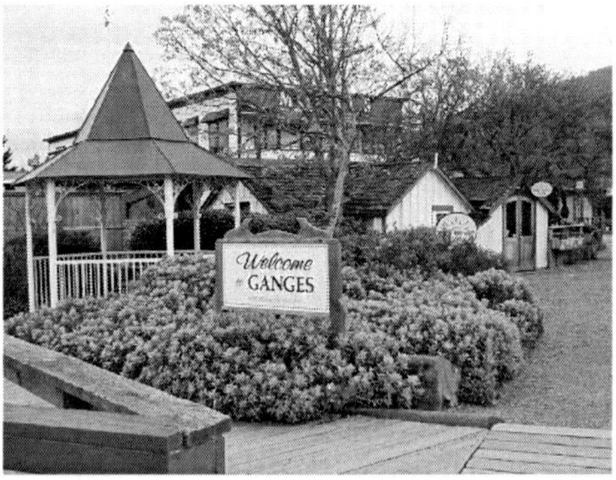

Vesuvius Bay Wharf

In the 1860's, ships traveling to Vancouver Island sailed past both the east and west sides of Salt Spring. Passengers were landed by boat, off *Trincomali Channel* on the northeast side of the Island, or in *Vesuvius Bay* on the northwest side of the Island.

The first wharf was built in Vesuvius Bay in the 1870's. It accommodated ships coming through the waterway called *Stuart Channel*.

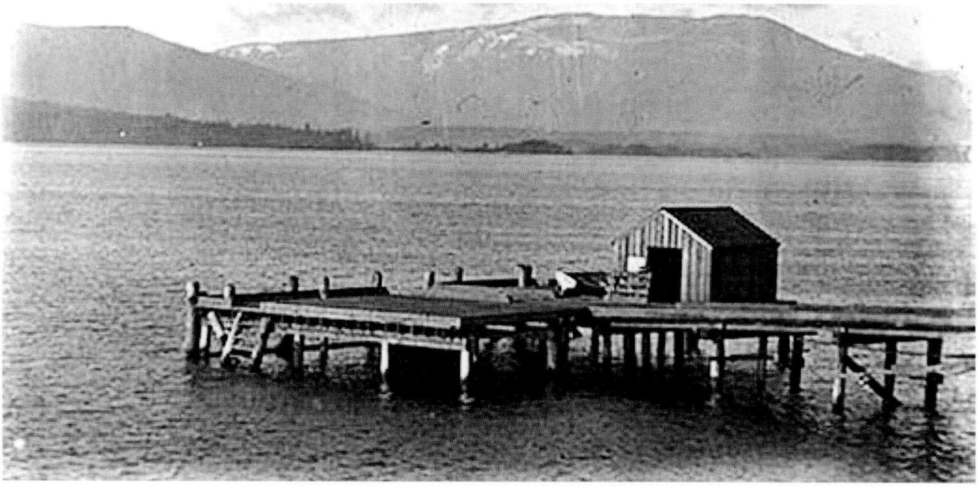

Vesuvius Bay wharf at the turn of the century – Salt Spring Archives 50532

By the 1890's, five wharves had been constructed on Salt Spring. A wharf in **the Postman's** community of *Fernwood* serviced the northern tip of the Island.

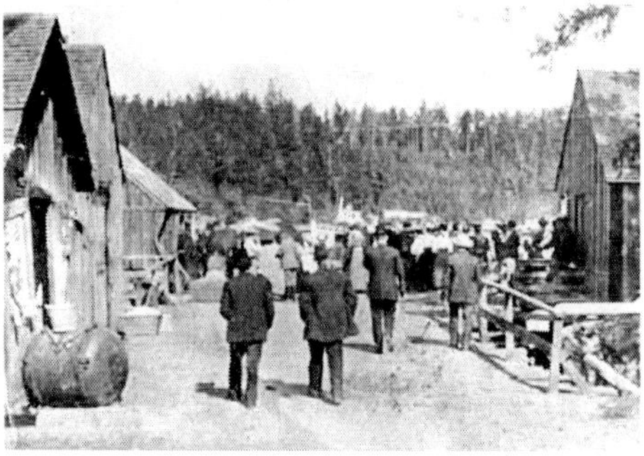

Wharf in Ganges Harbour in 1907
Salt Spring Archives 1994137002

Wharves in *Vesuvius Bay* and *Ganges Harbour* serviced the communities on the northwest and northeast sides, while wharves in *Fulford Harbour* and *Burgoyne Bay* serviced the southeast and southwest sides.

At the onset of World War I, a new 300 m wharf was constructed in Ganges Harbour to provide deepwater docking on any tide. By the 1930's, it had replaced the wharf in Vesuvius Bay as the main port of call.

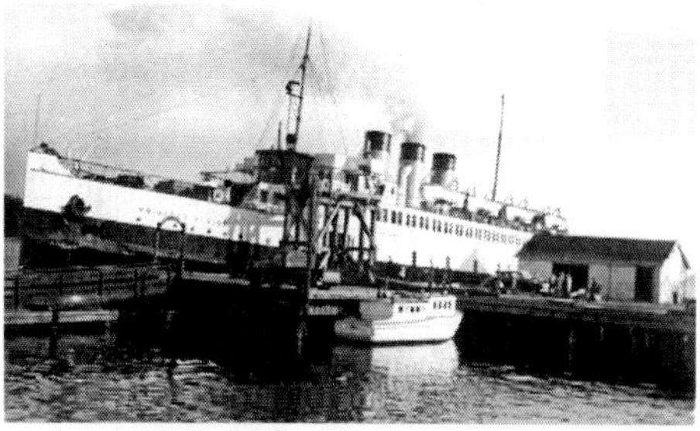

S.S. *Princess Elaine* at Ganges wharf in 1928
Salt Spring Archives CKC998162123

Today, there are three main wharves on Salt Spring. The newest wharf is located at *Long Harbour*, just north of Ganges Harbour. Acquired in the 1960's, it services large ferries traveling to and from the mainland.

The wharf in Fulford Harbour provides for the most demanding ferry terminal on the Island, servicing ferries traveling to and from the tip of Vancouver Island.

The Vesuvius Bay wharf still serves as a port of call, but for smaller ferries traveling to and from the southeast side of Vancouver Island.

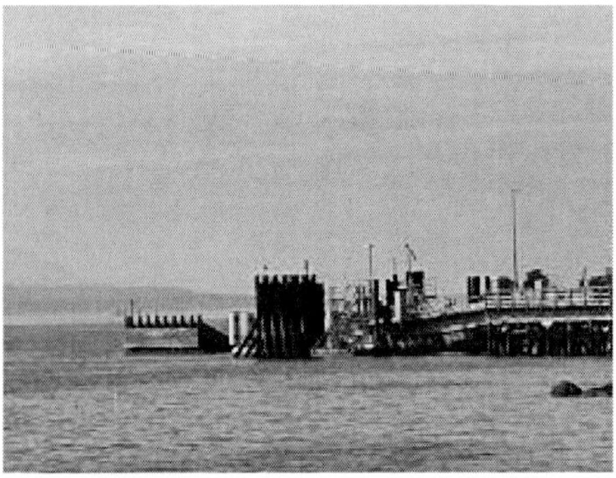

Vesuvius Bay wharf as it appears today

Ganges Post Offices

In the late 1850's, **the Postman** began offering a postal service from the store he owned in Fernwood. A schooner would pass by his property three times a week and he would row out into the Channel to collect the mail from one of the crew.

The store was initially named the *Salt Spring Island Store*, but was later renamed the *Balmoral Store*.

Although it soon became a gathering place for the families living in Fernwood, **the Postman** sold the business three years after it opened and the post office closed.

Later, in the 1870's, the *Salt Spring Island Post Office* opened in a little, one-room shack in Central Settlement.

An obstinate mule delivered the mail. Whenever the mule decided to run past a mail delivery point, its rider would drop a note apologizing for not delivering the mail that day.

Around that same time, a Portuguese storekeeper opened a second post office, from his store in Vesuvius. He would sail to Vancouver Island to purchase goods for his store. At one time, it was the only store on the Island.

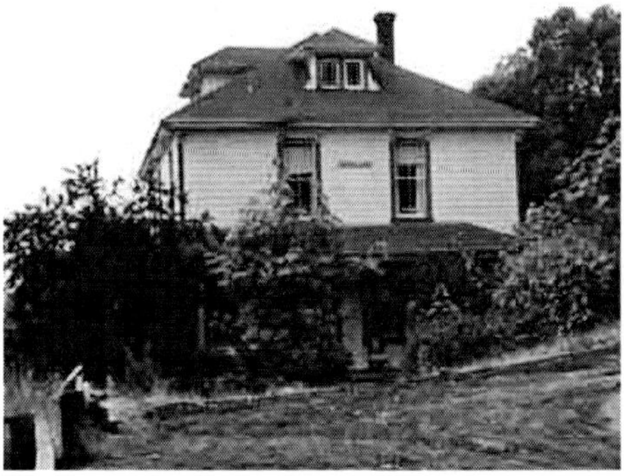

Vesuvius Post Office in the 1950's
Salt Spring Archives 02186028

The post office in Vesuvius closed shortly after it opened. Much later, in the 1970`s, the 100-year old building was destroyed by fire. Today, the *Vesuvius Inn Neighborhood Pub* sits on the site.

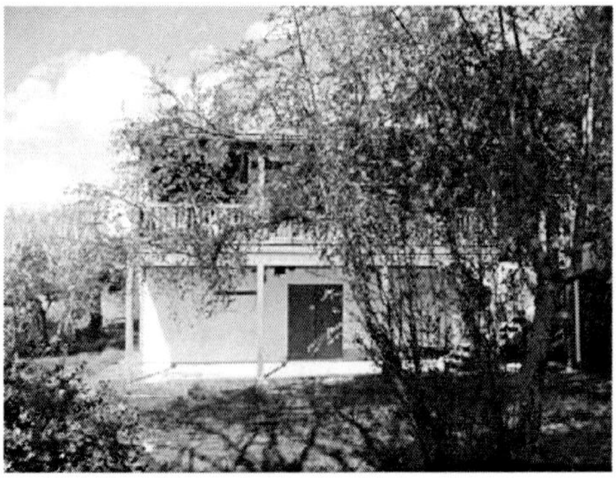

Site of the Vesuvius Post Office
as it appears today

In the 1890's, a settler opened another store on the Island, from his home in Central Settlement. Then, he took over the Salt Spring Island Post Office and moved it into his store.

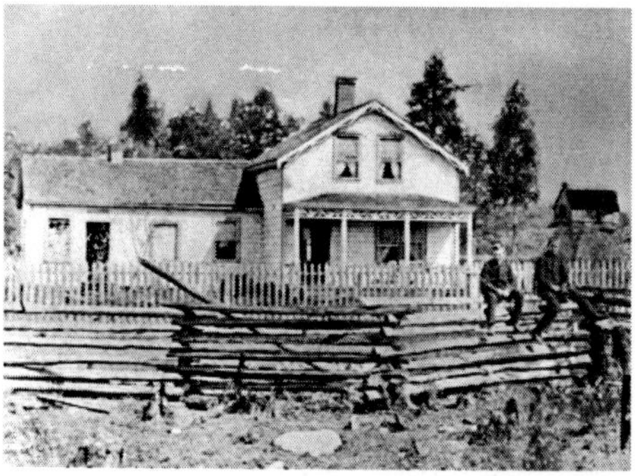

Salt Spring Island Post Office, 1890's
Salt Spring Archives 2005009001

The settler called his store *Broadwell`s Store*. It was the largest store on the Island. In the 1930`s, the Salt Spring Island Post Office closed. Today, a fire hall sits on the site.

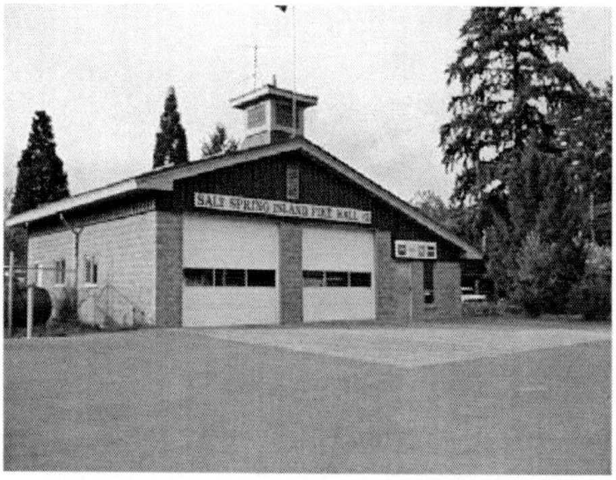

Site of the Salt Spring Island Post Office as it appears today

At the turn of the century, another post office opened, near the Ganges wharf. It operated from a building that was attached to the back of a boarding house.

The S.S. *Iroquois* would deliver the mail to the Ganges wharf, at which time the ship's purser would often open up the ship's bar to the settlers who were waiting for their mail.

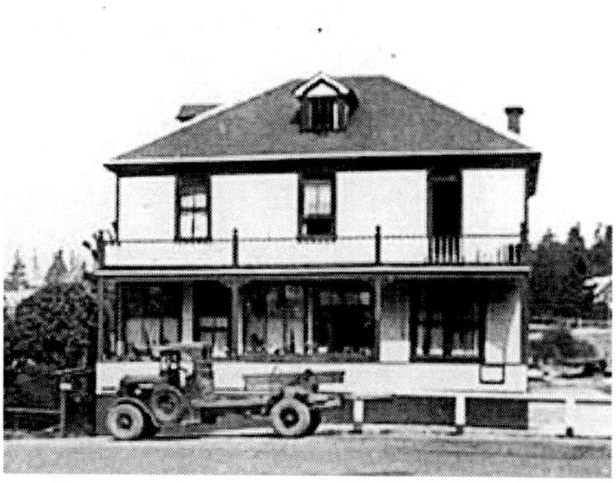

Ganges Post Office in the 1930's
Salt Spring Archives 1994137010

Much later, in the 1950's, the boarding house in Ganges was demolished, along with the attachment that had served as the post office. Today, a toy store, called *West of the Moon*, sits on the site and two post offices in Ganges serve the north end.

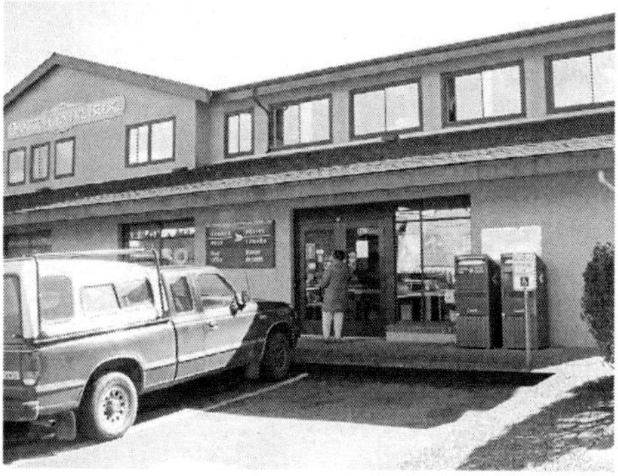

Fulford Post Office

Between 1880 and 1893, three post offices opened at the south end. At the turn of the century, two of them were moved into a valley called the *Fulford-Burgoyne Valley*.

When they were moved, they were consolidated as one post office called the *South Salt Spring Island Post Office*. It served the two communities there.

The consolidated post office operated from a store called *R.P. Edwards' Store*. The storekeeper was known locally as 'Old

Edwards'. He would wait until he heard the ship's whistle before loading the mailbags into his cart. The ship's Captain would then wait very impatiently as Old Edwards would take his time wheeling the cart down the long road to the Fulford Harbour wharf.

During its final voyage of 1911, the S.S. *Iroquois* was delivering the mail to the post office. When the ship sank during a storm, a mailbag that was on board washed ashore. One of the letters the mailbag contained was addressed to a settler who lived in the valley. It was from the government, appointing him Justice of the Peace.

At the end of World War I, the post office was moved into a hotel overlooking the harbour. It was called the *White Lodge*.

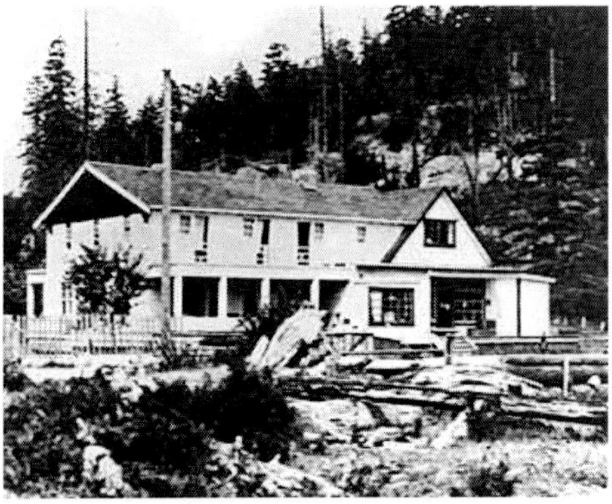

Fulford Post Office in 1920
Salt Spring Archives 1994137040

In the 1920's, another post office opened, at a small south end community called *Musgrave Landing*. Once again, there were three post offices serving the south end.

Shortly thereafter, the post office at Fulford Harbour was renamed the *Fulford Harbour Post Office*. In the 1930`s, the hotel from which it operated was destroyed by fire and rebuilt. Today, the *Fulford Inn* sits on the site.

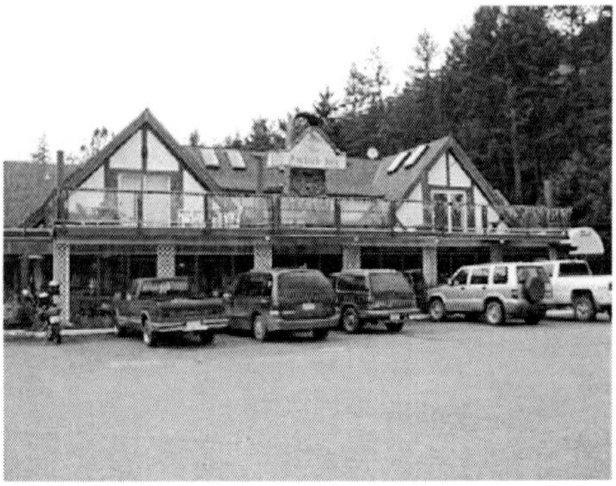

Old Fulford Harbour Post Office
as it appears today

In the 1940`s, the post office was moved into a store at the wharf. A decade later, the store was converted into a concession called *Mary Lee's Snack Shop*. Four years later, new owners changed the name to *Nan's Coffee Bar*.

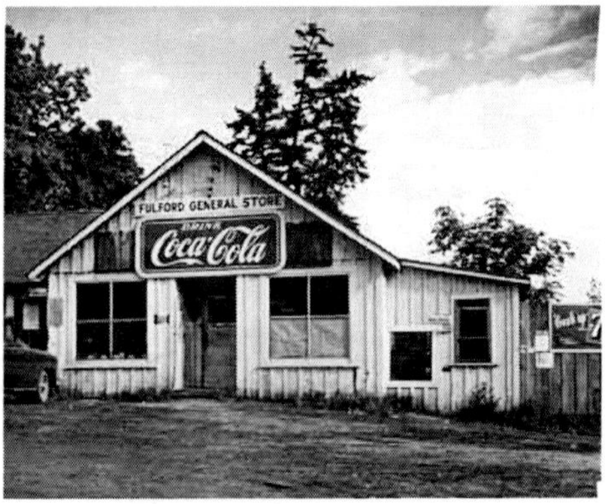

Fulford Post Office in the late 1950`s
Salt Spring Archives 02186003

Around that time, the other post offices at the south end closed, leaving only the Fulford Harbour Post Office in operation.

Today, the building that housed the post office at the wharf is home to the *Tree House Café South* and the post office operates from around the corner.

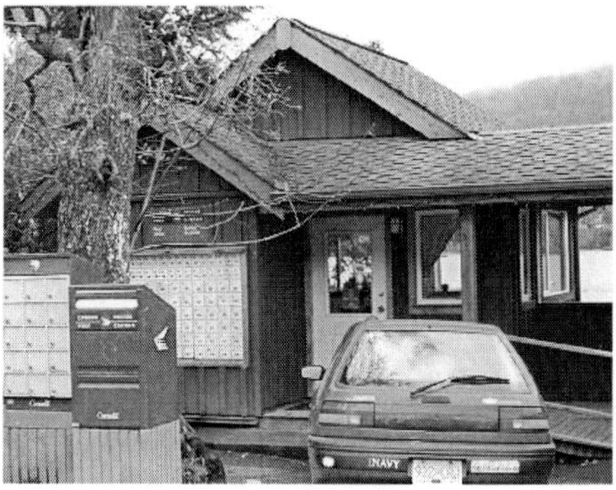

Mouat's Mall

At the turn of the century, two settlers went into partnership and purchased the store in Central. Then, they constructed a large building in Ganges and moved the store there.

Their new store included a blacksmith shop and some sheds that sat near the Ganges wharf. Using two boats, the partners operated a large export business from their store.

When one of the partners died three years later, a widow and one of her sons purchased the business. They sold everything from groceries and shoe polish to tools and furniture. They also operated the post office in Ganges.

Initially, the widow and her son named the store *G.J. Mouat and Company*. When her oldest son joined the business later, it was renamed *Mouat Brothers Company Ltd.*

By then, the wharf had become known as *Mouat's Landing*. Customers would gather there to socialize on *boat days* (when boats would dock at the wharf). They would leave their saddle ponies, ox teams, buggies and wagons all around the wharf.

Just before the outbreak of World War I, a new building was constructed next door and the store was moved there.

The new store had a wide staircase and a long counter that spanned the length of the store. The staircase led to a landing, and then split into two sets of stairs that continued up to the second floor.

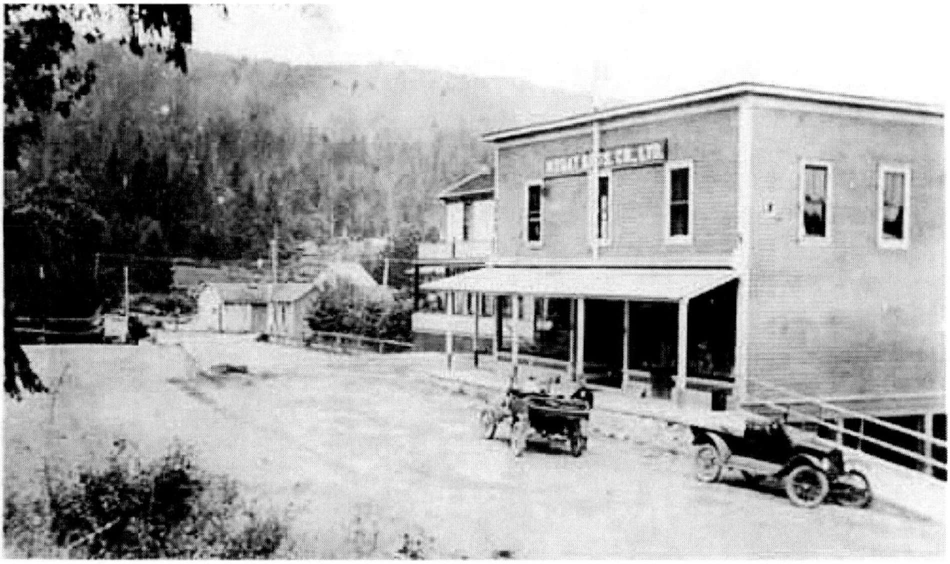

Mouat's Mall in the 1920's - Salt Spring Archives CKC998162061

There was a large feed shed at Mouat's Landing, with a separate room for kerosene, naphtha gas and lubricating oil. The shed had an office inside. It had a stand up desk on which sat a telephone that was connected to the store.

In the late 1960`s, the company assets were purchased by a group of individuals that included the widow's grandsons. At that time, a new company was formed and the store was renamed *Mouat's Trading Company Ltd.*

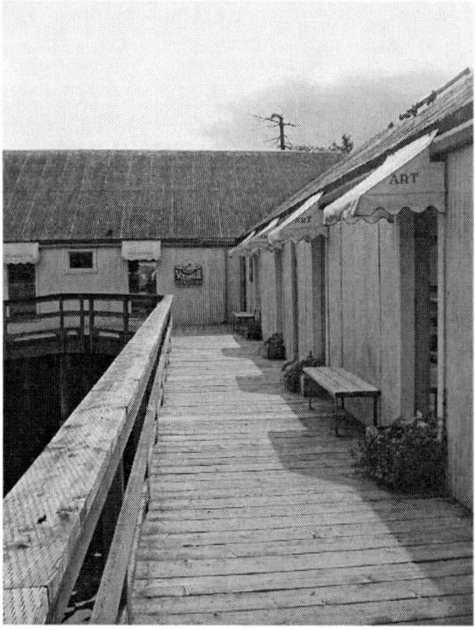

Over time, the feed shed was connected to the store to form a building complex. It was called *Mouat's Mall.*

Today, the store provides for hardware and housewares and the mall is leased to businesses that are known collectively as *Seaside at Mouat's.* At the time of this writing, the businesses in Mouat's Mall included a salon, a bookstore, a gallery and a restaurant.

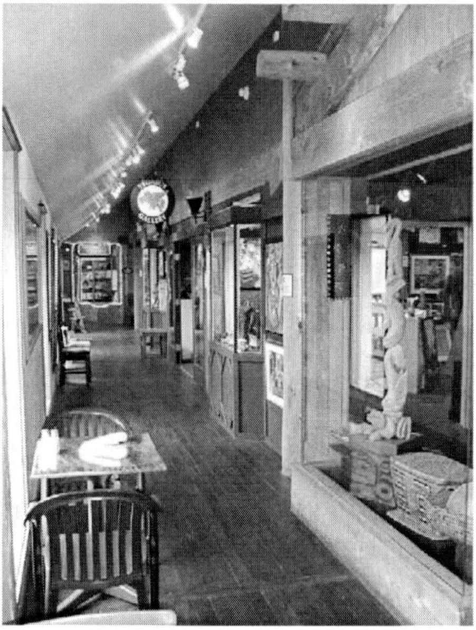

Mouat's Trading Company celebrates its centennial in the year 2007. The mall is located in Ganges at the end of Fulford-Ganges Road.

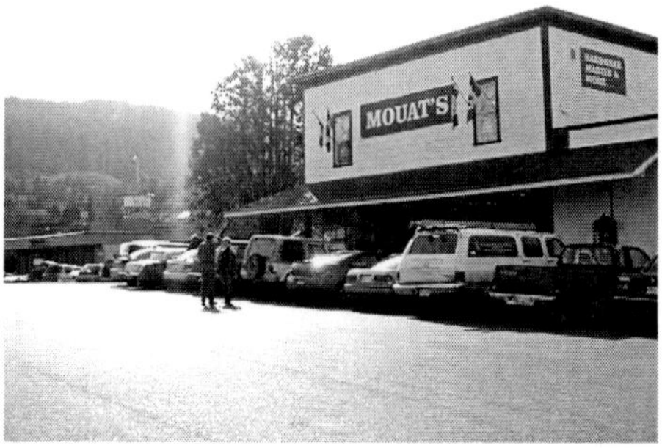

Mouat's Mall as it appears today

Grace Point Square

Grace Point Square is a building complex that offers a variety of shops, restaurants, galleries and other businesses. It is located in Ganges, at the end of Fulford-Ganges Road.

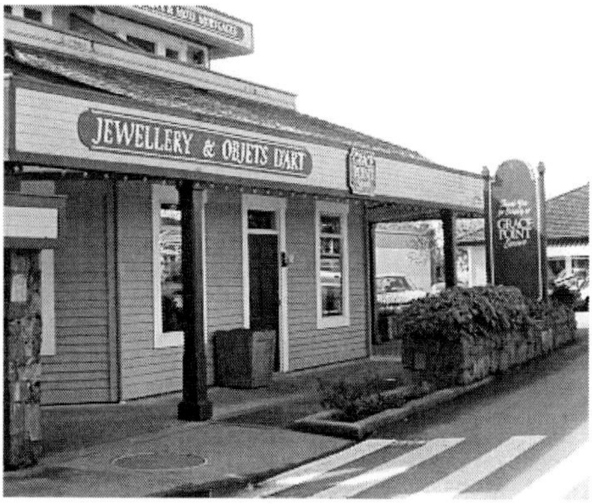

Salt Spring Island Trading Company

In the 1890's, a wealthy, but generous, Englishman immigrated to Salt Spring. He was always formally dressed, with a satin top hat and a long black frock. He liked to be called 'the Squire'.

Just before the outbreak of World War I, the English Squire and some other settlers built a general store in Ganges called the *Salt Spring Island Trading Company*.

Soon, the Squire's store became a direct competitor of the Mouat brothers' store. Nevertheless, the relationship between the store owners remained friendly.

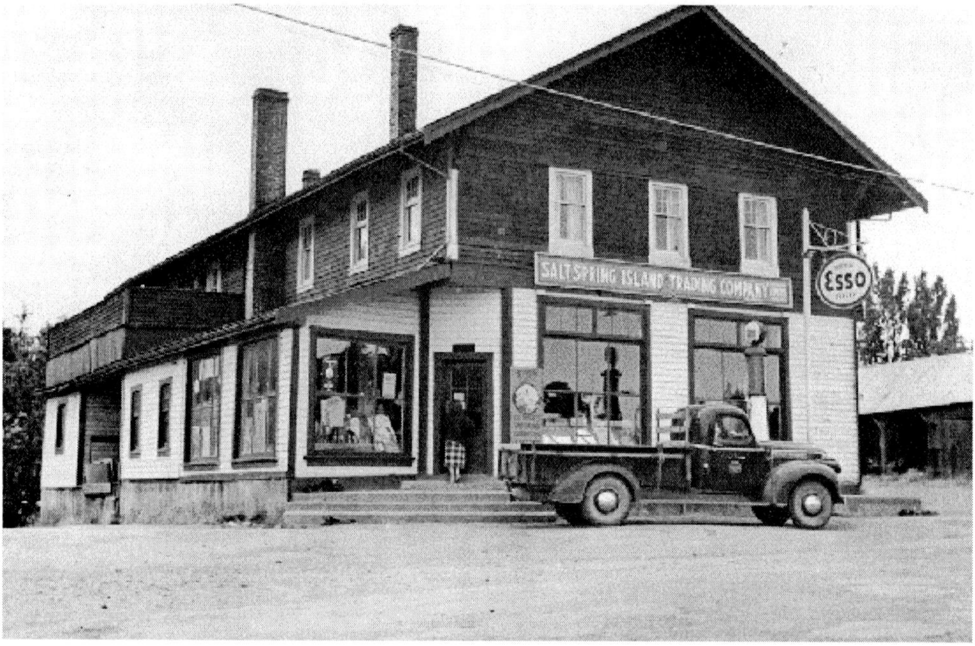

Salt Spring Island Trading Company in the 1930's - Salt Spring Archives 02186020

The store operated until the late 1960`s when it was bought out by the Mouat brothers. At that time, it was renamed the *Gulf Islands Trading Co. Ltd*. Over time, additional businesses were established alongside the store.

Today, the building complex is once again called the Salt Spring Island Trading Company. At the time of this writing, the businesses included a long-lived shoe store, as well as a health food store, a fitness center, a bookstore and a café. The building complex is located in Ganges, on Lower Ganges Road.

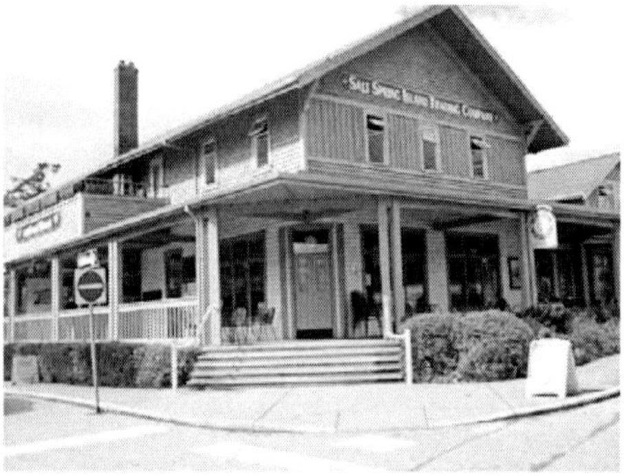

Salt Spring Island Trading Company as it appears today

Creekhouse & Creekside

Built across a creek in Ganges, which flows between Fulford-Ganges Road and McPhillips Avenue, Creekhouse & Creekside are building complexes that house local businesses.

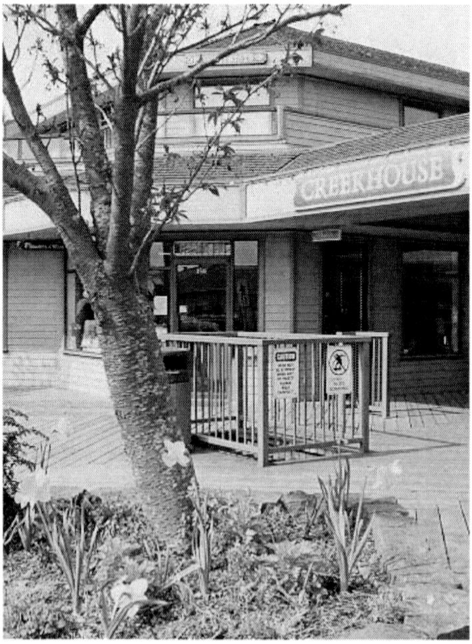

At the time of this writing, the buildings provided for a breakfast café, photographic studio, video store, and numerous shops and services.

Thrifty Foods

Initially, the Salt Spring Island Trading Company looked out over the ocean. The area in front of it was still a tidal inlet that contained log booms.

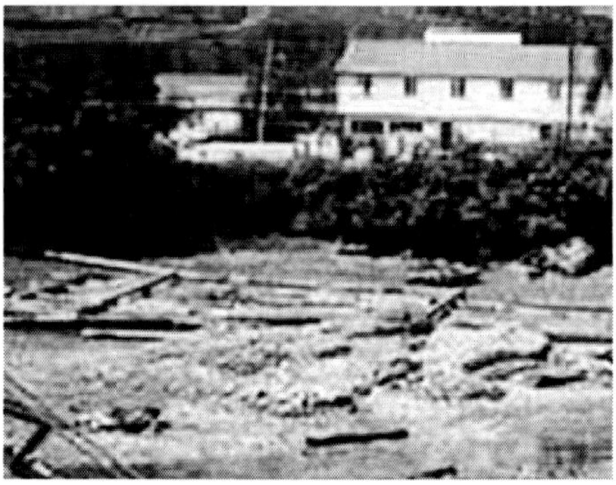

Site of Thrifty Foods in the 1960's Salt Spring Archives CKC998162110

In the year 1970, the site was filled in to provide more parking and retail space for Mouat's Store. Soon, a grocery store opened in part of the space.

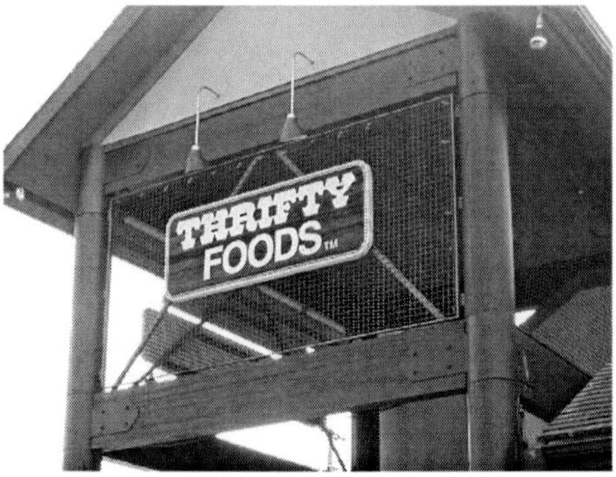

Today, *Thrifty Foods* is one of the busiest grocery stores in all of Canada. The supermarket carries fresh baking, produce and dairy products, as well as meats. It is located at Ganges Harbour beside Mouat's Landing.

Ganges Village Market Centre

The *Ganges Village Market Centre* is a busy mall in Ganges. At the time of this writing, the businesses included a pizza parlor, fitness center, pharmacy, video store and department store.

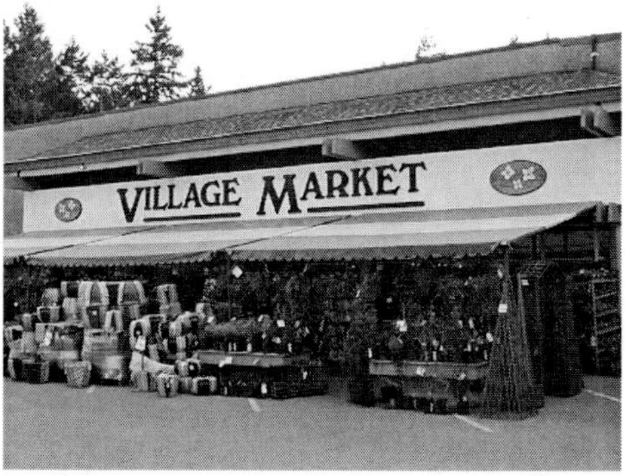

The mall, which is located on Lower Ganges Road, also provides for a supermarket and post office. The supermarket carries fresh baking, produce and dairy products, as well as meats.

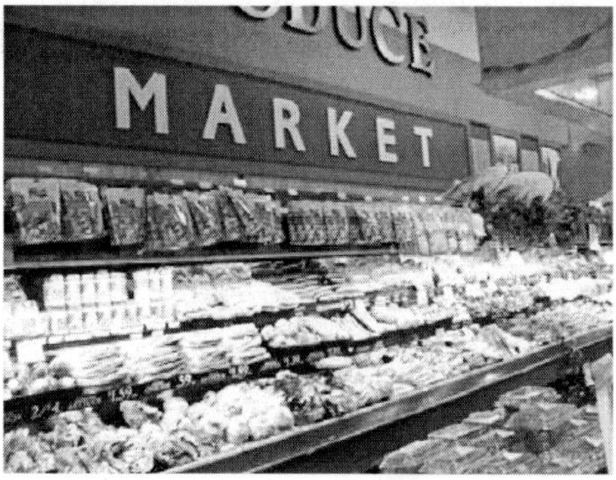

Booth Bay Bed & Breakfast

Just before the onset of World War I, a boat builder purchased some property on a bay. There, he began construction of a large, waterfront, frame house.

The following year, the boat builder sold his property. The new owner completed the house, adding upswept ends that gave the building a unique characteristic.

In the 1940's, the property was sold to a couple who converted it into a resort called *Aclands*. Several years later, new owners built some guest cottages on the property and changed the name of the resort to the *Booth Bay Resort*.

Later, in the 1970's, the property was sold yet again and a restaurant, called *The Bay Window*, was opened on the property. The resort ceased to operate in the 1990`s.

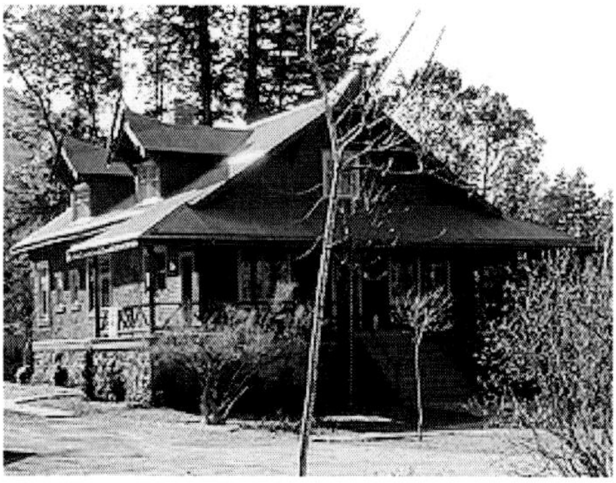

Today, the property is operated as the *Booth Bay Bed and Breakfast*. The B&B is located at the north end, near Vesuvius on Acland Road.

Harbour House Hotel

In the 1890's, a settler emigrated from Ireland to Salt Spring. Initially, he worked on a farm overlooking Ganges Harbour. A decade later, he purchased the farm and renamed it *Harbour House*.

While the settler was serving in World War I, his wife and brother-in-law converted the farmhouse into a guesthouse, adding several bedrooms and a dining room. They also set up some tents on the property. They called their guesthouse the *Harbour House Hotel*.

The hotel became a popular destination and, soon, they expanded it and added a tennis court. In the 1920`s, they added two additional tennis courts, a beer parlor and a glassed-in dance pavilion called the Sun Room. There was also a drawing room and a lounge, in which they kept roaring fires.

The guests participated in crab races on the billiard table, bridge, beachfront swimming and scavenger hunts. The hotel dances attracted as many as 100 people.

In the 1940`s, the tents on the grounds were replaced with cabins and by the 1960's, a swimming pool had replaced one of the three tennis courts.

A decade later, the hotel was destroyed by fire and rebuilt. Today, it offers 35 rooms, as well as facilities for small conferences, weddings and other special events. The hotel is located in Ganges, on Upper Ganges Road.

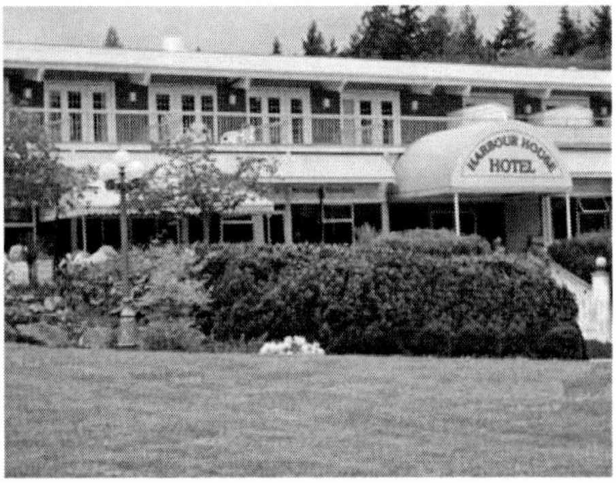

Hastings House Country Estate

In the mid-1800's, the Hudson's Bay Company established a fortified trading post at Ganges Harbour. The trading post was the first structure ever built on Salt Spring.

Much later, in the 1930`s, a naval architect immigrated to Canada from England. Shortly thereafter, he purchased the waterfront property overlooking the harbour.

When he began to establish a farm on the property, the architect moved the trading post inland and built a Sussex-style Manor House on the site. In his home, he worked on secret designs for the British Royal Navy.

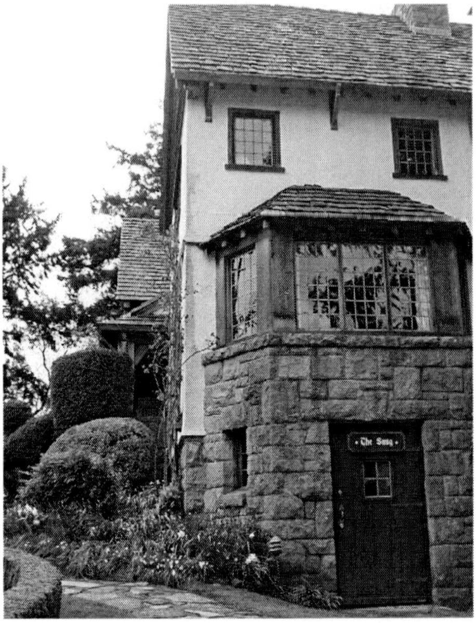

Today, the property operates as a world-renowned luxury Inn called the *Hasting's House Country Estate Hotel*. The Inn, which has won numerous awards, offers 18 guest suites in seven restored buildings.

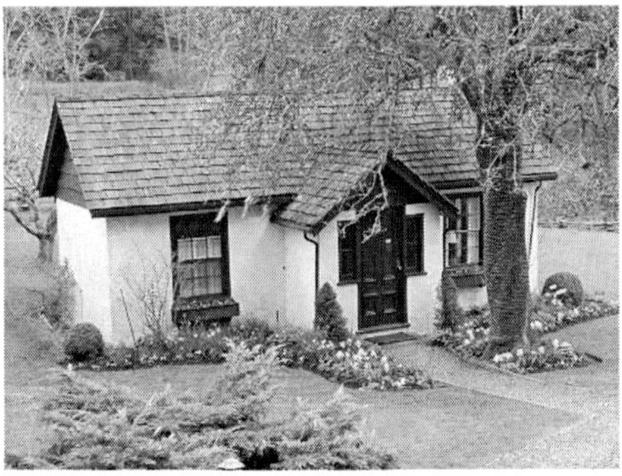

The Tudor-style home and farmhouse each provide for two suites. The original Hudson's Bay trading post serves as a two-room cottage called The Post. The original barn contains additional suites and a spa.

The Inn and spa are located on the shores of Ganges Harbour, on Upper Ganges

Road. At the time of this writing, the Inn was celebrating its centennial.

The Old Farmhouse Bed & Breakfast

In the 1890's, a British dairyman settled with his family on Salt Spring. A few years later, he purchased some property at the north end where he built a farmhouse. Over time, an Arbutus tree could be seen growing near the house.

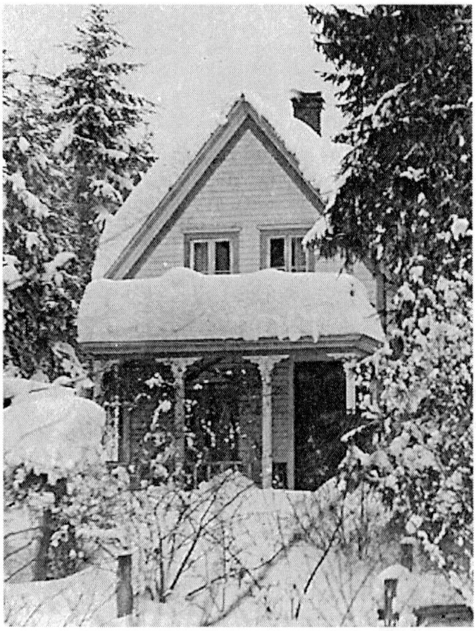

Old Farmhouse B&B, early 1900's
Management of Old Farmhouse B&B

One hundred years later, new owners converted the property into a bed and breakfast. Today, it is operated as the *Old Farmhouse B&B.* The Arbutus in the yard is now the largest on the Island.

The bed and breakfast is adult-oriented and pet-friendly. There are also facilities for weddings. It is located at the north end on North End Road.

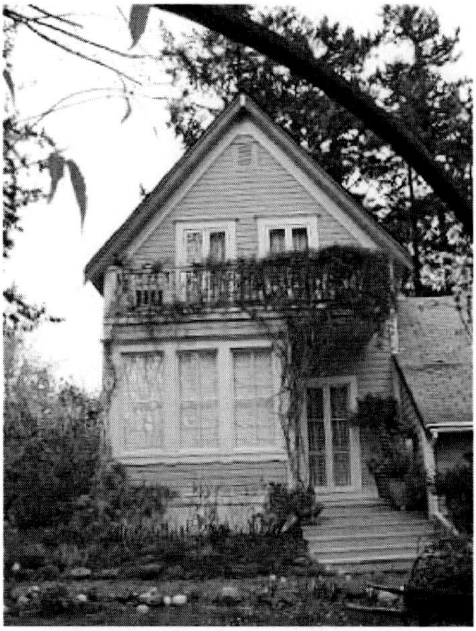

Old Farmhouse B&B as it appears today

Fulford Creek Guest House

At the turn of the century, a settler established a farm for his family in the Fulford-Burgoyne Valley. Initially, a small cabin was their homestead.

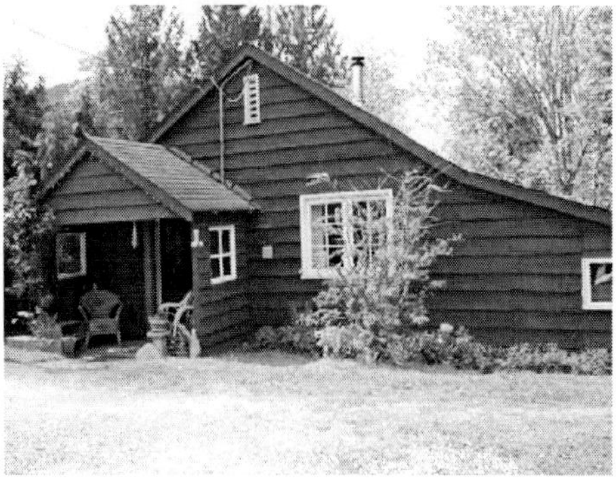

When the family outgrew the cabin in the 1920's, they built a four-bedroom farmhouse nearby. During the 1940's, the house was used as a boarding house for migrant farm workers. A decade later, it became a nursing home.

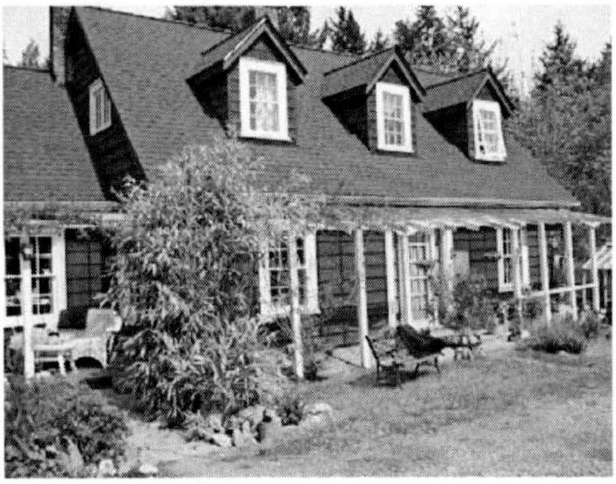

Today, the farmhouse operates as the *Fulford Creek Guest House*. The pet-friendly cottage rental is located near Fulford Harbour on Fulford-Ganges Road.

Fulford Inn

By the 1890`s, a tavern, called *Roger's Saloon*, had opened at the head of Fulford Harbour. At the turn of the century, it was destroyed by fire and the property was sold.

One day, the new owner heard a rumor that the highways crew were planning to build a road over the bank across the nearby creek. He was worried that it would cut off the corner on which his property sat.

The owner of the property knew that a bylaw existed, which prohibited the destruction of a fruit orchard during the construction of a highway. So he promptly planted fruit trees all over his newly acquired property. Subsequently, a bend in the road from Fulford to Ganges was created at the head of the harbour.

A few years later, the property changed hands again. The new owner, who was known locally as 'Pop', erected a store on the property.

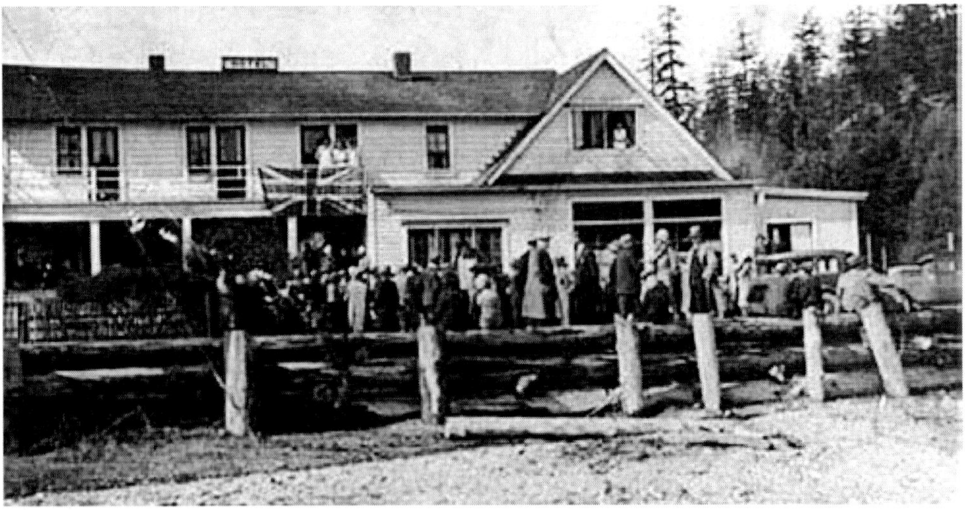

The Fulford Inn in 1920 - Salt Spring Archives 1994137041

Soon, the storekeeper expanded his store and opened a hotel. Initially, the hotel was called the *White House Hotel*, but was later renamed the *White Lodge*. During the 1920's, it also served as the home of the post office in Fulford.

The hotel was destroyed by fire in the 1930`s. When it was rebuilt, it was renamed the *Fulford Inn*. In the 1950`s, it was again destroyed by fire and rebuilt.

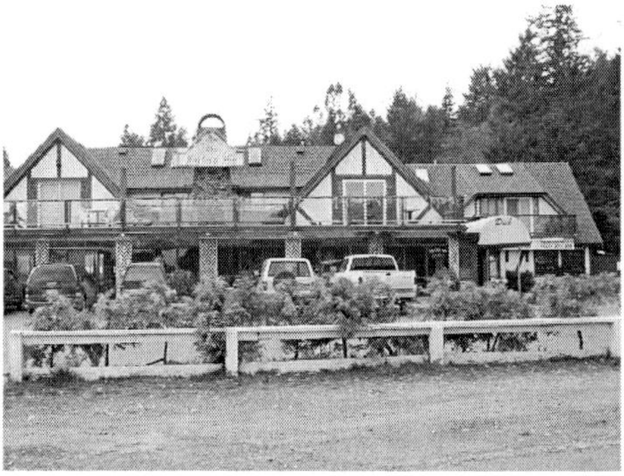

Fulford Inn as it appears today

Today, the hotel, which was designed as a Tudor-style Inn, is one of the oldest Inns in all the Gulf Islands. The Inn is located on the shores of Fulford Harbour on Fulford-Ganges Road.

Embe Bakery

At the turn of the century, the brother of the Portuguese storekeeper in Vesuvius constructed a stone building in Ganges, for use as a creamery. Named the *Salt Spring Island Creamery*, it was a cooperative of dairy farmers.

Initially, only farmers in the Ganges community sent their cream there. However, over time, other farmers starting supplying cream to the creamery. By the 1920's, the creamery was producing over 60,000 kg of butter.

During that time, a truck driver would drive around the Island, picking up the cans of cream from all the farms along the road.

When the ships would dock at the Ganges wharf, the driver would leave the empty cream cans at the wharf and wait for the full ones to be unloaded from the ship. Some of the cans came from neighboring Galiano, Mayne and Pender Islands.

One year, the creamery's butter was entered in the Canadian National Exhibition. It was awarded the distinction of being the best in all of Canada.

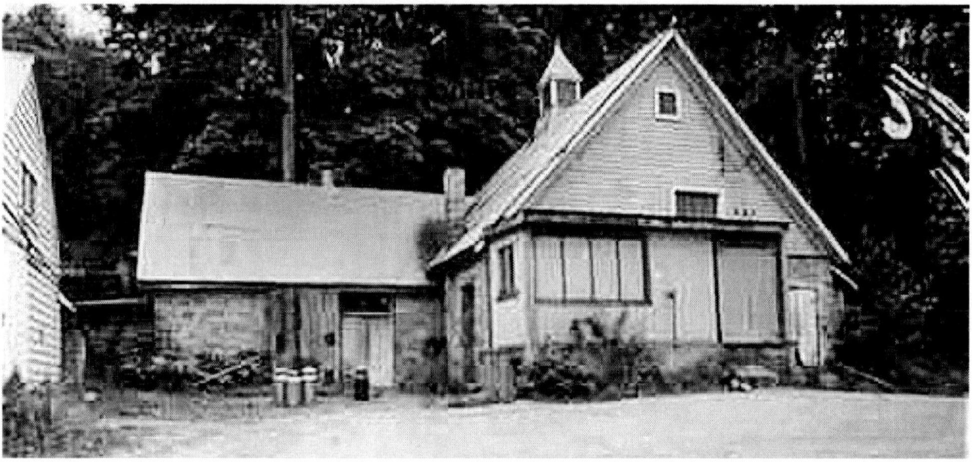

Embe Bakery in the 1950's - Salt Spring Archives 02186016

The Salt Spring Island Creamery closed in the 1950's. After several additions were attached to the front of the building, it became home to the *Embe Bakery*.

Today, the bakery offers soups, subs, breads, pastries and cakes. It is located in Ganges on Fulford-Ganges Road.

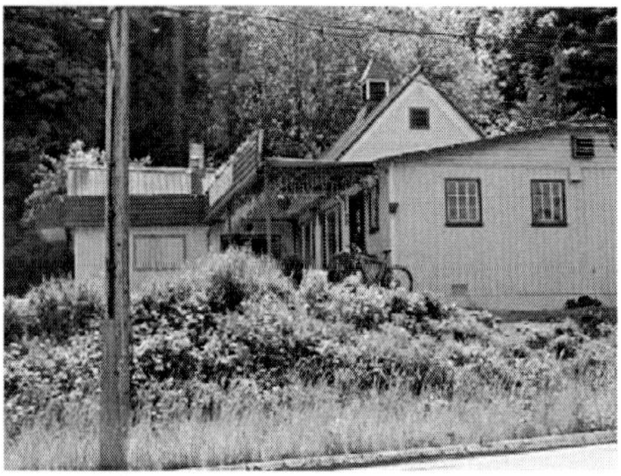

Embe Bakery as it appears today

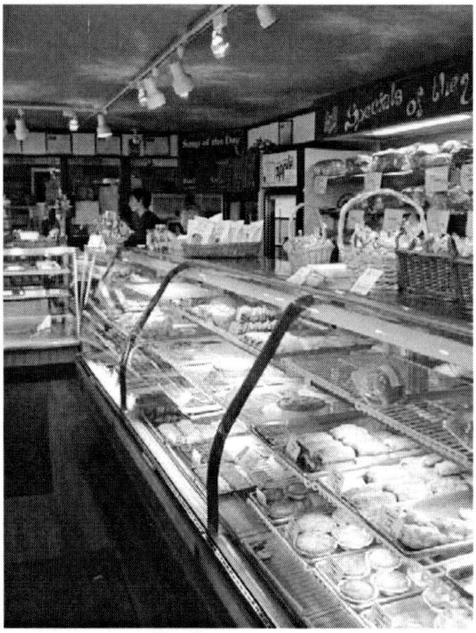

House Piccolo

In the 1940's, the Dominion Government Telegraph and Telephone Company constructed a building to house a telephone exchange on Salt Spring.

When the telephone company changed its system to dial telephones in the 1960`s, the building became the home of an ice cream and candy store. Since then, it has operated as various restaurants.

Today, the building is home to the *House Piccolo* restaurant, which features European and Scandinavian cuisine. Located in Ganges, on Hereford Avenue, the restaurant is open for dinner.

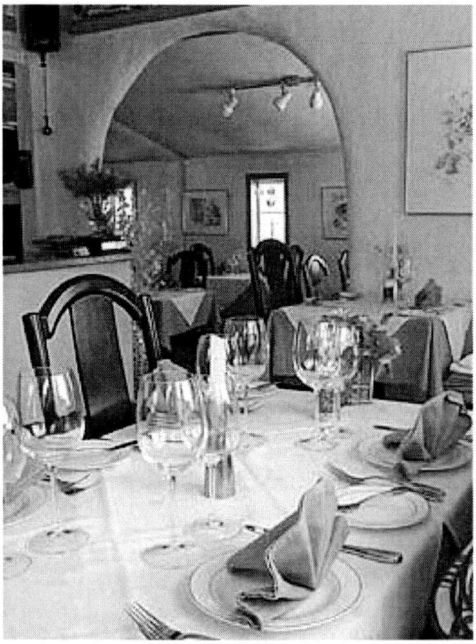

Salt Spring Cottages

In the 1860's, the Portuguese settler immigrated to Salt Spring and settled in Vesuvius.

Around the 1880's, the settler constructed three houses on Vesuvius Bay. The houses were built as dowries for three of his six daughters.

Because the vacant homes were built to be lived in after his daughters were wed, they were often rented out.

Eventually, the houses were sold and remodeled. One of the homes was moved up a hill where it overlooked the bay.

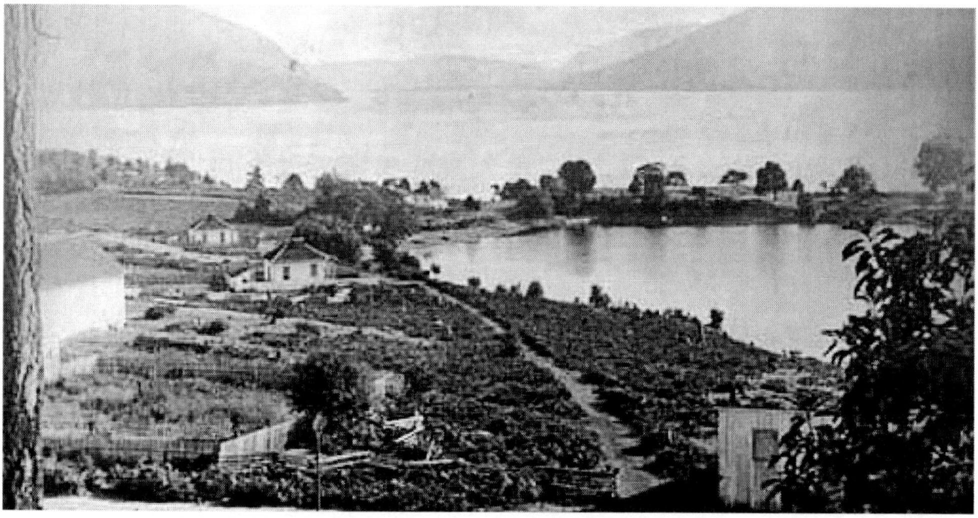

Dowry houses on Vesuvius Beach in the 1890's - Salt Spring Archives 093a

Today, the house on the hill is a pet-friendly cottage rental operated by *Salt Spring Cottages*. The cottage still looks out over the bay. It is located in Vesuvius on Langley Road.

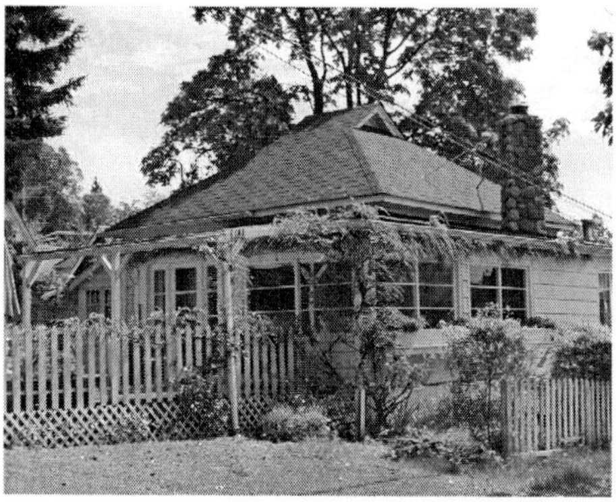

The Dowry house as it appears today

Tree House Cafés

In the 1920's, a small building was built behind Mouat's Store. It housed an electric generator that powered the store. Later, it became a place where the butcher made sausage and prepared hams for smoking.

Today, the building is home to an outdoor café called the *Tree House Café North*. The café is open for breakfast, lunch and dinner. It also provides for live entertainment and features over 50 entertainers during 123 consecutive nights of music. On Thursday nights there is an open mike under a plum tree.

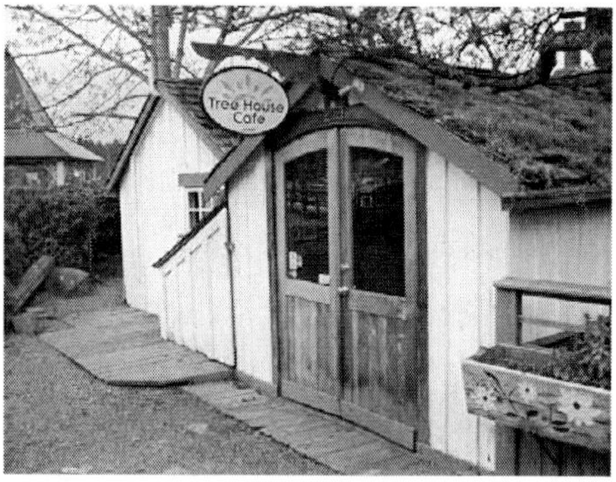

The café is located in Ganges at Mouat's Landing. Another location, called *Tree House Café South* exists in Fulford.

Salt Spring Island Sights & Activities

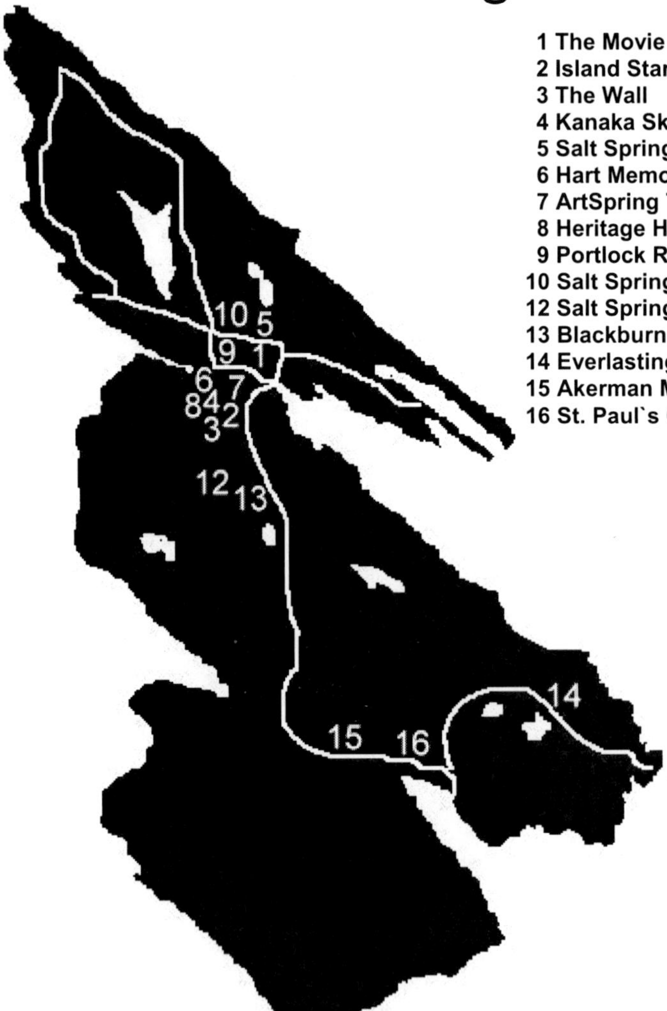

1 The Movie Gallery
2 Island Star Video
3 The Wall
4 Kanaka Skate Park
5 Salt Spring Golf & Country Club
6 Hart Memorial Disc Golf Course
7 ArtSpring Theatre
8 Heritage House Museum
9 Portlock Recreational Park
10 Salt Spring Cinema
12 Salt Spring Center of Yoga
13 Blackburn Meadows Golf Course
14 Everlasting Summer
15 Akerman Museum
16 St. Paul`s Catholic Church

Things to See & Do

Salt Spring Island offers its visitors a variety of things to see and do. It provides for concerts, theatre productions, art shows and museums. Recreational activities include bowling, billiards, swimming, kayaking, sailing, fishing, golf, frisbee golf, skateboarding, tennis and climbing.

The Island consists of five major routes. Fulford-Ganges Road runs north and south, connecting Ganges to the Fulford ferry terminal. Upper Ganges Road, which turns into Vesuvius Bay Road, connects Ganges to the Vesuvius ferry terminal. Long Harbour Road connects Ganges to the Long Harbour ferry terminal.

Lower Ganges Road turns into North End Road, which turns into Sunset Drive, circumventing the north end. Beaver Point Road connects the Fulford ferry terminal to the communities at the south end.

St. Paul's Catholic Church

In the year 1880, the construction of a Catholic church began on Salt Spring. Much of its construction was performed by Hawaiians, who were later buried in the adjoining cemetery. Thereafter, the church was the center of Hawaiian life for many years.

The windows, the door and the bell for the church came from an Indian reserve on Vancouver Island. The materials were transported by canoe to Burgoyne Bay, and then by stoneboat to Fulford.

Eventually, the exterior siding and part of the interior were faced with imitation stone, making it one of the most beautiful churches on Salt Spring.

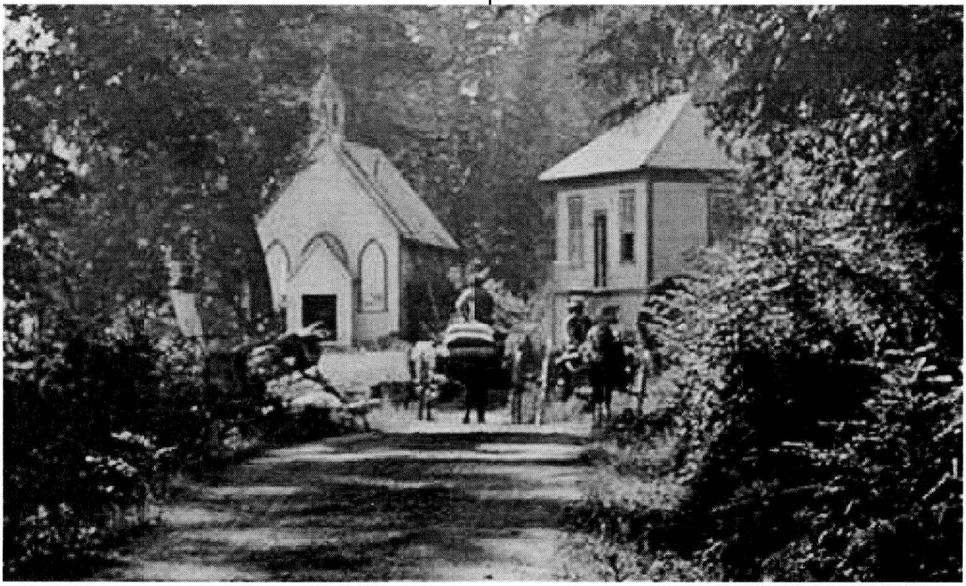

St. Paul's Catholic Church and rectory at the turn of the century - Salt Spring Archives 083a

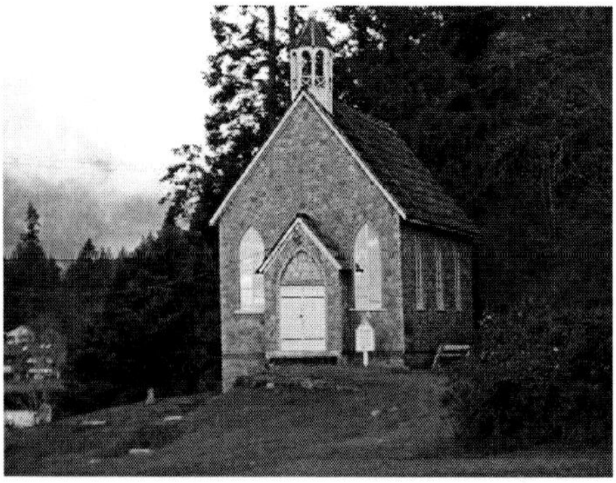

St. Paul's Catholic Church as it appears today

Today, there are at least six historic churches that visitors to the Island can admire. Located in Fulford, on Fulford-Ganges Road, *St. Paul's Catholic Church* is the oldest church on the Island. (#16 on the map)

For a first-hand introduction to the heritage buildings in Ganges, you can contact Salt Spring Walking Tours. They provide one-hour strolls through the *rancherie* (village). Phone: (250) 537-1833

Heritage House Museum

In the 1870`s, the Portuguese storekeeper constructed a grand home on Vesuvius Bay for his growing family. Soon, he converted his home and store into a hotel called the *Vesuvius Bay Hotel.*

In the 1880`s, the storekeeper built a little house to be used as overflow accommodations whenever there was no vacancy at his hotel. Unfortunately, one hundred years after its construction, the hotel was destroyed by fire.

Fortunately, the little house survived. However, it soon became threatened by the expansion of the Vesuvius ferry terminal. So, in the year 1980, the Farmers Institute moved it to their grounds and a seniors group obtained a grant to convert it into a museum.

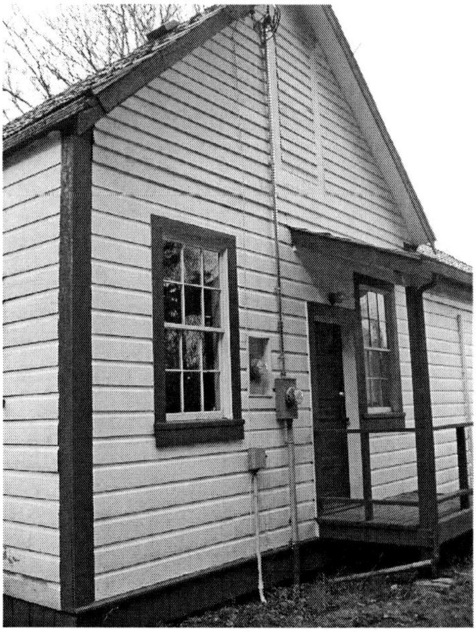

Today, the four-room house is the home of the Island's first museum. Named the *Bittancourt Heritage House Museum*, it can be viewed by appointment. The museum is located in Ganges on Rainbow Road. (#8 on the map) Phone: (250) 537-4895

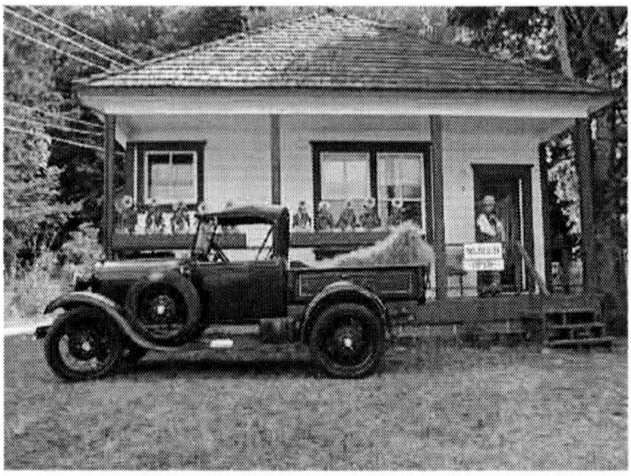

Akerman Museum

In the early 1860's, an English settler purchased some land in the Fulford-Burgoyne Valley. There, he built a log home.

Two year's later, he and his new wife built a larger, two-storey house beside a creek on their property. It was made from hand-hewn, squared timbers.

In the 1880's, the couple converted part of their new house into the first store ever to operate in Fulford. Later, they converted it into the Island's first Inn and pub. Called the *Traveler's Rest*, the Inn operated until the year 1910. The property was sold a decade later.

One hundred years after the settler had acquired the property, his grandson purchased it.

Throughout his life as roads foreman, the settler's grandson had collected artifacts and craft pieces from Indian village life. After he had been living on the property a while, he built a museum beside the old Inn, in which to house his artifacts. He was over 80 years old at the time.

Although the 140-year old Inn was recently demolished, the museum still operates on the property. It is located near Fulford on Fulford-Ganges Road and can be viewed by appointment. (#15 on the map) Phone: (250) 653-4228

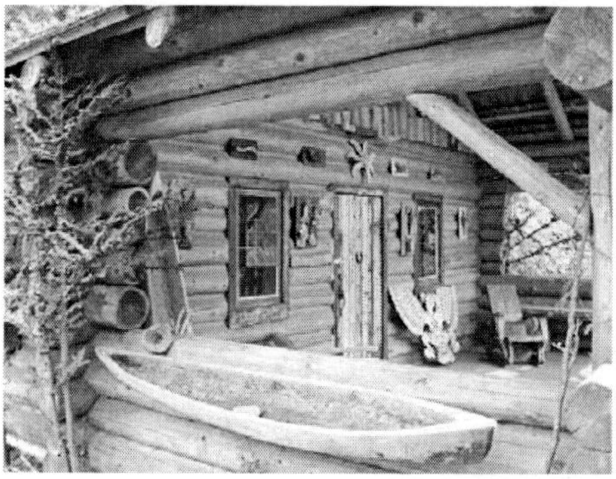

ArtSpring Theatre

In the late 1980`s, a teacher, an actor and an architect began planning the creation of an arts centre on Salt Spring. When the centre was completed a decade later, it was called *ArtSpring*.

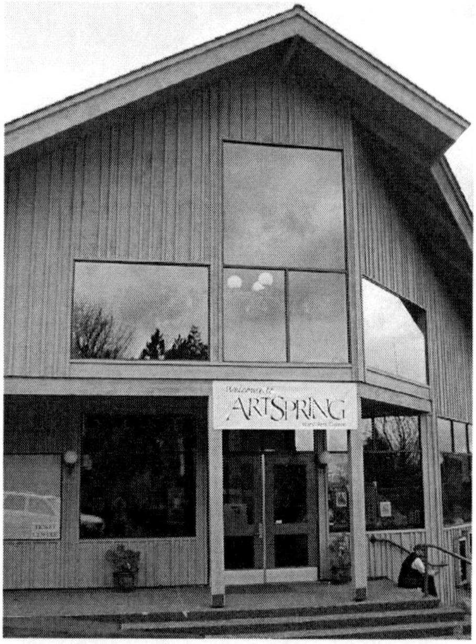

Today, ArtSpring is a 265-seat performance and visual arts theatre. Open year-round, it is the Island's premier venue for concerts, theatre and exhibitions.

The presentations by many artists and performers at ArtSpring have a worldwide audience. The Salt Spring Singers, who have been making music for 30 years, put on concerts throughout the year. The Graffiti Theatre uses local talent to produce professional theatre. The Salt Spring Painters' Guild hosts various art exhibitions.

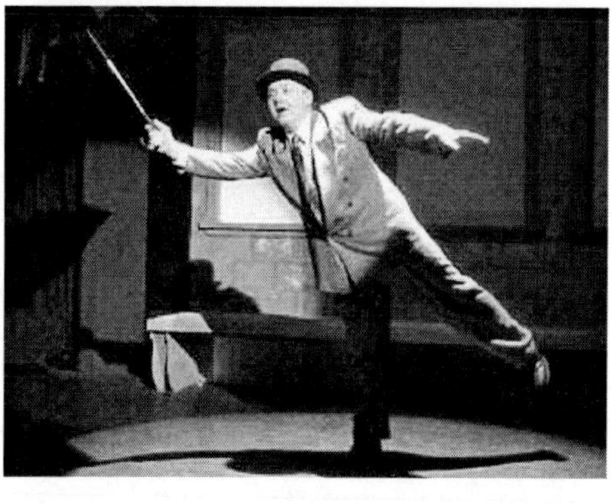

During its *Sizzling Summer Nights* music festival in July and August, ArtSpring hosts musical performances in all genres. The theatre is located in Ganges on Jackson Avenue. (#7 on the map)

Salt Spring Cinema

The very first hall to be built on Salt Spring was constructed in the 1890`s beside a school in Central. It was called the *Central Community Hall.*

That year, the hall hosted the Island's first agricultural fair. However, when it became apparent that the building was more suited to hosting indoor events, thc fair was moved and the hall went on to serve as a community center.

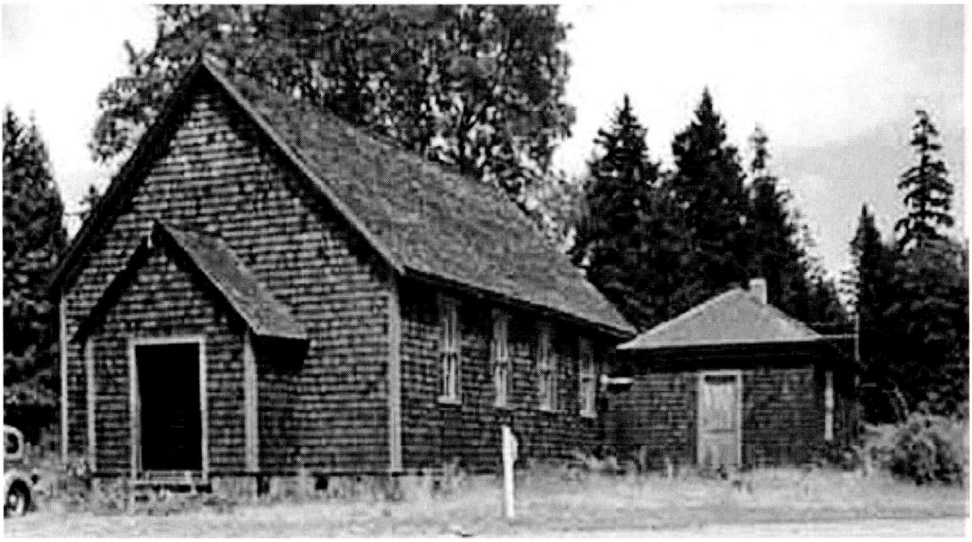

Salt Spring Cinema in the 1930's - Salt Spring Archives 02186024

During the 1950's, events organizers would set up wooden folding chairs in the hall for special events. Then, a projectionist would display slides on a screen, while the local piano teacher played background music for the audience. In the 1970's, two wings, a stage and a porch were added to the hall.

Today, the hall serves as a movie theatre, called *Salt Spring Cinema*. Located in Central, at the corner of North End and Vesuvius Bay Roads, it seats 120 people and offers a full concession stand.

A highlight of the cinema is the dynamic slide show that is shown before the feature film. (#10 on the map)

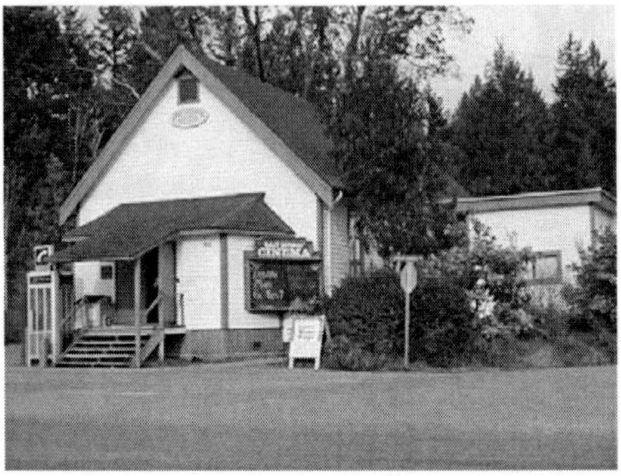

Salt Spring Cinema as it appears today

Hart Memorial Disc Golf Course

The *Hart Memorial Disc Golf Course* provides for frisbee golf. Once a popular camping location, the course now occupies an old camping oval in a beautiful old-growth forest.

The course is located in Ganges, in Mouat Provincial Park on Seaview Avenue. The *Hart Memorial Disc Golf Tournament* takes place there each year. (#6 on the map)

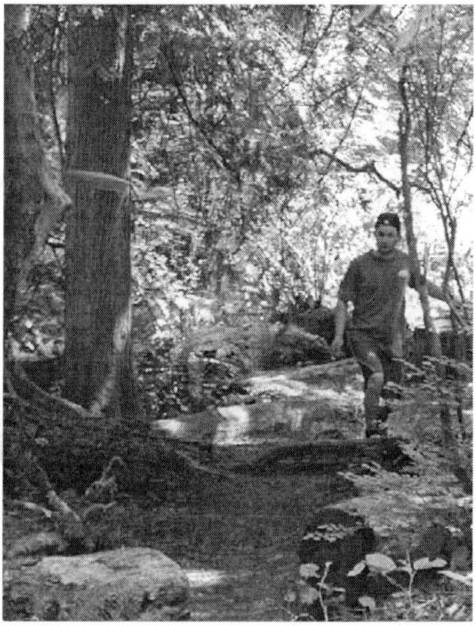

Salt Spring Golf & Country Club

In the 1890's, a Reverend took over a run-down farm in Central where he lived in a log cabin on a dirt floor. Later, when his family arrived, a new home was built on the property. Eventually, the Reverend turned the property into a successful farm called *Barnsbury Grange*.

In the 1920`s, the Reverend's son took over the property. He converted the farm into a golf course and the farmhouse into a clubhouse. Much later, in the 1960`s, the clubhouse was destroyed by fire.

Today, the farm is the home of the *Salt Spring Island Golf and Country Club*. The 9-hole course, which is open year-round, plays as a par 36. It features 10 tees and various teeing areas. One of the more challenging holes is a 454-yard, par 4 hole seven, which includes both a water hazard and a two-tiered green.

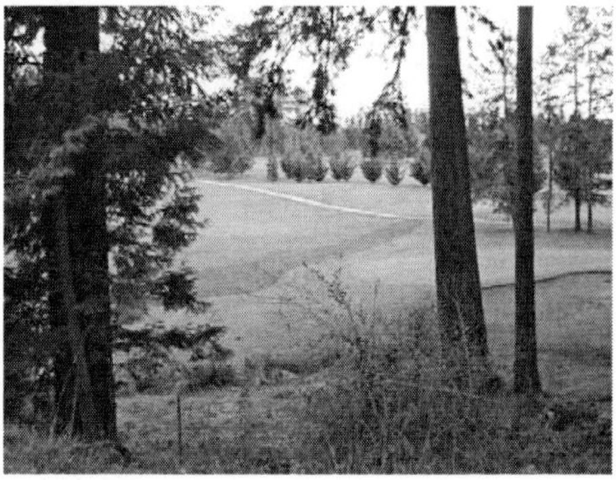

Club cars and pull carts are available for rent. Facilities include a driving range and fully stocked pro shop. The course is located in Ganges, on Lower Ganges Road. (#5 on the map)

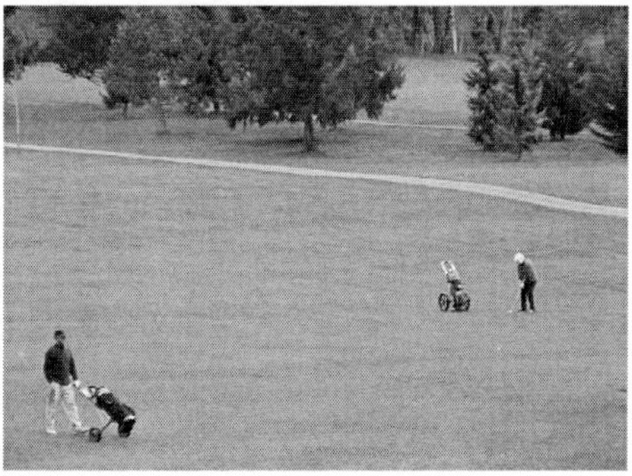

Blackburn Meadows Golf Course

The *Blackburn Meadows Golf Course* is a 9-hole links-style golf course and driving range located near Cusheon Lake on Blackburn Road. As Canada's first organic golf course, the greens and fairways of the Blackburn Meadows course are maintained using only organic methods. (#13 on the map)

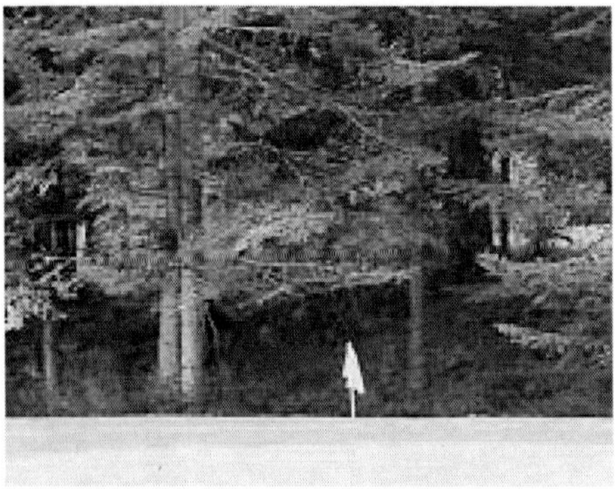

Salt Spring Centre of Yoga

Just after the turn of the century, a Scottish settler bought an acreage on Salt Spring. Then, he hired a British builder to begin construction of a large, two-storey house. The plans for the house included a turret, a tower and a chapel.

Unfortunately, just before the onset of World War I, the Scotsman ran out of money and abandoned the unfinished house. In the 1920's, he passed away, leaving his wife to rent it out.

Eventually, the government took over the property. They renovated it, and then used it to run rehabilitation programs until after World War II. Later, in the early 1980's, the Dharma Sara Satsang Society converted the home into an holistic center.

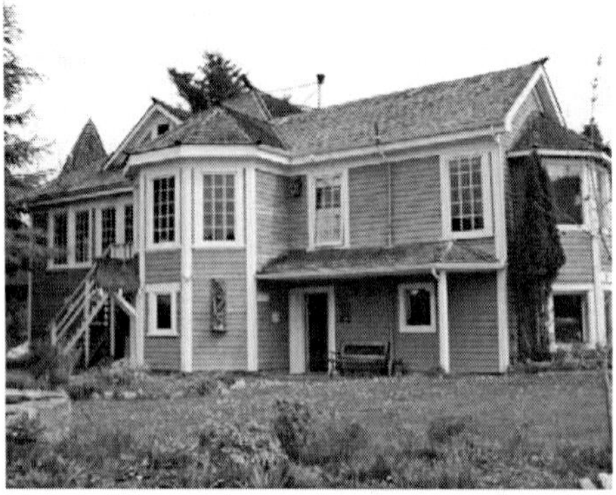

Today, the elegant house, which is known locally as the *Blackburn House*, is home to the *Salt Spring Centre of Yoga*.

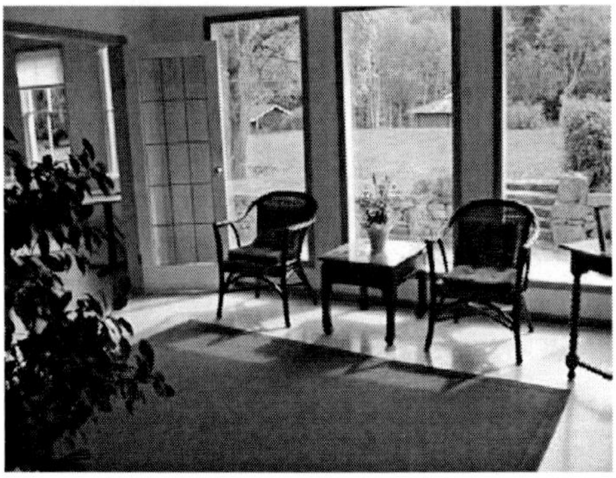

The center offers programs that concentrate on body and spiritual awareness, and self-help techniques, such as yoga and tai chi. Located near Cusheon Lake, on Blackburn Road, the center is famous for its Swedan massage. (#12 on the map)

Kanaka Skate Park

The *Kanaka Skate Park* is a brand new skate park that features a small outdoor climbing wall. The park is located in Ganges on Kanaka Road. (#4 on the map)

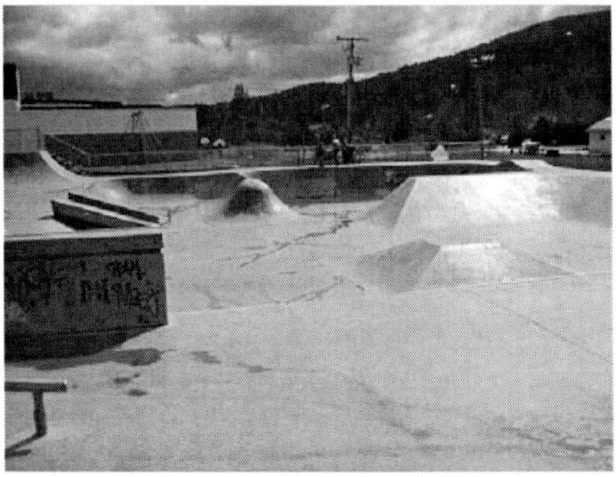

The Wall

The Wall is an indoor climbing facility. The facility, which is 7 m high, is located on Ganges Hill on Fulford-Ganges Road. (#3 on the map)

Everlasting Summer

At the turn of the century, a settler purchased some land in the Fulford-Burgoyne Valley. By the 1920`s, the 81-year old man had become well known for his wonderful flower garden, which could be seen through an ivy-covered gate.

The gardener tended his flower garden from morning until night. When visitors came for a tour, he would take them on a circular walk. He used a large, yet simple device, called a water-ram, to control the watering of his flowers. It stood taller than his two-storey home.

Much later, in the 1980`s, a large flower, herb and rose garden, called *Everlasting Summer*, was established near that same valley.

Today, the vast nursery produces over 200 plants and 75 varieties of roses. Thousands of flowers are then picked for drying.

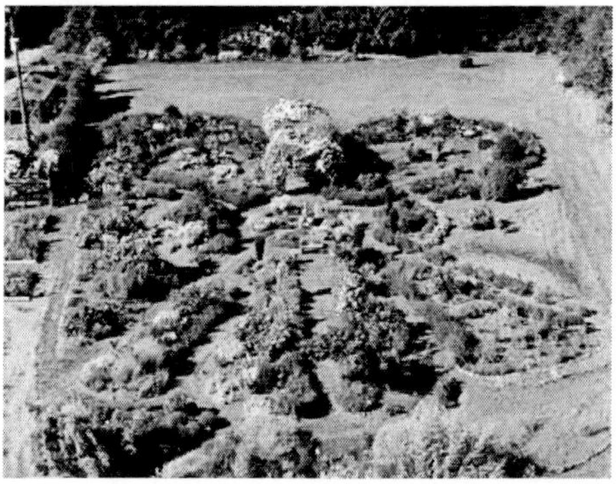

Dried flowers and floral arrangements can be purchased in a gift shop on the premises, which are located at the south end on McLennan Drive. (#14 on the map)

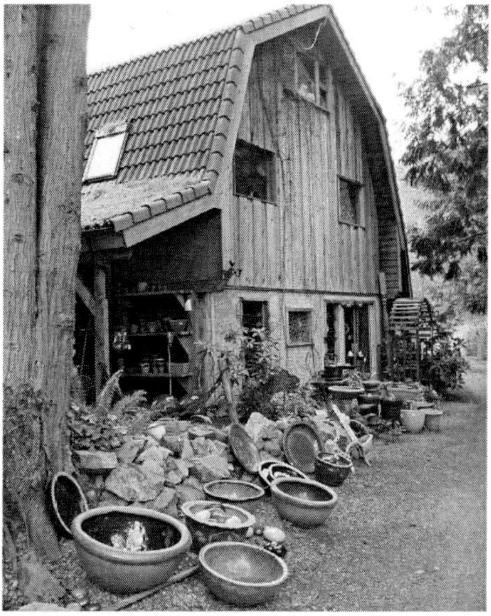

Portlock Recreational Park

In the 1970`s, a recreational area was developed in Central. It was called *Portlock Recreational Park*.

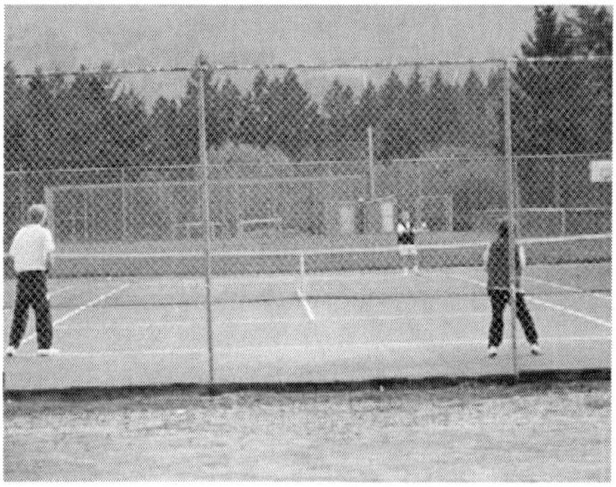

Today, the park provides for a heated swimming pool, tennis courts, a soccer field, baseball diamonds, playgrounds and a .4 km track. It is located at the corner of North End and Vesuvius Bay Roads. (#9 on the map)

Places to Shop

In the year 1900, the brother of the Portuguese storekeeper opened his own store, in Ganges. Four years later, he built a splendid house at the foot of Ganges Hill, and then moved his store there.

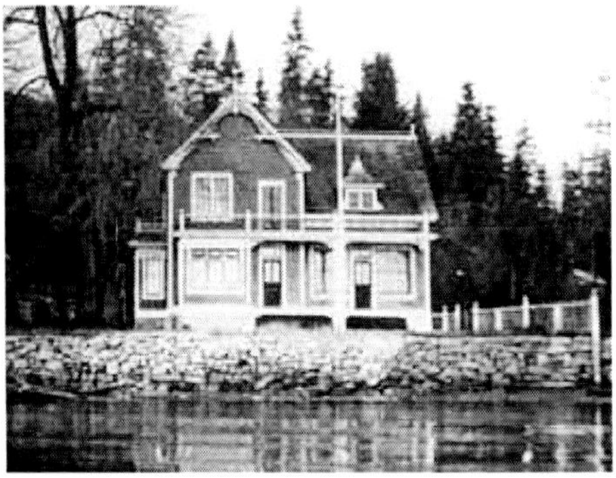

Store in Ganges in 1920
Salt Spring Archives CKC998162131

Today, there are a variety of stores on Salt Spring Island where visitors can pick up a *potlatch* (gift) for *tillicum* (a friend). The Island offers numerous places to shop 'til you drop.

Salt Spring even has its own currency. Called Salt Spring Dollars' it is the very first alternative currency in Canada that is backed 100% by the Canadian dollar.

The currencies, which can be obtained at the Visitor Information Centre in Ganges, work like gift certificates and are accepted by most Salt Spring businesses. Each bill features the work of local artists.

Aroma Crystal Therapy

Aroma Crystal Therapy offers aromatherapy, jewelry, crystals, stones and healing gifts. The store is located in Ganges, at Gasoline Alley on Fulford-Ganges Road.

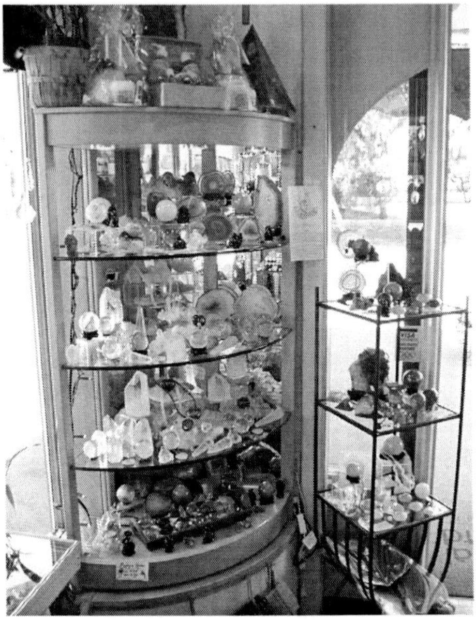

Mouat's Clothing Company

Mouat's Clothing Company offers two floors of casual Island wear for men and women, including clothing, footwear, accessories and athletic wear. The store is located in Ganges at Mouat's Landing.

Side B Clothing Company

The *Side B Clothing Company* offers quality clothing for active men and women. It is located in Ganges at Creekside.

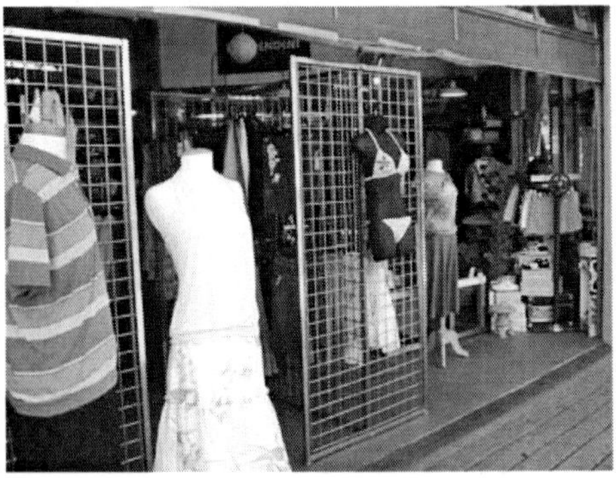

Watermark Books

Watermark Books is a general bookstore that offers quality books. It is located in Ganges on McPhillips Avenue.

Old Salty Greetings, Gifts & Gourmet

Old Salty Greetings, Gifts and Gourmet offers a trendy collection of gifts and greeting cards for all ages. The store is located in Ganges at Mouat's Landing.

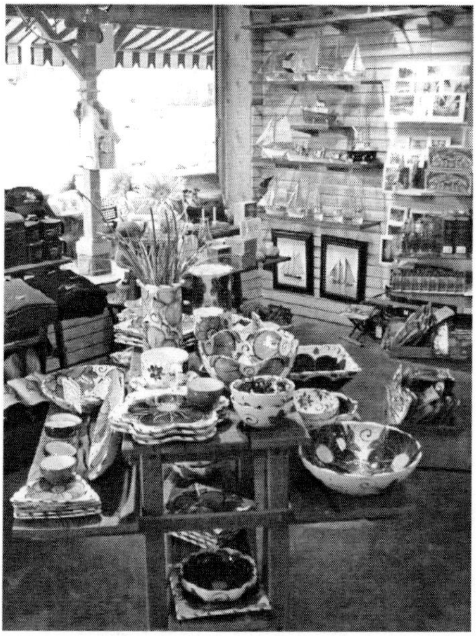

The Housewares Store

The Housewares Store offers nearly 4,000 sq ft of space dedicated solely to quality housewares. The store is located in Ganges at Mouat's Mall.

Saltspring Soapworks

Saltspring Soapworks was started as a home-based business in a small cottage. Today, the business operates in the heart of Ganges. It offers hand-made natural soaps using fragrances from the Gulf Islands. The store is located in the Harbour Market Building on Fulford-Ganges Road.

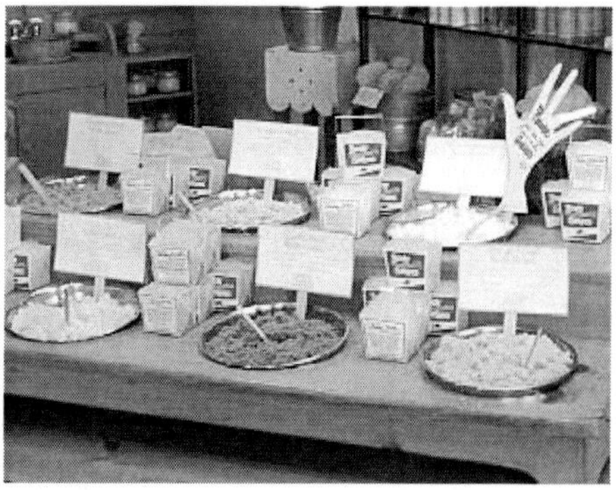

Jambalaya

Jambalaya is a bead shop that also features a great selection of hats and scarves. The store is located in Fulford on Fulford-Ganges Road.

Solace Aromatherapy & Tea

Solace Aromatherapy and Tea offers quality aromatherapy products. The store is located in Fulford on Morningside Drive.

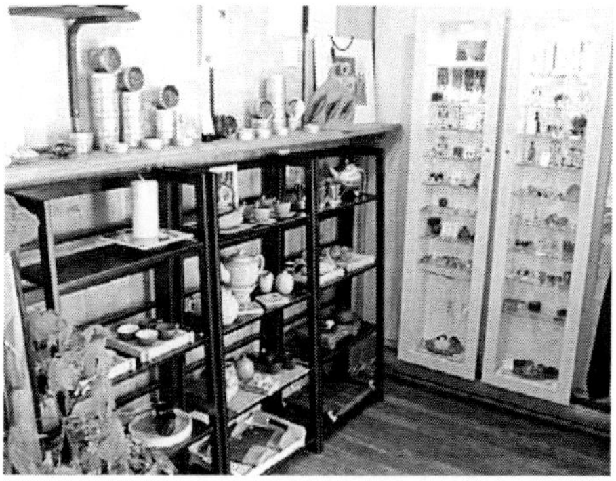

Ganges Garment Company

The *Ganges Garment Company* specializes in quality clothing made in Canada. The store is located at Ganges Harbour in Grace Point Square.

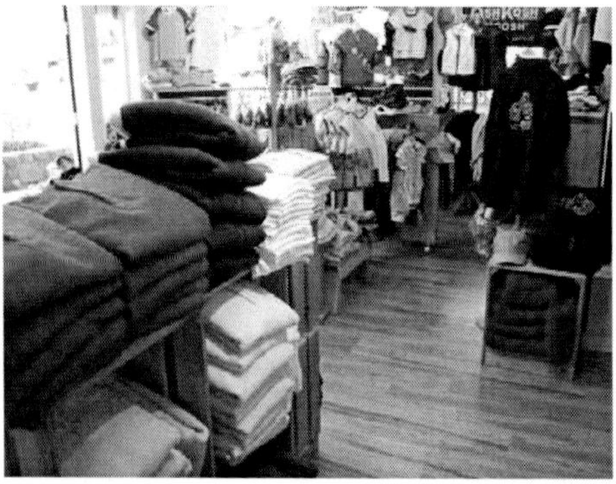

The Wardrobe

The Wardrobe is an eclectic clothing store that also offers hats and jewelry. The store is located in Fulford on Morningside Drive.

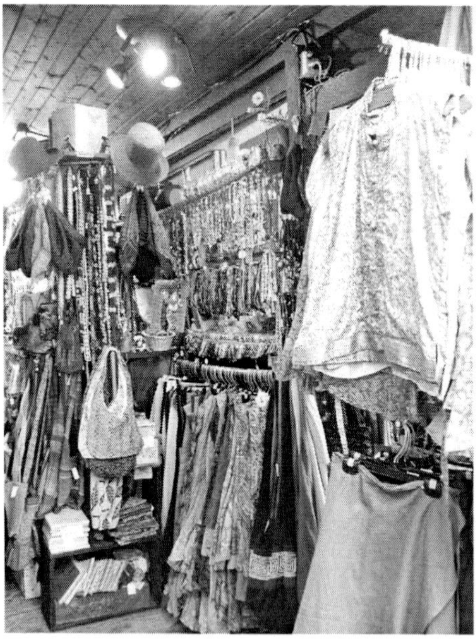

Houseboat

Houseboat offers housewares and accessories for West Coast home decor. The store is located in Ganges on Hereford Avenue.

Windflower Moon

Windflower Moon is a full range, metaphysical boutique that offers unique clothing and gift items produced by Island artists and other global locales.

They also carry books on spiritual awareness, childbirth and mindful parenting. The store is located in Ganges, in the Harbour Market Building on Fulford-Ganges Road.

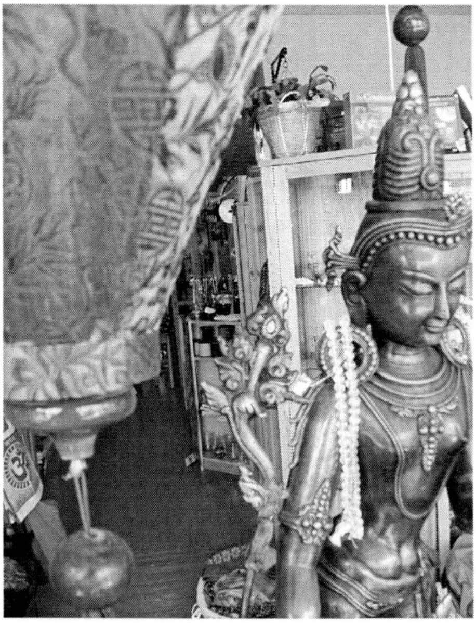

Island Escapades

Island Escapade's offers quality athletic clothing and gear for the whole family. The store is located in Ganges on Fulford-Ganges Road.

Stitches Quilts & Yarns

Initially, Methodist services at the north end took place in private homes, schools and community halls.

At the turn of the century, the building of the *Vesuvius Bay Methodist Church* began in Central. The businesswoman who would later start Mouat's Store drove her horse and buggy across the Island to raise the necessary funds.

In the 1920's, when several Protestant churches joined to form the United Church of Canada, the front portion of the church building was moved to Ganges and became the *Ganges United Church*.

By the 1950's, the church had outgrown the structure. So they sold it to the Royal Canadian Legion, who converted it into their hall.

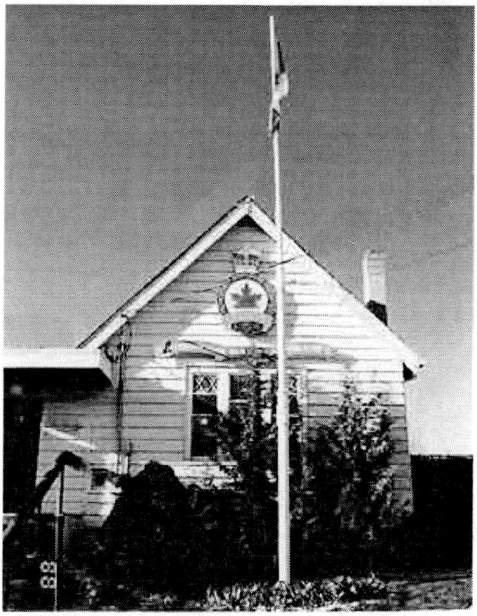

Stitches Quilts & Yarns in the 1960's
Salt Spring Archives L1

The structure served as the centre of Legion and Auxiliary activities until the 1980's.

Today, the front of the Vesuvius Bay Methodist Church is the home of *Stitches Quilts & Yarns*. Located in Ganges, on Hereford Avenue, it carries notions, fabric art supplies, embellishment kits, yarns and fabrics.

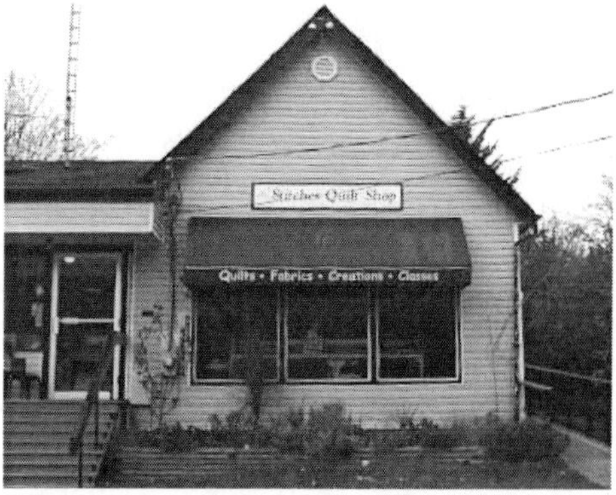

Stitches Quilts & Yarns as it appears today

Flowers & Wine

Flowers & Wine offers wine, flowers and unique gifts. The charming store is located in Ganges at Creekhouse.

Fables Cottage

Four years after the front portion of the Ganges United Church was moved to Ganges, a manse was built for the Reverend and his wife. Today, the manse is home to *Fables Cottage*, an incredible children's store.

The store, which is located on Hereford Avenue, features books, toys and crafts. The owners are both former Montessori teachers.

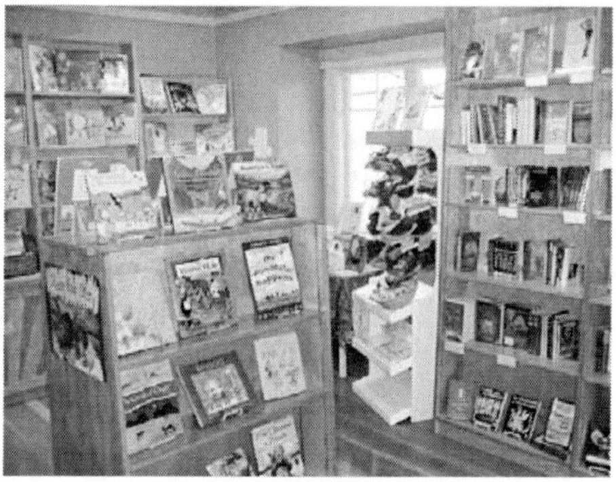

Gypsy Island Tribal Boutique

The *Gypsy Island Tribal Boutique* offers trendy clothing and accessories. It is located in Ganges on McPhillips Road.

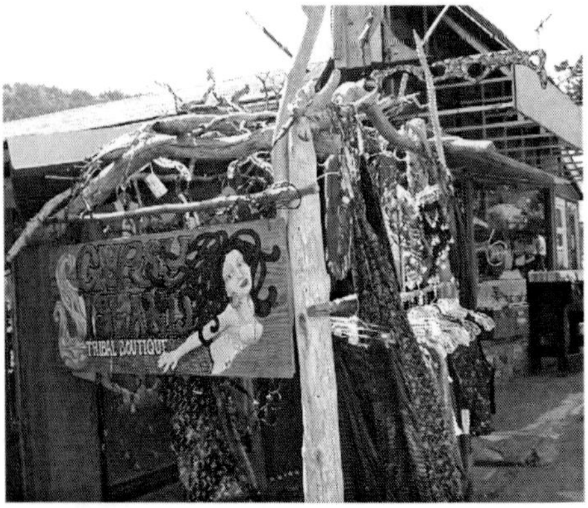

Boardwalk Greens

Boardwalk Greens is a charming, outdoor garden shop located in Ganges at Mouat's Landing.

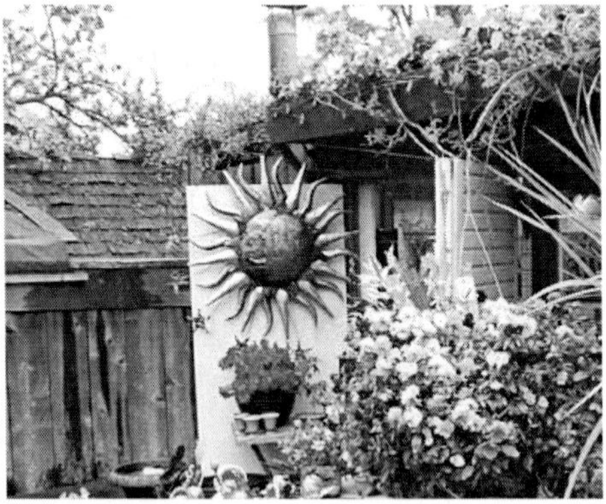

Stuff & Nonsense

Stuff and Nonsense offers an eclectic mix of fun and practical clothing, linens, dishware, home accessories, books and jewelry. The store is located in Fulford on Fulford-Ganges Road.

Volume II Island Books

Volume II Island Books is a bookstore that specializes in Gulf Island publications. The store is located in Ganges at Mouat's Mall.

West of the Moon

West Of The Moon sits on the site of the first post office ever to exist in Ganges. They offer alternative children's toys and activities made by local craftspeople and the finest international toy manufacturers. The store is located in Ganges beside Mouat's Mall.

Love My Kitchen

Love My Kitchen is a gift store that specializes in kitchen and housewares. It is located in Ganges, in the Harbour Market Building on Fulford-Ganges Road.

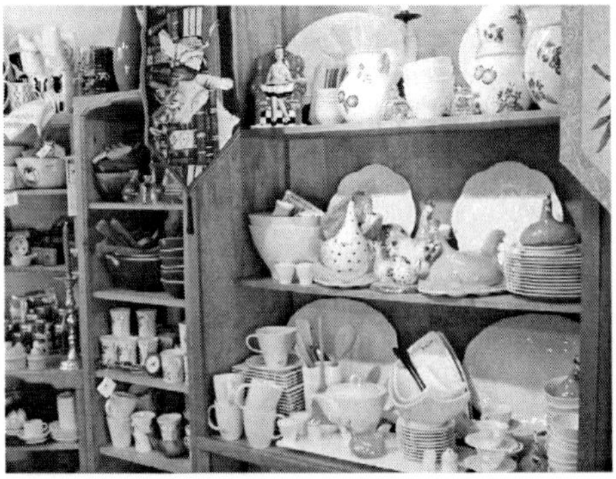

Sabine's Bookshop

Sabine`s Bookshop offers fine, used and rare books, and features a large maritime collection. The bookstore is located at Ganges Harbour in Grace Point Square.

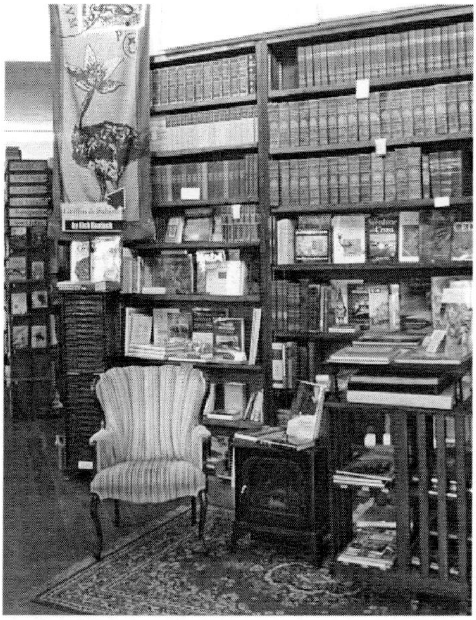

Salt Spring Books

Salt Spring Books carries an eclectic mix of books, magazines, nautical charts, and art cards and supplies. It is located in Ganges in the Salt Spring Island Trading Company building.

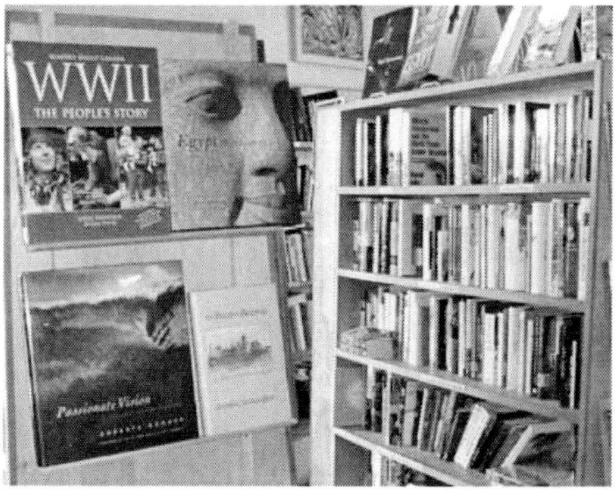

Family Jewels

The *Family Jewels* offers a wide selection of quality jewellery. The store is located in Ganges on Fulford-Ganges Road.

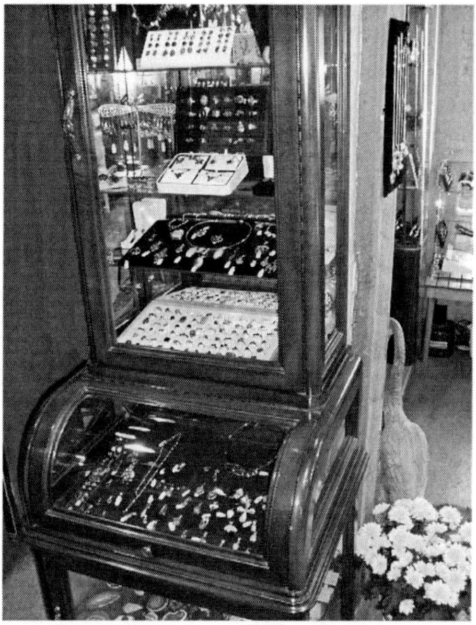

Galleries to Admire

In the 1850`s, when the first group of settlers arrived on Salt Spring Island, a former Black slave from the U.S. proceeded to establish a farm, in what would later become the community of Fernwood. More than one hundred years later, a painter moved into the farmhouse that had once belonged to the slave's family.

Around that time, a group of aspiring artists formed the Salt Spring Painters' Guild. Today, the Guild has about 100 active members.

Along with other artisans, some painters work all winter long, in their homes and studios, to fill the demand of tourists in the summer. During the tourist season, the Guild puts on an annual art show, and holds arts and crafts exhibits around the Island.

Salt Spring is famous for its *Self-Guided Studio Tour*, which allows visitors to see the work of artisans in their private studios from

May to September. On Thursdays, visitors can watch them demonstrate their craft.

A Studio Tour map, which is available at the Visitor Information Centre, displays the locations of the 40 participating studios. Look for the white road signs and the chance to meet an artist working in their studio.

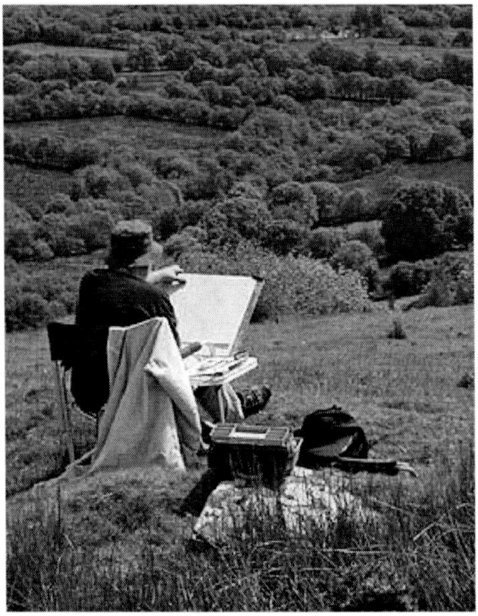

There are numerous art galleries located on the Island. On Friday nights, most galleries keep extended hours. If you prefer to participate in a guided tour of Salt Spring's finest art, you can contact Island Gourmet Safaris. They provide for full day tours of the Island's art and studios. Phone: (250) 537-4118

ArtCraft

In the 1960's, the Gulf Islands' Community Arts Council was formed and an annual art show began on Salt Spring. It featured arts and crafts produced by artists throughout the Gulf Islands. In the year 1980, the art show was moved to a heritage hall.

Today, the art show is called *ArtCraft*. The internationally renowned exhibition is the largest and longest-running art show in all the Gulf Islands. The show represents over 200 local artists and artisans.

ArtCraft is open from May to September. Other, shorter ArtCraft exhibits are held in the spring and during the Christmas season. The exhibit is located in Ganges, at Mahon Memorial Hall on Lower Ganges Road.

Stone Walrus Gallery

At the onset of World War I, the first bank on Salt Spring moved into a new building in Ganges. At that time, the building that had originally been its home became the private residence of the manager of the Salt Spring Island Trading Company down the street.

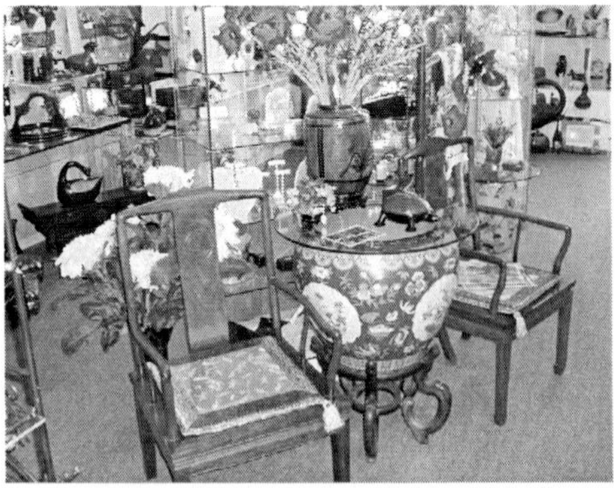

Today, the building is the home of the *Stone Walrus Gallery*. The gallery offers a collection of world art. It is located in Ganges on Lower Ganges Road.

Meredith Studio Gallery

In the 1980`s, a Salt Spring Islander started creating beautiful and functional pottery. Later, a painter starting painting landscapes, seascapes and florals. Recently, the two artists were wed. At that time, they transformed their art studios into the *Meredith Studio Gallery*.

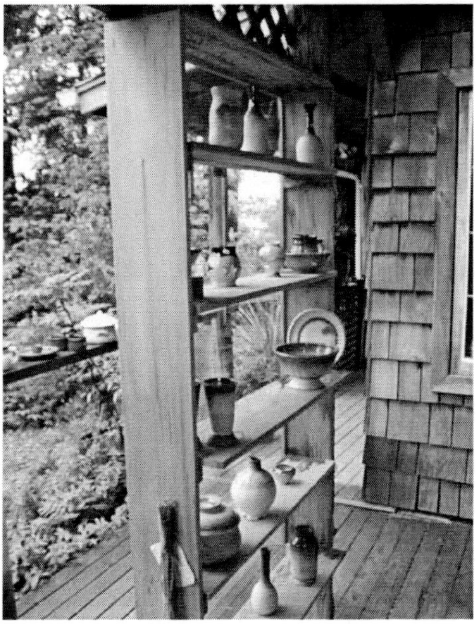

Today, the gallery offers paintings and pottery by these local artists. It is located in Vesuvius on Vesuvius Bay Road.

Thunderbird Gallery

The *Thunderbird Gallery* features native and local works of art. Sculptures in stone, bronze and wood highlight the collection. The gallery, which also hosts a monthly wine tasting and art show, is located at Ganges Harbour in Grace Point Square.

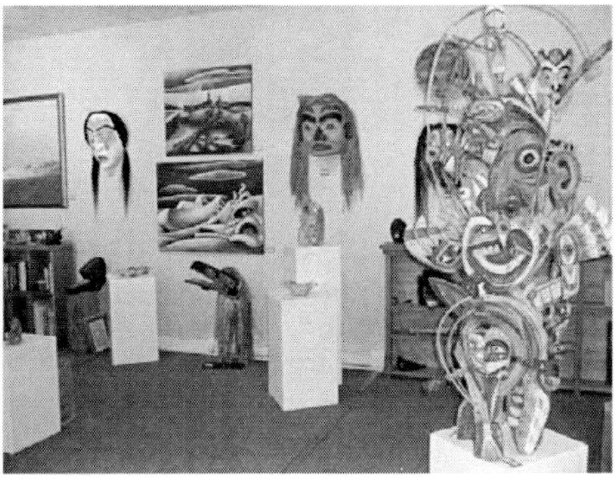

Galleons Lap Photography

In the 1930's, one of the Mouat brothers donated some land for *St. George's Anglican Church*.

Much later, in the 1990's, the church was moved across the street and became *All Saints By The Sea*. However, the church hall was not moved and, today, it is the home of a gallery called *Galleons Lap Photography*.

The gallery promotes the work of both contemporary and historic photographic artists. Located in Ganges, on Park Drive, it hosts shows in a broad spectrum of themes.

Stone Fish Sculpture Studio

The *Stone Fish Sculpture Studio* features creations set in stone. The artist chips, sands, shapes, and then polishes rock into beautiful pieces of art. His work is found in collections throughout the world. The gallery is located in Ganges on Lower Ganges Road.

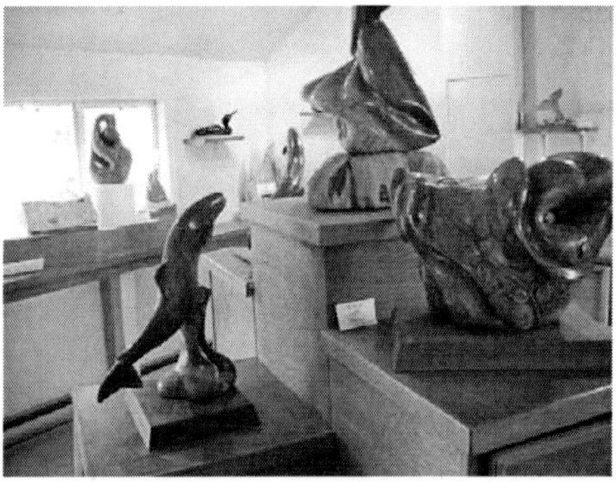

Pegasus Gallery of Canadian Art

In the 1960's, an established art gallery was moved to Salt Spring and became the *Pegasus Gallery of Canadian Art*. Today, the gallery provides for contemporary jewellery, paintings, sculptures, glassware and West Coast aboriginal masks.

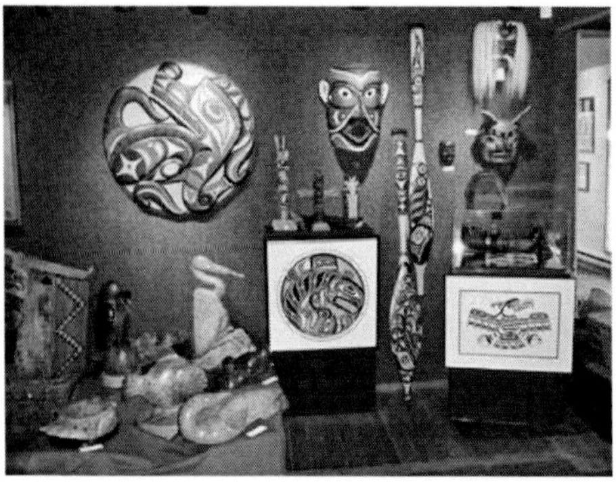

The gallery specializes in museum quality antique basketry and work by Northwest Coast native carvers. It also features paintings by local painter Carol Evans, who is renowned for her limited edition prints and watercolors, as well as by Robert Bateman, who is one of Canada's most well known wildlife artists and environmental activists. The gallery is located in Ganges at Mouat's Mall.

Morningside Folk Art Studio

The *Morningside Folk Art Studio* offers unique and interesting paper mache sculptures. It is located in Fulford on Orchard Road.

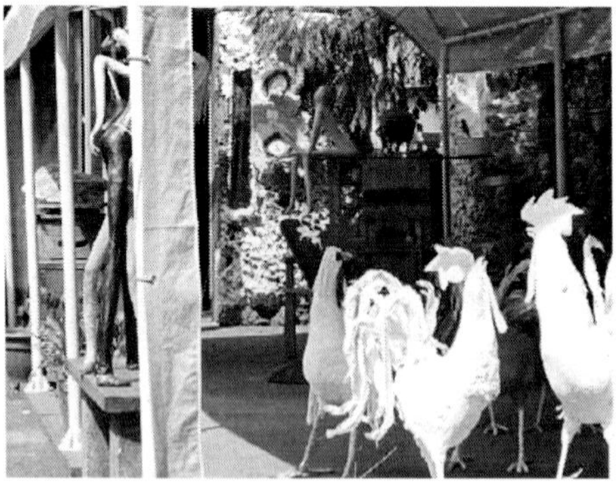

Frankly Scarlet

Frankly Scarlet is a fine jewelry store that is located at Ganges Harbour in Grace Point Square.

The Ark

In the late 1880's, the Portuguese storekeeper constructed a small Catholic chapel on Vesuvius Bay. A church bell was hung from the front gable.

The chapel was sold during World War II. At that time, it was converted into a private residence called *The Ark*.

Today, The Ark is a studio that offers artistic reproductions of dog portraits. The studio is located in Vesuvius on Vesuvius Bay Road. Unfortunately, the church bell went missing in the 1980's.

Waterfront Gallery

In the 1970's, an office building was constructed in front of the Salt Spring Island Trading Company. It was called the *Ganges Centre Building*. Soon, a small group of artisans founded an artist's co-operative, and then opened a gallery in the building.

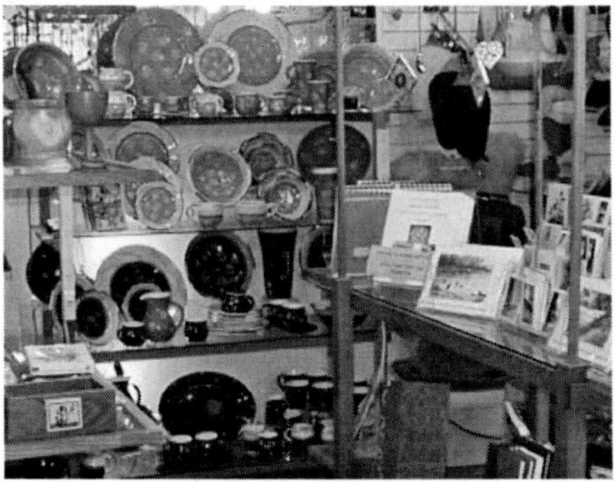

Today, the gallery, which represents over 75 Gulf Islands' artisans, is called the *Waterfront Gallery*. It is located in Ganges, at the Ganges Centre building near Mouat's Mall.

J. Mitchell Gallery

The *J. Mitchell Gallery* features quality artworks crafted from the studios of 38 first-class local artists.

The original works featured in the gallery are created from a variety of mediums, including clay, stone, brass, wood, paper, pottery and fibre. The gallery is located at Ganges Harbour in Grace Point Square.

Jill Jouise Campbell Gallery

The *Jill Louise Campbell Gallery* is the largest gallery on Salt Spring. It features impressionist watercolors from the American Southwest, Europe and the Pacific Northwest. The gallery is located in Ganges, at Mouat's Landing.

Events to Attend

During World War I, Mouat's Trading Company sponsored a Ford Model 'T' Car Rally. The car rally started in Ganges, in front of Mouat's Store, and then ended in Vesuvius. There, the participants enjoyed a picnic.

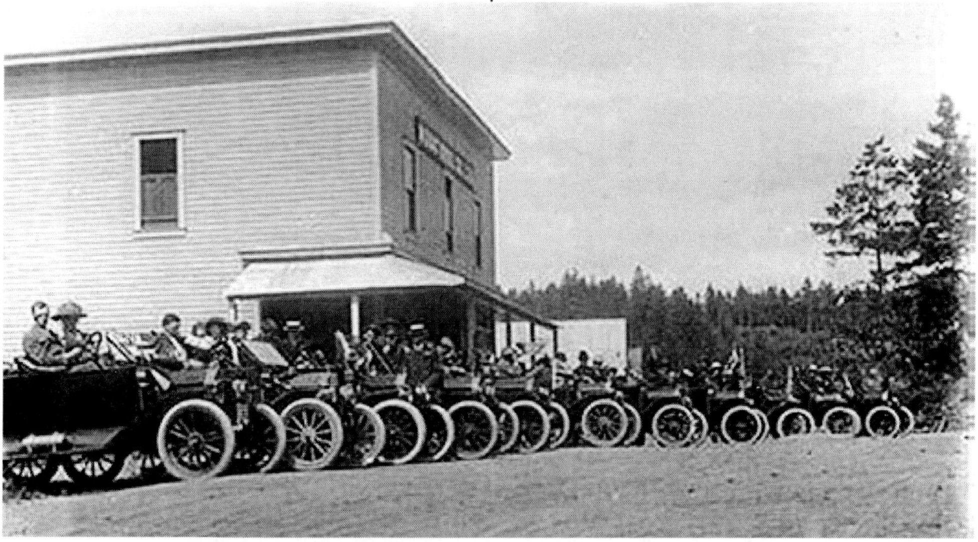

Mouat`s Ford Car Rally in 1914 - Salt Spring Archives 50571

Today, there are a variety of events on Salt Spring Island to watch or participate in. In addition to numerous festivals and exhibitions, other Island events include parades, tournaments and fairs. There is always something to take in on Salt Spring.

Erotica Festival

Salt Spring Islanders start the year with an erotic art show called the *Erotica Festival*. The week-long show is put on by ArtCraft and features a number of mature extremes in the performing and visual arts, in celebration of Valentine's Day.

Sensual dances, erotic art exhibitions and fashions shows are generally part of the venue, which takes place in February. The event is held in Ganges, at Mahon Memorial Hall on Lower Ganges Road.

Antique & Classic Car Parade

Although Mouat's Car Rally is long gone, the Salt Spring Antique and Classic Car Club puts on shows and parades throughout the year.

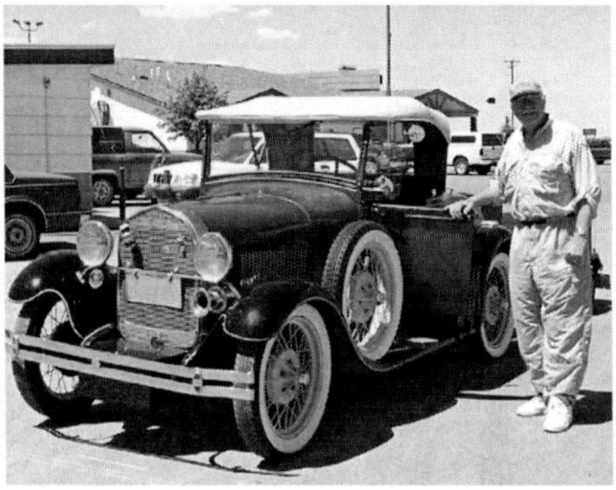

The *Antique and Classic Car Parade* is an annual event that takes place at Easter in Ganges. Participants frequently dress in clothing from the period, in keeping with the age and style of their car.

Saturday Market in the Park

The infamous *Saturday Market in the Park* began on Salt Spring in the 1970`s. At that time, vendors could sell virtually anything. However, today, market vendors must make, bake or grow their wares themselves.

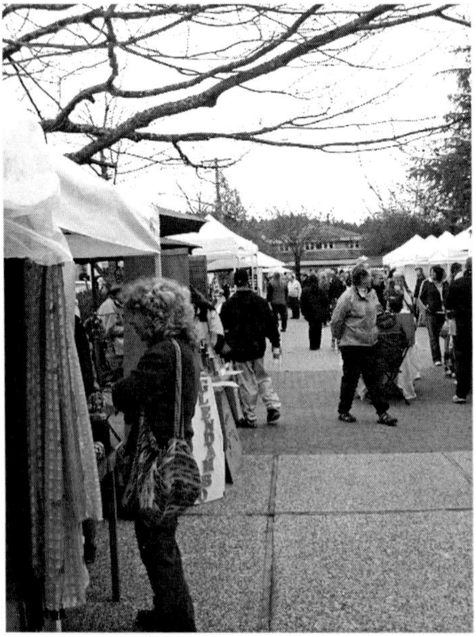

Over 100 artisans of various types contribute to the Island's international reputation for fine, world-class artists and organic farmers. The market frequently provides for live music, crafts, food and activities. It takes place every Saturday, from April to October, in Centennial Park at Ganges Harbour.

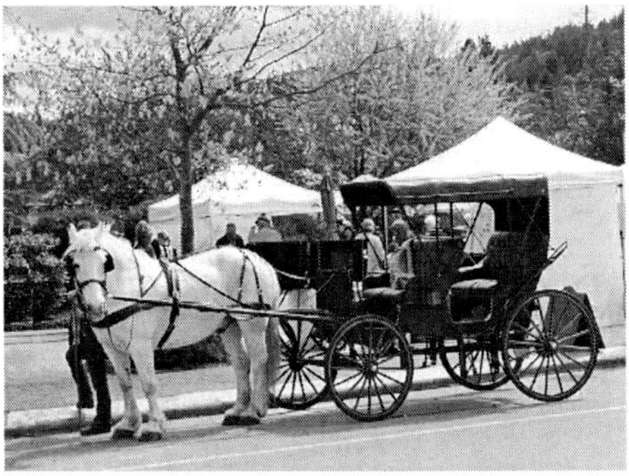

Painters' Guild Art Show

The annual *Salt Spring Painters' Guild Art Show* is a highlight for visitors to the Island. It is a colorful showcase of eclectic paintings produced by Island artists. The event is held in May at ArtSpring.

Round Salt Spring Race

The *Round Salt Spring* sailboat race began on Salt Spring in the 1970's. Today, over 80 boats compete in the 65 km long race, which is hosted by the Salt Spring Island Sailing Club.

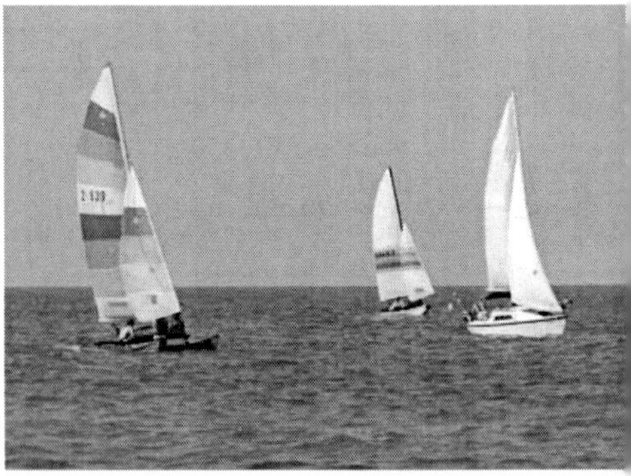

The race, which takes place in May, starts and ends in Ganges Harbour. There are prizes for all classes and categories.

Music and Munch

Music and Munch provides for a music festival with an eclectic selection of musical forms. The performances take place every Wednesday, at noon, from June to September. The event is held in Ganges, at the All Saints' Church by the Sea on Park Drive. Lunch is available.

SeaCapers Festival

SeaCapers is a long-lived seaside festival that has taken place most years in June. Events are held all around the Island. The festival often provides for a parade, biathlon, boat building competition, sand castle building competition and treasure hunt.

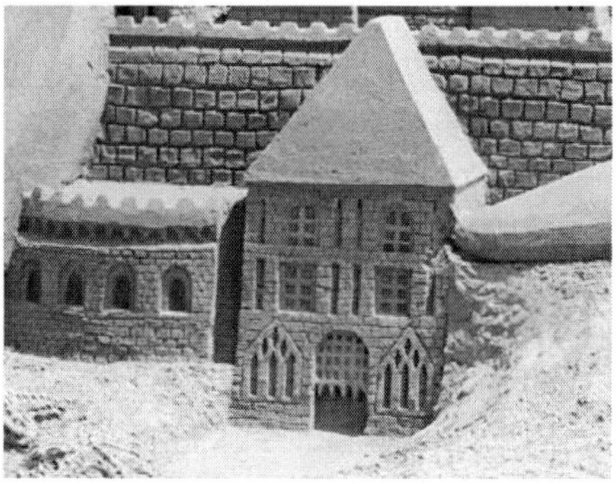

Contestants in the Build-a-Boat competition are each given a small sum of money from the local lumberyard to spend on materials. Then, they have just two hours to build a waterproof boat. The winner must demonstrate his craft by paddling it out and back in Ganges Harbour.

Canada Day Celebration

Canada Day Celebrations take place each year on July 1. Food, music and entertainment are provided. There is also a fireworks display.

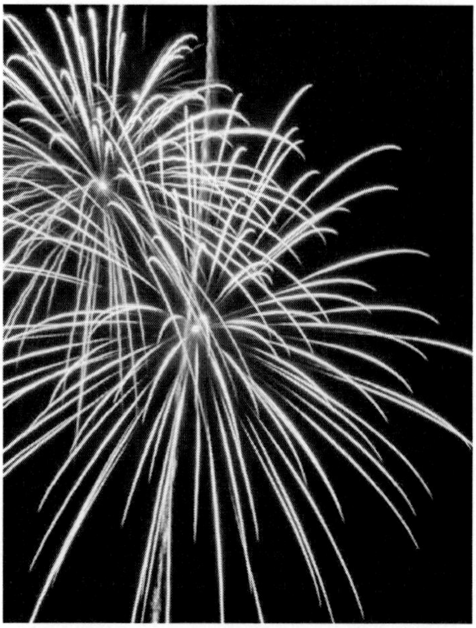

The main event is held in Centennial Park at Ganges Harbour. Other activities include a concert at ArtSpring and an Antique and Classic Car Show.

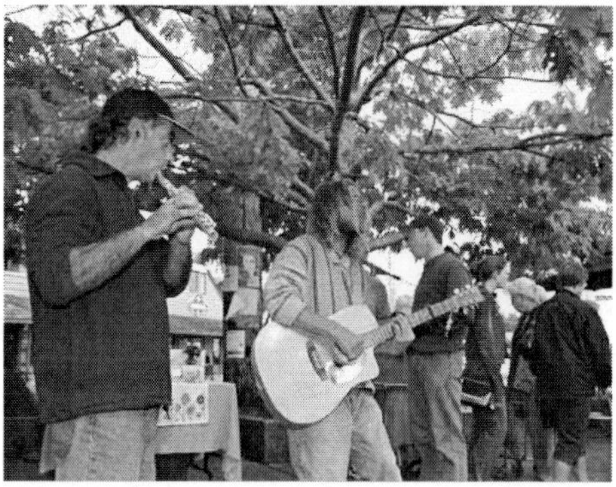

Sizzling Summer Nights

The *Sizzling Summer Nights* music festival is a festival of exceptional music. It is held each year at ArtSpring, from July through August.

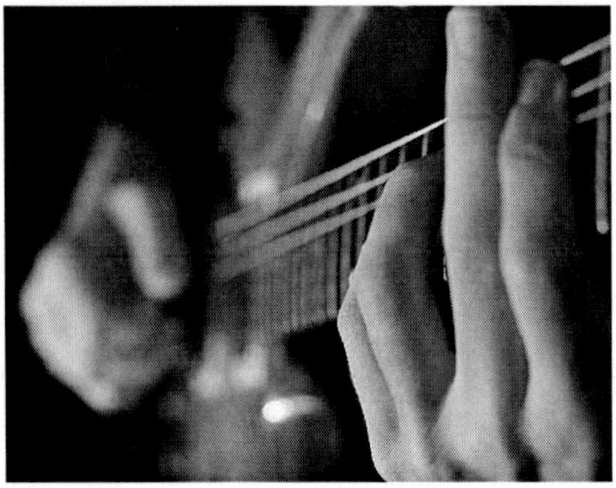

Festival of the Arts

The *Festival of the Arts* is an annual summer event that has been taking place since the 1980's. The month-long festival provides for a diverse and culturally rich array of talent, which includes performances by local, national and international artists and musicians around the Island. The event takes place throughout the month of July.

Fibre Festival

In the early 1970's, a Salt Spring Islander conceived of the idea of starting weaving classes. She purchased several two-harness table looms, and then persuaded the only known professional weaver on the Island to conduct the classes from her home. When five students enrolled in the classes, the Salt Spring Island Weavers Guild was formed.

The Guild warped late into the night, creating white cotton samplers and a set of four place mats. That summer, they exhibited their works at ArtCraft. Later, in the 1990's, the Guild held their first, annual Sheep-to-Shawl competition. That fall, their works were raffled off at the fall fair.

The third competition was held by the Guild at the Farmers Institute. It was called *Fibre Day* and included a Fibre-to-Fabric competition, as well as sheep shearing demonstrations and sheepdog trials. The Guild also held a fun Waulking the Cloth demonstration.

Over the years, as the interest in fine, traditional spinning and weaving grew, Fibre Day evolved into the *Fibre Festival*, a three-day long event that provides for demonstrations and tours of various local fibre arts studios.

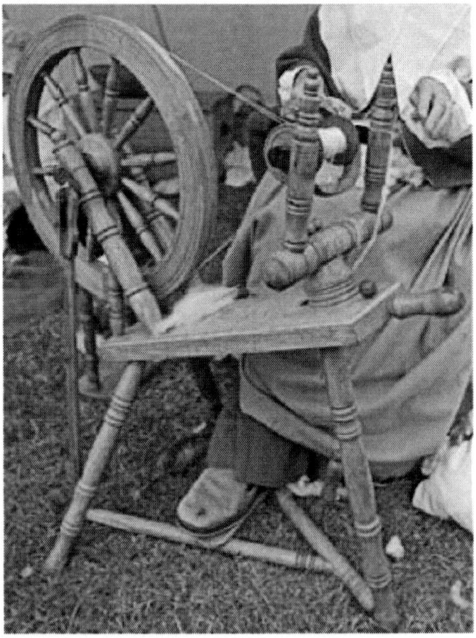

The festival celebrates weavers, felt-makers and spinners, as well as craftspeople who use a variety of techniques to make beautiful clothes, wall hangings, rugs and other works of art.

The Fibre Festival takes place in July, at the Farmers Institute on Rainbow Road. It is followed by a fashion show at ArtSpring.

Salt Spring Lavender Festival

The annual *Salt Spring Lavender Festival* is a celebration of lavender that is held each year in July. The event is hosted by Sacred Mountain Lavender, the Island's first fully integrated lavender farm. The farm is located at the south end, on a rocky road called Musgrave Road.

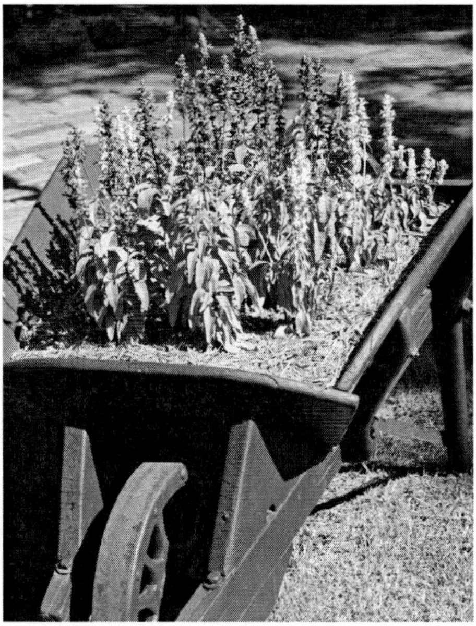

Fulford Days

In the early 1920's, the South Salt Spring Island Women's Institute constructed a hall in Fulford. Thereafter, the *Fulford Community Hall* became a venue for several events at the south end, such as fairs, dances, card parties and movies.

Four years after it was built, the furnace was overloaded with paper, causing the chimney to set the roof on fire. The fire destroyed the hall and the Women's Institute was forced to reconstruct it.

In the 1930`s, an arsonist burned the hall to the ground. However, fortunately for the Women's Institute, members of the community rebuilt it.

In the 1940`s, the resident who would later build the Akerman Museum purchased 100 pairs of second-hand roller skates. Soon, the neighborhood children were roller-skating in the hall.

Over the years, a lean-to entrance was added to the west end of the hall. It included a balcony where people could watch the roller hockey games.

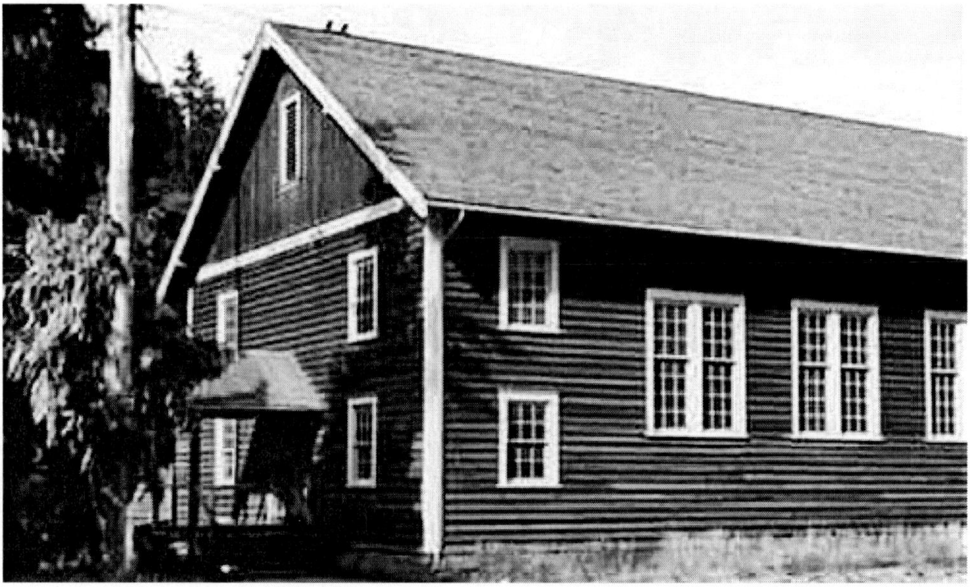

Fulford Community Hall in the 1950's - Salt Spring Archives 02186006

Today, the hall is host to some of the events that take place during *Fulford Days*, a week-long festival that is held in August.

Fulford Days began in the late 1980's. The main event is held in Drummond Park on Fulford Harbour. It provides for good food, music, competitions and other activities, as well as a fireworks display. A feature of the festival is the pies baked by the Fulford Pie Ladies.

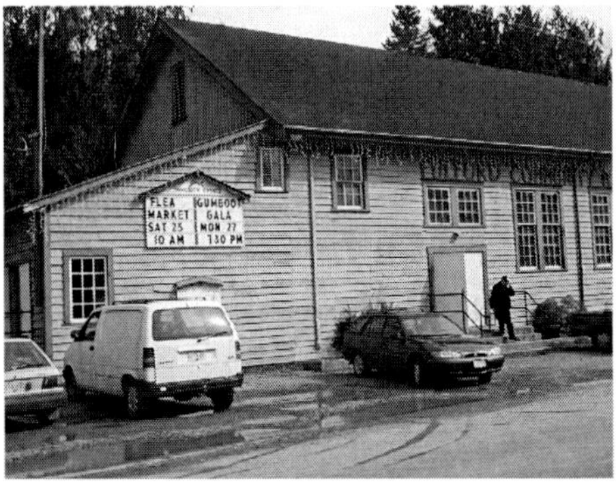

Fulford Hall as it appears today

Garlic Festival

The annual *Garlic Festival* takes place in August, at the Farmers Institute on Rainbow Road. The event provides for a variety of activities, as well as live music and a lot of food made with a lot of garlic.

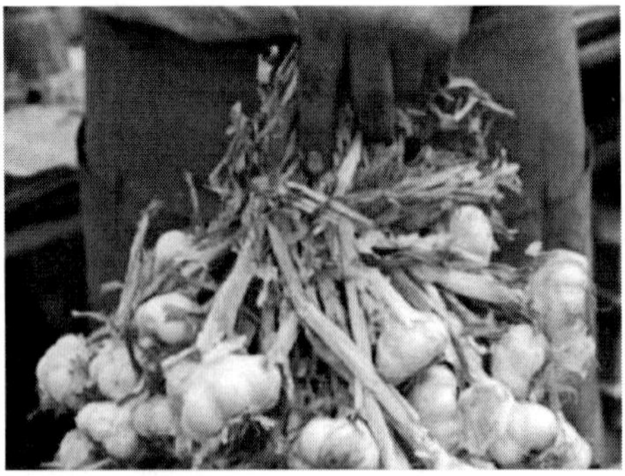

Street Dance

The *Street Dance* is a festival that is held in August, at Moby's Marine Pub on Upper Ganges Road. Dancers can dance the night away on the streets of Ganges.

Garden Faire & Music Festival

The annual *Garden Faire & Music Festival* takes place in August, at Everlasting Summer on McLennan Drive. Live music and activities are provided.

Labour Day Paint-In

During the *Labour Day Paint-In* artists set up their easels around Ganges and demonstrate their painting skills. The event takes place in September.

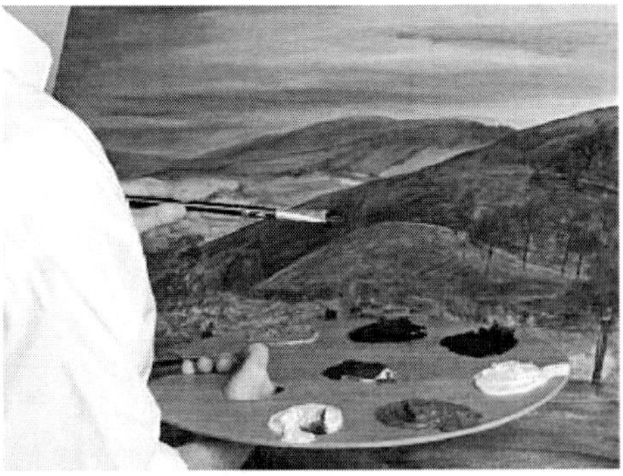

Terry Fox Run

In the 1980's, Terrance Fox, a 20-year-old amputee from British Columbia, inspired all Canadians with his 'Marathon of Hope'. His marathon was a run across the country to raise funds for cancer research. The annual *Terry Fox Run* takes place in September.

Salt Spring Fall Fair

After the Mahon Memorial Hall was built in Ganges at the turn of the century, it hosted the *Salt Spring Agricultural Exhibition* for several decades. The exhibitions were so spectacular that they rivaled the famous exhibitions in Vancouver.

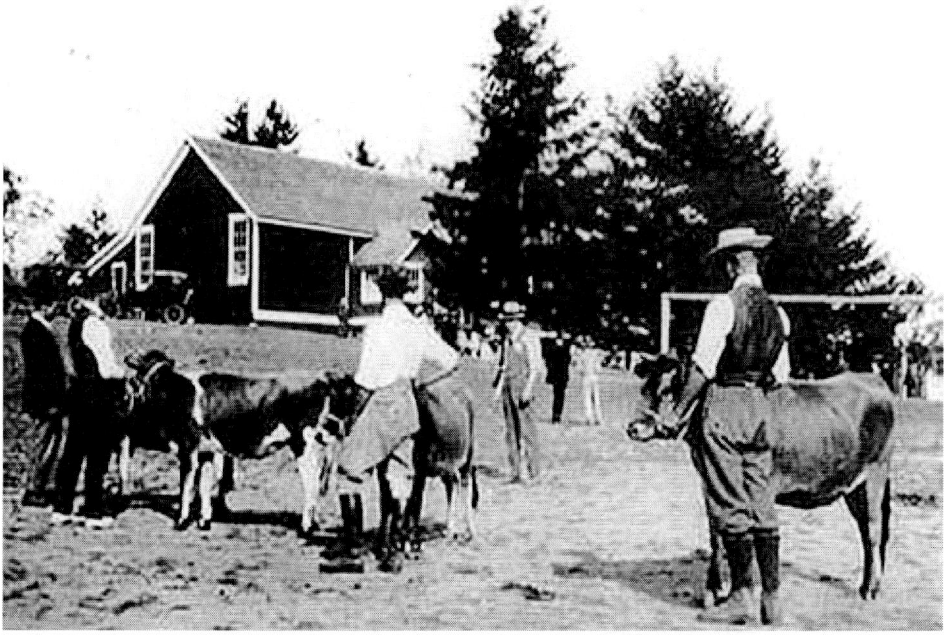

The Fall Fair in the 1920`s – Salt Spring Archives 1994137111

Unfortunately, the Salt Spring exhibition was terminated during World War II. After the war, much smaller exhibitions were held, but those soon ceased, as well.

Much later, in the 1970`s, the Salt Spring exhibition resumed on the elementary school grounds in Ganges. Three years later, the Farmers Institute purchased its own exhibition grounds nearby and held its first fall fair in the early 1980`s.

Today, the exhibition is called the *Salt Spring Fall Fair.* It provides for a farmer's marketplace and a variety of on-site food vendors. There are riding exhibitions, a midway and live entertainment.

The two-day fair attracts thousands of visitors who attend to see more than 1,500 entries of award-winning displays of produce and livestock. There is judging in a variety of categories, from produce and baking, to sheep shearing and crafts.

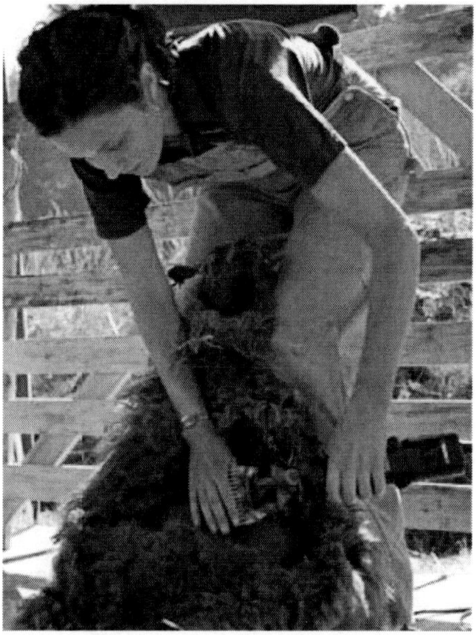

As the biggest Island event of the year, the fair takes place in September, at the Farmers Institute hall and fair grounds on

Rainbow Road. A shuttle bus is available to transport visitors between Ganges and the fair grounds. The fair is one of the oldest and longest, continuously running, fall fairs in all of British Columbia.

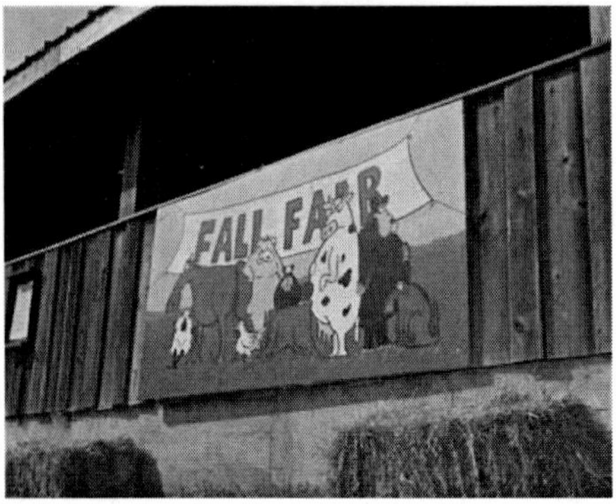

Apple Festival

By 1860, **the Postman** had established the Island's first nursery. Named the *Balmoral Nursery*, it produced fruit trees that grew very fast and yielded large fruit. As a result, he was able to meet all the demands for fruit trees from the population of British Columbia in just two years.

The following year, **the Postman** sold his nursery. At that time, it was reported to be the largest nursery in the entire Colony of Vancouver Island.

Later, in the 1890's, the British builder, who would later build the Blackburn House, planted an orchard of 500 trees on his property, from seeds that his family had gathered while traveling.

Eventually, the builder's family grafted cuttings from over 40 varieties of apples that had been sent to them from Ireland. To survive the trip, the sender had meticulously embedded each cutting in a potato. Reportedly, one of the varieties of apple trees produced as much as 545 kg of apples.

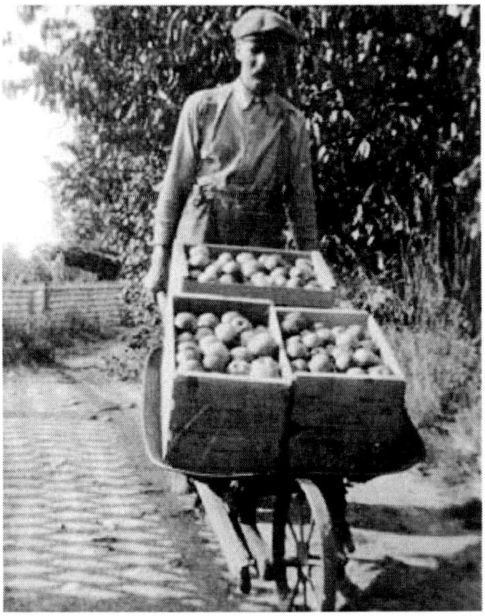

Wheeling in apples from the orchard, 1920's
Salt Spring Archives 1994137225

Today, Salt Spring Islanders celebrate the apple with an *Apple Festival*, which takes place each year in September, at the Fulford Hall at Fulford Harbour. The event is considered to be the best apple festival in all of North America, offering over 350 varieties of Island-grown apples.

Visitors can participate in an apple tasting event and travel to over one dozen orchards, most of which are organic. For an added treat, they can sample baking by the Fulford Pie Ladies.

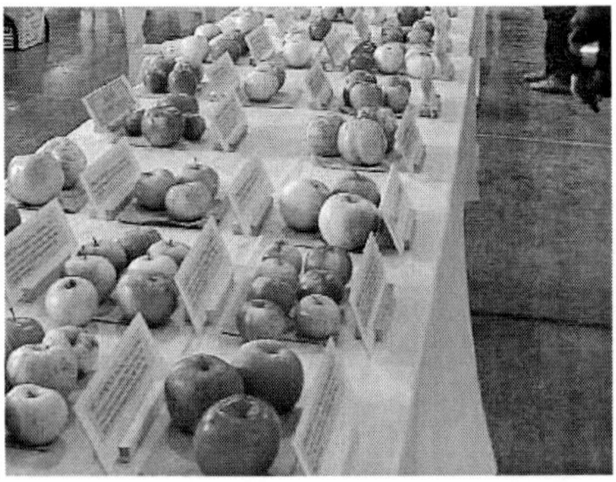

Halloween Howl

The *Halloween Howl* is an annual event that takes place at Halloween. It features a fireworks display and a haunted house. A masquerade ball is often held at the Beaver Point Hall on Beaver Point Road.

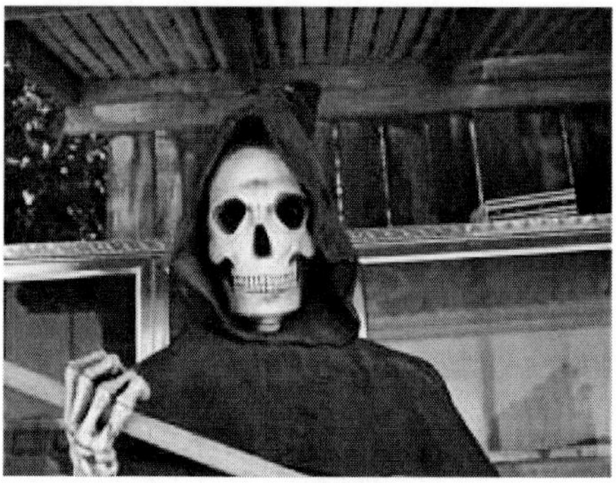

Christmas Celebrations

One winter, during the 1890's, a family's first Christmas on the Island came with a heavy snowfall. To celebrate, they set up a small Christmas tree in their equally small home. Then, they made decorations out of tiny candles that they clipped onto the tips of the branches.

The family made simple, hand-made Christmas gifts for one another and prepared roasts and mincemeat pies for dinner. The steamed plum puddings received a splash of brandy, which they lit on fire. After dinner, they sang carols and roasted chestnuts on the hearth.

Today, Salt Spring Islanders start the Christmas season with a November art show called the *Wintercraft Festival*. The 10-day sale is put on by ArtCraft and the Guilds of Christmas, and features the works of over 100 artists in 12 different craft guilds. The event is held in Ganges, at Mahon Memorial Hall on Lower Ganges Road.

In December, the Bellingham Central Lions Club, in Washington State, loads the *Christmas Ship* with toys and gifts, and sends it to Salt Spring. Known locally as the *Santa Ship*, the Christmas Ship is greeted in Ganges Harbour, and then Santa and his 'helpers' distribute gifts to the kids.

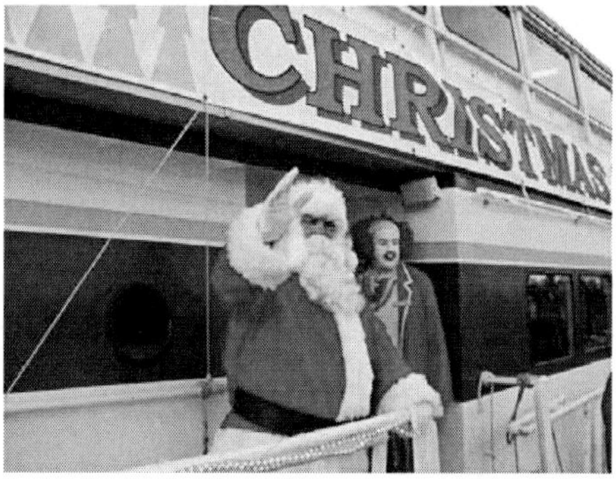

The Christmas season continues with a craft fair, which is held at the south end, at the Beaver Point Hall on Beaver Point Road. The season finishes with carols sung by the Salt Spring Singers.

Polar Bear Swim

The *New Year's Polar Bear Swim* takes place in Vesuvius Bay on New Year's Day. Hot chocolate is provided to those who brave the cold.

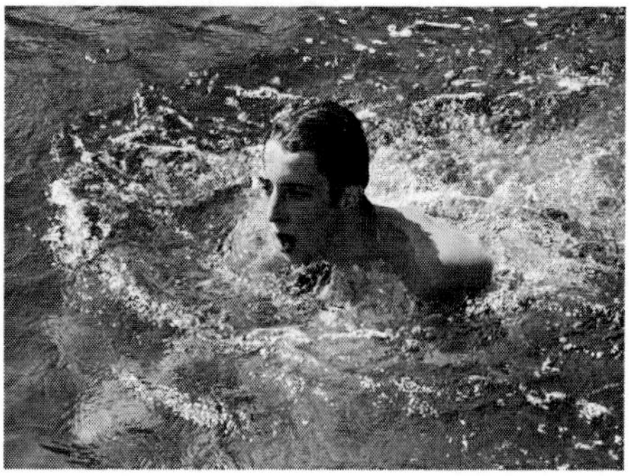

Salt Spring Island Parks & Beaches

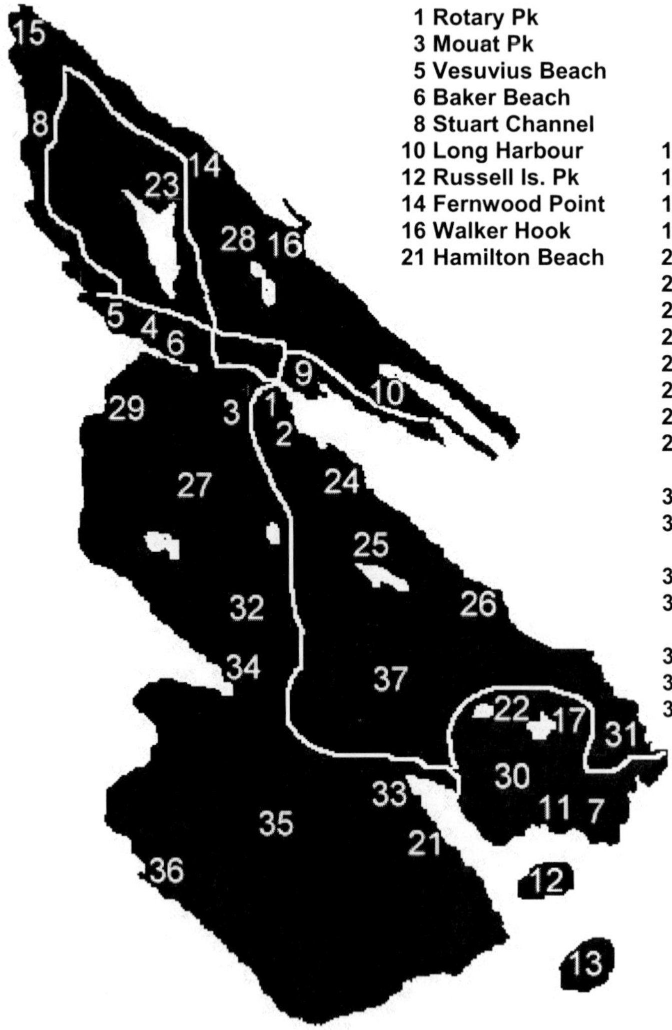

1 Rotary Pk
2 Centennial Pk
3 Mouat Pk
4 Quarry Drive Pk & Booth Canal
5 Vesuvius Beach
6 Baker Beach
7 Eleanor Point
8 Stuart Channel
9 Ganges Harbour
10 Long Harbour
11 Seabright Beach
12 Russell Is. Pk
13 Princess Margaret Pk
14 Fernwood Point
15 Arbutus Beach
16 Walker Hook
17 Weston Lake
21 Hamilton Beach
22 Stowell Lake
23 St. Mary Lake
24 Ganges Harbour
25 Cusheon Lake
26 Beddis Beach
27 Manzanita Ridge Pk
28 Dunbabin Pk
29 Mount Erskine Pk & Bader's Beach
30 Reginald Hill Pk
31 Ruckle Pk & Beaver Point
32 Mount Maxwell Pk
33 Drummond Pk & Fulford Harbour
34 Burgoyne Bay & Pk
36 Musgrave Point
37 Andreas Vogt Reserve

Parks & Beaches to Explore

By the year 1858, the English had named the largest of the southern Gulf Islands *Admiral Island*, after a Rear Admiral who was commander in chief of the Pacific Station in Victoria.

When **the Postman** and some other settlers arrived on that same Island the following year, they discovered 14 saline springs at the north end, the largest of which was 27 m in diameter. Subsequently, they named that settlement *Salt Spring*.

As more settlers arrived on the Island, they began to refer to the entire Island as *Salt Spring*. So, at the turn of the century, the Geographic Board of Canada conceded to the settlers by officially renaming the Island after its springs.

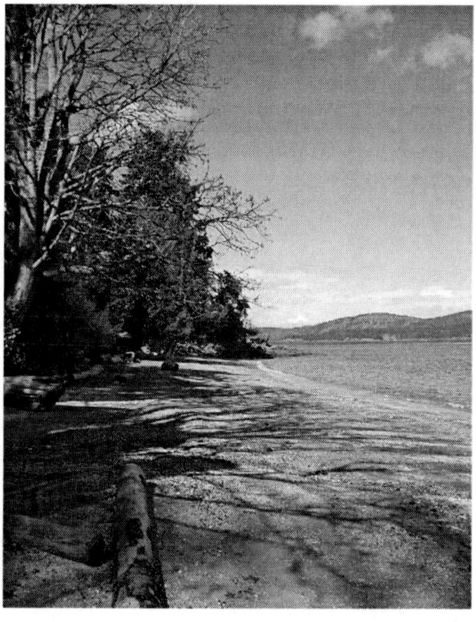

Today, visitors to Salt Spring Island enjoy numerous ocean access beaches. Although there are very few lakes on any of the other Gulf Islands, Salt Spring has 11 lakes, five of which have public beaches. Additionally, it is the only island that contains salt springs.

Much of Salt Spring Island is parkland. Island Pathways works year-round to establish and maintain a network of pathways and trails. The trails range from short, seashore access, walking trails to forest hikes, so you might want to invest in a pair of *waffle stompers* (hiking shoes).

Andreas Vogt Nature Reserve

The *Andreas Vogt Nature Reserve* is located near Fulford. It provides for a forest of Garry Oak and Arbutus trees, as well as views of many of the Island's peaks.

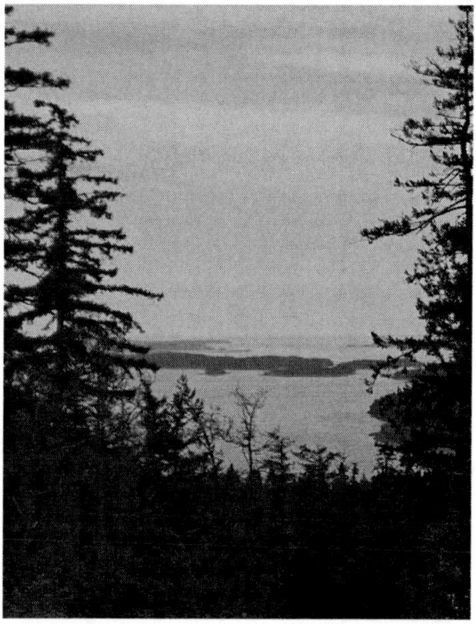

The attractive, 4 km trail through the reserve is of moderate difficulty. It is accessible from the end of a gravel road off Sarah Way. At the gate entrance, the trail to the left crosses a stream bed, and then leads to another trail on the left that heads to the nature reserve. (#37 on the map)

Beddis Beach

In the 1880's, the British builder purchased a sailing sloop and loaded it with food, a tent and some household items. Then, he set sail up the West Coast with his family. Eventually, the builder and his family landed on a beach, where they constructed a log home.

Later, when the builder contracted pneumonia and died, his sons took over his business. At the turn of the century, they built a new, two-storey, frame house for their family to live in.

Beddis Beach was named after this family of builders, whose home and orchard can still be seen standing nearby.

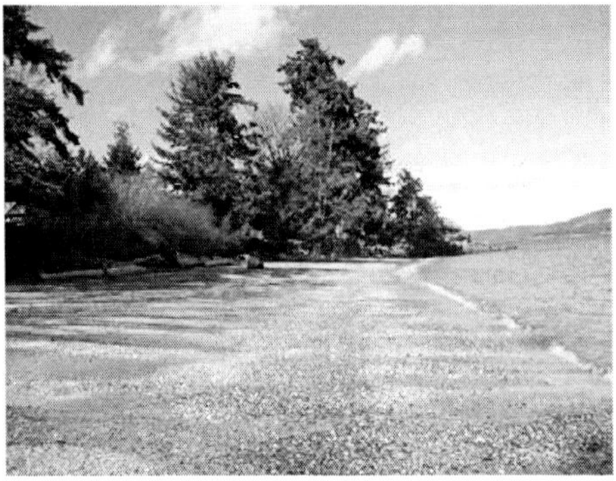

The stunning white-shell beach is located near Ganges Harbour. It is one of the most beautiful beaches on the Island and provides for views of Prevost and Pender Islands.

A buoy on a rock off the beach commemorates the family who, for many years, left a light burning in the front window of their home to guide ships through the Pass.

At the north end of the beach is a five-storey Cedar and stone structure called Winsor Castle. It was built from thousands of kilograms of stone, which were hand-picked by an artist, from beaches all over the Gulf Islands.

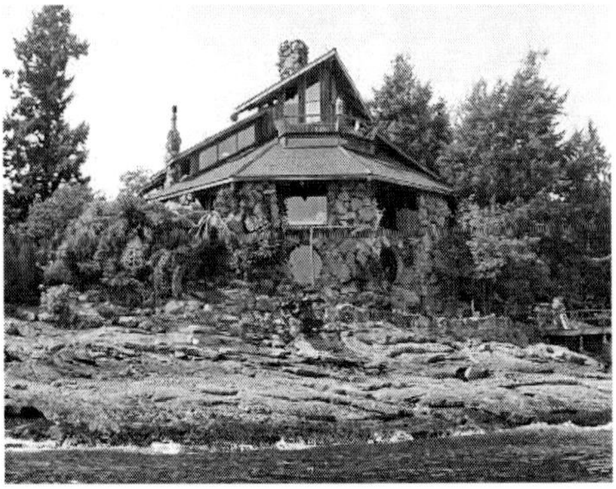

You can launch a boat from the beach and travel south along the shoreline to the Channel Islands. Alternatively, you can sail to Prevost Island. The beach is accessible from the end of Beddis Road. (#26 on the map)

Booth Bay

In the 1850's, one of the first settlers to arrive on Salt Spring purchased some land surrounding a canal. About a decade later, the settler became the first representative of Salt Spring in the Legislative Assembly in Victoria.

During his reign as Salt Spring's main politician in the 1870's, letters patent were issued for the incorporation of the Township of Salt Spring Island.

The first meeting saw a number of municipal by-laws passed, which started a battle over the incorporation and divided the Islanders politically for more than a decade.

In the 1880's, the people charged the politician with retaining his political position without election since no one else was nominated to oppose him. Eventually, the incorporation was cancelled and the politician went on to lose two provincial elections.

Fortunately, in the year 1890, he won again, in a new riding called The Islands. He held the seat until he passed away. His funeral was the most impressive ever held on Salt Spring.

Booth Bay was named after this politician, whose name also commemorates the adjoining canal.

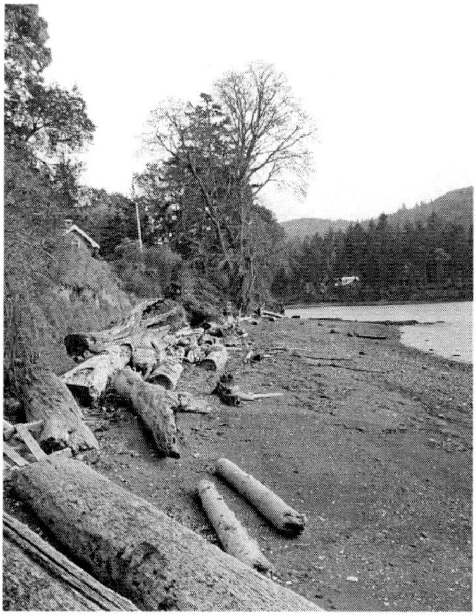

Booth Bay is located near Vesuvius. The beach on the bay is called *Baker Beach*. Accessible by way of steps at the end of Baker Road, it is a good place to watch the Bald Eagles soar. (#6 on the map)

Quarry Drive Park is located on the north side of the bay. The 2 km trail through the park is of moderate difficulty and provides for views of Vancouver Island. Accessible from Quarry Drive, it also provides access to the beach. (#4 on the map)

Burgoyne Bay Provincial Park

Burgoyne Bay Provincial Park is located on the southwest side of the Island. The park sits in a Douglas-Fir, Garry Oak and Arbutus forest and provides for views of rocky bluffs on Bold Bluff Point.

Numerous trails wander through the historical park with its heritage structures. The trails also provide access to Mount Maxwell to the north and Mount Sullivan to the south.

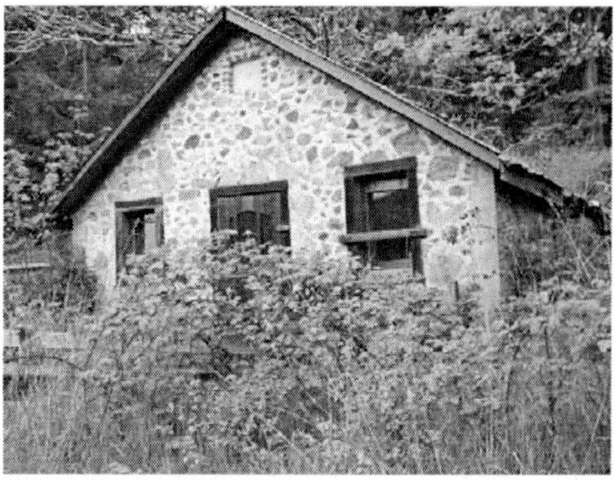

Burgoyne Bay is located in the park. It contains significant conservation, recreation, wildlife and fish. Two salmon streams run into the bay. At low tide, you can walk along the rocky beach for *lele* (a long time) looking at the Sea Stars.

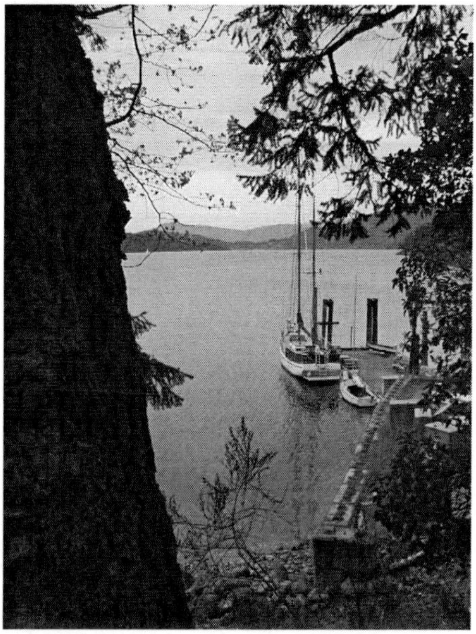

The beach also provides for a public dock. If you launch a boat from the beach, you can sail north to the Cranberry Outlet or south to Musgrave Landing. However, the bay is exposed to winds from the southeast and northwest. The beach and park are accessible from the end of Burgoyne Bay Road. (#34 on the map)

Dunbabin Park

Dunbabin Park is a pristine park on the northeast side of the Island. The easy, 1.5 km trail through the dense, lush park provides for large ferns, Western Red Cedar and Douglas-Fir trees. The trail can be accessed from Stark Road or Robinson Road. (#33 on the map)

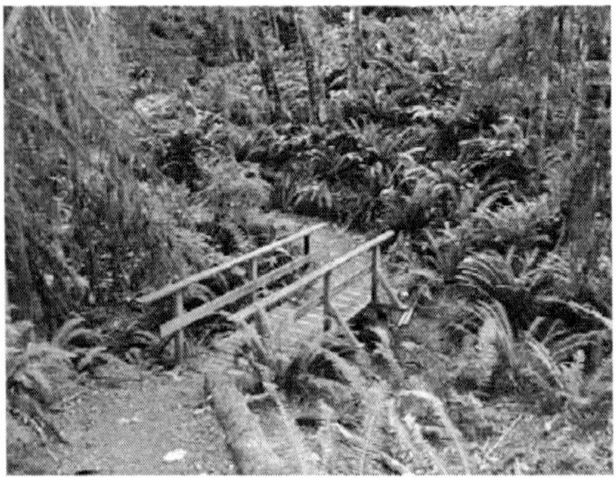

Eleanor Point

Eleanor Point is located in Forest Ridge Park near Fulford Harbour. As the most southeastern tip of the Island, it provides for views of Russell Island. The trail to the point is accessible from the end of Eagles Way. A road to the right leads to the beach on the point. (#7 on the map)

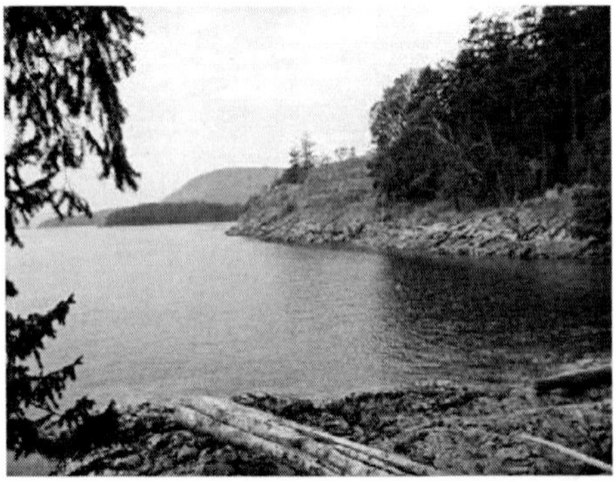

Fernwood Point

Upon landing on Salt Spring in the late 1850's, a few of the first settlers drew straws for their choice of sections of land.

As the second settler to choose, the man who would later become **the Postman** chose a parcel of land overlooking a little bay on the northeast side of the Island. On his property, he encountered one of the Island's 14 valuable salt springs.

Within a few months, **the Postman** had built a small log cabin on his valuable property. The cabin had a mud floor and was covered with shakes on poles. It was heated by a small fireplace.

By 1860, he had established the Island's first store and post office. To save postage on his letters, he established a method of writing a message down the page, rotating the paper, and then writing a second message across the first.

In his Balmoral Store, he sold groceries, dry goods and hardware. He would trade with the other settlers for goods in his store, but would not extend them credit. He would also not allow spitting in his store, nor would he allow swearing if ladies were present. He used a broom to enforce his strict policies.

Over time, the area in which **the Postman** had lived and conducted his business was named in his honor. Today, the area is part of the community known as Fernwood.

Fernwood Point is located in Fernwood. There are three beach accesses on the point, all of which provide for views of Galiano Island.

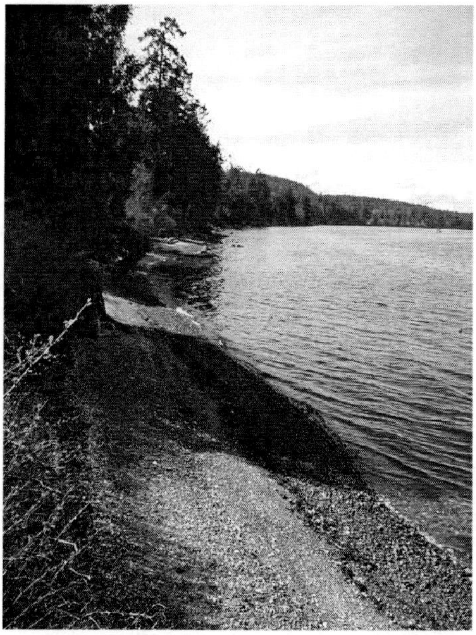

The access at the end of Fernwood Road leads to a public dock, which is surrounded by the only live Sand Dollar beds on the Island.

Two other beach accesses also exist. One access is at the end of Maliview Drive and the other is on North Beach Road. The latter leads to Hudson Point, where the McFadden Creek Heronry is located. (#14 on the map)

If you launch a boat from Hudson Point, you can sail along the shoreline or across to Wallace Island. The marine park on Wallace Island is a great place to see Seals and Bald Eagles.

The protected anchorages in the coves on the west side of Wallace Island make it easy to anchor in for the poolakle (night). Keep in mind that there are sudden winds in Houstoun Passage.

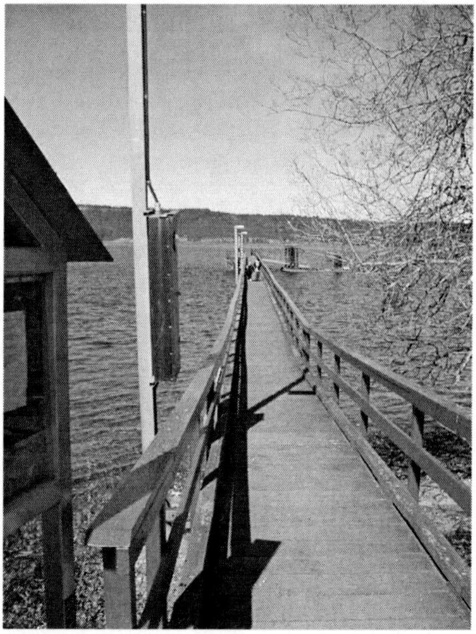

Fulford Harbour

In the 1860's, the gunboat, HMG *Forward*, was lost in a storm among the Gulf Islands. As the ship was being tossed about, the crew suddenly sighted a beacon light. So they pulled into a harbour to ride out the storm.

By the 1890's, a wharf was built in the harbour. It provided a way for a very comfortable passenger vessel, called the *Joan*, to take settlers to and from Vancouver Island.

At that time, most of the area was owned by Hawaiian settlers. However, by the 1920's, a white settlement began to develop around the harbour and a general store, church, community hall and Inn were built nearby. There was even an ice cream kiosk at the wharf.

Around that time, a carpenter built a ferry in the harbour. It was called *Hepburn's Ferry* and was powered by a farm tractor. It could carry four cars to Vancouver Island in two hours.

There were several pulleys on the ferry's drive shaft. So, if it needed more power during the voyage, the owner would just attach to the drive shaft a belt from the rear wheel of one of the cars aboard, and then start the car.

In the late 1920's, the Gulf Islands Ferry Company was formed. At that time, a ship that had been purchased from the Canadian Pacific Railway was converted into a ferry called the MV *Cy Peck*. It could carry 20 small cars.

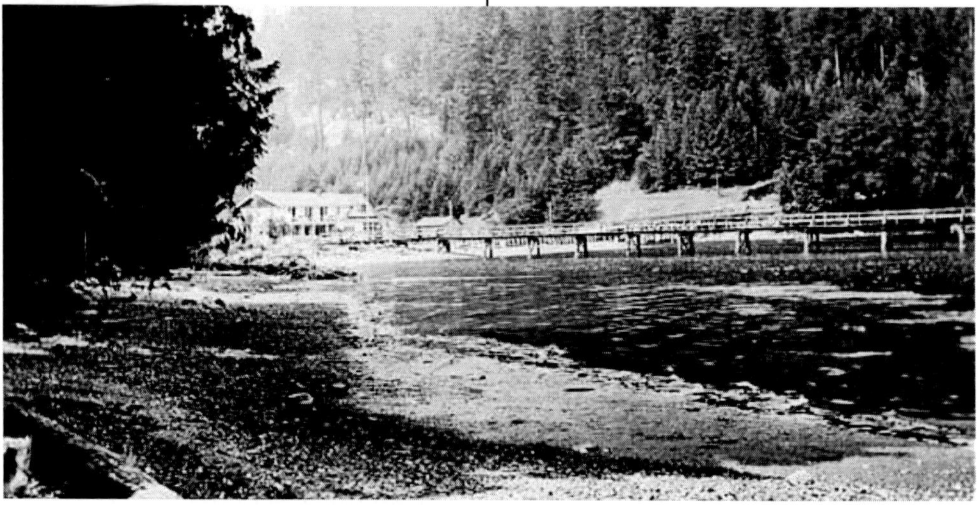

Fulford Harbour in the 1920's - Salt Spring Archives 0011179041

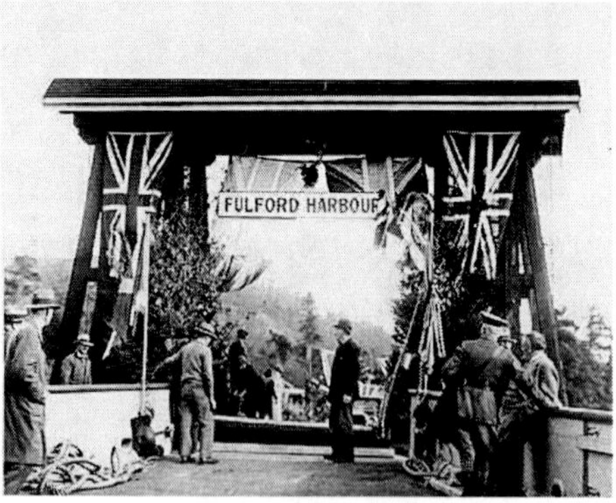

Fulford Harbour wharf in the 1930's
Salt Spring Archives 1994137295

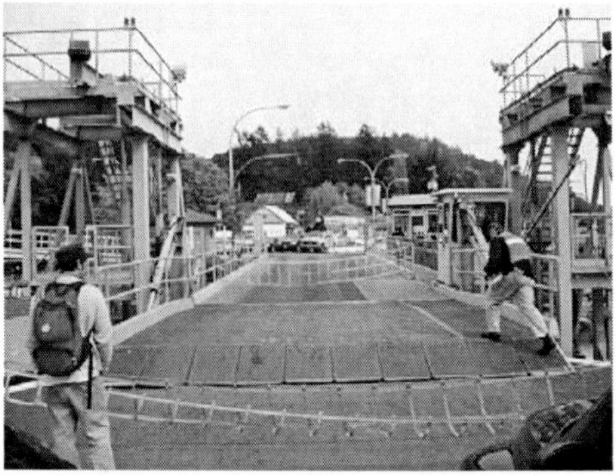

Fulford Harbour wharf as it appears today

In the early 1950's, one of the owners of Mouat's Store purchased the Gulf Islands Ferry Company, and then drastically improved it. The following year, the *Cy Peck* was carrying over 17,000 cars. At that time, it provided the only connection to Vancouver Island.

Fulford Harbour is located on the southeast side of the Island. The wharf in the harbour provides for the busiest ferry terminal on the Island. It still services ferries traveling to and from the tip of Vancouver Island. There are also two public docks in the harbour and a marina that provides for all season overnight moorage.

A recreational park, called *Drummond Park*, offers playgrounds and a beachfront swimming area on the west side of the harbour.

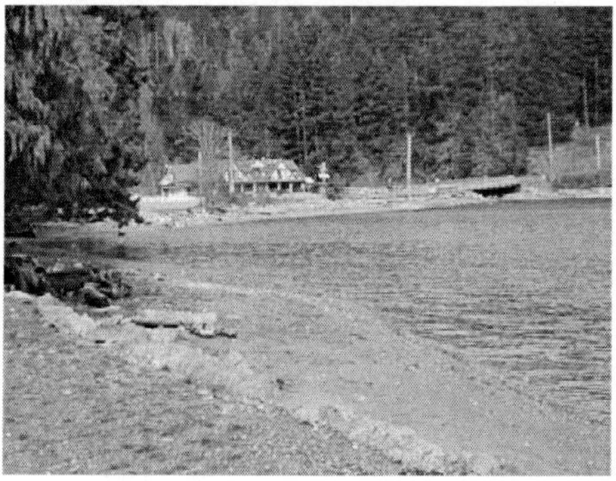

Fulford Harbour as it appears today

The beach at the park was once known as *Jackson`s Beach* but is today called *Hamilton Beach*. It is accessible from Isabella Point Road. (#21 and #33 on the map)

If you launch a boat from the beach, you can sail around around the south end and up to Musgrave Landing. Near Cape Keppel is a marine ecological reserve.

Ganges Harbour

In the year 1860, 14 Bella Bella Indians were carrying a load of furs in a canoe. Accompanying them was a renegade white man.

The Indians stopped in a harbour where about 50 Cowichan Indians were already camped. The two tribes were long-time rivals and, as a result, a battle ensued.

During the battle, the white man made his way to the home of a settler who lived nearby. When he told the settler about the battle, the settler went to the harbour to investigate.

At the harbour, the settler discovered that eight Bella Bella Indian men had been killed and the remainder taken prisoner. It was a massacre.

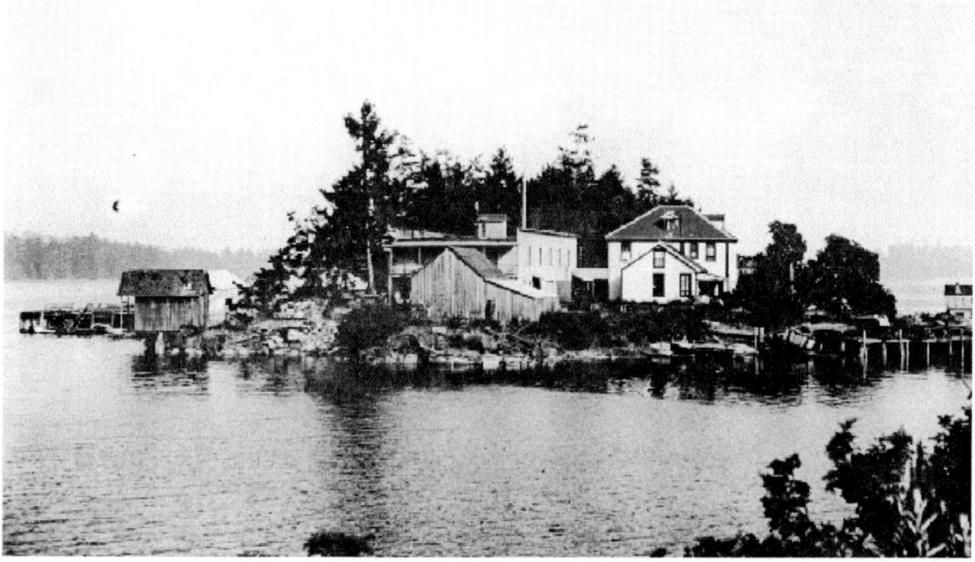

Ganges Harbour in 1912, the post office in the background - Salt Spring Archives 1994137020

Ganges Harbour is located on the northeast side of the Island. First named *Admiralty Bay*, it was the site of what is now known as the Massacre of Admiralty Bay.

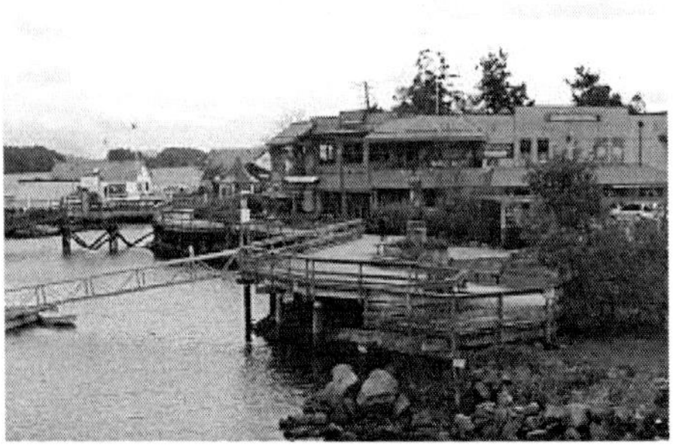

Ganges Harbour as it appears today

The harbour provides for two marinas and two government docks. There is an active Salt Spring Sailing Club and an outpost station for the Royal Vancouver Yacht Club.

Sea Star Point, on the north side of the harbour, provides for a lovely beach with wonderful views of Goat Island and the Chain Islands. The beach is accessible from the end of Churchill Road. (#9 on the map)

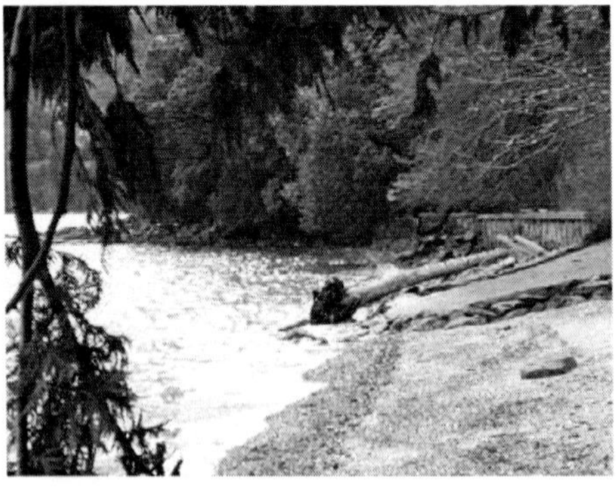

A second beach access is located further south, off Price Road. (#24 on the map) If you launch a boat from either beach, you can sail out to the little islands.

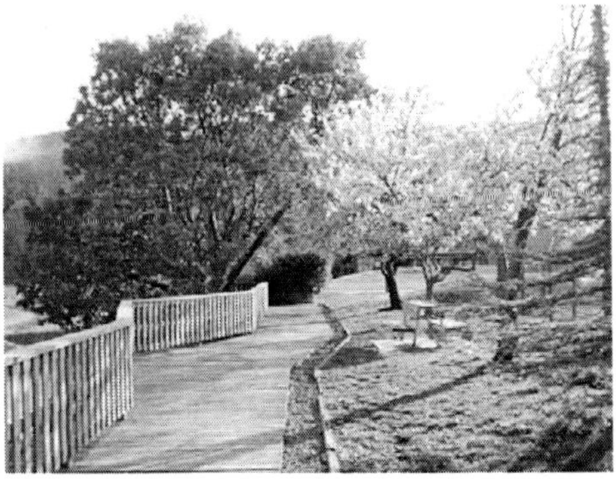

Centennial Park, which is located at the south end of the harbour, is the site of the *Saturday Market in the Park*. The bandstand in the park provides for outdoor entertainment, while the boardwalk offers a wonderful view of the harbour. There are facilities for picnics if you want to stay a while. (#2 on the map)

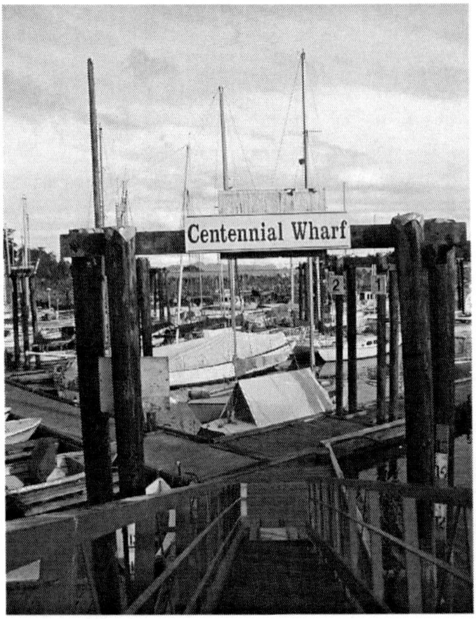

The park also provides for a marina, wharf and playgrounds. The wharf is secluded behind a secure breakwater and isolated from the floatplanes and powerboats that pass through the harbour.

Another park, called *Rotary Marine Park*, is located at the north end of the harbour. It also provides for a beautiful seaside boardwalk. (#1 on the map)

Recently, the Rotary Club of Salt Spring organized a fundraiser whereby visitors to the park could personalize commemorative paving stones that were then used to pave the entrance to the park.

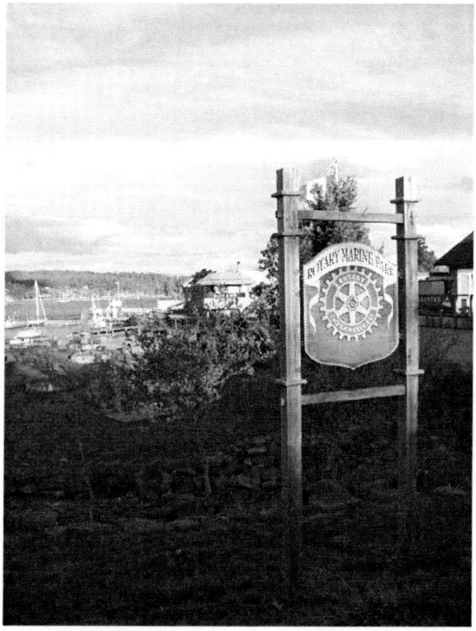

Long Harbour

In the 1940's, the Canadian Pacific Railway provided ferry service to and from the mainland. The ferry docked at Fulford Harbour four days a week. The trip took eight long hours.

In the 1960's, another ferry terminal was built, in Long Harbour. It took over the sailings to the mainland.

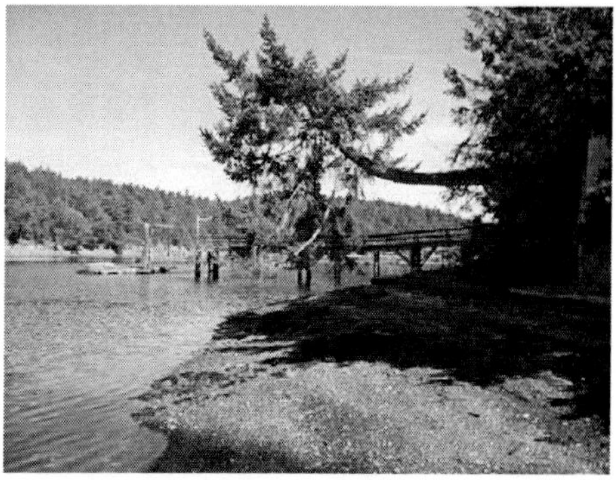

Long Harbour sits snugly between Nose Point and Scott Point, just north of Ganges Harbour. There are two accesses to the beautiful beach at the harbour. One access is from Beachside Drive and the other is from Ontario Place. (#10 on the map)

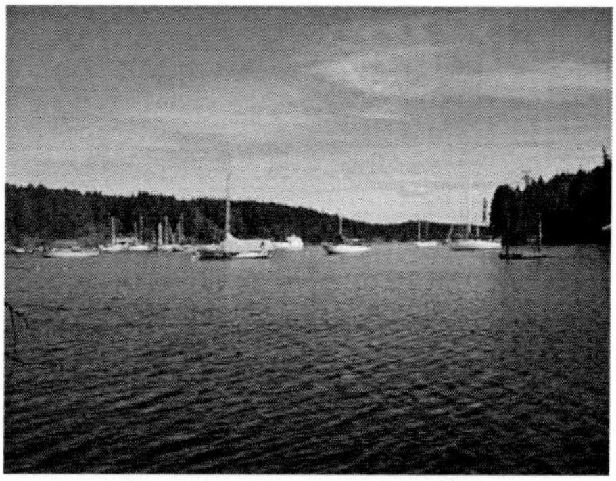

If you launch a boat from the beach, you can travel to the tip of Nose Point. From there, you can continue to Prevost Island, which is part of the Gulf Islands National Park Reserve. It offers some of the most scenic shoreline in all the Gulf Islands. However, be careful of the *skookumchuck* (strong currents) around Nose Point.

Manzanita Ridge Park

Manzanita Ridge Park is a beautiful nature reserve near Ganges. It was acquired only recently, from a long-time Salt Spring Islander.

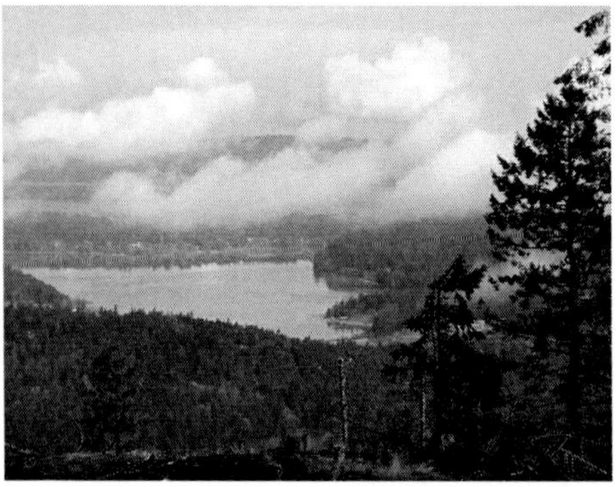

The park provides for views of neighboring Galiano Island. The strenuous 3 km trail through the park travels through a forest of 200-year old Douglas-Fir trees. It is accessible from Toynbee Road. (#27 on the map)

Mouat Provincial Park

After running Mouat's Store in Ganges for three years, the businesswoman who purchased it converted it into a boarding house. Then, she moved herself, her sons and her store employees into it.

By the onset of World War I, the woman's sons had become successful businessmen. As Mouat Brothers Company Ltd., they acquired the Island's Ford automobile dealership, installed a gas pump at the corner of the store and built a garage across from the boarding house. They also started a taxi service.

Unfortunately, one of the brothers soon contracted polio, which left him paralyzed. Nevertheless, he continued to conduct business from his wheelchair.

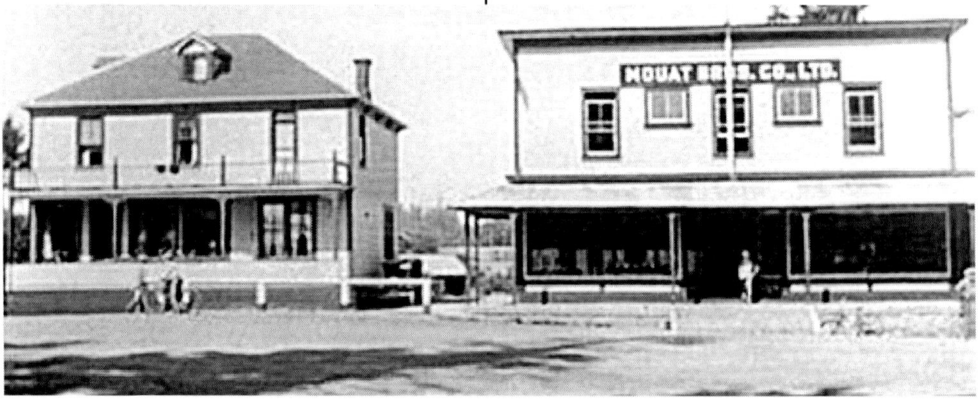

Mouat's property holdings in 1912 - Salt Spring Archives 1994137008

In the 1930`s, the woman expanded her boarding house, calling it the *Ganges Inn*. It was known locally as *Granny's Boarding House*.

Mouat Provincial Park was named after this family of entrepreneurs, whose company will be celebrating its centennial in the year 2007.

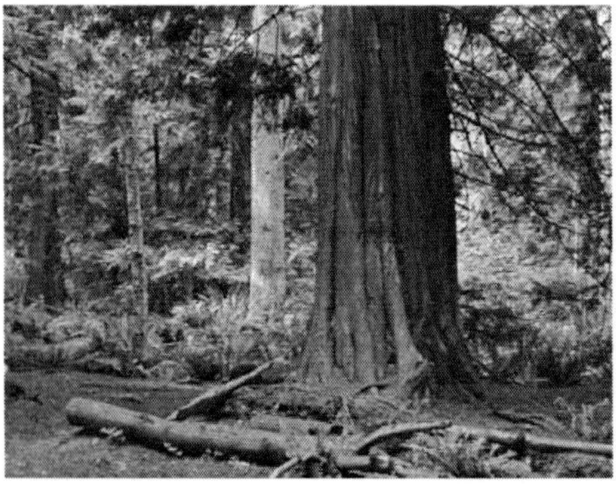

At one time, the park was the Island's only drive-in campground. Today, it provides for a disc golf course. There are also facilities for picnics if you want to stay a while. The forested park provides for beautiful Western Red Cedar trees. It is located in Ganges, on Seaview Avenue. (#3 on the map)

Mt. Erskine Park

Mount Erskine Park is located on the northwest side of the Island. The strenuous 2.5 km trail through the park is called the *Jack Fisher Trail.*

The trail, which travels through Arbutus groves, is accessible from the east side of Collins Road. At the junction, the trail to the right leads to a spectacular viewpoint.

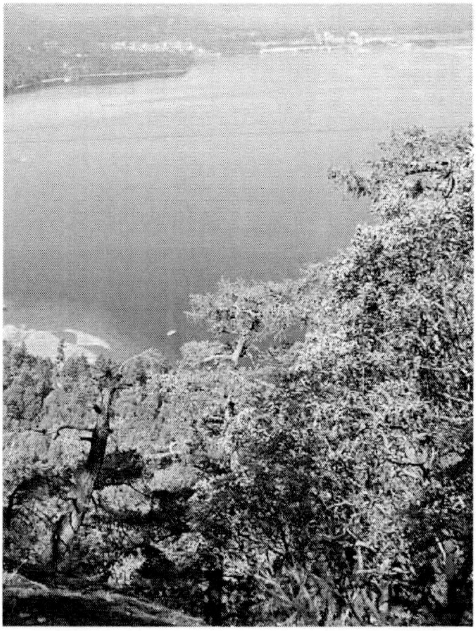

Bader's Beach is located beside Mt. Erskine Park. The sandy beach is also known as *Erskine Beach* and *Collins Beach.*

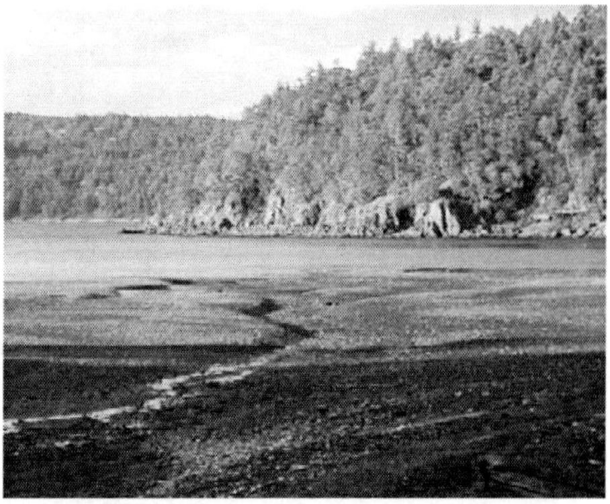

At the forest edge of the beach, *Cranberry Creek* provides for a waterfall that flows down from Mount Erskine and into an outlet called *Cranberry Outlet.* The beach is accessible from the end of Collins Road. (#29 on the map)

Mt. Maxwell Provincial Park

In the early 1860`s, an Irishman moved to Salt Spring where he purchased some land in the Fulford-Burgoyne Valley. There, he built a cabin at the foot of a mountain. He was the Island's first legal land owner.

The Irishman started farming with 100 imported, Texas Longhorn cattle. Over time, he became the Island's largest exporter of food, shipping about 20 head of cattle to Vancouver Island each month. Unfortunately, Indian cattle rustlers continuously plagued him.

When the government failed to provide him protection from the Indians, the stubborn Irishman and some other settlers set up an ambush on the mountain range.

When the Indians arrived in their canoes, the renegade white man accompanied them. Upon seeing the Indians, the settlers fired down from the mountain. This panicked the Indians and they fled. Later, they slit the throat of the white man, blaming him for the attack.

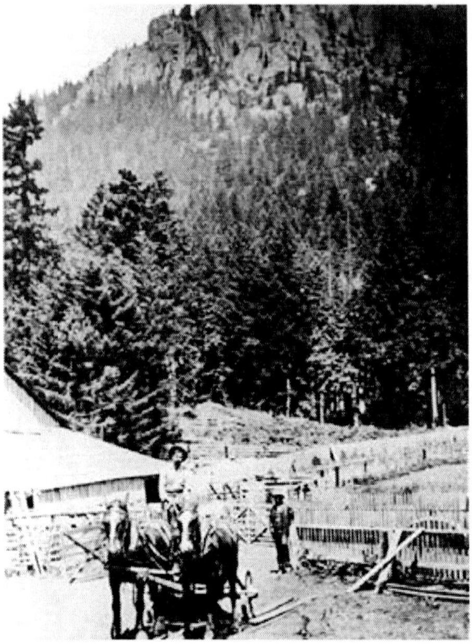

Mt. Maxwell in the 1890's
Salt Spring Archives 1994137251

Mount Maxwell was named after this Irishman, whose house was also the home of the post office at Burgoyne Bay.

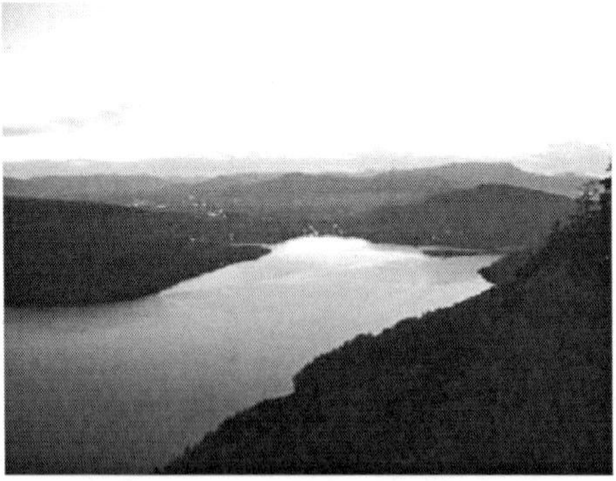

Mount Maxwell is also known as *Baynes Peak*. The 590 m peak is accessible by way of Mt. Maxwell Road and can be reached by car. The views seen from the mountaintop at sunset are spectacular. (#32 on the map)

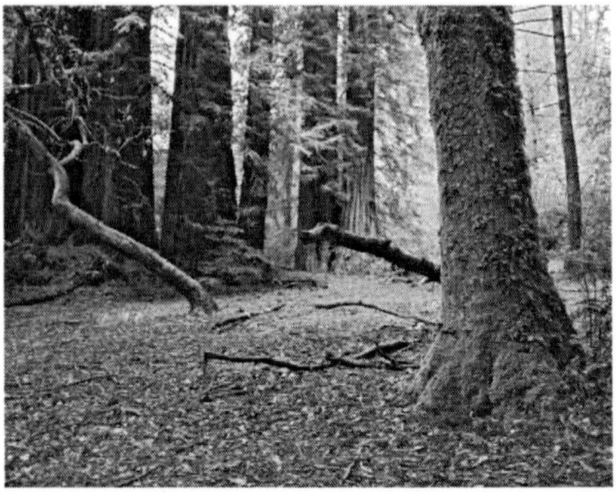

The mountain sits in *Mount Maxwell Provincial Park*, which is located in a secluded area on the west side of the Island. Established in the 1930's, it is the Island's first provincial park.

The old-growth forest park contains the largest Garry Oak, Western Red Cedar, Arbutus, Western Hemlock and Douglas-Fir trees on the Island. It provides for off-road cycling and there are facilities for picnics if you want to stay a while.

Musgrave Point

In the 1870's, four brothers emigrated from England to Salt Spring where they established a large sheep farm in a very secluded area. A decade later, a prominent settler purchased their farm.

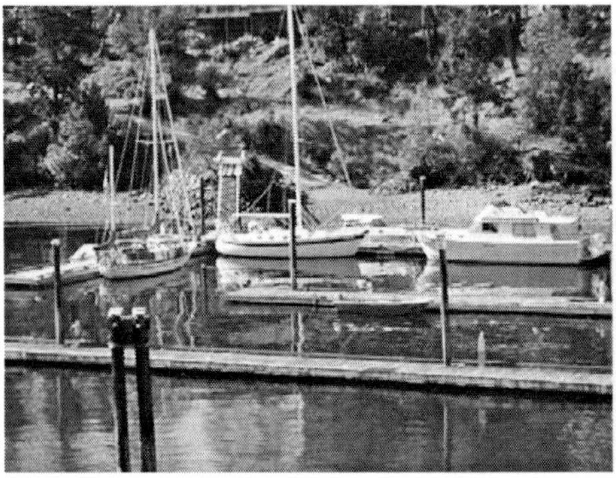

Musgrave Point was named after this settler who also purchased the brothers' 350 sheep.

The point is located on the southwest side of the Island. Until the 1920's, it was accessible only by water.

The pebbled beach on the point provides for a government wharf. The beach is accessible from the end of a long and rocky road named Musgrave Road. (#36 on the map)

Princess Margaret Park Reserve

In the 1870's, an Hawaiian settler came to the Gulf Islands bringing with him a few other Hawaiians. Soon, they settled on a small Island, which they registered in their names.

The Hawaiian had a unique way of curing tobacco. He would cut a round off a log, bore a hole through the middle, and then fill it with crushed, cured tobacco leaves. Then, he would pour in molasses and rum. When the hole was tightly packed, the log-round would split, producing a long tobacco stick that was ready for smoking.

The Hawaiian's family liked to hold luaus. The parties would begin in his house, and then everyone would travel from home to home. They would stay at each house until they had consumed all of the food and drink. Sometimes, the parties would last for weeks.

Around the turn of the century, the Island was sold. The Hawaiian had lived there for over 30 years. When he died two years later, his descendants carried on his unique method of curing tobacco.

Princess Margaret Park is part of the Gulf Islands National Park Reserve. Located on Portland Island, off the southern shore of Salt Spring, it provides for camping and there are facilities for picnics if you want to stay a while. (#13 on the map)

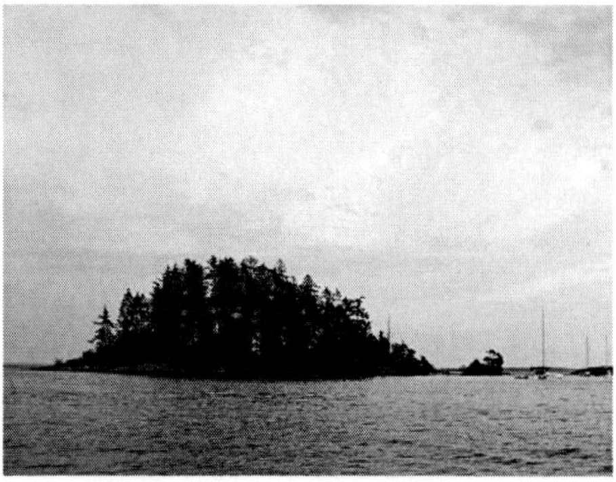

On the network of trails through the park can still be seen the fruit trees, roses and other plants that were grown by the Hawaiians who originally settled there. Bald Eagles and Turkey Vultures are also frequently seen there.

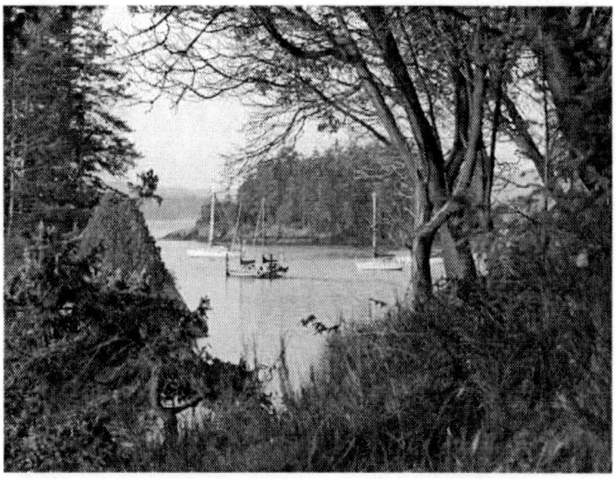

Reginald Hill Park

Reginald Hill Park is a small public park near Fulford Harbour. The strenuous 1.5 km hike through the park is accessible from the end of Morningside Drive. (#30 on the map)

Reginald Hill, which is located in the park, provides for views of the Fulford-Burgoyne Valley and of Vancouver Island. The breathtaking viewpoint also provides for the only view of the head of Fulford Harbour.

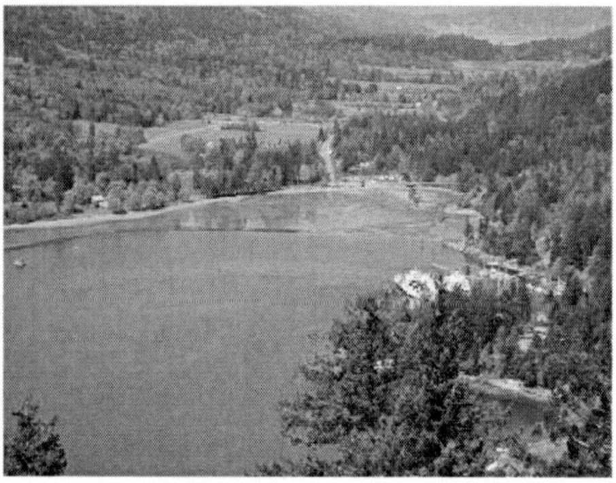

Ruckle Provincial Park

In the 1870's, a settler purchased some land on Beaver Point. There he established a farm. Three years later, he married a woman who had a son from a previous marriage.

At that time, the settler built a one and one-half storey frame house and the couple started a family of their own. As the family grew, a small addition was added to the house.

In the 1880's, the settler built a wharf, from which he operated the post office at Beaver Point. On his farm, he planted an orchard of 600 trees, establishing a variety of pears, called Ruckle Bartlet. Reportedly, it was the first fruit orchard in all of British Columbia.

The settler also raised dairy Jersey cattle and transported cream to the creamery in Ganges. He grew seed potatoes that produced as much as 60,000 kg of potatoes each year.

A decade later, two of the settler's sons built homes on his property and brought their brides to live there. At that time, the farm was the largest on the Island.

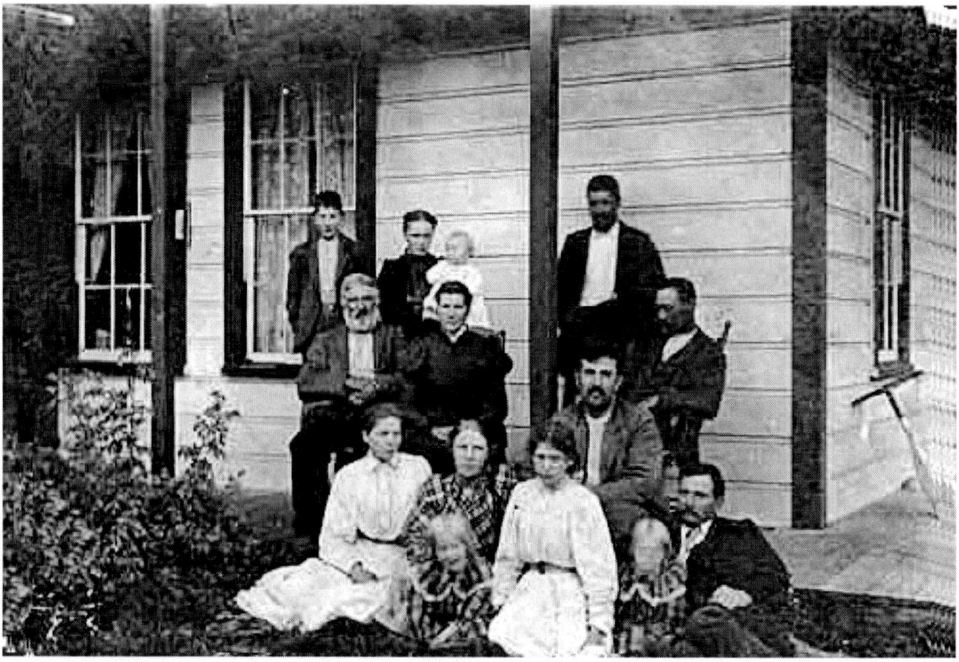

Ruckle farmhouse in the 1890's Salt Spring Archives 992112004

The settler's adopted son became very adept at woodworking. His magnificent home was fashioned in the Queen Anne style, with handcrafted woodwork and a sharply curved staircase with a gleaming cherry banister.

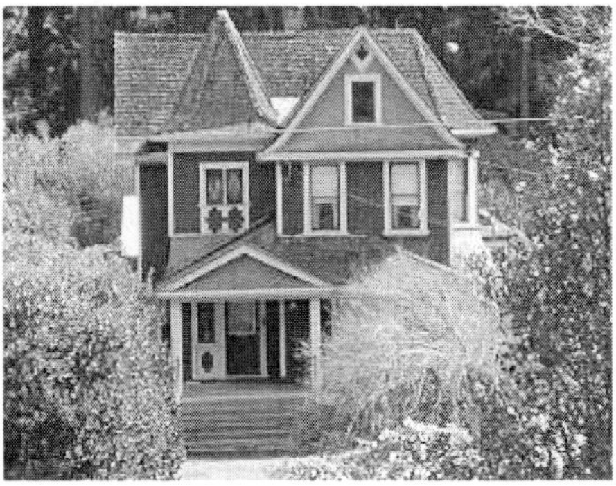

In the 1930`s, the family built yet another home on the property. The house was built for the settler's grandson who planned to live in it with his bride. Unfortunately, their wedding was cancelled and, thereafter, the house was used to store their potatoes.

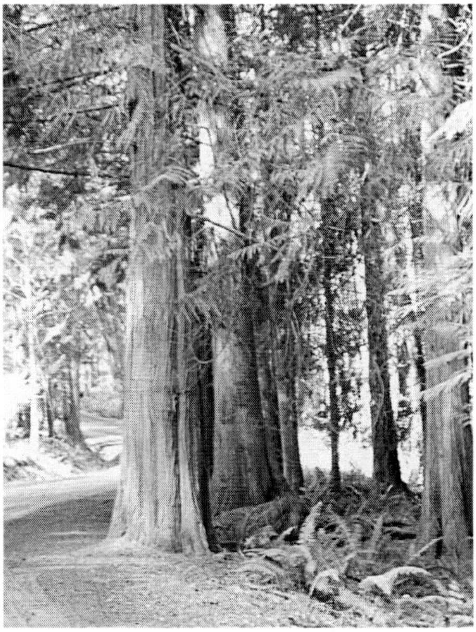

Ruckle Provincial Park was named after this family, whose farm is the oldest family farm in all of British Columbia today. The family was granted a life-long tenancy on the property and continues to work it.

The historical park, which was purchased in the 1970`s, is located near Fulford Harbour. As the largest park in all the Gulf Islands, it provides for some of the best hiking, through some of the largest Douglas-Fir and Western Red Cedar trees.

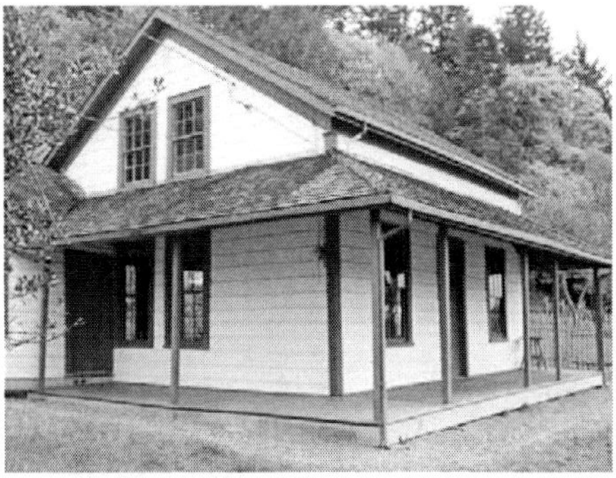

Ruckle Farmhouse as it appears today

Ruckle Park also provides for off-road cycling and there are facilities for picnics if you want to stay awhile.

Beaver Point is located in Ruckle Park. There are numerous little coves and bays surrounding the point. The park is accessible by way of Beaver Point Road. (#31 on the map)

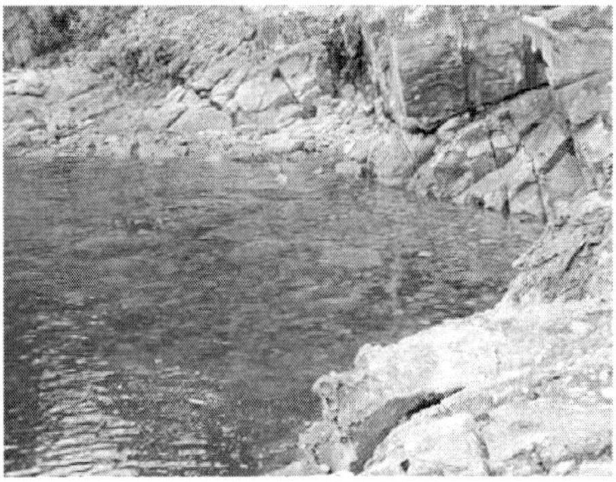

Russell Island Prov. Marine Park

In the 1870's, an Hawaiian settler emigrated to a tiny island. There, he developed a farm where he established an orchard, and raised sheep and cattle.

At the turn of the century, the Hawaiian passed away, leaving his entire farm to a young Hawaiian woman. She and her husband built a small frame house on the property, and continued to raise sheep and care for the orchard.

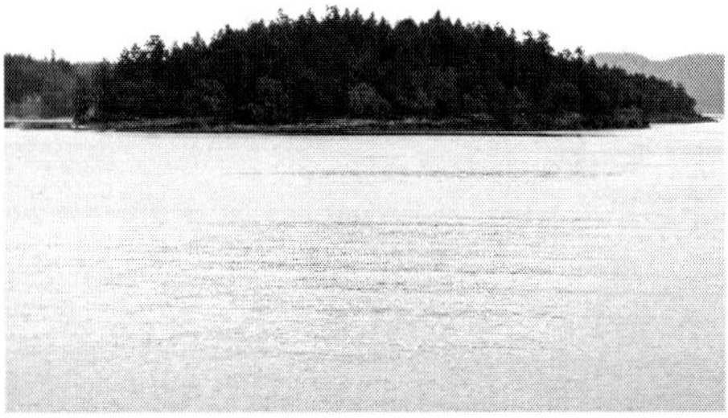

Russell Island Provincial Marine Park is located on Russell Island, which sits off the southeastern shore of Salt Spring. (#12 on the map)

The park is part of the Gulf Islands National Park Reserve and provides for a forest of Douglas-Fir, Arbutus and Garry Oak. There are stands of Shore Pine that grow around its perimeter.

The frame house that was owned by the Hawaiian immigrant still stands on the Island. The Island is protected by a resident caretaker.

Seabright Beach

In the 1870's, First Nations was allotted a reserve on a beach between what are now known as Fulford Harbour and Beaver Point. The Indians would set up elaborate camps on the reserve and live there throughout the summers, digging for clams along the shores of the harbour.

The Indians would make holes in the beach, into which they would place kindling. Then, they would light the kindling and throw rocks into the holes. The bonfires and torches they used would light up the shoreline like a city.

When the rocks became hot, the freshly-dug clams were dumped into the holes and covered with mats and bags. When the clamshells opened, the Indians would scoop the partially cooked clams out of their shells and thread them onto long, slender sticks. Each stick was then bent to form a hoop and hung over the fire until the clams browned.

The clamshells the Indians left behind on the beaches produced lime in the soil. Later, when the settlers put in crops of potatoes, the lime caused them to become scaly.

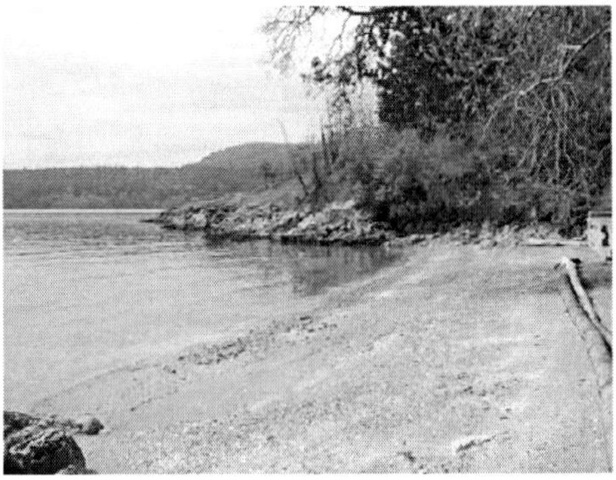

Located near Fulford Harbour, *Seabright Beach* sits beside Salt Spring's only Indian Reserve. The beach provides for some of the loveliest shoreline on the Island. It is accessible from the end of Menhinick Drive. (#11 on the map)

The North End

There are several beach accesses at the north end of Salt Spring. Two beaches are located on *Stuart Channel* on the northwest side of the Island.

One beach access is just south of West Eagle Road and the other is just south of Sunset Drive. The latter sits on a little bay and provides for views of Idol Island and Tent Island. (#8 on the map)

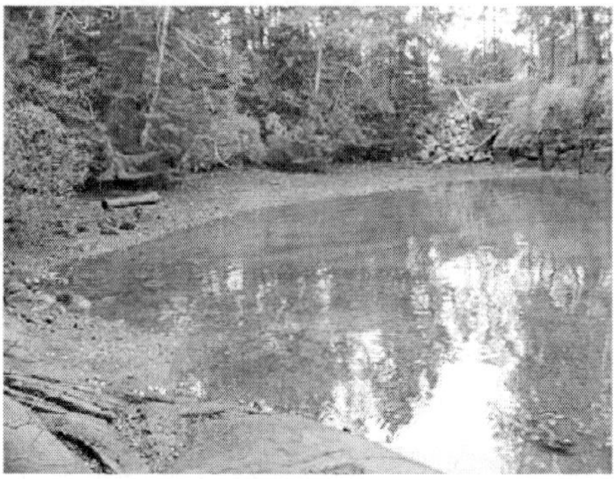

Southey Point is the most northern tip of the Island. The sandstone beach on the point is called *Arbutus Beach*. It is one of the prettiest spots on the Island and provides for views of several nearby islands. Accessible from Arbutus Road, it is a good place to see Sea Stars and a great place for a *soak* (swim).

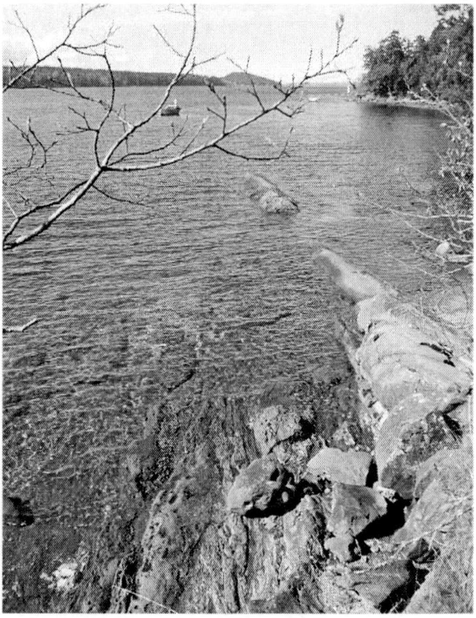

Another access to Arbutus Beach exists at the end of Southey Point Road. It also provides for good swimming. (#15 on the map)

If you launch a boat from the beach, you can travel south along the shore to Vesuvius. Alternatively, you can travel east to Wallace Island or west around the sandstone formations of Tent and Kuper Islands.

Vesuvius Beach

The first settlers on Salt Spring were landed on a beach from a Hudson's Bay Company steamer. However, the local Indians were aggressive. So the Black immigrants left the beach and moved further inland. There, they chose their land claims.

In the late 1850's, a Black settler and his family arrived on the Island with several head of cattle. Upon landing on the beach, he immediately sent one of his helpers to the property of **the Postman**, to ask for assistance in transporting his family's belongings.

Suddenly, the Indians landed on the beach in their canoes. They were accompanied by the renegade white man.

When the Black settler pointed his gun at the Indians, they climbed into their canoes and proceeded to leave the beach.

Just then, a swarm of canoes appeared in the bay, carrying Indians from another band. This prompted an Indian battle at sea, which culminated in another massacre.

Vesuvius Beach is located in Vesuvius. It is the most popular bathing beach on the Island and is one of the best places to watch the sun set. The pebbled beach is accessible by way of steps at the end of Langley Street. (#5 on the map)

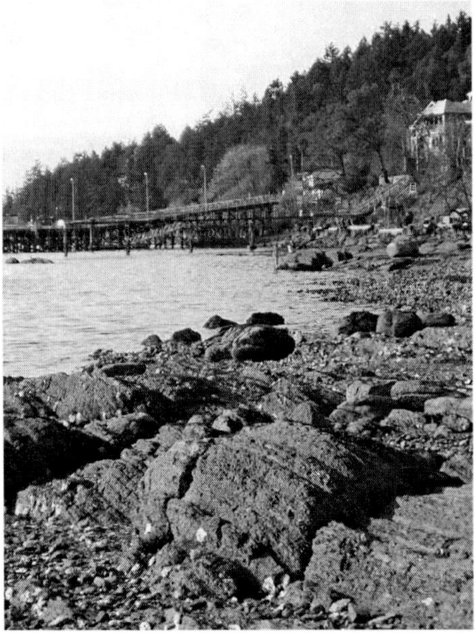

The wharf in Vesuvius Bay provides for a small ferry terminal that services ferries traveling to and from the southeast side of Vancouver Island. There is also a public dock in the bay.

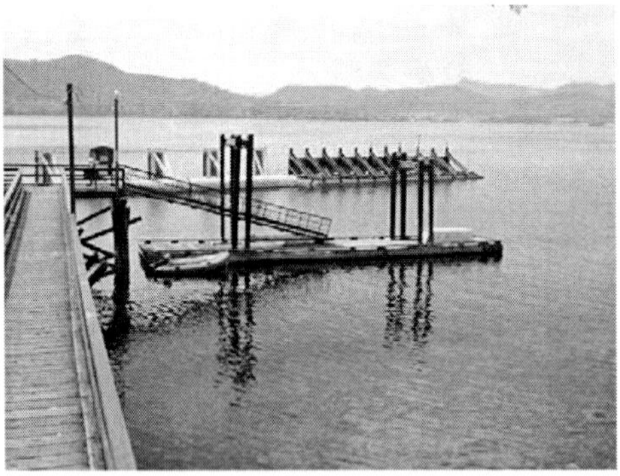

Walker Hook

Walker Hook is a small, privately-owned peninsula that hooks around to create an islet off the northeast side of Salt Spring.

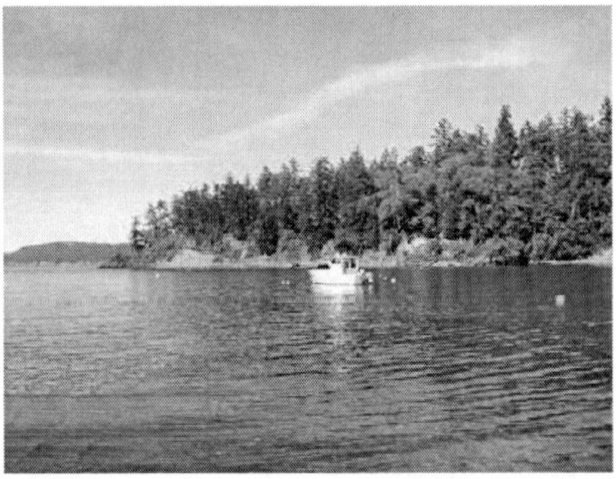

The quaint pebbled beach at Walker Hook is accessible from the end of Grantville Road. (#16 on the map)

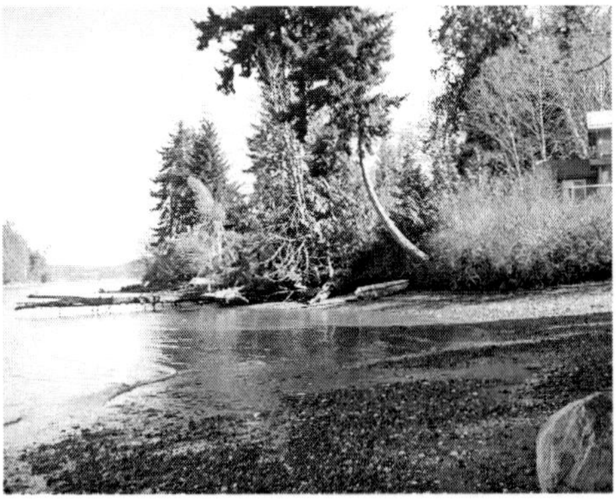

Credits

Historical Photos

British Columbia Archives and Records Services

Royal British Columbia Museum

British Columbia Ferry Services Archives

Salt Spring Archives (Salt Spring Island)

Galiano Museum & Archives (Galiano Island)

Pender Islands Museum Society (Pender Islands)

Mayne Island Volunteer Firefighters Association (Mayne Island)

David Spalding (South Pender Island)

Donald New (Galiano Island)

Hope Bay Rising Holdings Ltd. (North Pender Island)

Jim and Lorraine Campbell (Saturna Island)

Management of the Saturna Lodge (Saturna Island)

Management of The Old Farmhouse B&B (Salt Spring Island)

Credits

Current Photos

Kevin Oke Photography
Pender Island Fall Fair, Magic Lake Lantern Festival, Salt Spring Island Fall Fair, Saturday Market in the Park, Saturna Island Vineyards Harvest Celebration, Canada Day Lamb Barbeque, Cabbage Island Provincial Marine Park, Portland Island

Georgia Strait Alliance
Orca Pass International Stewardship Area

Goats and Stoats and Badgers Too
Feral Goat

Joanie McCorry (Mayne Island)
Mayne Island Quilters Guild

Darrel Perfumo (Mayne Island)
En-Vision Gallery

Brian Haller (Mayne Island)
Bonfire in Miners Bay Community Park, Easter Egg Hunt

Charles Andre (Mayne Island)
The Hobbit House B&B

Efraim Gavrilovich (Mayne Island)
Japanese Garden lights

Ken Smith (Galiano Island)
Halloween, Galiano Fiesta, Montague Harbour Marina, Island Time 5 Star B&B, Spanish Longboat, Clowns, Slow Pitch Tournament, Galiano Triathlon

Pender Island Taxi & Tours (Pender Island)
Pender Island Taxis

The Pender Islands Artisan Co-Op (Pender Island)
Rembrandt`s Birthday Art Show, Christmas Craft Fair Exhibit

Stella Roberts (Pender Island)
The Garden Party

Greg Gerke (Pender Island)
Easter Egg Hunt

Saturna Island Vineyards (Saturna Island)
Saturna Island Vineyards, Saturna Vineyards Wine Shop

Boot Cove Art Studio (Saturna Island)
Boot Cove Art Studio

Everlasting Summer (Salt Spring Island)
Everlasting Summer Garden Aerial View

Credits

AppleLuscious Organic Orchards (Salt Spring Island)
Apple Festival

Graffiti Theatre (Salt Spring Island)
Seven Stories Theatrical Production

Dreamstime™
Tony Campbell, David Coleman, Galina Barskaya, Paul Wolf, Scott Pehrson, Marilyn Barbone, Steffen Foerster, Steve Degenhardt, Melissa King, Randy McKown, Kutt Niinepuu, Dennis Sabo, Jason Cheever, Ryan Tacay, Costin Cojocaru, Marilyna Barbone, Nick Stubbs, Francois etienne Du plessis, Pete Setrac, Penny Riches, Dwight Hegel, Tom Hirtreiter, Elena Ray, Norman Pogson, Hannu Liivaar, Patricia Marroquin, Franc Podgorsek, Keith Naylor, Andrew Barker, Elina Gareeva, Richard Gunion, Silas Brown, Jannelle Althoff, Bobby Deal, Yula Zubritsky, Dick Sunderland, Elena Elisseeva, Dan Bannister, Jaimie Duplass, Marilyn Barbone, Natthias Nordmeyer, Svetlana Tikhonova, Jackie Egginton, Vlad Turchenko, Emin Kuliyev, Fred Goldstein, Jennifer Westmoreland, Sue McDonald, Mark Rasmussen, David Kay, David Pruter, Mehmet Alci

Credits

Acknowledgements

The Post Offices of British Columbia: 1858-1970 - George H. Melvin

The Gulf Islanders: Sound Heritage, Volume V, Number 4

Island Heritage Buildings – Thomas K. Ovanin, Islands Trust

A Gulf Islands Patchwork: Some Early Events on the Islands of Galiano, Mayne, Saturna, North and South Pender – British Columbia Historical Association

More Tales from the Outer Gulf Islands: An Anthology of Memories and Anecdotes – British Columbia Historical Association

Homesteads and Snug Harbours: The Gulf Islands – Peter Murray

The Terror Of The Coast: Land Alienation And Colonial War On Vancouver Island And The Gulf Islands – Chris Arnett

The Gulf Islands Explorer: The Outdoor Guide – Bruce Obee

Hiking the Gulf Islands: An Outdoor Guide to BC's Enchanted Isles – Charles Kahn

Plants of the Pacific Northwest Coast – Pojar and Mackinnon

Birds of the Pacific Northwest Coast – Nancy Baron & John Acorn

Mammals of the Northwest: Washington, Oregon, Idaho and British Columbia – Earl J. Larrison

The Beachcomber's Guide to Seashore Life in the Pacific Northwest– J. Duane Sept

WetCoast Words: A Dictionary of British Columbia Words and Phrases – Tom Parkin

Mayne Island & The Outer Gulf Islands: A History – Marie Elliott

Galiano: Houses And People, Looking back to 1930 – Elizabeth Steward

The Campbells of Saturna: An Oral History – Saturna Community Club

Salt Spring: The Story of an Island – Charles Kahn

Salt Spring Island: Bea Hamilton

Author

Vicky Lindholm moved with her husband to Mayne Island, British Columbia, in December of 2004. Having authored over 30 pieces of computer courseware, she brought with her more than 20 years of writing experience.

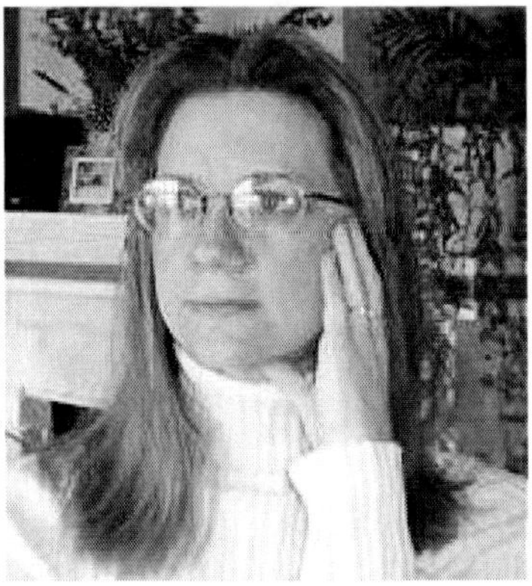

The *Facts And Folklore* series are the first books of their kind to be written by this author, who reviewed over 50 existing pieces of literature and explored parks, beaches and wildlife in order to produce these historical views of the southern Gulf Islands.

The books are historical guides to the events, landmarks, parks, beaches, shops, restaurants and wildlife in the southern Gulf Islands. They include over 1000 photos, past to present, most of which the author photographed herself.

Vicky currently lives and works on Mayne Island. In addition to making a living as a writer, she manages a small gift store, as a home-based business, from her residential property.

First Nations, 52

W

Y